The Russian Liberals and the Revolution of 1905

There is a widespread notion that Russia is forever fated to be an authoritarian country where liberalism and democracy can never make real progress. However, at the beginning of the twentieth century there was an extremely influential "liberationist" movement which culminated in the formation of a modern, Western-style liberal party, the Constitutional Democrats or "Kadets". The book provides a comprehensive history of the rise of the Kadets, focusing, in particular, on the revolutionary years 1905–6. It outlines how they dominated the First Duma elected by the people and analyses their policies, social composition and political tactics. The book challenges the view (shared by many historians) that the Kadets were inherently extreme, doctrinaire or unwilling to compromise, and argues that their eventual failure was primarily due to the intransigence of the old régime. *The Russian Liberals and the Revolution of 1905* illustrates, in detail, that the Kadets offered a moderate alternative to reaction on the one hand and revolution on the other.

Peter Enticott was formerly a researcher at the School of Slavonic and East European Studies, London, and the University of Wales, Cardiff; he has also been employed at the British Institute and at Folkuniversitetet in Stockholm, Sweden.

Routledge Studies in the History of Russia and Eastern Europe

15 **The Baltic States from the Soviet Union to the European Union**
Identity, discourse and power in the Post-Communist transition of Estonia, Latvia and Lithuania
Richard Mole

16 **Life Stories of Soviet Women**
The interwar generation
Melanie Ilic

17 **Brezhnev and the Decline of the Soviet Union**
Thomas Crump

18 **Women and Transformation in Russia**
Edited by Aino Saarinen, Kirsti Ekonen and Valentina Uspenskaia

19 **Competition in Socialist Society**
Edited by Katalin Miklóssy and Melanie Ilic

20 **Young Jewish Poets Who Fell as Soviet Soldiers in the Second World War**
Rina Lapidus

21 **The Vernaculars of Communism**
Language, Ideology and Power in the Soviet Union
Edited by Petre Petrov and Lara Ryazanova-Clarke

22 **The Warsaw Pact Reconsidered**
International Relations in Eastern Europe, 1955–1969
Laurien Crump

23 **Reassessing Orientalism**
Interlocking Orientologies during the Cold War
Edited by Michael Kemper and Artemy M. Kalinovsky

24 **Governing Post-Imperial Siberia and Mongolia, 1911–1924**
Buddhism, Socialism, and Nationalism in State and Autonomy Building
Ivan Sablin

25 **Creating Nationality in Central Europe, 1880–1950**
Modernity, Violence and (Be)Longing in Upper Silesia
Edited by James Bjork, Tomasz Kamusella, Timothy Wilson and Anna Novikov

26 **The Russian Liberals and the Revolution of 1905**
Peter Enticott

27 **The Politics of Culture in Soviet Azerbaijan, 1920–40**
Audrey L. Altstadt

The Russian Liberals and the Revolution of 1905

Peter Enticott

LONDON AND NEW YORK

First published 2016 by Routledge

2 Park Square, Milton Park, Abingdon, Oxfordshire OX14 4RN
711 Third Avenue, New York, NY 10017

Routledge is an imprint of the Taylor & Francis Group, an informa business

First issued in paperback 2017

Copyright © 2016 Peter Enticott

The right of Peter Enticott to be identified as author of this work has been asserted by him in accordance with sections 77 and 78 of the Copyright, Designs and Patents Act 1988.

All rights reserved. No part of this book may be reprinted or reproduced or utilized in any form or by any electronic, mechanical, or other means, now known or hereafter invented, including photocopying and recording, or in any information storage or retrieval system, without permission in writing from the publishers.

Notice:
Product or corporate names may be trademarks or registered trademarks, and are used only for identification and explanation without intent to infringe.

British Library Cataloguing in Publication Data
A catalogue record for this book is available from the British Library

Library of Congress Cataloging in Publication Data
Names: Enticott, Peter, author.
Title: The Russian liberals and the Revolution of 1905 / Peter Enticott.
Description: Abingdon, Oxon : Routledge, [2016] | Series: Routledge studies in the history of Russia and Eastern Europe | Includes bibliographical references and index.
Identifiers: LCCN 2015041385| ISBN 9781138638990 (hardback) | ISBN 9781315629933 (e-book)
Subjects: LCSH: Konstituětisionno-demokraticheskaěiia partiěiia–History. | Russia–History–Revolution, 1905–1907. | Russia–Politics and government–1904–1914. | Elections–Russia–History–20th century.
Classification: LCC JN6598.K95 E58 2016 | DDC 947.08/3–dc23
LC record available at http://lccn.loc.gov/2015041385

ISBN: 978-1-138-63899-0 (hbk)
ISBN: 978-1-138-47723-0 (pbk)

Typeset in Times New Roman
by Wearset Ltd, Boldon, Tyne and Wear

This book is dedicated to the memory of my brother John Trevor Enticott.

Contents

Foreword ix
Preface xii
Acknowledgements xiii
List of abbreviations xiv

1 Prelude 1
The background 1
The liberationists 10
Publication of journal Liberation *11*
The Union of Liberation 14

2 Reform or revolution? 22
Sviatopolk-Mirskii and the political "spring" 22
Bloody Sunday 23
The Third Congress of Liberation 25
The Union of Unions 27
The deputation to the Tsar of 6 June 29
Plans to establish a New Liberal Party 31
The Fourth Congress of Liberation 32

3 The birth of the Kadet Party 36
The Foundation Congress (12–18 October 1905) 38
The October Manifesto 46
Witte's attempts to gain public support 50
The December crisis 59
Party organization 62
The party press 64

4 The run-up to the First Duma 72
The Kadets' Second Congress (5–11 January 1906) 73

The election campaign 77
Party organization 78
The election results 83
The laws of 20 February 85
The loan which "saved Russia" 88
The Fundamental Laws 90
The fall of Witte 93
The Kadets' Third Congress (21–25 April 1906) 94

5 The First Duma (27 April–9 July 1906) 103
Kadet tactics and policies in the Duma 103
Discussions on the formation of a new ministry 119
The Kadets and the left 131
The grassroots 133
The Vyborg Manifesto 135

6 Kadet Party policy 146
The constitution and civil rights 146
Local government and regional autonomy 150
Social reform 154
Agrarian policy 154

7 Who were the Kadets? 170

8 Some conclusions 183

Glossary 193
Further reading 194
Bibliography 196
Index 203

Foreword

Although the Kadets were essentially moderates, they have frequently been criticized for their radical policies during the Revolution of 1905 and the First Duma. It has often been argued, principally by V.A. Maklakov and his disciples, that the Kadets were too doctrinaire and unwilling to compromise with the ancien régime. They needlessly sought confrontation with the ministry and insisted on a parliamentary constitution for which Russia was not ready. In view of the imminent dangers of violent revolution, anarchy and totalitarian democracy, they should have made peace with the Tsarist régime and entered a coalition cabinet together with government ministers.

Although such views were often expressed with the benefit of hindsight (particularly after the political watershed of 1917) they do raise fundamental questions, *inter alia*: Was Russia mature enough for a liberal-democratic constitution in the years before the First World War? Was there sufficient stability and cohesion in Russian society to underpin a liberal régime?

Half a century ago, Leonard Haimson in *The Problem of Social Stability in Urban Russia 1905–1917* painted an unduly pessimistic picture of the fragmented state of Russian society in the early years of the twentieth century. According to Haimson, urban society was dually polarized between the ancien régime on the one hand and privileged, educated society and urban workers on the other. Moreover, Robert McKean in "Constitutional Russia" observes that the division of the population into obsolete legal estates continued to hinder social cohesion and stability. The educated classes and estates were themselves fragmented internally, further inhibiting the emergence of a middle-class basis (whether liberal or conservative) for constitutional democracy. Meanwhile, in the countryside, the peasantry remained a class apart, with their own *soslovie* (estate)-based administration, complicating still further the formation of modern civil society, which McKean suggests is a "sine qua non for a democratic order".

Whether or not one fully accepts the validity of this analysis, it is evident that in 1905, urgent reform was needed to modernize Russia, to shore up the stability and cohesion of the Empire and promote the development of civil society.

Traditionally in Tsarist Russia, the initiative for reform had come from above, as in the reigns of Peter the Great and Alexander II. However, Nicolas II was a myopic reactionary who had little or nothing in common with the Tsar-Liberator.

He simply did not understand the need for co-operation with society and was even mistrustful of his own administration. Even his support for far-sighted ministers like Count Witte and Stolypin was at best reluctant and equivocal.

Until the end of the nineteenth century, most liberals hoped that the initiative for reform would once again come from the Tsar and his ministers. Only when such hopes were frustrated did moderate liberalism develop into radical opposition to the régime and demands for a democratic constitution.

Unlike the Octobrists on the one hand, or the socialists on the other, the Kadets did not seek to represent the narrow interests of a particular class or ethnic group. Instead, they sought to promote the common interest of society as a whole. At a time of conflict, they sought to pacify and unify the country. Far from seeking to divide Russia, liberal reforms were intended to create a more stable, cohesive community. Above all, Russian society should be founded on the rule of law and a common citizenship. In principle, all Russian citizens, whatever their differences, should share the same fundamental civil rights. Consequently, all citizens, including the peasants and minority nationalities, should have an equal right to participate in political life and feel that they had a stake in society. Hence the Kadets' demands for universal, equal, direct and secret suffrage instead of an estate-based electoral system.

Moreover, Kadet politicians considered it essential that the peasantry, the vast majority of the Russian people, should have a material interest in the consolidation of the new, constitutional régime. Accordingly, their insistent demands for enlarged peasant plots could not simply be ignored. Even though this was not a long-term solution to the agrarian crisis, it was of crucial importance if the peasantry were to be pacified and included in an all-Russian democratic consensus.

To facilitate the necessary reforms, an effective parliament with substantial powers was essential. However, in the absence of co-operation and good will on the part of the government, the emasculated constitution which emerged from the Laws of 20 February 1906 proved quite inadequate. And after Stolypin's coup d'état of 3 June 1907 guaranteed an ultra-conservative majority in the Third Duma, the "constitution" often tended to obstruct reform rather than to promote it. When it came to the rights of Jews and other minority nationalities, it could even hinder the development of cohesive civil society.

However, in the final analysis, was Russian society, after all, simply too underdeveloped to underpin a liberal, constitutional régime? In the light of recent research, many historians have begun to take a more positive view of social development in Russia in the first quarter of the twentieth century. Wayne Dowler (in *Russia in 1913*) insists that "a vibrant, public sphere existed in Russia, supported by a plethora of institutions of civil society". He totally rejects "the extreme reductionism that sharply polarizes workers, educated society and the state". According to Dowler, life in the cities had fostered a complex, interactive urban society. In particular, "a differentiated functional middle-class had come into existence", drawn from all social estates and including professional men and salaried employees in the private and public sectors. Even in the countryside, where the legal estate structures still dominated, a more open society was emerging, stimulated by wider literacy, the penetration of the market, mass commercial culture and the growth of cooperatives.

In *Voluntary Associations in Tsarist Russia*, Joseph Bradley also chronicles the remarkable growth of civil society, as mirrored in the existence of thousands of professional associations and other voluntary bodies by the early years of the century. And although he, like Dowler, cites many examples of co-operation, as well as tension, between society and the administration, Bradley ultimately concludes that: "Russia's failure to develop viable democratic institutions was not a failure of civil society, but of autocratic intransigence."

Of course, not all historians will concur with this analysis. However, it is difficult to disagree with Bradley's observation that "many different forms of civil society can exist under a variety of régimes, only one of which is liberal democracy and associations by themselves cannot create a liberal régime". Quite evidently, the preconditions for constitutional democracy vary greatly from time to time and from country to country. International experience has shown that even in the absence of some of the features of modern civil society, a democratic constitution can function in countries with widely different social cultures (multi-ethnic India being the prime example).

Consequently, even though a modern social order had not fully matured in Russia by 1905–6, this does not mean that demands for constitutional democracy were premature. On the contrary: given the "hopeless ossification of the autocracy" (to quote Marc Raeff), a liberal constitution, civil rights and the rule of law had become the precondition for social progress and the modernization of Russia.

Preface

There is a widespread notion that Russia is forever fated to be a land of authoritarian rule where liberalism and democracy can never make real progress. However, at the beginning of the twentieth century, the rise of an extremely influential "liberationist" movement, culminating in the foundation of a modern Western-style liberal party, suggests that this negative conception is essentially a myth. Moreover, the leaders of the Kadet Party (the "Constitutional Democrats") proved to be capable cultured public men, who played a pivotal rôle during the revolutionary years 1905–6. The first Duma elected by the people was dominated by the Kadets, who proposed a civilized, moderate alternative to reaction on the one hand and revolution on the other. Had it not been for the obduracy of the autocracy, the year 1906 might well have led to the participation of the liberals in government and the eventual establishment of a basically parliamentary system, with positive consequences for the future of Russia and for Europe as a whole. That this did not happen was not primarily the fault of the essentially moderate Kadet Party leaders. It was, above all, the fault of the old régime which had shown that it could not be trusted to meet the liberals even halfway.

This book is based on research conducted at *inter alia*: the School of Slavonic and East European Studies, London, the University of Wales, Cardiff, research facilities in Moscow and at Stockholm, Sweden. The book is far more than a mere narrative of events. It includes a comprehensive analysis of the Kadets' policies, their tactics in the Duma, their negotiations with the government and the social composition of the party membership. Finally, it addresses the question of whether a liberal régime would have been viable in Russia during the early years of the twentieth century. While the book will be of particular interest to historians, it should also appeal to a wider public.

Acknowledgements

The author wishes to express his profound gratitude to the following institutions: the School of Slavonic and East European Studies, London; the British Museum Reading Room (prior to 1997); the British Library; Cardiff University Library; the Lenin Library, Moscow; the State Archive of the Russian Federation; the National Library of Sweden, Stockholm; and Stockholm University Library. Special mention should also be made of the British Library's former Colindale branch with its exceptional collections of Russian journals and newspapers of the period.

Finally, the author wishes to thank Anette Hellström for her indispensable assistance and co-operation in the editing of this book.

Abbreviations

The following abbreviations have been frequently employed either in footnotes/endnotes or in the Bibliography.

A.R.R.	*Arkhiv russkoi revoliutsii*
A.S.E.E.R.	*The American Slavic and East European Review*
GARF	Gosudarstvennyi Arkhiv Rossiiskoi Federatsii
I.Z.	*Istoricheskie zapiski*
K.A.	*Krasnyi arkhiv*
K.-D.	Konstitutsionno-demokraticheskaia
OTCHËT	*Konstitutsionno-demokraticheskaia partiia – OTCHËT tsentral'nogo komiteta k.d.p. za dva goda*
P.G.D.	*Pervaia Gosudarstvennaia Duma*
Protokoly	*Protokoly Tsentral'nogo komiteta*
ROSSPEN	Rossiiskaia Politicheskaia Entsiklopediia
R.Z.	*Russkie zapiski*
S.E.E.R.	*The Slavonic and East European Review*
S.O.	Gosudarstvennaia Duma, *Stenograficheskie otchëty*
S.P.B.	St. Petersburg
S.Z.	*Sovremennye zapiski*
Ts.k.	*Tsentral'nyi komitet*
Vestnik	*Vestnik Partii Narodnoi Svobody*

1 Prelude

The background

Speaking to an American audience in 1903, the great Russian liberal Pavel Miliukov attempted to minimize the differences between Russian political parties and those of the West. In combatting government propaganda, which portrayed political life on the Western model as something alien to the Russian way of life, he attempted to endow Russian political parties with a firmer base and more durable roots than they had in reality:

> "Beneath the surface of the official uniformity", claimed Miliukov, "differences of political opinion have long existed which correspond in every way to the differences of political opinion in Western Europe; and those who adhere to the same opinion in politics to a certain extent acknowledge such party ethics and party discipline as are necessary for combined political action."[1]

Miliukov did not deny that organized political parties were still only in the process of formation in Russia. He was referring merely to movements of political opinion. But nevertheless, it is difficult to avoid the conclusion that Miliukov was overstating his case. In reality even the crystallizing of *opinion* among party lines had begun only in the mid-1890s, during the literary battles between the Legal Marxists and the Legal Populists.[F1] Even then, the political awakening was confined, for the most part, to the educated intelligentsia and to cultivated "society", which comprised only a small fraction of the population as a whole. Before this date, political opinions of a well-defined party type were mostly restricted to small circles of intellectuals, or to underground revolutionary organizations like the "Narodnaia Volia" (the "People's Will").[F2] The political ideas of the rest of educated "society" remained essentially moderate and incoherent. As for the great majority of the population – the largely illiterate peasantry – their political ideas were virtually non-existent.

F1 Their publications tended to be academic and theoretical, and so were usually permitted by the censorship.

F2 Narodnaia Volia was responsible for the assassination of Tsar Alexander II on 1 March 1881.

Prelude

In fact, a vast gulf separated Russian political life from that of the West. This was not merely the result of the repressive policies of an autocratic state. It was a reflection of the fact that in Russia there was no *tradition* of popular opposition to the autocracy. Moreover, for a long time there was no real social basis for an opposition movement. And this had a profound effect upon the history of liberalism in Russia, the subject of this study.

In the West, the growth of liberalism had been largely dependent on the rise of a powerful individualistic bourgeoisie – a phenomenon related to the gradual development of a modern market economy and the disintegration of feudalism. However, owing to Russian economic backwardness, there had been no real historical counterpart in Russia of the bourgeois classes of Western Europe. Capitalism in Russia had lagged far behind that of the West. Indeed, serfdom had been abolished only in 1861, and it was only after this date that capitalism could make significant progress. And even at the end of the nineteenth century industrial capital remained dependent on government patronage and protection, and tended to be politically subservient.

In the absence of a powerful bourgeoisie, there was, for many years, no social class able or willing to stand as an effective counterweight to the power of the autocracy. The only significant classes in Russian life before (and long after) the Emancipation were the nobility and the peasantry. The latter was much too primitive to spontaneously produce anything in the nature of constructive political opposition. Its active rôle in Russian history had been confined to the sporadic jacquerie against the seigneur, of which the greatest was the Pugachëv rebellion under Catherine II. Following such elemental eruptions of largely destructive violence, the peasants tended to slip back into almost complete passivity. Moreover, peasant disturbances were directed against the landowning classes rather than against the principle of absolute rule.

The nobles had likewise no tradition of political independence or opposition to the autocracy. The old boyar nobility, which had once been able to claim a degree of independent influence within the state, had long ago been replaced by a "service nobility", largely of plebeian origin. This process, which reached its climax under Peter the Great, created a nobility whose very rank and privilege originated in service to the state, and which came to see such service as its ideal. It is true that in the second half of the eighteenth century the nobles' obligations to the state were weakened, and their privileges strengthened, but nevertheless, they retained a very strong sense of their duty to serve the government. The traditions of the nobility did not provide a very favourable soil for the growth of a spirit of liberal opposition to the old régime.

It is a significant fact that liberal ideas were first introduced into Russia as a plaything of the autocracy – of Catherine II and later of Alexander I – rather than by a discontented nobility or peasantry. It is true that liberal ideas provided the inspiration of the Decembrist uprising of 1825, which attempted to overthrow the absolutist régime. But this abortive coup by army officers influenced by their experience of Western Europe during and after the Napoleonic Wars was the work of an isolated minority without wide social support. And neither the Emancipation of the Serfs in 1861, nor the other Great Reforms which followed it, were the result of a powerful and coherent liberal opposition in the country (although the Emancipation itself was partly motivated by the need to avoid a new "pugachëvshchina"). The Great Reforms were, in fact – and this was typical of Russian history – not so much the fruit of liberal agitation from below, as the result of an autocratic decision from above. Just as Peter the Great had seen the need to modernize Russia technically and administratively if it was to survive, Alexander II, following the Crimean defeat, realized that if Russia was to meet the competition of Western states, its military, administrative, legal, economic and social structure had to be modernized. Hence his borrowing, however incomplete, of European models in the shaping of the Great Reforms.

Although the latter were liberal *reforms*, they were scarcely *liberalism* in the full sense of the word, since they were intended to make autocracy work better rather than to undermine it. However, they did establish the chief arena of liberal activity for Russian society in the latter part of the nineteenth century and the first five years of the twentieth – the system of provincial and district ("zemstvo") self-government founded in 1864.[F3] Eventually the zemstvos were to play a major part in preparing the ground for Russia's first Western-style liberal party, and for this reason there has been a tendency to read back into the early history of the zemstvo something of the oppositionist spirit which it later displayed.

In fact, as Veselovskii has made clear (in *Istoriia zemstva III*), until the eve of the twentieth century, the opposition activity of the zemstvos was very limited. The zemstvo was almost always dominated by the middle nobility or "gentry" (the greater nobles being largely involved in state service in the "bureaucracy") owing to a curial system of voting designed in their favour, and to their own social influence and education. And this section of the nobility, like the rest of its class, had little tradition of political opposition. It is true that the Emancipation had weakened their ties to the state, by undermining their social and economic position. Before 1861 the pomeshchiks had represented the main source of authority for the rural population, whereas after this date, despite their domination of the zemstvos, their influence was to a great extent replaced by the bureaucracy and the courts. Moreover, the interests of the middle nobility were often adversely affected by the abolition of serfdom. In the long term all this was not without its effect upon the political attitudes of the "gentry". But old traditions died slowly, and this class remained for a long time psychologically tied to the state. Moreover, they tended to look to the government for the protection of their material interests in the difficult economic climate following the Emancipation. Such conditions were not particularly favourable for the growth of a liberal opposition. This does not mean that liberal ideas were entirely absent in this section of society. A smattering of such ideas – in favour of the rule of law, civil rights and

---

F3 The zemstvos were responsible, *inter alia*, for the building and maintenance of roads and bridges, schools, hospitals and veterinary and agricultural services. In 1870 a similar system was established in the cities: the city (gorodskie) dumas.

sometimes some form of public representation – was fairly widespread in the zemstvos. But the demands for such measures were rather muted, and were often conceived not as a means of limiting the monarchy, but rather as a means of perfecting it. Moreover, the reformers' aspirations were inchoate and uncoordinated and did not constitute a well-defined body of "party" opinion. It is true that, during periods of heightened social tension or animation, these hazy aspirations did tend to crystallize. For example, at the time of the Great Reforms, the Moscow nobility demanded some form of central representation for their own class, and their initiative evoked a sympathetic response in St. Petersburg "society".² Similarly, during the social unrest at the end of the 1870s and the beginning of the 1880s there was an upsurge of political activity among the zemstvos. Largely on the intiative of I.I. Petrunkevich, "the father of Russian constitutionalism", a constitutionalist movement began to grow up among the zemstvos, and a minority of provincial assemblies passed resolutions in favour of liberal or constitutional reforms. However, their views were not taken up by the zemstvos as a whole.³

The level of political activity during such periods has, in fact, been much exaggerated. Moreover, such times were only intervals separating long periods of inactivity or reaction, including social reaction, as in the 1880s. Most of the time the zemstvos occupied themselves overwhelmingly with their day-to-day business of raising the cultural and economic standards of their localities – with what became known as "small deeds". There was little continuity or coherence in liberal activity in the zemstvo, and therefore little real party feeling, except perhaps among the zemstvo gentry of Tver', who had a long history of radicalism. In the final analysis, this can only be explained by the fact that the gentry were still not very opposition-minded. Liberal ideas among this section of the population remained for a long time very undefined and moderate,[F4] while gentry with Slavophile or openly reactionary views continued to be in a majority.

The presence of a large reactionary element in this class was, however, for a long time obscured by the fact that until 1906, the more progressive elements of the nobility tended to be more active in the zemstvo than the rest of the gentry. The over-representation of the more enlightened members of the gentry – who brought a certain amount of idealism into zemstvo work – encouraged the later legend which exaggerated not only the zemstvos' liberalism, but also their supposed transcendence of the interests of the landowning classes in their day-to-day "economic" work. In fact, even in this field the legend is not entirely true – at least until the 1890s, zemstvo "economic" work was heavily biased in favour of the interests of the landlord. This is apparent not only from the favourable (from the nobles' point of view) distribution of zemstvo taxation, which even Miliukov admitted,⁴ but also from the reluctance of many zemstvos to commute natural obligations into money after the Emancipation.⁵ There were, of course, elements in the zemstvos which supported a more democratic approach, but they were for a long time in a small minority.

F4 For the moderate non-party humanitarian liberalism mirrored in the journal *Vestnik Evropy* (*The Herald of Europe*), see Anton Fediashin, *Liberals under Autocracy*, Madison 2012.

The belief in the economic altruism of the zemstvo was, in fact – like the exaggeration of its liberal tradition – largely the product of hindsight. For by the later 1890s a marked change had come over the zemstvo, a change especially well-marked in the economic field, where there was a massive increase in work directed at improving the conditions of the peasantry. At the same time there was a growth in the political activity of the zemstvos. Despite a ban on intercourse between the zemstvos of different provinces ("guberniia"), their personnel increasingly employed various exhibitions and technical congresses, together with such bodies as the Free Imperial Economic Society, as a forum for mutual discussion of their problems. As a consequence of this, the zemstvos began to show a tendency to collaborate in support of common political and economic demands – for a zemstvo press organ, more rights for the peasantry and the abolition of corporal punishment; for the permission to hold congresses on zemstvo questions; for the granting of wider competence to local self-government; for the establishment of the rule of law and for a change in the government's economic policies.

It is true that these proposals had a definitely liberal flavour, but few zemstvo demands in the 1890s went much further into "politics" than these requests for partial reforms – many of them directed at zemstvo rather than state affairs. Even the period following the accession of Nicholas II, when hopes of reform were for a time high, provides no real exception to this rule. The most radical zemstvo address to the Tsar following his succession – that of Tver' – demanded popular representation only obliquely, and in the vaguest of terms.[6] Moreover, when, in a moment of weakness, Goremykin (Minister of the Interior) permitted a private congress of the presidents of the provincial zemstvo boards – held at Nizhnii-Novgorod in August 1896 – it limited itself entirely to problems of local government, eschewing "politics".[7] But this was nevertheless a time of the slow clarification of liberal views even if this had not yet led to strong opposition to the government. The more progressive elements of society still tended to hope that – as in the time of Alexander II – the autocrat himself might take the initiative in effecting radical reforms "from above". They feared that a campaign of strident opposition might alienate the Tsar, and preferred to follow the essentially loyal path of moderation and peaceful persuasion.

The 1890s then, and especially the later 1890s, saw a democratization of the "economic" work of the zemstvo, coupled with an increase in its political consciousness. Why was this? Firstly, in 1891 there was a disastrous famine which decimated the rural population of several provinces, and this had a considerable effect upon public opinion. It increased the realization that reforms were necessary, and underlined the urgent need for greater expenditure on raising the material and cultural level of the people. Secondly, the growing complexity of zemstvo work entailed by the gradual development of its economic and cultural tasks had brought with it a considerable growth in the numbers of professional men working for the zemstvo: agronomists, statisticians, teachers, doctors, veterinary experts and the like – the so-called "Third Element". The latter were now increasingly gaining greater influence on the course of zemstvo work. Their interests were not in sharp conflict with those of the peasantry, and they were more politically radical than the gentry. Because of this, they tended to have a powerful democratizing influence on the zemstvos' day-to-day work.

Meanwhile, a marked change was taking place within the gentry itself; a change which was inevitably reflected in zemstvo life. After the Emancipation, the ownership of land was undergoing a process of rapid redistribution. Many nobles were unable to adjust successfully to the new conditions of farming which the Emancipation had imposed. Moreover, all sections of landowners were affected by the disastrous fall in grain prices from the 1870s onwards. As a result, in the decades following the Emancipation many nobles were compelled to sell at least part of their estates – one-third of the land which the nobles had held in 1861 had been sold by 1900, mostly to the peasantry. This process was now speeding up. From the point of view of the vendors, a prosperous peasantry was important in so far as it meant higher prices for land – and zemstvo measures to benefit the masses were therefore in the gentry's own enlightened self-interest. The liquidation of the nobles' landed property had another important consequence. It tended to compel many of the gentry to enter the professions for at least part of their living.[8] Many of these men were highly active in zemstvo life, and largely as a result of their European-style education and professional training, they tended to be more politically Westernized than other zemstvo men. On the other hand, a small section of those landlords who retained their land did so primarily because they had become more or less successful capitalist farmers. Dependent largely upon their own initiative and capital, the latter were also more independent of the state than the older style nobility.

The state now chose this moment to tread very heavily on the toes of all sections of landowners. By the end of the 1880s it had become increasingly clear to the autocracy that Russia could not survive as a great power unless it developed a massive industrial base. Government policy therefore began to concentrate on the promotion of industry at the expense of agriculture. The 1890s witnessed a brilliant flowering of Russian industry presided over by the far-sighted Minister of Finance, Sergei Witte. But Russia remained overwhelmingly an agrarian country, and industrial progress was achieved only at the cost of imposing crippling financial burdens on the agricultural population. Indirect taxes were raised to unprecedented levels, and prohibitive tariff barriers were erected against foreign manufactures. In so far as this impoverished the peasantry, it hit those landlords who wished to sell their land. In so far as it raised, for example, the cost of imported agricultural machinery, it hit the capitalist farmer, and helped ruin inefficient landowners. The age-old links between the interests of the gentry and the autocracy had already been weakened by the Emancipation. And now, under the impact of Witte's policies, these links were gradually being severed, or at least being made to undergo a heavy strain. The autocracy was, in fact, creating a hard core of potential opposition among a traditionally subservient class of the population – a process which was accelerated by the changes which were already taking place in the social position of the gentry. And these changes were themselves speeded up by Witte's policies.

From the mid-1890s onwards the oppositionist elements among the gentry increasingly tended to group around the provincial zemstvo institutions where they soon established close relations with the Third Element's more liberal members.

At first the opposition was formless and unorganized. The zemstvos remained overwhelmingly absorbed in day-to-day "cultural" and economic activities. It was the government itself that gave the opposition its greatest stimulus, by adopting policies which were openly hostile to the zemstvos. In the 1860s the autocracy had taken the initiative in reforming society. However, the remaining years of the century were marked by a growing government reaction. After 1881 the assassination of Alexander II by terrorists ushered in a period of extreme political conservatism dominated by the stern figure of the autocratic Tsar Alexander III. The zemstvo institutions were one of the chief casualties of the reactionary movement. The bureaucracy's attitude to local self-government had been ambivalent almost from its foundation, and had subjected it to a series of restrictions upon their authority and competence. In 1890 this culminated in a major "reform" of the zemstvo designed to tie it more closely to the regular administration and to strengthen the control of the nobility at the expense of the peasantry.

The accession of a new Emperor – the youthful Nicholas II – in 1894 brought fresh hope to the moderate zemstvo liberals. Many anticipated a relaxation of the reaction, or even a return to the era of the Great Reforms. Such hopes were to be rudely shattered almost from the outset. When, following his accession, the new Tsar received a mildly liberal address from the Tver' zemstvo, he reacted sharply. At a reception for representatives of the zemstvos and other public institutions he publicly rebuked the liberals:

> "I am aware", declared the Tsar, "that of late in some zemstvo assemblies there have been heard the voices of persons who have been carried away by senseless dreams of the participation of zemstvo representatives in the affairs of national administration. Let it be known that I, while devoting my energies to the good of the people, shall maintain the principle of autocracy just as firmly and unflinchingly as my never-to-be-forgotten father".[9]

The influence of Alexander III upon his son had been decisive. The young Tsar had been brought up under the heavy shadow of his powerful father, and he retained a simple faith in the conservative principles of autocracy, nationalism and Orthodoxy. Although he was not unintelligent his understanding of politics was limited and he was more at home in private than in public life. He had no real conception of the size or nature of the problems facing Russia, and he tended to ascribe all opposition to the seditious activities of a tiny minority of Jews and intellectuals. But although fundamentally a weak man, ill-suited to the rôle of absolute ruler at a time of crisis, he believed he had a religious duty to preserve his autocratic power and hand it down to his successor. And the Emperor's power remained almost completely unlimited. Individual ministers were responsible only to the Tsar, and reported directly to him. There was still no prime minister to coordinate policy, nor even a united cabinet of ministers.

Given the Tsar's support a strong far-sighted prime minister – a statesman cast in the mould of Bismarck – might well have transformed the future of the Empire. But like many weak men, Nicholas feared being dominated by a more powerful personality. Instead, he preferred to surround himself with people of inferior stature who shared his own, essentially negative, reactionary views.

The appointment of the unimaginative bureaucrat, D.S. Sipiagin, as Minister of the Interior in 1898 was the signal for a renewed spell of reaction. In the face of a growing mood of opposition among all classes of the population, the government attempted to strengthen its position by a series of repressive measures. As time went on, more and more areas of the country were placed under forms of exceptional law or "extraordinary protection", which vastly increased the arbitrary power of the bureaucracy. Meanwhile, the government stepped up its persecution of minority nationalities. Discrimination against the Jews went hand in hand with attempts to Russify other national groups. The Russian authorities even made a determined effort to undermine the special constitutional rights enjoyed by Finland.[10] At the same time the government attempted to eliminate unrest in the universities by carrying out purges of university staff and conscripting rebellious students into the army.

Once again the zemstvos were one of the reactionaries' main targets. A full-scale assault was launched upon the organs of local self-government, which threatened to strip them of many of their most important functions. In 1900 the growth of zemstvo taxation was severely limited, and famine relief work was removed from zemstvo control. In 1902 the government proposed to put an end to the zemstvos' veterinary activity, while following peasant disturbances, their statistical work was suspended in 18 provinces. In 1903 V.K. Plehve, Sipiagin's successor, carried out a purge of individual zemstvo institutions, including those of Moscow and Tver'.

The government's measures proved essentially counter-productive. The government's policy served only to rally public opinion behind the zemstvo, and made an increasing number of zemstvo men feel that "small deeds" were no longer enough. Indeed, it now appeared that not even the work of "small deeds" would be secure without major reforms in the political system and a change of government.

Moreover, cultivated "society's" faith in the government's ability to rule the country had been severely shaken by the development of serious disturbances among the masses – the workers and peasants. The popular discontent was to a large extent the direct result of Witte's policies as Minister of Finance. The development of large-scale industry had led to a rapid growth in the numbers of industrial workers; but there had been no corresponding growth in workers' welfare. By Western standards their wages and conditions were often appalling, and genuine trade unions were illegal. There was no proper provision for workers' housing, and many workers remained essentially displaced peasants without a settled family life. In these circumstances the proletariat formed a rootless, unstable element in Russian society. Following 1899 the position of the working class was aggravated by a serious industrial depression which resulted in severe unemployment and a fall in standards of living. Left-wing agitators began to have increasing success among the industrial labour force, and there were a growing number of strikes. The Ministry of the Interior's attempts to control the workers' movement by means of repression and experiments in so-called "police socialism" for the most part ended in failure.[11]

Discontent among the peasantry was also partly the result of Witte's policy of favouring industry at the expense of agriculture. But the roots of the problem went far deeper than this. Although the Emancipation had abolished serfdom it had failed to provide the conditions for the growth of a free capitalist peasantry. The peasants still remained a class apart, without full civil rights and governed by special laws and usages. Unlike the other classes of the population the majority of peasants in agricultural Russia had no individual property rights to their land, which remained under the control of the archaic village commune, or "obshchina". The holdings of individual peasants consisted of scattered strips within an antiquated three-field system, and were subject to periodic redistribution among the members of the commune. In these circumstances the productivity of peasant agriculture remained extremely low, and there was little incentive for individual cultivators to raise the technical level of their husbandry. In many areas the size of peasant allotments was inadequate, but even where they had a relatively large acreage, peasant agriculture was increasingly unable to feed a rapidly growing rural population, or to bear the heavy burden of state and zemstvo taxation. As a consequence, there were periodic famines and a growing number of rural disturbances. The peasants were gradually turning envious eyes upon the lands of the nobility, many of which they already farmed under an iniquitous leasehold system.

The unrest among the masses deeply disturbed large numbers of the zemstvo gentry, and many became convinced that only radical reforms could pacify the country. The serious agrarian disorders of spring 1902 underlined their fears. The Voronezh uezd (district) zemstvo reflected the mood of a growing number of landowners when, *in calling for wide reforms*, it proclaimed that: "*It is no longer possible to live like this in a remote province, fearing for one's life and one's property.*"[12]

Opposition to the government was rapidly increasing among the zemstvo men. However, until the turn of the century progressive zemstvo circles were dominated by the moderates. Many of the most influential zemstvo leaders continued to hold vaguely "Slavophile" views. Although they were hostile to the bureaucracy, they did not oppose the autocracy itself. Indeed, their chief spokesmen, such as Shipov, believed that constitutions were alien to the Russian way of life. In their view, the failings of the régime were the result of the growth of an arbitrary bureaucracy which formed an impenetrable barrier between the monarch and the people. Russia's problems could be solved only by curbing bureaucratic power, and establishing mutual confidence and constant intercourse between the Tsar and "society".

Much of the growing constitutionalist opposition was also very moderate in its aims. Pointing to the outmoded nature of Russia, they claimed that it was not ready for democracy. Their demands went no further than proposals for the establishment of a limited monarchy, civil liberty and the rule of law. These aims would, they hoped, be realized by the act of a liberal Tsar, who would turn to "society" for co-operation in governing the country. Their views were, in fact, not so different from those of the Slavophiles in that they too looked primarily for "confidence" between the Tsar and "society". They differed mainly in that they demanded a written constitution to guarantee civil liberty and ensure that the administration was accountable to the law. They were not prepared to accept the Slavophiles' mystic beliefs in the special nature of Russian life, and the possibility of an ideal autocracy. But both Slavophiles and moderate constitutionalists looked to the Tsar as the most hopeful source of reform. They still hoped that, as in the 1860s, the autocracy would itself take the initiative in transforming Russian life "from above". Both currents of opinion tended to idealize the era of the Great Reforms and the "Tsar-Liberator". In 1898, for example, the presidents of the provincial zemstvo boards met to unveil a memorial to Alexander II.[13] However, being an essentially "loyal" opposition the zemstvo moderates shrank back from overt anti-government activity, and were reluctant to advance far beyond the era of small deeds, of day-to-day cultural work in the zemstvos. In 1898 they even postponed plans to publish a journal devoted to zemstvo affairs in order to avoid offending the government.

The liberationists

In these circumstances the initiative was seized by the more radical constitutionalists who were later to form the nucleus of the "Union of Liberation". By 1901 the radicals, led by such men as Ivan Petrunkevich, the veteran leader of the Tver' zemstvo liberals, and Pavel Miliukov, one of Russia's most eminent historians, began to discuss the publication of an illegal political journal. Meanwhile, in June of the same year, a private meeting of liberals circulated an appeal from "the old zemstvo men", which demanded an end to the era of "small deeds" and called for far-reaching local government reforms.[14]

Zemstvo men, of course, played a prominent part in these new liberal initiatives, but they were by no means alone. Liberal ideas were now making rapid progress in other social circles. It has already been pointed out that many members of the Third Element had established close ties with the more liberal zemstvo gentry. But now, other professional men, unconnected with the zemstvos, began to move towards liberalism, rejecting their previous allegiance to the extreme left. During the 1890s the radical intelligentsia had been overwhelmingly socialist in complexion – either Marxist or Populist, and this continued to be true of a majority. But the turn of the century witnessed the gradual conversion of large sections of the professional intelligentsia to liberalism or a reformist socialism closely related to it. Among their number were many of the leaders of Legal Marxism, Legal Populism (i.e. agrarian socialism), and Economism (moderate trade-unionism).

The most influential of these men was Peter B. Struve, formerly the most celebrated of the Legal Marxists. Although his ideas still had a socialist tinge, he was now moving away from orthodox Marxism. By late 1900 he was making plans for the publication of a liberal journal abroad to unite all opposition elements around a common demand for a constitution. After unsuccessful attempts to obtain the cooperation of the Social Democrats in a joint liberal-socialist publishing venture, Struve[15] eventually secured the backing of the zemstvo radicals for an independent liberal journal.

In March 1901 Struve was involved in a demonstration in Kazan' Square, and was exiled to Tver', the centre of zemstvo radicalism. Once there he carried on conversations with leading zemstvo liberals such as I.I. Petrunkevich and A.A. Bakunin about his proposed paper.[16] The latter agreed to merge their own zemstvo project with that of Struve, who then fled the country to prepare for its publication. However, the preparations for an effective illegal journal required considerable time. It could not succeed without the support of a large body of sympathizers and agents in Russia. When Struve fled he left behind a close friend (V.Ia. Bogucharskii, another Legal Marxist) to help prepare the ground.[17] Bogucharskii first made contact with a number of writers and public men who had fled to Finland after Kazan' Square, and solicited their support. (This later became the St. Petersburg group of the Union of Liberation.) Following this initial success Bogucharskii travelled elsewhere in Russia, recruiting further support for the new venture. However, it was not until 1902 that Struve's plans began to take definite shape. In March of that year an exhibition of domestic crafts was used as a "front" for a wide discussion of the paper by its supporters in Russia. At about the same time Miliukov wrote the journal's first leading article,[18] which was subsequently approved at a conference of the paper's supporters.

Publication of the journal *Liberation*

On 18 June 1902, *Liberation* (*Osvobozhdenie*), a fortnightly journal under the editorship of Struve, began to be published in Stuttgart. Although Struve had insisted that his paper should be independent, it in fact became the semi-official organ of the "Friends of *Liberation*" in Russia. The latter, whose main task was contributing to the paper, and distributing it in Russia, were to provide the basis for the later Union of Liberation. *Liberation* formed, in fact, the centre around which the liberal movement was to grow.

Struve had originally intended to produce a paper designed to unite all opposition elements upon the basis of a common demand for a constitution, and this was still, to some degree, the task to which he addressed himself in his first editorial. In No. 1, he declared that "Our task is not to disunite, but to unite".[19] He made conciliatory gestures towards the moderate right by praising the Great Reforms, and also suggested that an accommodation was possible with the revolutionaries: "Even the extreme Russian parties", he said, "go no further in their practical demands than wide political and economic reforms in a democratic spirit". But he made it clear that he was addressing himself, primarily, to "the moderate elements of Russian society". Although he stressed the liberals' need to organize themselves, he refrained from laying down a programme for them.

The working out of a political platform was to be left to "the public men of our country, and, above all, to the leaders of (local) self-government".

Miliukov's leading article,[20] reflecting the views of the "friends of *Liberation*" in Russia, laid down the possible lines of a political programme for the paper's supporters. It outlined only general principles, eschewing anything which might be a source of disunity – such as social reform, or too much detail. Miliukov represented his proposals as a mere starting-point of discussions from which a party programme might later emerge. Nevertheless, despite its essentially provisional character, Miliukov's article went far beyond the outlook of the Slavophiles and the moderate liberals. The article was, for example, thoroughly Westernist: "In themselves", wrote Miliukov, "free forms of political life are as little national as the use of the abacus or the printing press, of steam or electricity". And in true Western positivist style, he depicted the victory of constitutionalism as inevitable. The article did not limit itself to demands for civil rights, the rule of law and legal equality – with which even the most moderate liberals would have agreed. It also demanded a representative body based upon the principle of "classless popular representation", an oblique reference to universal suffrage. Although Miliukov did not spell out in detail the powers which popular representatives should enjoy, he did stipulate that they should have the right to approve legislation and the state budget. However, he still looked to the Crown as the source of reform. The object of society, and more particularly the zemstvo liberals, should be to persuade the Court and ruling circles that radical constitutional change was essential. The fundamental principles of the constitution should be proclaimed by an Imperial Manifesto as a unilateral act of the Tsar. However, in view of society's distrust of the bureaucracy, the details should be worked out by representatives of reformed zemstvo institutions.

The articles by Struve and Miliukov in No. 1 of *Liberation* provide an illuminating insight into the attitudes and objectives of the Russian liberationists. Both men clearly envisaged the future formation of a widely-based constitutionalist movement, but as yet they were still reluctant to lay down a detailed programme for it, and were still casting around for the social and political elements upon which it would be based. However, it was evident that the zemstvo men were still their main target. The liberal leaders were by no means indifferent to gaining the support of the masses. But despite a number of ominous popular disturbances they remained an uncertain *point d'appui*. In the circumstances it was felt that quick results could be obtained only if the zemstvo men and educated "society" in general made a united effort to convince the Tsar and his advisers of the need for radical reform. However, unlike the Slavophiles and moderate liberals, the liberationists were ultimately prepared to appeal to the people if they met with no response from above. They felt that popular pressure might make the Crown more willing to listen to the arguments of liberal society, and as time went on they increasingly began to cultivate support from below. But they at no time supported violence, or a bloody revolution. They believed that the necessary reforms could be obtained peacefully without using extreme methods. However, they felt that if positive results were to be achieved, "society", with its special influence upon ruling circles, would have a vital rôle to play in their conversion to the liberal cause.

However, the government continued to display a profound suspicion of the zemstvos. Following the assassination of Sipiagin in early 1902, his place as Minister of the Interior was taken by V.K. Plehve, who saw police methods as the chief answer to the growing disturbances among the peasants, workers and intelligentsia. And as time went on he increasingly displayed bitter hostility towards the zemstvo liberals. Moreover, in 1902 liberal opinion was deeply antagonized by a decision to exclude official zemstvo representatives from a major government inquiry – Witte's Special Conference on the Needs of the Countryside. Agriculture was facing an acute crisis, and an inquiry into this problem was long overdue. This question was of direct interest to the zemstvo men, and they bitterly resented their exclusion from the conference. All shades of the opposition combined in organizing an unofficial zemstvo congress to consider the agrarian problem and to protest against the government's decision. The invitations were sent out by D.I. Shipov, the Chairman of the Moscow Zemstvo Board, and the congress met at his Moscow home.[21] The demands of the congress were essentially moderate. However, the assembly made it clear that it believed that the agrarian problem could be solved only by fundamental reforms and not by mere palliatives.[22]

The government's reaction to the convocation of the congress was hostile, and it issued a severe reprimand to those who had taken part. Later, following conversations with Witte and Plehve, Shipov and the moderate right were induced to abandon the most radical part of the congress's proposals.[23] (This had called not only for the inclusion of elected zemstvo representatives in the Special Conference but had also demanded their inclusion as permanent members in a council of Rural Economy in the Ministry of Agriculture.)

Among the more radical liberals, the news of the retreat by the zemstvo moderates was greeted with shock and indignation. Many liberationists saw it as a betrayal, and there was a chorus of demands for a change in *Liberation*'s editorial policy. In order to appeal to the widest possible spectrum of society, Struve had initially made overtures not only to the left, but also to the Slavophile, Shipovite element in the zemstvos. This policy now came increasingly under fire,[24] and the liberationists began to move towards the formation of a more homogeneous, more coherent political movement.

In the autumn of 1902 the initiative was taken, not so much by the zemstvo gentry, as by the largely non-zemstvo intelligentsia from the professions. Among this section of the population socialist ideas were still predominant, but liberal influence was increasingly making itself felt. St. Petersburg was the main centre of the radical intelligentsia, which tended to be more left-wing than the zemstvo men. And it was in Petersburg[25] that the so-called "Culinary Committee", composed mostly of liberationist writers and journalists, grew up, acting as the spearhead of pressure for a more coherent political grouping.

However, it was not until early 1903 that *Liberation* itself took heed of the growing impatience with the zemstvo right. As late as December 1902 it was still paying court to this section of opinion,[26] but by February 1903 it had abruptly changed course. Miliukov declared that "*Liberation* is serving too wide a circle of people and social classes", and demanded a more definite, more left-wing policy, and an end to overtures to the Slavophiles.[27] The reason for this article was clear: the "Friends of *Liberation*" were now thinking of forming a closer political union. "Before organizing", said Miliukov, "it is necessary to know whither and with whom to set off together". Struve, endorsing Miliukov's arguments, called for the formation of "a decisively democratic party". Universal suffrage was now made an official plank of *Liberation*'s platform. *Liberation* was, then, beginning to turn towards a more homogeneous, more left-wing basis of support. Its social demands also moved to the left: by the summer of 1903 it had even begun to call for radical agrarian and labour reform.[28]

Meanwhile, government policies were making the formation of a more coherent liberal movement seem a matter of special urgency. Within Russia the persecution of the zemstvo was being stepped up, and in the Far East the government's adventurist foreign policy had now put the Empire on a collision course with Japan. In the circumstances the need for a liberal organization capable of taking political initiatives and responding to current events was becoming increasingly self-evident. On 20 April 1903 the "Friends of *Liberation*" met to discuss this matter,[29] and within three months their efforts led to the establishment of the Union of Liberation.

The Union of Liberation

The "Union of Liberation", as the new liberal organization was named, had its somewhat unspectacular inauguration at Schaffhausen in Switzerland on 20–22 July 1903. It is true that its official début did not take place until January of the following year, but nevertheless D.I. Shakhovskoi gives Schaffhausen a "central significance"[30] in the foundation of the Union.

Shakhovskoi claims that the participants were unrepresentative, so it is, perhaps, unwise to attribute too much importance to their composition. Petrunkevich divides them, somewhat arbitrarily, into two groups of ten, one of zemstvo men and the other of liberationists unconnected with local self-government.[31] However, Fischer's division of the participants into three roughly equal groups – "gentry liberals", like Petrunkevich and Shakhovskoi, "intelligentsia liberals", such as P.I. Novgorodtsev, and "intelligentsia socialists", such as Struve, S.N. Bulgakov and S.N. Prokopovich,[32] is a more revealing one, even if he does tend to underemphasize the number of gentry liberals. In particular his inclusion of F.I. Rodichev among the "intelligentsia liberals" is rather misleading. Although he was an advocate by profession he had very strong links with the zemstvo. The proportion of intelligentsia present was, however, high, illuminating the importance of the movement away from orthodox socialism which was currently taking place in this section of society. However, the purely liberal intelligentsia were still in a minority at Schaffhausen where they were represented by three professors – P.I. Novgorodtsev, I.M. Grevs, V.I. Vernadskii – and

V.V. Vodovozov, a journalist and assistant professor. They were overshadowed by a group – seven in all – whose ideas still had a socialist tinge. Their presence indicates that *Liberation* had had some degree of success in obtaining socialist co-operation with the liberals upon the basis of a common demand for a constitution. From the very first number of *Liberation* Struve had suggested that such an alliance was possible, at least for the time being, until the triumph of constitutionalist principles. And now such arguments seem to have had an effect, at least upon the reformist socialists. However, this success involved the Union in corresponding disadvantages, for this group, mostly friends of Struve, apparently retained a certain awareness of its own identity,[33] which derived from its consciousness of its long-term socialist objectives. The presence of the socialists was, therefore, probably one of the reasons why Schaffhausen saw the creation, not of a party, but of a *Union* – a federal association of autonomous groups united around the common demand for an end to the autocracy and the establishment of a constitution. The presence of moderate zemstvo men like N.N. L'vov, was probably another factor in inducing the conference to arrive at this decision. Moreover, the differences of opinion among the participants made agreement on such vexed questions as agrarian policy difficult to obtain, and they were accordingly shelved. But, nevertheless, the general lines of future activity were laid down, including plans for holding a future Congress of Liberation.[34]

In the autumn of 1903 the "Friends of *Liberation*" held two meetings devoted to the task of organizing the Union and preparing for its forthcoming congress. Of the two meetings the more significant was at Kharkov. In addition to laying the groundwork for the congress, it concerned itself with influencing the moderate constitutionalists in the zemstvos. One of the most important actions of the Kharkov meeting was its decision to establish a liberal organization exclusively for zemstvo men. This "Union of Zemstvo Constitutionalists" held its first congress in November.[35]

Meanwhile, in the period before the First Congress of Liberation, the liberationists' ideas continued to move to the left under the influence of increasing government repression and the darkening outlook in the Far East. At the same time, the continued growth of unrest among the peasants and workers increasingly prompted the liberationists to seek more support from below, from the people, by supporting demands for social reform. The high-water mark of this tendency was expressed in No. 33 of *Liberation*, by "L's" article on the agrarian question, which had editorial support.[36] Rejecting purely political liberalism, and declaring liberalism's indissoluble links with "social economic democracy", "L" called for wide agrarian and labour reforms, including measures to help the masses obtain the land. Although this article was more radical than the view of the liberationists as a whole (it was apparently the work of Sergei Bulgakov, a former Legal Marxist[37]) it demonstrates the prevailing leftward trend.

The swing to the left was not confined to the pages of *Liberation*. It was also much in evidence at the First Congress of Liberation in January 1904, when the Union was officially founded in St. Petersburg. The programme adopted by the congress[38] reflected the liberationists' increasingly radical mood. It demanded universal, equal, direct and secret suffrage, called for a constitution "in the spirit of wide democratisation", and recognized the "right of self-determination for the different nationalities entering into the composition of the Russian state". And although it stressed that: "the first and main aim of the Union of Liberation is the *political* liberation of Russia" it also turned its attention to social and economic questions. The Union gave a pledge that it would base its attitude to such questions on democratic principles, and declared that "the defence of the interests of the toiling masses" would be "the direct object of its activity".

However, the congress limited itself to declarations of principle; no long-term tactics or detailed programme were worked out. This appears to have been a reflection of the diversity of the elements represented at the congress, and the difficulty of arriving at formulae acceptable both to the left and to the right. The declaration on social policy, for example, was hotly contested by the more moderate constitutionalists, while on the left the socialists continued to be a divisive influence. According to Shakhovskoi, the socialists "were in general inclined to look upon the Union as a purely political and temporary combination". The reformist populists who participated even tried, unsuccessfully, to limit the Union's activity to the intelligentsia and the zemstvo men.[39]

The failure to work out a detailed plan of tactics at the congress meant that the newly-elected central organ of the Union – the council – obtained a wide degree of discretion in executive matters. The council consisted mainly of four liberal gentry – I.I. Petrunkevich, Prince Peter D. Dolgorukov, Prince D.I. Shakhovskoi and N.N. L'vov – whose activity centred on Moscow; and four literary men working in St. Petersburg – N.F. Annenskii, V.Ia. Bogucharskii, S.N. Prokopovich and A.V. Peshekhonov, all reformist socialists. In addition the council included the Kiev zemstvo leader M.M. Kovalevskii and Sergei Bulgakov, a Kharkov professor and former legal Marxist. The chief offices were all in the hands of the zemstvo gentry. Petrunkevich was chairman, Shakhovskoi secretary, and Dolgorukov treasurer. Moreover, although there was a substantial group of socialists – the genuinely liberal intelligentsia being notably absent – the council included two moderate constitutionalists – L'vov and Kovalevskii – whose presence emphasized that the Union had still not lost contact with the more moderate zemstvo liberals.

The council delegated the task of distributing *Liberation* to a special "technical commission" centred on Petersburg; while the Muscovites concentrated on maintaining intercourse with the provincial groups.[40] It was agreed that the council's chief priority should be the expansion of the Union and the strengthening of its organization.

However, for several months the council's work was impeded by the Russo-Japanese war. The war, which broke out in February 1904, led to a split in the Union almost at its outset. Almost all shades of liberationist opinion regretted the war, and opposed Russian imperialist ambitions in the Far East, but differences arose over the tactical position to be adopted now it had begun. The more moderate elements of the Union were afraid of losing contact with the opinion of "society" as a whole, which was inclined either to adopt a "defensist" attitude to the war or to adopt an openly "patriotic" position. Struve, taking the moderate view, which found most of its support among the zemstvo men,[41] argued that a campaign against the war would alienate public opinion.[42] On the other hand, Miliukov, who had strong backing from the intelligentsia, insisted that it was essential to avoid giving the impression that the liberationists supported the war.[43]

The deep division within the ranks of the liberationists proved a serious source of weakness and severely retarded the council's organizational work. In the circumstances the Union was unable to make any real progress; if anything it was forced onto the defensive. It is true that its protégé, the Union of Zemstvo Constitutionalists, was continuing to make headway, and held its Second Congress in May. But the congress's views were to the right of the Union of Liberation as a whole, especially its defensist attitude to the war, and the vaguely Slavophile overtones of its demand for "popular representation with the union of the monarch with the people".[44]

The work of the Moscow "A" group of the Union of Liberation on a model constitution, "The Fundamental State Law of the Russian Empire",[45] was also largely directed at the zemstvo moderates. This document was not an official publication of the Union: indeed it was never discussed by the liberationists as a whole.[46] It seems to have been primarily designed to have an educational influence upon the zemstvo men, and "society" in general. In his "Introduction", Struve directed his arguments primarily at the moderate elements of the country, and he stressed the rôle which the constitution could play in securing social and political stability. Struve admitted that this approach might be regarded as conservative, but it was "a far-sighted conservatism". The projected constitution carefully avoided extremes and left the monarch with considerable authority. The Emperor was to retain control over the executive, appoint ministers and have substantial authority over foreign policy. He would also have the power to dissolve "parliament" (within prescribed limits) and would retain a veto over legislation. Moreover, while parliament would have the right to initiate legislation and confirm the budget, and ministers were to be responsible to it, the dangers of direct democracy were diluted by provision for two chambers. In addition to a lower house elected by universal suffrage, there would be an upper house representing reformed zemstvo institutions. This was rather more than a design for a "limited monarchy"[47] but it did not go far beyond it.

The work of the Zemstvo Constitutionalists and the drafting of a model constitution continued, then, to go ahead during the first half of 1904. But for the most part the Union of Liberation underwent a period of stagnation, occupying itself mainly with the distribution of *Liberation* and with maintaining its imperilled unity. The actual corporate activity of the Union was confined almost entirely to the council, which met alternately in each of the capitals once a month. During this period of division and weakness, the local liberationist groups tended to be something of a law unto themselves.[48]

However, by July 1904, the conditions for political activity began to change sharply. The war in the Far East was going badly for Russia, undermining public confidence in the government. The liberationists rapidly began to close ranks in united opposition to the war. Meanwhile, the appointment of the moderately liberal Prince Sviatopolk-Mirskii as Minister of the Interior in August 1904, following the assassination of the reactionary V.K. Plehve by terrorists, led to a relaxation of repression, and rather more open political activity became possible. For the first time the liberationists were able to develop a fairly free, legal press within Russia. The existing liberal journal *Pravo* (*Law*), which was strictly speaking an organ of the legal profession, became more openly constitutionalist, and at the same time completely new papers were inaugurated: *Nasha Zhizn'* (*Our Life*), run by the revisionist Marxists, and *Syn Otechestva* (*Son of the Fatherland*), which had a revisionist populist flavour.

The liberationists now redoubled their efforts to unite the entire opposition behind a demand for a constitution. In September, the Union sent representatives to a conference of opposition and revolutionary parties in Paris.[49] For the most part the various social-democratic organizations refused to attend, but the Socialist Revolutionary Party participated, as did a number of opposition groups from the minority nationalities of the Empire. At the Conference it was decided, at least on paper, that the various groups represented would co-ordinate their efforts to end the autocracy and establish a democratic régime. They also demanded the restoration of the Finnish consitution and recognized, in general terms, the principle of self-determination for minority nationalities. None of the parties and groups represented intended to drop any of their own ultimate aims or abandon their own tactical methods. But they did recognize the need for a temporary alliance until the destruction of absolutism. In fact, the Conference had little practical result; its decisions had a mostly symbolic character and did not lead to a significant increase in cooperation among the opposition. However, the Conference once again underlined the liberationists' tendency to seek allies on the left in a common struggle for constitutional reform.

Meanwhile, encouraged by the new political conditions the liberationists were planning to achieve a breakthrough in their activity in the zemstvos. As a first step, Shipov and the bureau of the 1902 All-Zemstvo Congress were persuaded to call a new congress in the Autumn of 1904. When Mirskii gave permission for the congress, mistakenly believing that only local government affairs would be discussed, the liberationists hastened to make use of it. They determined to hold a second congress to consider means of swinging the zemstvo men behind the demand for a constitution.

In preparation for the Second Congress of Liberation, the council devised a detailed tactical programme for the Union.[50] In addition to its proposals on the Zemstvo Congress, it outlined three other objectives:

Firstly, the liberal intelligentsia were to organize a series of banquets on the lines of the French banquet campaign of 1848. Nominally, the festivities would be in honour of the fortieth anniversary of the judicial reforms of the 1860s, but in fact they were to be used a a front for stirring up a mood of opposition among the intelligentsia, and for making speeches and proposals more radical than those which could be expected from the zemstvo men.

Secondly, it was agreed that a concerted effort should be made to swing the Zemstvo Constitutionalists and the annual zemstvo assemblies to the left.

Finally, a proposal was made, but shelved, to form semi-political unions of professional men and unite them in a Union of Unions under liberationist influence.

The Second Congress of Liberation, which was held secretly in St. Petersburg on 20 October 1904, failed once again to decide on a detailed programme. According to Shakhovskoi, a draft had been prepared in Paris, but it arrived too late for discussion. The main achievement of the congress was therefore its adoption of the tactical plan drafted by the council. The adoption of new tactics signalled the end of the period of stagnation in the Union's affairs. The Union's work now assumed a more positive, purposeful direction.

The tactical programme agreed by the congress proved to be remarkably successful. For the first time the Union had committed itself to a major campaign amongst the intelligentsia. And the series of banquets which were held in the capitals and in many provincial cities proved highly effective in mobilizing Russia's professional classes behind demands for a democratic constitution. It is true that the Social Democrats made a number of attempts to disrupt the banquets.[51] But although this was a source of embarrassment to the liberationists, it did not seriously affect the success of the campaign.

However, the most important part of the Union's tactical plan was aimed, not at the intelligentsia, but at the zemstvos. On 2 November a conference of the Zemstvo Constitutionalists was held to coordinate radical opinion at the forthcoming All-Zemstvo Congress. The congress, which took place from 6–9 November, was a triumph for the liberationists. The zemstvo men openly demanded the establishment of Western-style civil liberties and the rule of law. At the same time they adopted a vaguely worded demand for a constitution.[52] Coming from the representatives of the zemstvos, this demand had an enormous impact on the opinion of "society". The liberationists' efforts to influence the regular provincial assemblies had decidedly less success – partly because of government pressure, and partly because the zemstvo leaders were more liberal than their rank and file.[53] Nevertheless, the regular zemstvo assemblies did respond to some extent to liberationist promptings, and a majority came out in favour of some form of representative body.[54]

Notes

1 P.N. Miliukov, *Russia and its Crisis*, Chicago 1905, p. 22.
2 B. Veselovskii, *Istoriia zemstva*, S.P.B. 1909–11, Vol. III, pp. 97–104 (hereafter referred to as Veselovskii). Terence Emmons, *The Russian Landed Gentry in the Peasant Emancipation of 1861*, Cambridge 1968, pp. 375–81. I.P. Belokonskii, *Zemskoe dvizhenie*, 2nd edn, Moscow 1914 (hereafter referred to as Belokonskii), p. 3.
3 I.I. Petrunkevich, "Iz zapisok obshchestvennogo deiatelia", *A.R.R.*, Vol. XXI, Berlin 1934, pp. 99–114; Veselovskii, III, pp. 230–40; S. Galai, *The Liberation Movement in Russia 1900–1905*, Cambridge 1973, pp. 11–20.
4 Miliukov, *Russia and its Crisis*, p. 288.

20   *Prelude*

5 Veselovskii, III, pp. 75–6; Petrunkevich, "Iz zapisok", p. 80.
6 Belokonskii, pp. 51–52; F.I. Rodichev, "Iz vospominanii", *S.Z.*, LIII, 1933, p. 291. The most radical part of the address was as follows:

> We look forward, Sire, to public institutions having the possibility and the right of expressing their opinions on questions which concern them so that the expression of the needs and thoughts, not only of the bureaucracy, but also of the Russian people, may reach the heights of the throne.

The main author of the address, F.I. Rodichev, later denied that there was even an indirect demand for a constitution. See F.I. Rodichev, "Avtobiografiia F.I. Rodicheva", *Vozrozhdenie*, Paris 1954, p. 69.

7 Shipov, *Vospominaniia*, Moscow 1918, pp. 70–3 (hereafter referred to as Shipov).
8 For the change in the nobles' social position see, e.g. Veselovskii, III, p. 203; Miliukov, *Russia and its Crisis*, pp. 559–60; Petrunkevich, "Iz zapisok", pp. 213–15, 307–8.
9 George Fischer, *Russian Liberalism*, Cambridge, MA 1958, pp. 74–5. Belokonskii, p. 52.
10 Alexander I had granted a constitution and a measure of autonomy to the Finns. After 1898 the Russian Governor-General Bobrikov followed policies which aimed at eliminating many of their special privileges.
11 Under the direction of S.N. Zubatov, a senior police official, a number of attempts were made to establish police-sponsored trade unions. The object of the "zubatovshchina" was to gain control of the workers' movement and exclude the influence of the socialist parties. Provided the workers could be kept out of "politics" the leaders of "police socialism" were prepared to support some of the workers' purely economic demands.
12 Belokonskii, p. 111.
13 Shipov, p. 80.
14 V.I. Lenin, *Sochineniia*, 3rd edn, Moscow-Leningrad 1931, Vol. V, pp. 74–8.
15 For an account of Struve's negotiations see Galai, *The Liberation Movement in Russia*, pp. 97–108; R. Pipes, *Struve, Liberal on the Left*, Cambridge, MA 1970. Both Galai and Pipes provide a detailed account of Struve's gradual drift to the right.
16 Petrunkevich, "Iz zapisok", pp. 336–7.
17 Belokonskii, pp. 92–3. Belokonskii merely refers to Struve's friend as "X", but S. Frank (*Biografiia P.B. Struve*, New York 1956, p. 31) confirms that it was Bogucharskii. Frank also names the publisher D.E. Zhukovsky as one of the paper's chief financial backers. However, the zemstvo liberals also provided substantial financial support. In the spring of 1901 Prince D.I. Shakhovskoi and N.N. L'vov went to Stuttgart to finalize arrangements for the publication of the journal and provided Struve with 100,000 rubles (see Petrunkevich, "Iz zapisok", p. 337).
18 Petrunkevich, "Iz zapisok", p. 337; Miliukov, *Vospominaniia 1859–1917*, 2 Vols, New York 1955, p. 236.
19 Editorial, *Osvobozhdenie*, No. 1.
20 "S.S." (Miliukov): "Ot russkikh konstitutionalistov", *Osvobozhdenie*, No. 1.
21 Shipov, pp. 160–8; Belokonskii, pp. 94–6.
22 The congress's proposals included demands for a radical reform of the zemstvo, equal civil rights for the peasantry, and a review of Witte's financial policies.
23 Shipov, pp. 170–91. Shipov was led to believe that provided they moderated their demands and kept out of "politics", the government would in future adopt a more sympathetic attitude to the zemstvos. However, administrative interference in zemstvo affairs continued and even Shipov came to believe he had been deceived (Shipov, p. 194).
24 See e.g. "Anton Staritskii" (A.V. Peshekhonov), "Lozhnyi shag" in *Osvobozhdenie*, No. 7, 18 September 1902.
25 The zemstvo men were centred on Moscow, which was geographically and spiritually closer to provincial Russia. St. Petersburg was far more of a Western city, and the centre of a highly sophisticated Westernized intelligentsia.

26 Editorial, *Osvobozhdenie*, No. 12.
27 Miliukov ("S.S.") and Struve, "K ocherednym voprosam", *Osvobozhdenie*, No. 17, 16 February 1903.
28 See Struve's article on the German elections in *Osvobozhdenie*, No. 25, 18 June 1903.
29 Belokonskii, p. 164.
30 D.I. Shakhovskoi, "Soiuz osvobozhdeniia, Vospominaniia", in *Zarnitsy*, S.P.B. 1909, p. 105 (hereafter referred to as Shakhovskoi). This work is also published in D.B. Pavlov (ed.), *Liberal'noe dvizhenie v Rossii 1902–05 gg.*, Moscow 2001, pp. 526–602.
31 Petrunkevich, "Iz zapisok", p. 164.
32 Fischer, *Russian Liberalism*, pp. 140–1.
33 S. Frank, *Biografiia P.B. Struve*, p. 38.
34 Shakhovskoi, p. 106.
35 Shakhovskoi, p. 106. The Union was a far more open organization than the Union of Liberation. Since it did not indulge in underground activities it was hoped that it would be possible to attract members from among the more moderate constitutionalists.
36 "K agrarnomu voprosu", *Osvobozhdenie*, No. 33, 19 October 1903.
37 Nathan Smith, *The Constitutional-Democratic Movement in Russia, 1902–1906* (PhD thesis, University of Illinois, 1958), footnote, p. 148.
38 *Listok Osvobozhdeniia*, No. 17.
39 Shakhovskoi, pp. 111–12.
40 Shakhovskoi, p. 117.
41 Shakhovskoi, p. 118.
42 "Pis'mo k studentam" in *Listok Osvobozhdeniia*, No. 1. In his "Letter to the Students", Struve argued that as far as possible the force of patriotism should be diverted into liberal channels. Students should participate in patriotic demonstrations and should join in the chanting of such slogans as "Long live the Army!" However, at the same time they should also add liberal slogans like: "Long live freedom!", "Long live free Russia!".
43 See letters from Miliukov ("S.S.") and Struve's reply in *Osvobozhdenie*, No. 43, No. 45.
44 Shakhovskoi, pp. 118–20.
45 "Osnovnoi gosudarstvennyi zakon Rossiiskoi imperii", in *Materialy po vyrabotke russkoi konstitutsii*, *Osvobozhdenie*, Paris 1905, Vol. I.
46 Shakhovskoi, pp. 135–6.
47 Fischer, *Russian Liberalism*, pp. 171–2.
48 Shakhovskoi, see also: E.D. Kuskova: "Kren nalevo: iz proshlogo", *S.Z.*, No. 44, p. 390. In the spring of 1904 Kuskova was sent to the provinces to establish new liberationist groups. To her dismay, she discovered that in a whole series of provincial centres the liberationists were split into mutually exclusive groups of zemstvo men and intelligentsia. In Kursk she was informed that the antagonism between the two factions was so great that it was impossible to unite them.
49 See: *Listok Osvobozhdeniia*, No. 17, No. 19, 1904. Miliukov, *Russia and its Crisis*, pp. 524–6. *Vospominaniia*, Vol. I, pp. 242–5. The liberationist representatives were Miliukov, Struve, Peter Dolgorukov and Bogucharskii.
50 Shakhovskoi, p. 135.
51 See, e.g., E.D. Kuskova, "Kren nalevo: Iz proshlogo", *S.Z.*, No. 44, 1939, pp. 390–1.
52 Belokonskii, p. 222. A minority led by Shipov opposed a representative body with legislative powers. Instead, they favoured a purely consultative body. Their opinon was recorded alongside that of the majority when the congress's decisions were published.
53 See, e.g., B. Veselovskii, "Dvizhenie zemlevladel'tsev" (Part 2), in L. Martov, P. Maslov and A. Potresov (eds), *Obshchestvennoe dvizhenie*, Vol. II, S.P.B. 1909–11, p. 5; Shipov, p. 103.
54 Shakhovskoi, p. 142.

2 Reform or revolution?

Sviatopolk-Mirskii and the political "spring"

The liberal campaign was not without its effect upon the government, and in particular upon Prince Sviatopolk-Mirskii the new Minister of the Interior. The latter had a reputation of supporting very moderate liberal tendencies, and on taking office he had given vague promises of obtaining the confidence of society. He would, he proclaimed, follow a policy of "true and broad liberalism, at least in so far as this liberalism is not of such a nature as to change the established order of things".[1] Mirskii's appointment led to a genuine relaxation of Plehve's régime of police repression, especially as far as the press and the zemstvos were concerned. However, the liberationists treated Mirskii and his policies with reserve and suspicion. In the columns of *Liberation* (*Osvobozhdenie*) Miliukov argued that Mirskii's attempts to gain the support of society without changing the basic nature of the autocracy were meant to deceive the public.[2] The liberals would not be carried away by the government's vague promises of reform: "We need facts", declared Miluykov, "we will not give any more credit". The government should accept the liberationist programme: "There is no half-way house between autocracy and consistent constitutionalism." Struve recognized Mirskii's good intentions but emphasized that nothing short of a constitution would be acceptable to the liberationists.[3]

Meanwhile, Mirskii was becoming increasingly ready to make concessions to meet the demands of at least the more moderate opposition. Following the Zemstvo Congress he had a discussion with Shipov about the zemstvos' demands.[4] Subsequently, at Mirskii's request, a group of zemstvo liberals drew up a detailed account of their proposals. Their memorandum,[5] which was drafted by the moderate liberal S.N. Trubetskoi, urged that the Tsar should take the initiative in implementing a programme of political reform, which should include the convocation of a representative assembly with legislative functions. Mirskii was favourably impressed by some of the liberals' arguments, and advised the Tsar to announce a programme of reform. He did not support the demand for a representative assembly with legislative power, but he did suggest that elected representatives should be brought into the existing State Council. This would not have given Russia a real constitutional system, but it would have gone some way to satisfying the more moderate elements of the Zemstvo Congress. At first the Tsar was inclined to accede to Mirskii's proposals, and asked him to draft an ukaz putting them into effect. However, eventually the idea of bringing elected representatives into the State Council was dropped.[6]

The amended ukaz, which provided for a programme of government reforms, was issued on 12 December.[7] In it the Tsar directed his attention primarily to the problems of the peasantry, and ordered that work should be undertaken to bring their legal rights into line with those of other classes. The ukaz went on to propose the reform of the zemstvos, including the widening of their sphere of competence and their electorate; a relaxation of restrictions upon the press and religious dissenters; and the provision of state insurance for industrial workers. At the same time it committed the government to a programme of legal reform, and undertook to review the exceptional laws used to maintain order in large parts of the Empire. However, the ukaz stressed that there was to be no change in the existing system of government. It was made clear from the outset that the "Fundamental Laws of the Empire" would remain inviolable. Moreover, on 14 December the government issued a stern communiqué condemning the liberal campaign of the previous month and declaring its demands impermissible.[8]

The tone of the communiqué and the failure to concede any kind of popular representation was a severe disappointment to the liberationists. Struve admitted that the ukaz contained concessions, but he pointed out that the autocracy remained intact. Moreover, the ukaz had not proposed to grant freedom of assembly or association, while its promises were to be implemented by the discredited bureaucracy.[9] Without totally condemning the ukaz, the liberal legal journal *Pravo* (*Law*) also severely criticized the communiqué and doubted whether the government sincerely meant to implement the proposed reforms.

Events in the Far East, where Port Arthur fell to the Japanese on 20 December, encouraged the liberationists to take a strong line with the government. And any prospect of their gaining confidence in the Ministry's good intentions were to be shattered by the events of "Bloody Sunday".

Bloody Sunday

On 9 January 1905, thousands of St. Petersburg workers were planning to hold a mass demonstration under the leadership of Father George Gapon. Gapon, a young Orthodox priest, was the head of the so-called "St. Petersburg Assembly of Workers". The assembly was not a revolutionary body; indeed, it had been established with police approval. Like other experiments in "police socialism" it had originally been designed as a means of keeping the workers out of the clutches of the socialist parties and ensuring their loyalty to conservative principles. However, under the pressure of the growing political crisis, the movement had begun to move to the left. Gapon himself had a sincere concern for the needs of the workers and came to share many of the ideas of the liberation movement. He finally conceived the idea of organizing an essentially loyal and peaceful march to petition the Tsar for social and constitutional reforms.

As the day of the procession drew closer there were growing indications that the government planned to stop the procession by force. On 8 January a deputation from *Pravo* made a last-minute bid to persuade the government to let the march take place.[10] But it was now too late. On the morning of Sunday 9 January many thousands of workers carrying icons and portraits of the Tsar began to converge on the centre of St. Petersburg from various parts of the city. Everywhere the unarmed marchers were systematically dispersed by a murderous hail of fire from government troops. Hundreds of people were killed and many more were seriously injured.

The apparently cold-blooded massacre profoundly shocked all shades of public opinion. Bloody Sunday deeply intensified anti-government feeling in the country, and led to a wave of unrest among the masses. The events of 9 January marked the beginning of the Revolution of 1905.

The liberationists shared in the popular sense of outrage and adopted a tone of extreme hostility towards the representatives of the existing régime. Struve even went so far as to launch a bitter attack on the Tsar himself, describing him as the "executioner of the people".[11] The liberationists now began to lose hope in the prospects of reform from above, without much greater popular pressure from below. Accordingly, they now turned their attention to gaining the support of the masses, especially as the latter were now, politically speaking, clearly on the move. And if the liberationists were to have a serious impact on the people, the formation of a properly organized political party with a clear-cut programme was essential.

The actions of the government following Bloody Sunday gave another cogent reason for organizing such a party. Mirskii had now been replaced at the Interior by the featureless bureaucrat A.G. Bulygin, while D.F. Trepov was put in charge of St. Petersburg, and granted exceptional police powers. The latter had great influence with the Tsar and presided over a harsh régime of repression against the revolutionaries and the opposition. Meanwhile, the government did little to prove that it intended to put the ukaz of 12 December consistently into effect.[12] On 18 February a sovereign manifesto[13] condemned the opposition movement and its attempts to subvert the existing political system and called on the population to co-operate with the Tsar in crushing "sedition". However, the government did not limit itself to repression. Paradoxically on the same day as the manifesto, the Tsar issued a rescript to A.G. Bulygin,[14] which directed the latter to set up a commission to draft proposals for some form of consultative representative assembly. A simultaneous ukaz to the Senate,[15] the Empire's supreme legal authority, apparently gave the people the right to petition it concerning reforms, including changes in the system of government.

In the eyes of the opposition the government's policy seemed equivocal and double-faced, and they were not inclined to believe in the sincerity of the concessions.[16] And not even the moderate liberals were now prepared to accept a merely consultative assembly. But nevertheless, the prospect of some kind of representation, which would for the first time legitimize open, organized political activity, made the organization of a fully-fledged liberal party a matter of added urgency.

However, if a party was to be established, a reasonably detailed programme was a fundamental necessity for the liberals. And given the mood of the country the programme would need to be radical if it were to attract popular support. In No. 67 of *Liberation* Struve called for a propaganda campaign among the people making use of the ukaz to the Senate, and declared that it was time "openly to organise cadres of a democratic party".[17] In the same issue, he put forward a tentative draft of a party programme.[18] The draft was well to the left of the Union's previous proposals. Struve now called for radical social reforms, including the compulsory purchase of pomeshchik land and measures to protect industrial labour. And, apparently echoing the demands of the socialist parties, his draft called for a "constituent assembly" elected by universal suffrage.

The influences which were affecting Struve had a similar impact upon the zemstvo liberals. At their Fourth Congress in February the Zemstvo Constitutionalists called for a representative system based on universal suffrage. And, like Struve, they now came out in favour of a "constituent assembly" and radical agrarian measures. There should be leasehold reform in the interests of the tenant, and a land fund to assist needy peasants. Moreover, the fund should include compulsorily alienated landowners' property.[19]

The Third Congress of Liberation

The trend towards a more definite programme with greater popular appeal culminated at the Third Congress of the Union of Liberation on 25–28 March. The political programme[20] agreed by the Congress was the Union's most comprehensive statement of its position, and deserves careful examination. In common with the entire radical opposition the Congress called for universal[F1] "four-tailed" suffrage, including votes for women. And like Struve and the Zemstvo Constitutionalists, the Union now lent its support to demands for a "constituent assembly". But, as with all liberal demands for such an assembly, it remained far from clear what this term implied. It could hardly mean a constituent assembly in the Leninist sense of a body with complete power to create a new political system exactly as it wished. This was unthinkable without a revolution. No monarch would voluntarily hand over power to such an assembly, and the Union of Liberation had no power to compel the Tsar to do so. Moreover, the liberationists were not violent revolutionaries. While they were prepared to ally with the extreme left for strictly limited purposes, the prospect of a popular insurrection filled them with unease. It seems, in fact, that what they had in mind was still much closer to Miliukov's proposals in No. 1 of *Liberation* than to the "Jacobin" constituent assembly demanded by the left. (In "Ot russkikh konstitutionalistov" Miliukov had suggested that popular representatives should work out the *details* of a constitutional settlement proclaimed by the Tsar owing to society's lack of faith in the bureaucracy.) Superficially the demand for a

---

F1 That is, suffrage should be universal, direct, equal and secret.

constituent assembly appeared extremely radical, even revolutionary. But in practice it was a vague formula open to wide differences of interpretation.

The programme's constitutional demands remained almost equally indefinite. Although the programme called for popular representation based on universal suffrage, it made few detailed constitutional proposals. Instead it confined itself to general principles, and made no attempt to prescribe even the number of chambers within the future Russian parliament. The programme also failed to define the powers of the popular representatives in detail. Even though it specified the confirmation of the budget, the right of legislative initiative and ministerial responsibility to parliament, enough was left unsaid to leave wide scope to both left and right to interpret the demand for a constitution in their own way.

The same is true of the programme's proposals on the rights of national minorities. Apart from a definite committment to restore Finland's ancient rights, the programme was very general, speaking of: "the widest regional self-government" for "regions" such as Latvia and Poland, and of "cultural autonomy". This formula seems to have been an attempt to mollify the left and the national parties, while simultaneously appeasing the right by avoiding talk of secession. However, there was no equivocation in the Union's proposals on the most fundamental liberal demands. Its belief in the rule of law, legal equality and the inalienable rights of the individual were unshakingly reaffirmed (Section 1).

Section 6 – upon the government's financial, economic and tariff policy – seemed equally unequivocal. The programme attacked the government's policies and demanded: "the end of the protection of individual undertakings and industrialists in favour of the development of the productive forces of the people". At the same time the programme called for a progressive income tax and the gradual abolition of indirect taxation. Such demands had a highly democratic, almost populist flavour. However, reforming the government's financial and tariff policies was desirable not only for the development of the productive forces of the people, but also from the viewpoint of the landowner. Moreover, many of the gentry were highly sympathetic to the idea of a progressive income tax, even if it involved them in some personal sacrifice. It was felt that this would at least compel the towns and the detested businessmen to pay their fair share to the national purse – something which the gentry had long desired.

The social, particularly the agrarian, programme of the Union appeared to represent a much bigger pill for the landowners to swallow. It is true that radical agrarian reform had been advocated in, for example, No. 33 of *Liberation*, but it had not then been official policy. However, in view of the changing mood of the masses, the inclusion of definite social reforms in the Union's programme now seemed essential for gaining social support. The Congress's agrarian proposals (Section 8), which provided for the compulsory purchase of landowners' property, have often been portrayed as extreme self-sacrifice by liberationist landlords. However, this is something of an overstatement. In fact, it was made quite clear that state and crown lands of various types would provide the main source of assistance to needy peasants. It was only where these were absent ("gde ikh net") that private landowners' property was to be alienated. It was not made clear *how much* would be taken, nor, indeed, *which* lands of the gentry would be purchased. It has already been mentioned that many nobles were only too willing to sell their land, or part of it, and this would clearly have been the first to be alienated. In analysing the realities underlying the liberationists' agrarian proposals it is instructive to examine the special congress of zemstvo men held to discuss the agrarian question in April 1905.[21] At this congress, which was under liberationist domination, and came to much the same conclusions as the Union itself, heavy stress was laid upon the need of reform for the "pacification of the land" (point 1). The gentry were, once again, being persuaded that reform was essential to stave off anarchy and revolution. At the same time, the congress made a most illuminating observation in connection with the purchase of landowners' property. It claimed that compulsory alienation should not be too costly "in view of the indebtedness of private landownership". This suggests that the land which the liberationists were considering alienating was not primarily the property of the successful gentry farmer. Their attention seems to have been focused mainly upon the land of the unsuccessful nobility who had been unable to adopt to modern agricultural conditions. And many of these might well have been prepared to cut their losses and liquidate their estates in return for suitable financial compensation.

The Union of Unions

Despite their aura of self-sacrifice the proposals of the Third Congress of Liberation did not reflect any real break with the enlightened self-interest of the gentry. The liberationists continued their work in the zemstvo and still hoped to gain the support of the landowning classes. But at the same time, they were now making a concerted effort to widen the social basis of their support. In addition to their zemstvo activities, the liberationists were now making serious attempts to recruit the intelligentsia and the masses.

The most successful liberal venture was directed primarily at the intelligentsia. As long ago as October 1904 the liberationists had considered forming semi-political unions of professional men. By the spring of 1905 their plans had become a reality. In May 1905 13 unions, mostly, but not all, of professional men, were united in the "Union of Unions" under the presidency of Miliukov.[22] The creation of the Union of Unions was an attempt to gather together all the relatively moderate members of the intelligentsia, including many socialists, behind a common demand for constitutional reform. It did not have a strictly "party" character, although Miliukov hoped that the elements composing it would later crystallize out in party form. But he recognized that they would not all necessarily join the *same* party. Miliukov stated that:

> We cannot predetermine for what number of individual groups of parties there may be material in this undifferentiated middle group [of moderate intelligentsia]. But first of all it is necessary to attract as much material as possible towards the forthcoming redistribution, and the unions which have

already taken shape and the programmes already formulated represent the most convenient starting-point for this.[23]

However, it is clear that the liberationist leaders hoped that by keeping the Union of Unions under their own wing, they could induce the majority of its members to support the future liberal party. At the same time, they also hoped to gain the backing of the majority of the zemstvo men. However, their more sanguine hopes were not fulfilled. The Union of Unions on the left, and the zemstvo men on the right, were composed of elements which proved increasingly difficult to reconcile. As Shakhovskoi points out,[24] although it was possible for the leaders of these elements to agree, on the periphery, to both left and right, it was a different matter. The more the movement grew, the further apart its individual elements became. Miliukov, for example, was forced to admit that the professional men nurtured "an invincible distrust" of zemstvo men.[25]

The Union of Liberation was, then, to a much greater extent than previously, directing its attention to organizing the professional classes. And at the same time a number of liberationists were now making a serious attempt to organize the workers and peasants. Following 9 January a group of revisionist socialists led by the former "Economist" S.N. Prokopovich carried on vigorous activity in the St. Petersburg labour movement.[26] Their main objective was the formation of a single labour union to unite all industrial workers behind demands for democratic reform. The projected union was to be based upon local workers' groups organized on a district and city basis and crowned by a federal all-Russian body. Although, strictly speaking, it was intended to be a non-party organization, it was hoped that its political programme would be on liberationist lines and that it would ultimately seek association with the Union of Unions. However, despite the liberationists' efforts, the scheme had little success, partly because it failed to take sufficient account of the economic needs of different trades and industries.[27] Although the Petersburg liberationists continued to be active in the trade union movement right up to the autumn of 1905, they were gradually isolated by the growth of the influence of the socialist parties.

Meanwhile, in Moscow, a number of liberationists from the professional movement and from the Moscow Agricultural Society were making a parallel attempt to achieve a breakthrough among the peasantry.[28] In the spring of 1905 the Moscow authorities, actively assisted by reactionary landowners, held a heavily weighted inquiry into the views of the peasantry. A number of conferences of conservative peasants were convened to demonstrate the basic loyalty of the rural population. As a counterweight to this a provincial conference of peasants was held to express the real opinions of the countryside. This conference, which was held in Moscow on 5 May, proved to be the first step to the formation of an All-Russian Peasant Union. Liberationists like A. Staal and A. Teslenko played a leading part in the conference, and were members of its organization bureau. Partly as a result of their influence, the conference's proposals were broadly on the same lines as those of the Union of Liberation. For a long time the liberationists nurtured serious hopes of keeping the growing peasant movement under their wing.

The Union of Liberation was now deeply committed to winning the support of the intelligentsia and the masses. But there can be little doubt that many of the leaders of the union, particularly those who later took the initiative in forming the Kadet Party, continued to focus their attention primarily upon the zemstvo movement. This makes it clear that despite their emotional outbursts after Bloody Sunday, they had still not abandoned their hope of reform from above. They still hoped that – under the influence of the difficult internal and external circumstances in which Russia found itself – the Tsar might pay heed to the arguments of respectable society in favour of reform. And they felt that it was up to them to ensure that the arguments of society were as radical as possible. They accordingly made a determined effort to bring their influence to bear upon the series of All-Zemstvo congresses inaugurated by the historic gathering of November 1904.

The liberationists' efforts met with considerable success. The constitutional demands of the Second Zemstvo Congress,[29] held in April 1905, moved to the left. The majority of the Zemstvo Congress now demanded a bicameral parliament and endorsed proposals for universal, direct and equal suffrage. They also agreed that the chief task of the first representative assembly should be to establish a new "state order", a proposal very close to the liberationist demand for a "constituent assembly". The congress's demand were, in fact, too radical for some of the delegates, and a minority led by Shipov demonstratively walked out.

The deputation to the Tsar of 6 June

However, under the influence of events in the Far East, the zemstvo leaders as a whole made a supreme effort to obtain the Emperor's consent to reform. Following the naval disaster at Tsushima, which marked final defeat in the war with Japan, the liberationists reluctantly tried to sink their differences with the Shipovites. At a Third Zemstvo Congress which was held in May[30] all shades of zemstvo opinion attempted to work out a joint address to the Tsar. In order to appease the moderate minority, the Congress majority retreated from their April demands, although they failed to avert a final walk-out by the Shipovites.

The address approved by the Congress[31] adopted an attitude of loyalty towards the Tsar himself. Its condemnation was reserved for the arbitrary behaviour of the bureaucracy, which had supposedly frustrated the Emperor's own sincere wish for reform. Referring to rumours that the bureaucracy favoured an assembly elected on a class basis, the address stressed that the only way to save Russia was for the Tsar to call popular representatives "chosen equally and without distinction" by all Russian subjects. In agreement with the Emperor, they should decide on the issue of war and peace, and establish a reformed state system. Even though this adress did not reflect the full demands of the Union of Liberation – indeed, it did not even give a clear call for direct and secret suffrage – it was heavily condoned by the majority of its leaders. Many of them, including Petrunkevich, Rodichev and Shakhovskoi,[32] actually took part in the deputation which presented the address to the Tsar on 6 June. During the audience they acquiesced in a speech by Prince S.N. Trubetskoi, which reflected the attitudes of the zemstvo moderates rather than those of the Union of Liberation. The tone of the speech was loyal almost to the point of sycophancy. Moreover, it displayed deep hostility towards the revolutionary movement. Trubetskoi even went so far as to depict constitutional reform largely as a means of averting class war, and combatting the spread of "sedition".[33] Although it is true that, in the delicate circumstances of the audience with the Tsar, the liberationists did not oppose Trubetskoi's words, it is clear that subsequently the Union of Liberation felt embarrassed by them. The liberationists realized that the speech might lead to their becoming discredited in the eyes of radical public opinion. Even Struve, who by now was in some respects drifting to the right, was moved to attack "the unpleasant, insincere notes of Prince Trubetskoi's speech".[34]

The atmosphere of disillusionment with the deputation was intensified by the actions of the Emperor himself. He had given only vague assurances to the zemstvo men, to the effect that it was his "inflexible will" to call some kind of representative body.[35] But he gave no indication that he intended to establish a genuine constitution, or even a democratic electoral system. Moreover, on 21 June he received a reactionary deputation with every sign of cordiality.[36] It is true that the Tsar was now willing to make some reluctant concessions to the opposition. Preparations for initiating some form of popular representation had been proceeding ever since the Rescript to Bulygin on 18 February. In July the Tsar presided over a conference at Peterhof[37] which finalized the details of the Bulygin proposals. Despite the reservations of some of his advisers, he seems to have been resigned to the idea of a purely advisory assembly. However, although the views of the most extreme reactionaries were rejected, the conference displayed little sympathy with the opposition's demands for universal, direct and equal suffrage. The electoral law which was finally agreed was highly conservative. The Bulygin Duma was to be an essentially consultative body, based upon a system of indirect, multi-stage elections.[38] The electorate were divided into social classes for the preliminary stages of voting and representation was weighted heavily in favour of property interests and the classes which were still considered the most politically reliable – the nobility and the peasantry. On the other hand, the minority nationalities received much less favourable treatment, and in the towns high property qualifications effectively disfranchised the working class and the majority of the intelligentsia. These proposals did not even go halfway to meeting the demands of the opposition. Moreover, the Tsar and his advisers seem to have been either unaware of, or oblivious to, the fact that public opinion was no longer prepared to accept a merely advisory assembly. The final impression which remains after reading the accounts of the conference is of a great gulf separating the position of its members from public opinion in general and from the liberationists in particular.

The Bulygin proposals were not officially announced until August. However, the opposition was aware of their main outlines well in advance of this date. The liberationists even obtained full details of the secret discussions at Peterhof.[39] Following the deputation of 5 June it became increasingly clear that the Tsar had no intention of making concessions acceptable even to the moderate opposition.[40] Once again it became evident that ruling circles would give way only under the impact of much stronger popular pressure. The emphasis of liberationist work now moved towards seeking support from below, towards the formation of a broad political party to influence the people.

Despite the liberationists' change of direction, they still continued their work in the zemstvos. In July, the Fourth All-Zemstvo Congress[41] was persuaded to accept at a "first reading" the so-called "Muromtsev Constitution" based on the proposals of the Second Zemstvo Congress and the Union of Liberation's model constitution.[42] But even in the zemstvo field the accent was now on appealing to the people. The congress showed a clear tendency to seek support from below, and to cultivate links with the peasantry and the professional unions.[43] In an article in *Liberation*, Miliukov emphasized that the zemstvos' chief objective was now to influence public opinion rather than the government.[44]

Plans to establish a New Liberal Party

The Union of Zemstvo Constitutionalists shared in the mood of disillusionment with the prospects of reform from above. At their Fifth Congress[45] on 9–10 July they denied any responsibility for the deputation of 6 June, claiming that it represented only the views of the May "Coalition" Zemstvo Congress. Moreover, by now they had begun to feel that their work in the zemstvos had been largely completed. They therefore decided to participate in the Union of Unions in order to influence the intelligentsia, and determined to take the first steps in the foundation of the Constitutional-Democratic Party ("Konstitutsionno-demokraticheskaia partiia").[F2] A commission of 20 was set up to negotiate with like-minded groups with a view to forming a temporary party committee.[46] The committee was to operate with the Zemstvo Constitutionalist bureau in working out a programme on the agrarian question, and in reviewing the labour, financial regional and national problems.

The historic decision to set up the commission was taken on the initiative of the Secretary of the Union of Liberation, D.I. Shakhovskoi. Most of the other leaders of the Zemstvo Constitutionalists were also members of the Union. According to Shakhovskoi 15 of the commission's 20 members were liberationists.[47] But although on 13 July, Struve called for the formation of a party[48] the Union of Liberation itself did not act immediately. Its leaders still held back a little, hoping that the Union of Unions might be persuaded to join the party, despite the fact that it was now veering further and further towards the left. However, they were unable to avert a fatal split with the Unions over the question of the prospective Bulygin Duma. Despite its misgivings about the Duma's imperfections, the Union of Liberation intended to make use of it for tactical purposes. Miliukov pointed out that the Union possessed no means of making a boycott effective.[49] There was no question of accepting the Duma as a satisfactory representative body, but it should be used as a tribune for further opposition. As Struve put it, "The Duma should be

---

F2 Later generally called the "Kadet" Party (derived from the initials K.D.).

employed as a new instrument of struggle with the autocracy".[50] The Union of Unions, on the other hand, took a different view. It was increasingly coming under the influence of the socialist parties and its suspicions of the Union of Liberation had already been aroused by the deputation of 6 June. It now tended to see proposals in favour of entering the Duma, as the first step towards betrayal – towards compromise with a government that could not be trusted. At its Second Congress (1–3 July) it voted for a boycott of the Duma, alleging that it was an attempt to confuse the nation with a mere facade of representation.[51] All the arguments of the Union of Liberation failed to change this position, despite weeks of effort.

It eventually became clear that the Union of Liberation's attempts to attract the Union of Unions, as a whole, into the future party had little prospect of success. Its leaders therefore turned, with a sense of partial failure, to a more limited objective – forming a party with the help of the Zemstvo Constitutionalists alone.

The Fourth Congress of Liberation

On 23 August the Union of Liberation held its Fourth Congress in Moscow.[52] The mood of the congress was one of determined opposition.[53] While it supported participation in the Duma it gave no indication that it was willing to compromise with the administration. It declared that the liberationists would use the Duma to struggle for freedom, "without being deterred by the prospect of an open rupture with the present government". The congress's attention was firmly directed towards gaining support from below rather than seeking concessions from above. The liberationists decided to maintain constant intercourse with the organs of the recently founded Peasant Union, which they themselves had taken an important part in promoting. Local liberationist groups were to take part in the formation of peasant unions in their areas in preparation for an all-Russian congress.

At the same time the liberationists finally took the decision to form a Constitutional-Democratic Party. A commission of 40 was chosen to enter into agreement with other appropriate groups and to make arrangements for holding the party's Foundation Congress. It was agreed that the Programme of the Union of Liberation would form a basis for the discussion of a party platform. Once this decision had been made, the Union of Liberation's work came to an end although the Union was never formally disbanded.[54] The diffuse elements that had clustered around the Union of Liberation now began to crystallize out into party form, even if they did not all enter the *same* party. They had been held together hitherto only by the absence of suitable conditions for regular party life and by the lack of precision, even ambiguity, of the Union of Liberation's demands.

During its relatively short life the Union of Liberation had endeavoured to rally all the more moderate elements of society around the liberal demand of a constitution. However, in doing so it had incurred a risk: the danger of seeming to be all things to all men. While wooing the left with talk of political democracy its leaders had simultaneously courted the zemstvos with displays of moderation. As a result, they inevitably incurred severe criticism from many political elements, both to their right and to their left. Right-wing liberals like Maklakov, and Slavophiles like Shipov, have accused them of adopting an unduly hostile and uncompromising attitude towards the old régime – an attitude stemming from abstract rationalism and leftism. Lenin, on the other hand, saw in their talk of "democracy" and a "constituent assembly" an attempt to deceive the people while they concluded a dishonourable deal with the Tsar. Maklakov's allegations do less than justice to the liberationalists' position. It is true that the failure to obtain reform from above drove the Union of Liberation to the left – to an increasingly uncompromising attitude of opposition. But this was not primarily the result of rationalistic leftism. It was based upon long and bitter experience of the government and the Tsar; experience which indicated that they were not even willing to meet the liberals halfway. To the government's record of repression and half-hearted promises of reform had been added the massacre of Bloody Sunday, and finally the fiasco of the deputation of 6 June. It was only when it became painfully clear that no help could be expected from above – at least without much greater pressure from below – that the liberationists turned towards apparently unremitting struggle with the autocracy.

The other charge – that of Lenin and other Marxist writers like S.E. Sef – appears to be equally unjustified. It is true that many of the leaders of the Union of Liberation seem to have been prepared to aid and abet a "deal" between Tsar and "society" at the time of the deputation of 6 June. On the other hand it is clear that even if the liberationists *were* prepared to dilute the demands of their March congress, they would not have accepted a settlement on the lines of the Bulygin proposals. Moreover, it should be remembered that their support for a compromise was the product of the exceptional international situation following Tsushima. Russia was in such a grave position that the good of the nation seemed to demand an urgent new initiative towards reform, even at the cost of a temporary compromise. The deputation of 6 June was, after all, the work of the Third Zemstvo Congress. It did not, strictly speaking, bind the Union of Liberation at all. Even if the Tsar *had* come to a compromise with society it would not have prevented the liberationists demanding further reforms. Once an initial "deal" had been arrived at between the Crown and "society", conditions might, indeed, have been much more favourable for more radical change.

In fact, there is no real reason to suppose that the liberals were plotting a dishonourable sell-out to the autocracy. Of course, they did not intend to demand the establishment of the democratic republic which Lenin called for. However, this had never been their objective, so they could hardly be accused of betraying it. It is true that they tended to use terms like "democracy" and "constituent assembly" somewhat loosely, and that they gave them an interpretation which was unacceptable to the extreme left. Moreover, owing to the diversity of the Union's composition, the Liberationists themselves often differed as to their exact meaning. But this does not mean that they were engaged in a calculated deception of the public. And although it is true that the liberals were not in

34 *Reform or revolution?*

favour of a violent revolution this was not necessarily evidence of bourgeois "treachery". On the one hand it stemmed from the fear that violence might engender an equally extreme outbreak of reaction on the right.[55] On the other, it derived from misgivings about violent revolution itself. Many liberationists feared that violence might call forth dark forces among the masses – forces which might imperil the political freedom which they valued so highly. The liberationists have often been condemned as treacherous and faint-hearted for harbouring such attitudes. But is it possible, in retrospect, to say that they were mistaken?

Notes

1 *The Times*, London, 12 September 1904.
2 "Novyi kurs", *Osvobozhdenie*, No. 57, 2 October 1904.
3 "Kn.Sviatopolk-Mirskii i vopros o konstitutsii", *Osvobozhdenie*, No. 59, 28 October 1904.
4 Shipov, Vol. I, pp. 278–80.
5 Shipov, pp. 581–7.
6 S.Iu.Vitte, *Vospominaniia, memuary*, Minsk-Moskva 2001, pp. 477–82; S.E. Kryzhanovskii, *Vospominaniia*, Berlin (1938), p. 26.
7 G.G. Savich, *Novyi gosudarstvennyi stroi Rossii*, S.P.B. 1907, pp. 6–8.
8 *Pravitel'stvennyi Vestnik*, 14 December 1904.
9 "Novye obeshchaniya i novye ugrozy", *Osvobozhdenie*, No. 62.
10 I.V. Gessen, "V dvukh vekakh", *A.R.R.*, XXII, pp. 209–10.
11 "Palach naroda", *Osvobozhdenie*, No. 64.
12 Vitte, *Vospominaniia*, op. cit., pp. 485, 507–32. Witte put the blame for this upon the Tsar and the Court continually dragging their feet.
13 *Pravitel'stvennyi Vestnik*, 19 February 1905.
14 Savich, *Novyi gosudarstvennyi stroi*, p. 13.
15 *Pravitel'stvennyi Vestnik*, 18 February 1905; Belokonskii, p. 263.
16 Even Shipov did not believe in the government's sincerity. See Shipov, pp. 294–7.
17 "Voprosy taktiki", *Osvobozhdenie*, 5 March 1905.
18 "Demokraticheskaia partiia i eë programma", *Osvobozhdenie*, 5 March 1905.
19 Shakhovskoi, p. 149. See also the article on this congress by "Zemskii glasnyi" in *Osvobozhdenie*, No. 67.
20 See Shakhovskoi, pp. 151–7 on the congress and its programme; Editorial on the programme in *Osvobozhdenie*, No. 69–70; V.V. Vodovozov (ed.), *Sbornik programm politicheskikh partii v Rossii*, 2nd edn, S.P.B. 1905, pp. 64–71.
21 Belokonskii, pp. 273–6. See also Prince P.D. Dolgorukov and I.I. Petrunkevich (eds), *Agrarnyi vopros*, Moscow 1905, Vol. I, pp. 299–352 for a full account of the congress.
22 The unions were as follows: writers, doctors, pharmacists, lawyers, journalists, engineers, veterinary surgeons, academics, agronomists, accountants, clerks, railway employees and associations devoted to obtaining equal rights for Jews and women.
23 "Partii, ili soiuzy", in P.N. Miliukov, *God bor'by*, S.P.B. 1907, pp. 41–7.
24 Shakhovskoi, p. 159.
25 Miliukov, *God bor'by*, p. 50.
26 S. Schwarz, *The Russian Revolution of 1905*, Chicago 1967, pp. 315–19.
27 Schwarz, *Russian Revolution*; see also S.N. Prokopovich, *Soiuz rabochikh i ikh zadachi*, S.P.B. 1905, p. 26.
28 E.I. Kiriukhina, "Vserossiiskii krest''ianskii soiuz v 1905 g", *Istoricheskie zapiski*, Vol. 50, 1955, pp. 95–141; Chermensky, *Burzhuaziia i tsarism*, Moscow 1939, pp. 116–19.

29 Belokonskii, pp. 276–82.
30 Belokonskii, pp. 286–7.
31 Belokonskii, p. 287.
32 Belokonskii, p. 288.
33 Belokonskii, pp. 288–9.
34 "Nezhnaia uvertiura k groznomu konfliktu", *Osvobozhdenie*, No. 73.
35 Belokonskii, p. 292.
36 Nikolai II (Imperator), "Dnevnik Imperatora Nikolaya II", Berlin 1923, p. 205.
37 For a full account of the conference, see: *Petergofskoe soveshchanie o proekte Gosudarstvennoi Dumy*, Berlin 1913. See also: Sir B. Pares, "The Peterhof Conference", *Russian Review*, Vol. II, No. 4, Liverpool 1913.
38 See Savich, *Novyi gosudarstvennyi stroi Rossii*, pp. 21–3.
39 Information on the Peterhof Conference was communicated to Miliukov by one of the participants, the great historian V.O. Kliuchevskii. See: P.N. Miliukov, *Vospominaniia*, New York 1955, Vol. I, pp. 298–9.
40 See, for example, the article by the "Old Zemstvo Men" in No. 73 of *Liberation*, which bitterly attacked naïve belief in the Tsar's good faith.
41 Belokonskii, pp. 292–332. For the first time the congress included delegates from the town dumas – organs of self-government representing urban propertied classes. By establishing a permanent secretariat and permitting its bureau freedom to co-opt members, the congress opened the way to the penetration of the zemstvo organization by non-zemstvo professional men like Miliukov.
42 "Proekt osnovnogo zakona Rossiiskoi imperii", Vol. III of *Materialy po vyrabotke russkoi konstitutsii*, *Osvobozhdenie*, Paris 1905. This project was often called the "Muromtsev Constitution". It was drafted by S.A. Muromtsev, together with N.N. Shchepkin, F.F. Kokoshkin and N.N. L'vov, the men who were chiefly responsible for the earlier draft constitution. See: P.N. Miliukov, "Sergei Andreevich Muromtserv: biograficheskii ocherk", in D.I. Shakhovskoi (ed.), *Sergei Andreevich Muromtsev*, Moscow 1911, p. 43. F.F. Kokoshkin, "Raboty zemskikh s''ezdov", in *Russkie Vedomosti 1863–1913, Sbornik Statei*, Moscow 1913, pp. 90–4. All of these men, with the exception of L'vov, were to later play prominent parts in the Kadet Party.
43 Belokonskii, pp. 323–32.
44 "Rossiia organizuetsia", *Osvobozhdenie*, No. 74, 13 July 1905.
45 An account of this congress may be found in an appendix to *Osvobozhdenie*, No. 78–9.
46 See the article by "Zemets-konstitutionalist" on the congress's decisions in *Osvobozhdenie*, No. 75.
47 Shakhovskoi, p. 162.
48 "Rozhdaetsia natsiia", *Osvobozhdenie*, No. 74
49 "Idti ili ne idti v Gosudarstvennuiu dumu?", *Osvobozhdenie*, No. 75.
50 "Iz ruk Tsaria", *Osvobozhdenie*, No. 75, p. 428.
51 *Osvobozhdenie*, No. 75, p. 428.
52 Shakhovskoi, pp. 164–9.
53 For the congress's decisions, see: "Postanovleniia IV-ogo s''ezda", *Osvobozhdenie*, No. 77.
54 Shakhovskoi, p. 169.
55 P.B. Struve, "Kak naiti sebia", *Osvobozhdenie*, No. 71.

3 The birth of the Kadet Party

During 1905 the Union of Liberation had striven to widen the sphere of its influence. While intensifying its work in the zemstvos, it had simultaneously attempted to extend its hegemony to the professional unions and the intelligentsia. At the same time it had made increasing efforts to woo the masses – the peasants and the workers.

By the time of the liberationists' fourth and final congress in August part of this policy was already in ruins. The Union of Unions, which had at first been dominated by the liberals, had by now come under strong socialist influence. It was to take no part, as a whole, in the formation of the new party. Meanwhile, the liberationists' efforts to gain the support of the masses do not appear to have had any lasting success. In particular, their attempts to organize the peasantry proved largely fruitless. At the First Congress of the Peasant Union[1] the new organization had veered sharply to the left. The insistent demands of many delegates for the expropriation of landowners *without compensation* were quite unacceptable to the liberationist leadership.[2] At the Fourth Congress of Liberation the liberals had still hoped to avert a left-wing takeover of the peasant movement, but in fact this did not prove to be possible.[3]

In view of all this, the future leaders of the "Kadet" Party were compelled to jettison some of their earlier hopes. Indeed, instead of being based upon a wider social spectrum than the old Union of Liberation, the new party was to have, initially, a more restricted base. The Union of Liberation had centred around a rather loose alliance of three main elements: firstly, the zemstvo "gentry" liberals, secondly, the revisionist socialists, and finally, a number of liberal professional men and intelligentsia. The second of these elements had long been a stumbling block to closer unity within the Union of Liberation. It was to prove impossible to weld it, as a whole, into the future, more homogeneous, Kadet Party.[4]

Moreover, during September, it became increasingly clear that even among the zemstvo gentry, the "Kadets" were not to have things all their own way. The month saw yet another Zemstvo Congress (with the participation of city dumas) heavily influenced by the former liberationists.[5] In many ways this congress marked the high-water mark of their success in the zemstvo movement. For example, the congress accepted completely the liberationist line on the Bulygin Duma, recognizing that it was "not popular representation in the proper sense of the word", but that it could serve as a "point d'appui for the social movement striving to attain political freedom and true popular representation".[6] In the circumstances participation in the Duma was a "heavy duty" ("tiazhëlaia obiazannost'") proclaimed the congress in its manifesto to the people.[7] The Duma should demand a "deciding voice" in legislation and the budget, and should insist that the ministry should be accountable to the Duma.

At the same time the congress turned its attention to social reform. It even accepted, "in cases of necessity", the need for compulsory purchase of private lands to assist the peasantry.[8] In one respect the congress even went beyond the programme of the Union of Liberation. For the first time the zemstvo men decided to support demands for Polish autonomy, provided this did not undermine the unity of the Empire.

But despite their success in gaining zemstvo support, the Kadets had no cause for complacency. For the September Zemstvo Congress saw the re-emergence of a right-wing opposition, for the first time since the Shipovites had walked out in the spring. The new right, headed by Alexander Guchkov, the future leader of the Octobrist Party, concentrated their attacks upon proposals for the decentralization of Russia and Polish autonomy, claiming that this would lead to the dismemberment of Russia.[9] It is true that their views were shared by only a small minority of the congress, but they were, nevertheless, significant. The reappearance of a right-wing in the zemstvo movement was a reminder to the radicals that they were by no means representative of the provincial gentry as a whole. The more reactionary "backwoodsmen" of the nobility, who normally took little part in zemstvo politics were slowly beginning to stir. As the revolution developed they began to fear for their lives and property, and their political apathy was undermined. They were shortly to take their revenge upon the liberals who had for so long claimed to speak on their behalf.[10]

But for the present it was the left-wing of the zemstvo men that remained in control and it was this group that now joined with the liberal intelligentsia in organizing the Constitutional-Democratic Party. Since the attempt to attract wider social support had failed, the new party was, in fact, to be constituted upon largely the same foundation as its predecessor. The party was to begin as the direct descendant of the Union of Liberation and the Union of Zemstvo Constitutionalists. It was these two bodies which alone, in the end, set about founding the party. Invitations to the Constituent Congress were sent out, primarily, via local groups of the Union of Liberation, and where these did not exist, to individual Zemstvo-Constitutionalist leaders. The latter were to hold provincial conferences of sympathizers to discuss the programme of the future party, and to choose three delegates per province to the forthcoming congress.

Every effort was made to ensure that the preparations for the congress were as complete as possible. There were very few provinces – in European Russia at least – which received no invitation to be represented at the congress.[11] However, outside events were to shatter the bureau's carefully laid plans. In the country at large, revolutionary forces were moving towards a showdown with the government. The prestige of the régime had now been brought to its lowest ebb by final defeat in the Japanese war – a war which had brought profound economic and political discontent in its wake. In mid-September a series of strikes broke out and by early October they began to take on a political character. The strike movement rapidly developed into a national campaign for a constituent assembly elected by "four-tailed" suffrage. Partly caused by left-wing agitation and partly by a spontaneous wave of discontent, the strikes rapidly began to bring Russia's urban, commercial and industrial life to a standstill. On 7 October they spread to the railways and then to the telegraph system (11–15 October). Meanwhile, following the granting of university autonomy in September, the universities became sanctuaries of free political life – not just for their students, but for society as a whole. They rapidly became a venue for turbulent revolutionary meetings, and this contributed still more tension to an already electric atmosphere. By 10 October the strike movement was nearing its peak. In Moscow a general strike began, and quickly spread to all other industrial workers and to the entire communications network. It embraced not only industrial workers and urban wage labour in general, but even the professional men of the Union of Unions. Not even the employers opposed the strike. Indeed, many continued to pay wages to their striking employees. The entire nation was apparently united in opposition to the government, and in a common desire for a new order.

The Foundation Congress (12–18 October 1905)

Gratifying though all this may have been to the Kadets, it could scarcely have been more inopportune in so far as it affected their plans for holding their First Congress. The congress met in Moscow from 12–18 October, at the very climax of the strike. As a consequence the glare of publicity was turned away from the congress towards the wider stage outside, and upon the chief organ of the striking masses, the St. Petersburg Soviet of Workers' Deputies born on 13 October.[12] Moreover, the severing of rail communications meant that a large number of the delegates heading for the congress were unable to be present, while the congress itself was held in an abnormal atmosphere and amidst constant interruptions.

Because of this it was decided that the First Congress of the new party could have only a provisional character[13] and that another would have to be called as soon as possible. However, in view of the exceptional course of events in the country, it was decided that the October Congress could not be put off,[14] despite its obvious deficiencies. And these were serious, especially in the composition of the congress.

The organization bureau of the congress had sent out invitations to 47 provinces.[15] However, in fact only 20 of these were even partially represented at the actual congress.[16] Indeed, leaving aside Moscow and Petersburg, 18 provinces were represented by only 32 delegates – not the 54 to which they ought, theoretically to have been entitled. Moreover, some provinces had only one delegate; others, like Tver', as many as five.

Representation was, in fact, anarchic – it was often not, strictly speaking, representation at all. Apart from properly elected delegates the congress included liberationists and constitutionalists, "finding themselves in Moscow by chance";[17] seven of the provincial "delegations" were made up in this way. In addition to the delegates from the provinces, there were 24 members of the organization bureau at the congress.[18] The composition of this group may partly explain, but not entirely, the enormous number of representatives from Moscow – 36 in all[19] – a representation outnumbering all the provincials combined. The Muscovites were, of course, the only group which had little problem in attending the congress and it would seem that they benefitted most of all from the loosening of the strictly representative principle. Petersburg, with 11 members, was much less heavily represented. Together with other factors the unequal representation was to have serious consequences at the end of the congress.

Its *immediate* effect seems to have been to give the congress's discussions a less conclusive nature than might otherwise have been the case. One of the main tasks of the congress was the working-out of a party programme. It had been agreed that the programme of the Union of Liberation would be the starting point for the discussions. But clearly a *provisionial* congress could not work out a *final* programme. Partly as a consequence of this, the party's platform was not taken much further than this "starting point". The programme worked out by the congress[20] was, basically, a refurbished version of the Union of Liberation's platform, rather more detailed, and amended to take the decisions of the September Zemstvo Congress into account. As such it shared many of the earlier programme's virtues, but also many of its defects.

The programme, adopted by the congress, unequivocally demanded all the classic Western political and civil rights, such as the freedom of speech, religion, movement and assembly (points 2–7). It demanded equality of justice, and the inviolability of the individual except as provided for by law (points 7, 8 and 27a). There should be no exceptional courts. In addition the party now recognized the right of minority nationalities to cultural self-determination, including the complete freedom to use different languages and dialects in public life, and in, at least, primary education (points 11–12). All these rights were to be guaranteed by a reform of the system of justice. Section 4 of the programme demanded the completion of the liberal judicial reforms of 1861. The administration and the judiciary should be separated, the "zemskii nachal'nik" (or "land captain")[21] should be abolished and the criminal code should be reformed. Finally, the legal reforms should be completed by the drafting of a new civil code.

Thus far there had been little equivocation. It was always in this field – in the sphere of civil rights and the rule of law – that the liberals were most fully in agreement. However, Section 2, which was concerned with the party's constitutional proposals, remained almost as vague and imprecise as the old liberationist programme. It is true that this section demanded universal suffrage upon the basis of the "four tails"[22] (point 14). But the programme then proceeded to grant freedom of opinion upon the question of whether parliament should consist of one or two chambers.[23] Matters of still greater constitutional importance were also left in mid-air. The programme made no attempt to elaborate its constitutional proposals in detail, and limited itself to the enunciation of certain general principles. The programme proposed that the representatives of the people should "participate in the execution of legislative power, in the establishment of the state budget ('rospisi dokhodov i raskhodov') and in control over the legality and advisability of the actions of the higher and lower administration" (point 15). The members of the popular assembly were to have the right of legislative initiative (point 18), and ministers were to be responsible to the assembly (point 19). At the same time the programme stipulated that no law, government order or tax should be put into effect without the sanction of the representatives (points 16–17). If these proposals had been implemented they would have led to the establishment of a basically parliamentary régime. However, the programme made no real attempt to outline the precise balance of power within the constitution. Even the question of whether the state should be a republic or a monarchy was passed over in silence. What did the programme mean when it said that popular representatives should "participate" in legislation? Did this mean that their legislative powers would be shared with the monarchy (and/or an upper chamber)? And if, as seems likely, this is indeed what it meant, what were the prerogatives of the monarchy to be? Should the Tsar have the right of an unconditional veto over legislation, or special powers over the executive, foreign affairs and the army? No answer was given to these vital questions. Their solution, like that of so many other issues, was (in the words of Miliukov), "presented to the future".[24]

The Kadets' proposals on local self-government and autonomy were almost equally vague. It is true that they demanded the restoration of the Finnish constitution, and supported proposals for Polish autonomy. They agreed that Poland should have a Seim (or legislature) elected by universal suffrage, provided that this did not conflict with the unity of the Empire. But the programme did not go beyond this loose formula (point 25). There was no attempt to define the powers of the Seim or to outline its sphere of competence vis-à-vis the central government.[25]

The section's proposals on local self-government were closely in line with those of the Union of Liberation. Point 20 stipulated that local self-government should be extended to all parts of the Empire, while point 2 demanded a small zemstvo unit elected by four-tailed suffrage. Article 22 seemed to lay down the principle of extreme decentralization. It proposed that the powers of local government should be extended as far as possible, "with the exception only of those branches of administration which in the conditions of contemporary state life must necessarily be concentrated in the hands of the central power". However, this statement of principle was fraught with contradictions. The Kadets were not a party of laissez-faire liberalism. Indeed, their radical social and economic programme presupposed a powerful redistributionist and interventionist state. And in view of this the branches of the administration which should "in the conditions of contemporary state life", be given to the central power were likely to be very large.

In financial and economic policy (Section 5), the programme adhered closely to the "liberationist" line. Once again the liberals demanded a complete change of government policy. Redemption charges on the peasants' existing allotment land were to be abolished (point 31), expenditure on popular needs was to be increased (point 30), and credit facilities for the small farmer improved (point 35). Taxation should radically be reformed upon a basis of direct rather than indirect taxation. This would lead to the "gradual abolition of indirect taxation on articles consumed by the mass of the people" (point 32). On the other hand, *direct* taxation should be increased; point 33 demanded progressive income and inheritance taxes. At the same time the programme resumed the attack on high tariff barriers, and proposed that they should be reduced in order to cut the cost of essential articles and to raise the technical level of industry and agriculture (point 34).

This entire section of the programme had a strongly democratic flavour, but at least part of it still coincided (see pp. 6, 26) with the complaints of the entire agricultural population, including the gentry, about government policies which favoured and cosseted industry at the expense of agriculture. This does not mean that the Kadets' economic and financial policies were primarily motivated by crude self-interest. In fact, there is abundant evidence that the Kadet gentry were prepared to make material sacrifices for the public welfare. The only issue which was not always clear was the *extent* to which they were willing to make such sacrifices.

This uncertainty was especially well-marked in the Kadets' agrarian proposals (Section 6). The liberationists had already proposed that state, appanage and monastic estates, together with some private land, should be compulsorily alienated to meet the needs of the peasantry. The Kadets now took this a stage further. The liberationist programme had restricted the alienation of private land to cases where there was no state or other lands available. This restriction was now no longer mentioned; instead, it was laid down that the land would be alienated in the "dimensions required" (point 36). The programme also stipulated that compulsory alienation should take place with compensation for the present owners based on a "just valuation", not the market value of the property. However, this formula still left wide scope for different interpretations. What were the "necessary" or "required" ("potrebnye") dimensions? How would a "just evaluation" be determined? Were all private estates to be subject to expropriation of only certain categories of estates?

In April (1905) the Agrarian Congress[26] had revealed a wide difference of opinion among liberals upon such subjects, but there had been strong support for preserving estates formed on modern capitalist lines. At the same time little sympathy had been displayed towards more feudal estates based upon the principle of leasehold. Did the present congress agree or disagree with such attitudes? No clear answer was given to such questions. The programme's demands for leasehold reform in favour of the tenant might, it is true, appear to be evidence of the congress's antipathy to estates of the more backward type. Point 39 stipulated that the tenant should be granted security of tenure, compensation for improvements and a means of appeal against high rents. But on the other hand, point 40 might equally be interpreted as being against the interests of the modern capitalist farmer, since it demanded the extension of workers' protection legislation to agricultural wage labour. The attitude of the party towards different categories of landowners was therefore not made clear in the programme. But one thing appears certain: the party was not considering the liquidation of all estates or even of all leasehold. If it had been, the importance which it gave to the reform of the conditions of lease and hire would have made little sense.

In many respects the Kadets' agrarian proposals remained vague or ill-defined. Nevertheless, they had apparently been worked out more fully than the programme of the Union of Liberation. For example, it had now been decided that private land should be alienated at *state* expense (point 36). At the same time, the programme had attempted to clarify the principles upon which the distribution of the land would be based. Point 37 indicated that whether the land would go into communal or individual use would depend on local custom. The party had therefore declared its *neutrality* in questions relating to land tenure and the viability of the peasant commune or "obshchina". But although the party appeared to have made a decision in this matter, their proposals concealed the same indecisiveness as before. The party could not really *afford* to be neutral in such a vital matter – methods of land tenure were a fundamental problem in the solution of the agrarian crisis. In fact, the party seems to have decided on a compromise that would offend no one rather than face up to the problem squarely.[27]

Agrarian policy was always a matter of keen debates and disagreements between the Kadets, so it is not surprising that many aspects of the party's programme in this field remained open or ill-defined. However, the Kadets appear to have been generally in agreement upon the remaining proposals in the party programme, namely: those on education, and on legislation concerning the urban worker. In the field of education, the Kadets called for wide reforms, including the provision of free, universal and compulsory primary education (Section 8). Their solution to the problems of industrial labour was progressive Western-style legislation (Section 7). There should be freedom to form unions, the right to strike, and universal legal protection for workers, especially women and children. Workers were to be insured against sickness, accident, incapacity and old age, and there were to be conciliation chambers composed of both sides of industry to settle disputes. There should even be an eight-hour day when conditions made this possible. This was indeed a radical policy, and as the Kadets were fully aware, it did not fall far short of the Social Democrats' demands in their party's "programme-minimum" (i.e. the programme which the socialists believed to be possible within the context of a purely "bourgeois" revolution).

In such fields as education, labour legislation, civil rights and the rule of law, the Kadet Party displayed little or no ambivalence. But as we have seen, on many vital matters the programme remained indefinite. Wide scope for different interpretations of party policy remained. This was, partly a consequence of the provisional nature of the congress. But at the same time it also reflects the fact that the congress was still based on precisely the same elements as the Union of Liberation. And it had always proved impossible in the past to weld the Union's heterogeneous membership into anything more than a loose confederation. It is, therefore, difficult to see how these diverse elements could now be united in a more or less homogeneous political *party*, or get to agree upon a common unambiguous party programme.[28] It was no coincidence that at the end of the congress the majority of the reformist socialists, who had long been the most difficult group to assimilate,[29] decided not to join the new party. The disagreement which led to this decision does not seem to have been based upon the party programme. As we have seen, the programme was elastic enough to permit widely differing interpretations. But the socialists seem to have been intensely suspicious of entering a closer union with the zemstvo "gentry" liberals for whom they harboured a deep distrust.[30]

The influence of the revisionist socialists had for a long time been centred on the St. Petersburg "Big" group of the Union of Liberation. This was composed almost exclusively of intelligentsia – particularly writers – under the leadership of such personalities as Prokopovich, Kuskova and Bogucharskii. It had always been exceptionally active in distributing *Liberation*, in carrying on propaganda, and in organizing and recruiting the intelligentsia, especially in the Union of Unions. It had also played an important rôle in the St. Petersburg workers' movement and in the banquet campaign of late 1904.

However, at the October Congress, this group found itself in a small minority, isolated among the Moscow-based zemstvo men and their purely liberal professional allies. As a result they seem to have concluded that the new party would be dominated by bourgeois-pomeshchik interests. Their reservations were reinforced by the fact that Miliukov was chosen to give the opening report to the congress. Although Miliukov was a professional man, and was a former president of the Union of Unions, he had increasingly taken an active part in the zemstvo movement. Indeed, he had even been elected as a member of the Zemstvo Congress Bureau. According to I.V. Gessen, the socialists were deeply suspicious of his close links with the zemstvo men.[31] Miliukov's memoirs tend to confirm his growing sympathy with the zemstvo representatives[32] and his own disaffection with the socialists. On his own admission he rejoiced at the absence of so many St. Petersburg delegates, claiming that they would have introduced "an element of implacability".[33]

This attitude was not explicable in terms of sheer anti-socialism. Miliukov had never been a prey to such a sentiment. Indeed, he had spent a great deal of time in 1905 promoting the idea of a common front with the socialist parties to obtain political democracy and liberty.[34] Miliukov was fully acquainted with the doctrines of orthodox Marxism; and for a long time he continued to believe that the socialists' immediate aims went no further than the establishment of a purely "bourgeois" or Western-style parliamentary régime. Why, then (Miliukov had argued) should not liberals and socialists march together towards this common goal? There was no need for their paths to diverge until their immediate object had been attained. Such ideas had long been popular with the liberationists, and had led to their earlier willingness to participate in the 1904 Paris Conference of opposition and revolutionary parties. And even now, despite the fact that the idea of a common front with the left had been somewhat shaken by the Sixth Social-Democratic (Bolshevik) Congress,[35] Miliukov continued to make overtures to the left.

In his opening report to the congress on behalf of the organization bureau, Miliukov said that a sharp line divided the party from the right – from the defenders of the class interests, of landowners and industrialists. On the other hand, said Miliukov "between us, and our, we would like to say, *not opponents but allies on the left* [author's emphasis], there also exists a certain border-line, but it is of a different character from the one which we draw on the right". At the same time, he boasted that the Kadet Party programme was "further to the left than all those proclaimed by Western European political groups which are analogous to us". Miliukov's hostility does not, therefore, appear to have been directed at the socialists or the left as such. But it does seem that he feared that continuing diversity within the Kadet camp might prevent the birth of a really united party. "If anything", he said, "has held up these aspirations (towards such a party), then this is in the first place the considerable diversity of the elements entering into the 'Union' or the 'Congress' but unable to enter a united and disciplined party". The St. Petersburg socialists had always formed a distinct group conscious of its own special aims and objectives. And Miliukov was fully aware that of all the elements represented at the First Congress, they would be the most difficult to assimilate into a united liberal party. He therefore made it clear that if they joined the party they would have to do so on the liberals' terms. A split could be avoided, but if they made any attempt to introduce socialist demands into the programme this would lead to an immediate "schism" ("raskol").[36]

However, the socialists were unwilling to accept such conditions. They had been willing to cooperate with the liberals on equal terms within the framework of a loose political union with limited objectives. But they were not prepared to enter a unified liberal-dominated party in which they would be very much the junior partner, and perhaps even a sleeping partner. Moreover, they apparently believed that the formation of a Western-style political party was premature. E.D. Kuskova later argued that parties of this sort needed a free parliamentary life if they were to be effective, and this did not yet exist.[37] It is significant that when this group refused to join the Kadets it did not form a new party itself, nor did it join, or help create, another. Instead, the majority of its members constituted a political group or *club* with the revealing name of "Without Title" ("Bez Zaglaviia"). In the circumstances the socialists' decision to leave the party was probably inevitable and even desirable. However, many Kadets appear to have experienced some difficulty in reconciling themselves themselves to the split. A party pamphlet written by A.A. Chuprov[38] regretted the exit of the left and so much of the intelligentsia, especially since the socialists seem to have taken most of the "Third Element" with them.

The eclipse of the Petersburg socialists was reflected in the new Central Committee of the party elected at the congress. Of the 30 members chosen to this temporary body[39] only four were from the Petersburg revisionist socialist wing, and they all declined to enter it (S.N. Prokopovich, E.D. Kuskova, V.Ia. Bogucharskii and V.V. Khizhniakov). On the other hand, 15 of the remaining 26 had been active in the zemstvos or town dumas as members of their boards or councillors in their assemblies.⁴⁰ However, it would be misleading to classify the group of zemstvo men as simply "zemstvo gentry". Of the group of 15 zemstvo men only six could be described as such with little qualification (Prince Peter Dolgurukov, Prince Pavel Dolgorukov, A.M. Koliubakin, N.N. L'vov, I.I. Petrunkevich and Prince D.I. Shakhovskoi). The remaining nine (F.F. Kokoshkin, V.I. Vernadskii, S.A. Kotliarevskii, N.A. Kablukov, S.A. Muromtsev, V.E. Iukushkin, I.V. Luchitskii, N.N. Shchepkin and V.D. Nabokov) also had professional occupations of considerable significance. All nine of them either were, or had been, university professors or lecturers. Together with two non-zemstvo men (P.N. Miliukov and A.A. Kornilov) they formed a bloc of 11 academics on the committee. Not surprisingly this helped to give the party a "professorial" image in the country – an image which it long retained. Equally noteworthy was the fact that of this group of academics, eight were either teaching or had taught at Moscow University. This reflected once again the predominance of Moscow at the Foundation Congress.

The 11 non-zemstvo committee members⁴¹ were almost all professional men. The only exception was M.A. Sabashnikov, a Moscow publisher, who was, properly speaking, from the world of business. However, this was a business which by its very nature had exceptionally strong links with the intelligentsia. The remaining members of this group were mostly involved in the professions of the law, university teaching and journalism, several of them combining more than one of these occupations. Two members of the committee had formerly been connected with the bureaucracy. Nabokov had been associated with high society and the Court⁴² and I.V. Gessen, the editor of *Pravo* (*Law*), had previously been an official in the Ministry of Justice.

The Central Committee was, then, recruited exclusively from the zemstvo men and from the professions. It is noteworthy that there was not a single member from the masses – from the peasants or the workers. Furthermore, the professional men were almost all from the higher levels of the intelligentsia. There was only one member (N.N. Chernenkov)⁴³ from the Third Element, and no petty officials or school-teachers. However, the committee still reflected a wide spectrum of liberal opinion. On the right there was the moderate constitutionalist N.N. L'vov, who later joined the Octobrists, while on the left there was the radical lawyer M.L. Mandelshtam, who continued to harbour reformist socialist tendencies.

Nevertheless, the new Central Committee was more homogeneous and contained fewer left-wingers than the Council of the Union of Liberation. Even if the socialists had agreed to enter the committee, they would still have been in almost total eclipse. This does not mean that the party was now turning its back on the left-wing elements in Russian politics. Indeed, the party congress went out of its way to declare its solidarity with the revolutionary movement. Largely as a result of the enthusiasm generated by the events of the October Days, liberal support for the doctrine of "no enemies on the left" now reached its high-water mark. In a declaration on 14 October the congress openly proclaimed its support for the general strike:⁴⁴

The demands of the strikers as they are formulated by (the strikers) themselves came in the main to the immediate introduction of the fundamental freedoms, and to the free election of popular representatives to a Constituent Assembly on the basis of universal and direct suffrage. There cannot be the slightest doubt that all these aims are common to the demands of the Constitutional-Democratic Party. In view of such an agreement in aims, the Constituent Congress of the Constitutional-Democratic party considers it its duty to proclaim its fullest solidarity with the strike movement. In its own sphere ("mesto") and with the means available to the Party, the members of the Party are striving towards the fulfillment of the same tasks and like all the rest of the struggling groups *have decisively rejected the idea of obtaining their ends by means of negotiations with the representatives of the Government* ("vlast'") [author's emphasis].

The party had lost faith in the government owing to the latter's "endless procrastinations and shuffling tricks". If it refused to give way to the demands of the people's "peaceful struggle" and decided on a declaration of war, "everything that is enlightened and conscious in Russia will stand on the side of the people".

The Union of Liberation had gradually come to despair of their hopes of reform freely granted "from above" and had progressively turned instead towards the people. This process now seemed to be complete. But if Maklakov is to be believed,[45] this mood of radical opposition had begun to crumble away even before the end of the congress. On the final day of the congress a messenger appeared with the news that the Emperor had apparently given way, and had promised to grant a constitution. According to Maklakov the news brought joy to the faces of many delegates. However, in his *Memoirs* Miliukov denies[46] the existence of any state of euphoria. According to Miliukov, the actual text of the Tsar's promises produced "a vague and unsatisfactory impression" upon the delegation.

The October Manifesto

At first glance the "October Manifesto"[47] appeared to concede much of what the Kadets demanded. It promised to grant political freedom and civil liberties (Article 1) and to widen the electorate to the future Duma, "as far as this is possible taking into account the shortage of time remaining before the convocation of the Duma" (Article 2). Further development of the principle of universal suffrage was to be left to the Duma itself. Finally, the manifesto promised as an "unshakeable rule" that no law should come into force without the agreement of the Duma (Article 3). Moreover, the Tsar gave a pledge that the people's representatives would be granted the "possibility of effective participation in the supervision of the legality of the authorities which we have set up". At the same time the implementation of the manifesto's promises was entrusted to a new "cabinet" of ministers under the premiership of Count Witte.

Whatever may have been the views of a minority, the congress as a whole was far from satisfied by such assurances. Above all, it was disturbed by the vague terminology in which so much of the document was couched. According to Miliukov, it was reminiscent of government promises in the past, with their ambiguity and their failure to lead to real reforms.[48] But even if the Kadets had entertained no doubts about the government's sincerity, they would not have been completely happy with the manifesto – for they clearly felt that it had not promised enough.

All this was reflected in a congress resolution of 18 October,[49] which displayed severe scepticism towards the manifesto's promises. The congress began by complaining that "the fundamental principles of political freedom, equality and universal suffrage put forward on its banner by the Russian liberation movement" had received "far from full recognition". The manifesto had been much too vague in its promises on civil rights. Moreover, the principles of civil equality and real constitutional government had been referred to only in Witte's report accompanying the manifesto, and then only in the vaguest of terms (point 1). Meanwhile, the implementation of the government's promises remained "in the hands of people whose political past inspires the people with no confidence whatsoever". Again (point 3), Witte's report had hinted that the State Council (the purely bureaucratic legislative body already in existence) would act as a check upon the power of the popular representatives. This was entirely unacceptable, as were the manifesto's proposals to limit the Duma's supervision of the administration's actions only to their legality but not to their advisability. Moreover, the congress pointed out that despite the manifesto the government was still employing repressive measures against the opposition with the assistance of various kinds of exceptional legislation (point 4). The government had also failed to meet the opposition's demands for a complete political amnesty. Because of all this, and because the Duma could not be regarded as satisfactory popular representation, the Duma could serve only as *one* of the means to be adopted in the struggle for a constituent assembly (point 5).

The congress demanded that the government should put the rights proclaimed by the manifesto into immediate effect, while instituting universal suffrage preparatory to a constituent assembly (point 6). At the same time the bureaucracy should be purged of elements of doubtful reputation and a new "businesslike" cabinet summoned. Following the convocation of popular representatives the ministry should be dissolved and be replaced by "a cabinet of the spokesmen (predstaviteli) of the majority". Lastly, a full religious and political amnesty should be granted (point 7). Such, then, were the congress's demands. However, the Kadets were extremely sceptical about the chances of receiving any satisfaction from the government. They therefore committed themselves to a policy of the de facto seizure of the political freedoms promised in the manifesto even if the government failed to implement them (point 8). The attitude of the congress seems to have been correctly summed up by Miliukov's alleged declaration (at a banquet on 18 October) that "nothing has changed, the war goes on".

Both at the time, and in later years, the Kadets' attitude came under fierce attack from the right. V.A. Maklakov, for example, would one day condemn it as evidence of Kadet irresponsibility and implacability. In all his later sets of memoirs, Maklakov played variations upon this theme. According to Maklakov, the Kadets had been so long in opposition that they had developed a kind of war psychology towards the government. In the course of the struggle they had increasingly fallen under the influence of the doctrinaire intelligentsia – a class which, while able to be destructive, was incapable of constructive work. Miliukov was cast in the rôle of chief malefactor – as the archetype of the doctrinaire intellectual. Maklakov's hero, on the other hand, was the much idealized figure of the sensible, practical zemstvo man. According to Maklakov, if the moderate zemstvo men had been in charge of the party, the liberals would have to come to an honourable agreement with the government after the October Manifesto. However, this had been frustrated by the implacability of the intelligentsia. According to Maklakov: "Society had won the war against the historical power (i.e. the autocracy), but did not intend to conclude peace with it." It had abdicated its chance of a peaceful settlement for doctrinaire reasons.[50] However, Maklakov's views were based largely on hindsight and speculation. They certainly did less than justice to the Kadet position. In fact the Kadets' hostility to the government was not primarily the result of abstract radicalism, nor was it the outcome of the supposed domination of the party by intellectuals. It was rather the consequence of long and bitter experience of governmental equivocation and unwillingness to make adequate concessions. The liberals had turned away from hopes of reform from the bureaucracy only when they began to be disillusioned by the government's endless evasions and "shuffling tricks". They had reluctantly come to the conclusion that the government could not be trusted to carry out a sincere programme of radical reform. And had the Kadets any real reason to trust the government now? Had the October Manifesto proclaimed a decisive change of heart? There had, it is true, been a change of *ministry*, with Witte as the new premier, but this in itself proved little.

Witte was, perhaps, the most able statesman of the old régime, but, despite his later assertions to the contrary, his reputation was scarcely a liberal one. In 1898 he had been responsible for a memorandum ("The Autocracy and the Zemstvo"), which had been used as a weapon against the extension of local self-government to the western provinces.[51] Moreover, in 1904, his attitude to Mirskii's proposals for bringing elected representatives into the State Council had been ambivalent. His reputation was that of an ambitious intriguer, of a worshipper of efficient autocracy, rather than that of a liberal. This does not mean that he was simply a reactionary or that he opposed reforms. According to T.H. von Laue, he believed that the government should keep in touch with influential sections of public opinion, and that there should be a greater respect for civil liberty and the rule of law;[52] but in the past he had always opposed any attempt to limit the authority of the Tsar. Like the Slavophiles he seems to have seen reforms as a means of perfecting the autocratic system rather than of limiting it. However, it is true that in the October Days Witte appeared as the chief advocate of a constitution. He seems reluctantly to have come to the conclusion that a constitution must, rationally, be regarded as historically inevitable. However, emotionally he remained a supporter of autocracy, and finally accepted the idea of a constitution only in the face of the wave of opposition in the country and, because of the absence of the bulk of the armed forces in the Far East.[53] He may well have contemplated the establishment of a limited monarchy on German lines with himself cast in the rôle of Bismarck. But he remained unwilling to concede a full parliamentary régime, and his support for a constitution was always inconsistent and ran counter to his own basic instincts. Moreover, he exhibited a strong tendency to slip back into bureaucratic habits and support for police repression, especially when the forces began to return from the East. Even in his autobiography, in which Witte tends to exaggerate his liberalism, he does not emerge as a sincere and wholehearted advocate of a constitution. It is true that he had recommended it to the Tsar as a way out of the revolutionary crisis. It even appears that he may have represented it as the *best* way out,[54] but he had never firmly identified himself with it. He had merely proposed it as one of the two alternative methods – the other was military dictatorship – which might pacify the country. Moreover, Witte admitted that he advised Nicholas against an imperial manifesto.[55] He had argued that the only document which should be published should be Witte's own "loyal report" to the Crown in favour of constitutional reform. Witte had advised the Tsar that this would be the most prudent course of action because it would "lay the responsibility on him, Count Witte, and will not be binding on His Majesty".[56] Now it is true that this does not in itself prove that Witte was not prepared to make genuine constitutional concessions. But it does suggest that his firmness of purpose was suspect. Witte's memoirs indicate that he advised the Tsar against the manifesto largely because he wished to avoid any subsequent blame for inducing the Tsar to make an irrevocable promise of a constitution. This suggests that Witte was not prepared to stake everything on a constitution by identifying himself with it. He was certainly not prepared to stand up and fight for it if this meant offending the Tsar and ruining his own career.

Like Witte, the Tsar had made the October concessions only reluctantly. From the first his support for the new course was at best half-hearted and inconsistent. The manifesto had been extorted by opposition pressure,[57] and did not reflect any fundamental change in the Tsar's deepest beliefs. At heart he remained a reactionary – the pupil of Alexander III and Konstantin Pobedonostsev, Procurator of the Holy Synod. And even his support for Witte's new "liberal" government proved to be far from absolute. Formally, the Emperor had granted Witte exceptional powers. Before accepting office Witte had obtained the Tsar's consent to the principle of a united cabinet of ministers under his premiership. Previously ministers had been individually responsible to the Crown; now, for the first time, the Tsar had accepted the principle of a ministry with collective responsibility coordinated by a powerful prime minister.[58] However, this principle was never fully implemented in practice. The ministers of War, Marine, Foreign Affairs and the Court remained responsible only to the Tsar; and the new Minister of the Interior, P.N. Durnovo, soon emancipated himself from Witte's control. Moreover, as time went on, the Tsar frequently ignored Witte and the cabinet, and initiated policies on the advice of General Trepov and other advisers.

All this made Witte's position an extremely difficult one. There was little in his record to inspire society with confidence in his government's liberal credentials. And if he were to have any real chance of gaining social support the ministry would have to demonstrate by its actions that the October concessions were sincere and irrevocable. Above all it would have to display consistency and firmness of purpose. In the circumstances this proved to be almost impossible. Moreover, Witte's own attitude remained ambivalent. Although he could see the need for reforms, he increasingly became convinced that exceptional, and often illiberal, measures were needed to suppress the revolutionary movement. And he remained essentially a bureaucrat, a man of the old régime. In the words of T.H. von Laue, he "lacked the temperament and experience for a successful public appeal".[59] Moreover, he could not have gone too far towards meeting the liberals' position without running a serious risk of antagonizing the Tsar and his reactionary advisers.

The Kadets were soon to have ample grounds for doubting the government's sincerity. The events of the first few days of the new ministry were hardly calculated to reassure them. No sooner had the ink on the manifesto dried, than all over Russia outbreaks of violence began, organized by right-wing extremists. Throughout the country, drunken mobs carried out vicious pogroms against Jews, intellectuals and zemstvo liberals. More horrifying still was the widespread connivance of officials of the local administration and police with the pogromists. Moreover, the new government displayed a marked reluctance to bring the culprits to book.[60] Demands for the removal, or punishment, of officials who had implicated themselves fell largely on deaf ears. On the other hand the government refused to grant a complete religious and political amnesty. The partial amnesty which *was* granted satisfied nobody, either on the left or on the right. Moreover, the number of political prisoners and exiles was soon to be swollen again. For, in defiance of the demands of the opposition, the government soon began to adopt severe repressive measures as a means of crushing widespread revolutionary disturbances. Larger and larger areas of the Empire were put under exceptional law or extraordinary protection. The whole of Poland was declared in a state of emergency and placed under martial law. Meanwhile, the government displayed no real sense of urgency about putting the promises of the manifesto quickly into effect. In these circumstances the Kadets could scarcely have much faith in the government's promises. Their feelings were mirrored in the liberal press. *Pravo*, for example, accurately reflected the Kadets' distrust: "In the circumstances of actual reality do not the solemn words of the Manifesto sound ironic? And is it surprising that society puts such little trust in these words?"[61]

Witte's attempts to gain public support

Although the opposition remained sceptical about the government's motives, Witte made a number of attempts to obtain public support. On 22 October an imperial decree restored Finnish autonomy, and on 3 November this was followed by a number of modest measures designed to improve the lot of the peasantry.[62] At the same time, the government began to issue temporary rules governing the exercise of civil liberties.[63] However, these concessions proved to be too little and too late to satisfy the opposition. Moreover, in many respects the temporary rules proved to be highly conservative, and they often received an illiberal interpretation at the hands of the bureaucracy.

In addition to implementing a programme of modest liberal reforms, Witte also attempted to attract representatives of the public into the cabinet. But it is significant that at first of all he approached the conservative minority of the zemstvo movement rather than the Kadets.[64] On 19 October he proceeded to invite D.N. Shipov to accept the post of State Comptroller in the new ministry.[65] Witte was therefore seeking to form the first "constitutional" ministry with the aid of a man who had never supported a constitution. Shipov, who was essentially a believer in an ideal autocracy, supplemented by purely advisory popular representation, had accepted the manifesto only reluctantly, as the act of the Tsar. On his own admission, he was "a constitutionalist by royal decree". However, Shipov was fully aware that his views were not shared by society as a whole. He felt compelled to remind Witte that he represented only a minority. If a new cabinet were to obtain the confidence of society it would have to include representatives of the majority of the zemstvo movement. If this was not done, Shipov would see little point in entering the government. He therefore proposed that Witte should approach the zemstvo bureau with a view to opening negotiations with I.I. Petrunkevich (for the post of Minister of Agriculture), S.A. Muromtsev (Justice), and G.E. L'vov (Interior). Witte agreed to approach the Zemstvo Bureau. But he had done so only on the initiative of Shipov. Clearly, he would have preferred to deal with public men a good deal to their right.

The Zemstvo Bureau was by now so completely under Kadet domination that in his *Memoirs* Miliukov made little distinction between it and the party. It therefore shared the Kadets' profound distrust of the government. Only a few days earlier the party had officially renounced the idea of a "deal with the government" – and any open negotiations with Witte might have seriously compromised it. And now, in view of their chronic lack of faith in the bureaucracy, the Kadet leaders suspected that the government was setting some kind of snare in an effort to mislead or discredit them. This attitude of distrust dominated their policy towards the meeting proposed by Witte. The bureau accordingly decided to send a delegation composed of men "who would not enmesh the new political party in a clumsily-laid net".[66] Muromtsev, an eminent professor of jurisprudence, was considered too liable to compromise and was not included in the deputation.[67] Instead, F.F. Kokoshkin and F.A. Golovin were chosen, together with the moderate Prince Georgii L'vov, the only member on the Witte–Shipov list (and who was destined to be the first prime minister of the Provisional Government in 1917). According to Miliukov, the choice of Kokoshkin signified that the bureau did not want to involve itself in compromise.[68] Golovin was also chosen for his inflexibility, while L'vov was to be a strong but silent partner.[69] These were not men to give hostages to fortune. To prevent any implication that they were seeking ministerial portfolios their rôle was strictly limited to the exchange of information. They would simply lay down the official party line, and elucidate Witte's views. There would be no bargaining. Moreover, to allay society's suspicions about the delegation, its interview with the premier would be published in the press.[70]

The meeting took place on 21 October, and proceeded as planned. The delegates responded to Witte's overtures by reiterating the views of the party congress. They demanded that the government should give evidence of its good faith. It should summon a constituent assembly elected by universal suffrage, put its promises of civil liberties into effect, and grant a complete political amnesty. Not surprisingly, Witte declared such conditions unacceptable in the current state of the country. And indeed, the Kadets must have known that Witte would find their conditions very difficult to swallow.

Many years later, Maklakov condemned the Kadets' proposals, especially their demand for a constituent assembly, as doctrinaire and utterly unrealistic. But in fact, as Miliukov has pointed out, the demand for a constituent assembly was not the real dividing line between the Kadets and the government.[71] It is true that the Kadet leaders were reluctant to abandon the slogans of their first party congress. An immediate volte-face on the issue of a constituent assembly might well have led to their becoming politically discredited. But the majority of the liberals had never supported a constituent assembly on "Leninist" or "Jacobin" lines. Their vague demands for a "constituent assembly" had been based not so much on inflexible democratic principles as upon distrust – upon the belief that the bureaucracy could not be trusted to work out an acceptable constitution. It seems probable, therefore, that if only the government could have proved that it sincerely intended to grant a constitution satisfactory to society, the Kadets would ultimately have ceased to demand a constituent assembly. This was, indeed, an argument that Miliukov was soon to put to Witte.

At the beginning of November or the end of October the premier invited Miliukov to come and see him for a private chat. Although he had no authorization from the party as a whole, Miliukov decided to accept the invitation.[72] According to Miliukov, in the course of the conversation he sought to "bring the argument down from the academic plane into the sphere of actual reality". He freely admitted that a constituent assembly was not a practical proposition at the moment. It would take too long to call a constituent assembly, which would be concerned only with drafting a constitution, and then wait for new elections to choose a legislative assembly. Instead, Miliukov suggested that the government itself should promulgate a constitution right away: "Summon someone today", said Miliukov, "and order him to translate the Belgian, or still better, the Bulgarian constitution, into Russian, take it to the Tsar tomorrow for his signature, and on the next day publish it". Despite the malicious capital which Maklakov later made of this, it is extremely doubtful whether Miliukov meant this advice to be taken literally. He did not imagine that foreign constitutions could be applied unchanged to Russian conditions. As Miliukov subsequently explained, he was speaking figuratively.[73] But nevertheless, he *was* demanding a published constitution as evidence of the government's good faith. And his reference to the Bulgarian constitution is a significant pointer to the sort of system the Kadets might have been prepared to accept. (Although this constitution was basically parliamentary and based on universal suffrage, it left the Crown considerable power in the fields of the armed forces, the executive and to some extent in foreign affairs.)[74]

When Witte cast doubt upon the opposition's willingness to accept a constitution proclaimed "from above", Miliukov's answer was equally significant. He explained that society was hostile to the idea largely because "it does not believe in the possibility of receiving such a liberal constitution from the bureaucracy". If such a constitution were proclaimed the public would certainly abuse Witte at first, but things would soon settle down again. Now it is true that this advice was unofficial. But, nevertheless, Miliukov was rapidly becoming the Kadets' most influential leader. He was in an excellent position to know the real political temperature of his party. And his evaluation was, clearly, that it would settle for something less than a constituent assembly: namely, for a constitutional monarchy conceded from above provided it guaranteed a basically parliamentary régime.[75] In the meantime, said Miliukov (until the convocation of a legislative assembly) Witte should form a "businesslike" government of honest bureaucrats acceptable to the public. At this point Witte for the first time displayed his pleasure. "Now at last", he said, "I have heard the first piece of good sense. That is what I have decided to do".[76] However, he remained non-committal about the rest of the Kadet leader's advice. He even failed to convince Miliukov that the government's support for constitutional principles was sincere and irrevocable. The government had never, even in the October Manifesto, actually pronounced the word "constitution". Miliukov therefore demanded that it should now be used: "If", he said, "your powers are adequate, why are you unable to pronounce the word 'constitution'?" "I cannot, because the Tsar does not wish it", Witte replied. At this Miliukov broke off the conversation. "Then it is useless", he concluded, "for us to talk together. I am unable to give you any useful advice".[77] This was not just a barren quibble about words, as Maklakov later argued. If the government was unwilling or unable to pronounce such a vital *word*, its sincerity and constancy in supporting a constitutional *system* was put in doubt. If Witte was unwilling to antagonize the Tsar by pronouncing a mere word, would he be prepared to fight for its substance in face of the possible displeasure of his reactionary master? If Witte had not been given a free hand in matters of policy, and if he was unwilling or unable to take a strong line with the Tsar, there was little point in trusting in the government's good faith. In the circumstances any accommodation with Witte would have been built upon shifting sand, and might have served only to discredit the liberals.[78]

During his interview with the premier Miliukov had abandoned the doctrinaire position which Maklakov has so much deplored and had adopted a more realistic attitude. But he had met little response from Witte. He had failed even to obtain an assurance that the government was sincere over the very idea of a constitution. Meanwhile, a similar fate had overtaken the moderate right in *their* negotiations with the government.

After his failure to come to an agreement with the Zemstvo Bureau, Witte had once again turned to Shipov and the minority of the Zemstvo Congress. Shipov and his friends could scarcely have been accused of doctrinaire hatred of the government. They represented precisely those elements of society which should (according to Maklakov's later analysis) have found least difficulty in coming to terms with the government. In fact, such an agreement proved impossible to reach. The leaders of the zemstvo minority willingly negotiated with Witte, but their negotiations merely served to undermine their trust in the latter's good faith.

On 22 October, the day after his ill-starred meeting with the Zemstvo Bureau, Witte once again invited Shipov to come and see him. But instead of negotiating with Shipov he attempted to force his hand by presenting him with a fait accompli. He informed Shipov that his appointment as State Comptroller had already taken place. However, the zemstvo leader refused to be pressurized. He insisted upon seeing the Tsar to explain his point of view and succeeded in obtaining an audience on the following day.[79] Although the attitude of the Zemstvo Bureau had made him less insistent about the need to represent the zemstvo majority, Shipov advised the Tsar to include a substantial group of public men in the ministry, claiming that his own appointment would otherwise be meaningless.

As a consequence of Shipov's advice, on 24 October Witte held a meeting with several representatives of the moderate right.[80] In addition to Shipov, M.A. Stakhovich (another zemstvo leader of Slavophile rather than constitutionalist views), and Alexander Guchkov, the future leader of the Octobrist Party, were also present.[81] However, the talks broke down over the vital question of who should hold the post of Minister of the Interior. Witte's candidate was P.N. Durnovo, a nomination which he supported with extreme tenacity. Despite Witte's statements to the contrary,[82] Durnovo was not a man to inspire the confidence of society. He was too closely associated with the bureaucracy, and had a most dubious and reactionary reputation. Because of this, the zemstvo leaders were adamant with Witte and insisted that Durnovo's appointment would be unacceptable. They would agree only to a compromise – that Prince Urusov, a moderately liberal provincial governor, should be minister and Durnovo his deputy.[83] Witte seemed to give way, and sent for Urusov. But according to Witte, he had second thought when he actually met Urusov. He came to the conclusion that the Prince was insufficiently experienced in police work for such a post at a time when a strong man was essential.[84] He renewed his support for Durnovo and without consulting Shipov, obtained Urusov's agreement to be his deputy. Witte would soon have ample cause to regret his decision. Durnovo's conduct in office justified the zemstvo men's worst suspicions. He rapidly emancipated himself from Witte's control and joined hands with the reactionaries at Court. Witte later admitted that "Durnovo's appointment was one of the greatest mistakes I made during my administration".[85] However, in October 1905 Witte's support for Durnovo was unshakeable. He even overcame the Tsar's own reservations about Durnovo and secured his appointment as acting Minister of the Interior.

On 26 October he announced the new appointment to the zemstvo leaders, and this time Witte was inflexible. Witte's behaviour convinced Shipov and Guchkov that he valued the appointment of Durnovo more than he wanted social support. His attitude suggested that his new cabinet would be dominated by reactionary bureaucrats. There was no guarantee that the zemstvo men would have any real influence on the ministry even if they had joined it.[86] The leaders of the moderate right came to the conclusion that they had been deceived. Shipov later attacked Witte for his "lack of sincerity and straight-forwardness", and his "obvious inability to free himself from the habits and methods he had assimilated from the bureaucratic system".[87] By the end of October even the moderate right had lost all confidence in the government's sincerity and good faith. In the circumstances it is very difficult to see how the Kadets could have come to any kind of understanding with the ministry. Any declaration of support for the government at this stage might have led to the party becoming completely discredited with the public, and committing political suicide.

However, the Kadets did not adopt a totally uncompromising attitude towards the ministry. On the contrary, they now began to assume a more flexible posture. On 6–13 November another Zemstvo Congress was held in Moscow. Now that Western-style political parties were being established, the zemstvo congresses were rapidly becoming something of an anachronism, and this was to be the last assembly of its kind. However, this did not prevent the Kadets from using it to prepare the ground for a possible détente with the government. The proposals which they now submitted to the zemstvo men marked a retreat from their position at the Foundation Congress. "In this respect", said Miliukov in his *Memoirs*, "it [the congress] was, as it were, a continuation of my conversations with Witte". These decisions of the congress were "a kind of personal success on the route of converting Party tactics to a more realistic direction".[88] And, indeed, it was Miliukov, on behalf of the Zemstvo Bureau, who played the major rôle in proposing the change of front.[89] According to Miliukov's resolution,[90] the October Manifesto was now recognized as "a precious conquest of the Russian people". The government should now demonstrate its good faith by displaying decisiveness and consistency in implementing its promises. In so far as it did so, it would be able to count upon the support of "wide circles of zemstvo and town leaders". It is significant that the use of the term "constituent assembly" was now abandoned. Instead, Miliukov proposed a more moderate, more flexible formula. The resolution now demanded that the government should establish universal suffrage, and assign "constituent functions" to the "first assembly of popular representatives". Moreover, it was stipulated that the assembly's proposals would require the *"confirmation of the Tsar"*. In addition to its constituent functions, the assembly should reorganize local government on democratic lines, examine the budget, lay down the principles of land reform and pass urgent measures in the field of labour legislation. Before the popular representatives met, the government should implement its promises of civil liberty and end all exceptional laws. At the same time officials guilty of crimes after 17 October should be punished, and the administration should be subjected to the rule of law. Miliukov's proposals were accepted by the congress as a whole without any significant modifications.[91] The message to Witte was clear – if the government demonstrated its good faith and its willingness to accept radical reform, the Kadets would drop their extreme hostility to the government, and with it the term "constituent assembly".[92] However, this more conciliatory attitude met no response from Witte. He even refused to accept a delegation from the Zemstvo Congress.

The congress apparently marked a substantial retreat by the liberal leaders. They had dropped the uncompromising pose which they had adopted at the October Party Congress and they seemed to have gone back on their commitment to a constituent assembly. But as we have already seen, the Kadets had always interpreted this term quite differently from the socialist parties. And a representative assembly working out a constitution subject to the confirmation of the Tsar was much closer to what the Kadet leaders had always meant by a "constituent assembly", than was the socialist conception of such a body. Moreover, the congress had by no means voted for support for the government; nor had it dropped the demand for a basically parliamentary régime. In fact, it appears that the congress's proposals were a closer *definition* of what the Kadet leaders had always wanted, rather than a real retreat from their basic programme.[93]

The Kadets had certainly moderated their *posture* and changed their *tone* since their Foundation Congress. However, the extreme language which they had adopted in October was not really typical of the Kadets. To some extent they appear to have been carried away by the wave of radical enthusiasm which was sweeping the country at that time. The ultra-radical pose which they had struck at the First Congress appears to have been largely the result of the exceptional circumstances of the moment.[94] It did not necessarily reflect their most fundamental attitudes and beliefs. It is therefore hardly surprising that as the intoxicating effects of the October crisis began to recede, the party gradually retreated to a more sober and more tenable position.

It is of course true that the Zemstvo Congress was formally a non-party organization, and that it could not officially speak on behalf of the Kadets. However, the zemstvo leadership was now very heavily dominated by prominent members of the party. Miliukov himself had been chosen to propose the zemstvo bureau's main resolution, and later on, three other leading Kadets were entrusted with the task of presenting the congress's views to Witte (F.F. Kokoshkin, S.A. Muromtsev and I.I. Petrunkevich).[95] It therefore seems clear that even if the congress did not necessarily put forward demands which fully reflected the Kadet's policies, it did put forward proposals which they were willing to endorse and promote.

Naturally enough, the Zemstvo Congress's demands did lead to some protests from the left against the apparent change of front. However, the November Congress also witnessed the emergence of a much more vigorous opposition on the *right*. The reason for this was not difficult to discern. Revolutionary disorder had grown alarmingly, accompanied on the extreme right by brutal pogroms. On 27 October a naval rebellion broke out at Kronshtadt, while at the beginning of November preparations had begun for a second general strike, of which the liberals disapproved.[96] The revolution seemed to be getting out of control. Against this background many of the prosperous zemstvo men were beginning to fear for their lives and property. According to *Pravo* many members of the congress had direct experience of the pogroms and had also been affected by "a senseless spontaneous movement, the burning of country seats" and the "destruction and annihilation of property". Because of this, said *Pravo*, "confusion", even "fright", had reigned at the beginning of the congress.[97] These circumstances proved favourable to the right-wing of the zemstvo movement which renewed the struggle on the issue of Polish autonomy. When a naval mutiny broke out at Sebastopol several zemstvo men even demanded that the congress should express its support for the government.[98] However, the right-wing minority did not succeed in dominating the congress, nor does it appear to have pushed the Kadets towards reaction. It is true that the congress delegation's message to Witte stressed the part which reform could play in the *pacification* of the country. It also pointed out the danger of class war, and of indiscipline in the armed forces. But this does not mean that the Kadet leaders had finally turned away from the revolutionaries to their left. The Kadets had often talked in this way in the past, for largely tactical reasons. They had hoped that by frightening the government with the spectre of revolution they would compel it to agree to reform. It is true that the Kadets had always feared anarchy – by no means a chimera in a backward country – and they had never supported violence, even if they had never entirely ruled it out in principle. To this extent their concern about disturbances was real. But although the revolutionaries were now beginning to turn their backs upon the Kadets,[99] the liberals were not ready to reciprocate. They realized that their only hope of reform lay in pressure upon the government from the left. The Kadets therefore adhered to their previous tactics. They continued to call for the unity of the opposition during the first, or "bourgeois" revolution.

As Petrunkevich put it:

> I do not fear revolution and consider myself and all of us to be revolutionaries. The danger is in *anarchy* [author's emphasis] whereas revolution has its own cultural tasks and is leading to the replacement of an inferior régime by a better one ... I say now that it is possible to hold out our hand to the socialists since we are still bound to them by a single ("odin") aim – the construction of a constitution.[100]

Nevertheless, the Kadets and the revolutionaries were now beginning to drift farther apart. Although the growth of violence and anarchy had not driven the Kadets to reaction it did incline them to greater caution. For even though the Kadets were not hostile to the revolutionaries as such they *were* beginning to fear that the left was itself losing control of the revolution. In their view the revolutionaries were allowing themselves to be swept off their feet by spontaneous revolutionary currents in the country at large. Because of this they were adopting ill-judged or even dangerous tactics – especially in their promotion of violence and their use of the strike weapon. The Kadets had never opposed political strikes in principle and had proclaimed their full solidarity with the October stoppage. But they did feel that such methods should be employed with circumspection – as a decisive weapon at a crucial moment. An editorial in *Pravo*[101] described the political strike as a method to be resorted to only in exceptional cases – it was an "extreme revolutionary means". If it was employed too frequently it would lose its impact and become devalued as a political weapon. Moreover, unless strikes began with the support of the whole opposition, they would lead to dangerous divisions which could benefit only the autocracy. They might also lead to a wave of popular reaction. Because of this *Pravo* condemned the Second General Strike as unwise. The grounds for the strike (the proclamation of martial law in Poland, the apparent threat to the lives of captured Kronshtadt mutineers and the demand for an eight-hour day), were insufficient to justify it, and the moment was ill-chosen.

Whether the grounds for a strike were in fact insufficient is questionable. It seems probable that to some extent the Kadets were losing their nerve. They always had a tendency to believe that omelettes could be made without breaking eggs. However, their anxiety about the tactics of the extreme left was largely justified. Both Trotsky and the Bolsheviks had by now gone beyond demands for the end of the autocracy, and were already fomenting class hatred against the liberals and the "bourgeoisie". Even the strikers' demand for the eight-hour day was directed against the employers rather than against the government. All this helped to divide the opposition, and engendered a growing reaction among the propertied classes. Many landowners and industrialists had been satisfied with the promises of the October Manifesto, and now an increasing number hastened to make their peace with the government. The tactics of the extreme left were now breaking down the unity of the whole nation against the government which had ben instrumental in extorting concessions in October. Without the sympathy and support of the employers – indeed, the strike met their bitter opposition – the workers soon became exhausted, and the strike came to an inconclusive end. So far from demonstrating the strength of the opposition, the strike, in fact, displayed its divisions and weaknesses.

As November drew to its close, and as disorder in the country grew, Kadet uneasiness over the tactics of the left deepened. In a leading article *Pravo* once again stressed the danger that extremism and violence might lead to a wave of reaction and a division of the opposition. *Pravo* emphasized that it was not hoping for the defeat of the revolution. It was, however, concerned that there should be "common tactics in the struggle", that "the opposition should not be a prey to chimeras", and that it should not "fawn upon anarchy". The revolutionaries should cease to heap accusations upon the liberals, and should hold out the hand of friendship to them.[102]

Implicit in this argument was the belief that the extreme left might still be induced to limit their immediate aims to the demand of the "bourgeois" revolution of Marxist orthodoxy – a revolution which would usher in, not socialism, but a Western-style democratic régime. Clearly, then, notwithstanding its uneasiness over the tactics of the left, *Pravo* did not realize the full implications of Bolshevism and the "democratic dictatorship of the proletariat and peasantry", or still hoped that such extremists would be held in check. However, the Kadets' complacency was clearly being undermined. On 1 December, Miliukov, writing in the Kadet journal *Svobodnyi Narod* (*The Free People*),[103] gave a stern warning to the revolutionaries. The left should not, he said, overestimate its own power or embrace extremes. There was a certain limit, beyond which,

> revolutionary propaganda becomes destructive, and yesterday's ally becomes a fierce enemy. We come close to this limit if we resort too often and too lightly to such powerful methods as, for example, the political strike – methods which depend upon revolutionary enthusiasm, and which upset the normal course of life in the country more or less profoundly.

Again, the revolutionaries would be losing sight of the common aim if they "built their calculations upon the sharpening of class antagonisms". Provided the revolutionaries remembered that they and the Kadets shared the same objective, they would have the liberals on their side. "But", Miliukov warned the left, "you will isolate yourself and will be digging your own grave if you pose the revolution unattainable aims, unleashing its anarchic forces; and proclaiming the revolution to be permanent ('nepreryvnyi')". The socialists could not escape from the laws of history – they should have learnt this from Marx himself. "To replace Marxism by Jacobinism" meant "going back 30 years and harming (the socialists') own cause".

Clearly, then, the Kadets were at last becoming painfully aware of the dangers of Bolshevism and "Trotskyism", with their emphasis on proletarian leadership of the revolution. But nevertheless, they hoped that such extremes would be a temporary phase. What they really seem to have wanted was the eventual repetition, at a crucial moment, of the more or less peaceful pressure which had exacted the October Manifesto; pressure limited to the aim of obtaining a more or less democratic constitution. However, they did not welcome the idea of chaos or an armed revolt, which would utterly destroi all existing authority, and bring the revolution to the frontiers of socialism. To the Kadets this seemed a route fraught with dangers. However, they still refused to equate revolutionary violence with that of the government.

The December crisis

Meanwhile, events in Russia were leading up to another showdown between the government and the revolutionaries. On 3 December, Witte finally summoned up his courage, and arrested the entire St. Petersburg Soviet – the headquarters of the revolution. The revolutionaries retaliated with the Third General Strike, which began on 8 December, and a Bolshevik armed uprising centred mainly in Moscow – a revolt suppressed with exceptional savagery by the government. The Kadets were unable to sympathize fully with the actions of the revolutionaries.

Miliukov pointed out that the strike, which no longer had the full support of society, and which was backed by workers who were already starving, had little chance of success.[104] Moreover, he was convinced that the government was deliberately making use of the strike to fan the flames of social reaction.[105] But the strike did not drive the Kadets into the reactionary camp. Not even the Moscow uprising made the party finally turn its back on the revolutionaries. While Octobrists like Guchkov hastened to support the government in Moscow, the Kadets refused to do so. It is true that they regarded the rebellion as a mistake, but they reserved their invective purely for the government. Miliukov even accused Witte of wishing to provoke a rebellion in order to be able to crush it and demonstrate the weakness of the revolution.[106] Moreover, he brought government atrocities in Moscow under fierce attack.[107] This was not just the view of Miliukov, or of the Kadet "centre" or "left" – it seems to have reflected the opinion of the party as a whole. For example, in an article in *Narodnaia Svoboda* (*Freedom of the People*)[108] Struve bitterly attacked government barbarism. According to Struve, the rising was a terrible mistake, but it displayed a kind of heroic and tragic greatness. The left should now unite with the rest of the opposition to obtain their main aim (i.e. a constitution and civil liberties).

Struve, who had for a long time been moving slowly towards the right, was now once again in Russia. Upon the proclamation of the October Manifesto[109] he had ceased publication of *Liberation*, rushed back to Petersburg and laid the groundwork for a new liberal periodical. The result was *Poliarnaia Zvezda* (*Pole Star*) which finally appeared on 15 December and which has been generally regarded as the mouthpiece of the Kadet right-wing. However, the evidence suggests that Struve's later moves towards a more conservative standpoint have led many commentators to exaggerate *Poliarnaia Zvezda*'s right-wing tendencies. In most cases they have sought to confirm their analysis by referring to the views expressed in the editorial of the journal's first issue.[110] This declared that "We are sworn enemies, in reason, conscience and feeling of any violence whether it proceeds from the Government or from anarchy". This has often been interpreted as meaning that Struve had decisively turned his back on the revolution and the revolutionaries. Struve's later accounts of his position in 1905–6 have tended to confirm this interpretation.[111] However, Struve's reminiscences appear to have been strongly coloured by hindsight. Their accuracy is cast seriously in doubt by contemporary evidence relating to his political position at this time.

His article in *Narodnaia Svoboda* does not support the thesis that Struve had broken decisively with the revolutionaries. It suggests that while Struve was opposed to violence he was still prepared to come to terms with the revolutionaries if they would become more realistic and adopt different tactics. However, *Poliarnaia Zvezda*'s fiercest attacks were reserved not for the left but for Guchkov and other supporters of government actions in Moscow. In No. 6 Struve heaped invective upon Guchkov for his "services to Dubusov" (the suppressor of the revolt), and poured scorn upon the propertied class he represented. According to Struve, Guchkov and his friends had supported the government because of ignoble "bourgeois fear" for their own lives and property. It was clear, said Struve, "that the Russian reaction is only another face of property-owning Russia and that this propertied-bureaucratic Russia is barring the way to the Russia of the people".[112] This was scarcely the language of the right, and it makes any crude classification of Struve as "right-wing" impossible. In fact, in some spheres, especially in social questions, Struve was still to the left of the party. He had still not entirely discarded his socialist outlook. Semeon Frank, Struve's closest associate, did not hesitate to link *Poliarnaia Zvezda*'s programme to gradualist socialism – to English Fabianism in particular – and he made it clear that he was not merely expressing his own opinion but that of the journal as a whole.[113]

However, Struve's radicalism in social and economic matters was not reflected in his views on purely *political* affairs. It is true that he was still willing to ally with the revolutionaries in order to exert peaceful pressure upon the government. However (as he himself admitted), he would have preferred the government itself to have stood at the head of the revolution and to have imposed a compromise solution to the crisis.[114] At the same time he now expressed his support for a constitutional monarchy and his opposition to republicanism,[115] and severely criticized the doctrinaires of the left, as unrealistic. However, these views do not entirely justify the idea that Struve, even purely politically, was far to the right of his party. As we have seen the Kadet leaders as a whole were already moving away from the transient enthusiasm of the Constituent Congress towards a not very different standpoint. And neither the December uprising nor the emergence of *Poliarnaia Zvezda* marked any new decisive point in the movement of Kadet opinion to the right, even though they may have marked another milestone in this process. The Bolshevik historian Sef asserts that after December Kadet enthusiasm for the revolution was increasingly on the wane. But even he admitted that "this curve of the Kadet mood declined extremely cautiously and slowly".[116]

In fact, the Kadets could not afford to be unduly hostile to the revolution, since their relations with the government had in no way improved. Their distrust of Witte had been reinforced by the government's atrocities in Moscow and by its adoption of severe repressive measures in the country as a whole. More and more regions were being subjected to exceptional or martial law, and in some areas punitive expeditions were employing Draconian methods to crush the revolution. The Kadets were also profoundly antagonized by the government's refusal to institute universal suffrage. Despite the fact that even the moderate right had insisted on this, their advice was rejected and on 11 December the government published an electoral law which was essentially merely a development of the Bulygin proposals.[117] Although the vote was now extended to a much larger number of citizens – indeed, it came close to the principle of universality – the elections were to be neither direct nor equal. The Kadets felt that the government had once again proved that it was not to be trusted and they bitterly attacked the new law. Petrunkevich insisted that "Universal suffrage is the three-cornered stone without which it is impossible to construct the edifice of the new Russia".[118] The Kadets were by now farther off than ever from a rapprochement with Witte, and could have little faith in voluntary reform from above. Their only hope, therefore, was that pressure from the opposition, including the left, would compel the government to concede what they wanted. And so, despite their misgivings about the revolution, the Kadets were in no position to wish for its total defeat.

At the end of 1905 the party lay in a political no-man's land between two warring enemies – the revolutionaries and the autocracy. Shot at and abused from both sides they were unable to play any decisive rôle in the conflict. They could not give their wholehearted support to either side. Most of their sympathy went to the revolutionaries, but they feared the total victory of either of the opposing forces. Their interests would have been best served by some form of stalemate since this might have led to a compromise suitable to them. But the Kadets could do little directly to achieve such an outcome. Unlike the government and the revolutionaries they were not prepared to resort to violence. They were, above all, a party of respectable men whose natural bent was towards parliamentary methods and legal opposition, not the barricades. Because of this, their future was to be determined largely independently of their own actions – by the outcome of the struggle between the government and the revolution – and much less by anything which they did themselves. The only independent weapons the Kadets possessed consisted of Western-style constitutional activity and the organization of peaceful public opinion. While these methods might well have suited Edwardian England, they were, unfortunately for the Kadets, to prove inadequate in the conditions of Tsarist Russia.

Party organization

The Kadets were the first major political party in Russia to model themselves wholly on Western lines. The socialist parties had been founded at an earlier date, but even in 1905 they continued to lay their chief emphasis on underground or conspiratorial activity. However, from the outset the Kadets planned to establish an open, parliamentary-style party dedicated to securing reform by peaceful, and essentially legal, methods. The October Congress had taken the first steps in laying down the foundations of such a party. But the circumstances in which it had been held prevented its decisions being absolutely authoritative. The congress therefore decided that the Central Committee which it had elected should be only provisional, holding office only until a new party congress, which would be held in the very near future.

However, the party's plans were frustrated by circumstances which were largely beyond its control.[119] In November, the Kadets' preparations for a new congress were severely retarded by a strike of postal and telegraphic workers, which reduced communications to chaos. Progress was further disrupted by the effects of a wave of revolutionary disorders and growing government repression. And as events built up towards the December crisis, it finally became clear that the congress could not be held before January.

The revolution had an equally disruptive effect upon the organization of the party in the country.[120] The postal-telegraphic strike cut off all communications between the Central Committee and the provincial party groups, and even interfered with links between Kadet groups in the same province. At the same time, in several provinces the Kadets encountered substantial administrative opposition to the formation of local party organizations.[121] All this tended to impede the orderly development of the party on the lines which had been laid down by the First Congress. The Party Statute adopted by the congress[122] had envisaged that the provincial group would be the centre of provincial party administration, with other local groups subordinate to it. Even the recruiting of members had been entrusted almost exclusively to the central and *provincial* organs. In order to ensure that the party would be established along these lines the congress had provided for the holding of local constituent conferences in each province.[123] But partly because of the chaotic state of the country, and partly because of administrative pressure, it often proved impossible to hold these conferences. As a result, the provisions of the Party Statute often remained a dead letter. Instead of a regular party organization centred on the provincial groups, there were frequently only uezd (district) branches, or groups uniting a number of districts.[124]

The party's organizational difficulties were matched by confusion in the party's finances. The First Congress had set a low individual subscription rate of 5 kopecks a month towards central party funds.[125] At the same time each provincial group would be obliged to donate a quarterly sum of 200 rubles to the party treasury. However, partly because of the weakness of the party organization, and partly because of the pressing needs of the local groups themselves, this plan proved very difficult to put into effect.[126] The Central Committee lacked adequate information about the composition of local party groups, and this made it impossible to distribute financial burdens equitably. Furthermore, the circumstances of the time seriously impeded the Kadets' efforts to recruit a mass membership. As a result of all this, very few subscriptions appear to have been sent to the Central Committee.

In many parts of the country there was still no effective party organization. It is true that some groups had found little difficulty in getting established. In Vladimir and Krasnoiarsk, groups had been formed even before the party congress,[127] and in Moscow and Nizhnii-Novgorod they were founded almost immediately afterwards. But in general, the party's development was slowed down by the effects of strikes, pogroms and government repression. Moreover, the refusal of the moderate socialists to enter the party retarded organizational work even in the capital.[128]

In view of the difficulties which the party experienced in organizing a new congress, the Central Committee decided to make use of the November Zemstvo Congress to assist the party in its work. On 12–14 November it held joint meetings with a number of zemstvo men,[129] including spokesmen from provinces not represented at the Foundation Congress. The discussions with the zemstvo men led to the formation of Kadet groups in a large number of provinces.[130] More provincial branches were founded in November than in any other single month.

The party officially[131] enumerated no less than 14 provincial branches founded in this period, together with independent groups in eight uezds and three towns (excluding the Petersburg city group).[132] By the end of the year the official tally of party branches came to 24 full provincial groups, 11 independent town groups and eight uezd (or district) groups. But although the party was making progress it had not yet established a comprehensive all-Russian organization.

At this stage of the party's history Moscow was undisputedly the chief centre of party activity. It was Moscow which had dominated the First Congress, and it was there too that the Central Committee took up its headquarters and set about its activity. As one of its first steps, the committee decided that it should meet regularly – once a week in plenary session, although if necessary, additional extraordinary meetings would be held.[133] At the same time the committee set up a secretariat to maintain correspondence and personal contacts with local party groups. This was composed, initially, of three members: Prince D.I. Shakhovskoi, formerly the secretary of the Union of Liberation; A.A. Kornilov, a well-known historian; and A.N. Maksimov, a leader-writer on the liberal paper *Russkie Vedomosti (The Russian Gazette)*.[134] The Moscow publisher M.A. Sabashnikov was appointed as the committee's treasurer. However, in general the committee seems to have paid litle attention to the formalities of internal organization: for example, there was no permanent president or official leadership.[135]

The Central Committee's relations with the Kadets' Moscow City group appear to have been equally informal. The committee tended to be dominated by Muscovites and it apparently had exceptionally close ties with the local Kadet group. Indeed, in his report to the Second Congress Kornilov found it appropriate to describe the activities of both organizations together. All this probably explains why the Moscow group obtained exceptional importance in this period of party activity. The Muscovites played a particularly active rôle in mobilizing public opinion and in propagating the party faith. In conjunction with the Central Committee they set up a school to train party orators (under the guidance of V.A. Maklakov).[136] During the same period the Moscow group also established committees concerned with the organization of public lectures and mass propaganda.

The party's publishing activity was also concentrated in Moscow. Following the First Congress, the Kadet industrialist landowner and publisher M.G. Kommissarov handed over the Moscow publishing house Narodnoe Pravo (The People's Right) to the party.[137] This soon began to produce a steady stream of books and pamphlets directed both at the intelligentsia and the masses.[138] By the time of the Second Congress, 100,000 copies of one pamphlet (*To the Peasants*) had already been distributed to the people.[139]

The party press

Although the achievements of *Narodnoe Pravo* were considerable, in itself publishing activity of this type could not provide an adequate channel for party propaganda. Nor could it keep the Kadet activists in close touch with the opinions of their leaders, or provide a satisfactory source of party news. The Kadets were now in urgent need of new party journals and newspapers. It is true that there were already several provincial papers which gave the party general support. Moreover, *Pravo* and the Moscow daily *Russkie Vedomosti* provided the Kadets with some kind of national press.[140] But the latter was directed at the educated classes and was not tied closely enough to the party line, while *Pravo* was still catering for a restricted and specialized readership. It was still divided between its political funcions and its rôle as a periodical of the legal profession. What the Kadets really needed was a journal directed at the party faithful, together with an extension of the Kadet popular press.

For some time progress was retarded by a combination of lack of funds and administrative repression. Nevertheless, attempts were made to broaden the Kadet press. At the end of November, S.M. Propper, the owner of the Petersburg *Birzhevye Vedomosti* (*The Bourse Gazette*) offered the editorship of his paper's morning edition to Miliukov and I.V. Gessen, who accepted the offer with alacrity.[141] The new journal, which was originally entitled *Svobodnyi Narod*, commenced publication on 1 December. However, on the following day the paper was seized by the censor for publishing an appeal from the St. Petersburg Soviet.[142] Although the paper was banned, its editors refused to accept defeat. It was retitled *Narodnaia Svoboda* and publication was resumed. But once again it was closed by the administration, this time on its sixth number (20 December).[143] Partly because of this, and partly because of the wave of social reaction in December, Propper withdrew his support for the venture and it finally foundered. It was more that two months before the Kadets developed any adequate replacement. Following the Moscow uprising the governmental reaction was at its height, and attempts to start a popular newspaper in Moscow were frustrated by the City Commandant.[144] Moreover, both before and after the rebellion, the administration continually imposed restrictions upon the Kadet provincial press.[145]

At their Foundation Congress the Kadets had resolved to establish political freedom by direct action, without waiting for government permission. However, they now began to find this policy increasingly difficult to implement, especially during the reactionary hysteria which followed the December uprising. The autocracy had suffered a reverse in October, but by no means a total defeat, and it was now rapidly mounting a counter-attack. Moreover, large sections of the bureaucracy had never acted as if they fully recognized the manifesto's promises. This was particularly true in the case of the provincial administration. In many areas the Kadets could not even be sure that they would be able to form party branches. Nor could they guarantee that their literature would be allowed to circulate freely, or that their public meetings would be permitted.

All this helps to explain the Kadets' failure to recruit mass support at this stage of the party's development. It is true that there were cases of entire peasant communities applying for party membership,[146] but these were clearly the exception rather than the rule. At the Second Party Congress one speaker complained about the almost total absence of representatives of the masses among the delegates.[147] The party leaders appear to have been fully aware of the seriousness of this problem and to have been anxious to find a solution for it. In February 1906 the party's official journal was forced to admit that "although the general spirit and programme of the Constitutional Democratic Party were broadly democratic, until very recently this was far less true of its composition".[148]

At the end of 1905 the Kadets were moving into a pre-election period. If the party was to have any real chance of success, it would have to make a concerted effort to enlist the support of the people. This would inevitably be the main task facing the party during the next stage of its existence – a period which would extend from the Second Party Congress in January 1906 to the Third Congress in April.

Notes

1 "Pervyi vserossiiskii s''ezd krest''ian", *Osvobozhdenie*, No. 77 and 78/79.
2 See, e.g., "K obrazovaniiu konstitutsionno-demokraticheskoi partii", *Osvobozdenie*, No. 78/79.
3 The liberals' aspirations were to be finally eclipsed at the Second Congress of the Peasant Union held 6–10 November 1905. See E.I. Kiriukhina, "Vserossiiskii krest''ianskii soiuz v 1905 g", *I.Z.*, 50, 1955, pp. 115–25.
4 The sobriquet "Kadet" was in future to be a very popular name for the Constitutional-Democratic Party. It was derived from the Russian words for the party's initials "K.D." ("Konstitutionno-Demokraticheskaia Partiia").
5 For the proceedings of this congress see: *Pravo*, No. 37 and 38, 1905.
6 *Pravo*, No. 37, pp. 3050–1.
7 *Pravo*, No. 37, p. 3054.
8 *Pravo*, No. 38, pp. 3178–9.
9 For the debate on this question, see: *Pravo*, No. 38. pp. 3171–6.
10 See Shipov, Vospominanii, 1918, pp. 518–19 on the reaction in the zemstvos in 1906–7. Almost everywhere progressive zemstvo leaders were dismissed by their propertied electorates in favour of reactionaries. See also Veselovskii, "Dvizhenie zemlevladel'tsev" (Part 2), p. 24.
11 *OTCHËT tsentral'nogo komiteta konstitutsionno-demokraticheskoi partii za dva goda*, S.P.B. 1907, pp. 16–18 (hereafter referred to as *OTCHËT*).
12 The Soviet's elected chairman was G.S. Khrustalev-Nosar, a St. Petersburg lawyer who had taken a leading part in liberationist attempts to organize the working class of the capital. However, he was shortly to join the Mensheviks.
13 *OTCHËT*, p. 3.
14 For the proceedings of the congress, see: "Pervyi s''ezd Konstitutsionno-demokraticheskoi partii, 12–13 oktiabria 1905 goda", in V.V Shelokhaiev (ed.), *S''ezdy i konferentsii Konstitutsionno-demokraticheskoi Partii*, Vol. I, ROSSPEN 1997, pp. 17–43.
15 *OTCHËT*, p. 16, footnote.
16 *OTCHËT*, p. 18.
17 For further details, see *OTCHËT*, pp. 1–27.
18 *OTCHËT*, p. 16–18.
19 *OTCHËT*, p. 18.
20 For the party programme see: "Programma konstitutsionno-demokraticheskoi partii", *Pravo*, No. 41, 1905; *Konstitutsionno-demokraticheskaia partiia – s''ezd 12–18 oktiabria 1905*, Moscow 1905, pp. 23–6; *Pervyi s''ezd K.d. partii 1905 goda*, Vol. I, pp. 34–42, in V.V. Shelokhaev (ed.), *S''ezdy i konferentsii konstitutsionno-demokraticheskoi partii*, ROSSPEN 1997 (GARF. f. 523, op. 1, d.38.).

The birth of the Kadet Party   67

21 The "land captain" had limited powers of disciplining the peasantry without recourse to the normal machinery of justice. They were appointed by the administration, and were normally members of the landed gentry.
22 That is, universal, direct, secret and equal suffrage.
23 The programme stipulated that if there were to be a second chamber, it should consist of representatives of local self-government, who would in future be elected by universal suffrage. However, in this case the suffrage would not have been *direct*. Section III (point 21) of the programme prescribed that the higher organs of local government should be elected indirectly by the lower organs.
24 Miliukov, *Vospominaniia*, Vol. I, p. 309.
25 This is equally true in the case of point 24. This envisaged the establishment of local autonomy and "regional representative assemblies". However, the assemblies' powers were not defined.
26 For the reports and debates at this Congress see: P.D. Dolgorukov and I.I. Petrunkevich (eds), *Agrarnyi vopros*, 1st edn, Moscow 1905, Vol. I., pp. 299–352.
27 Miliukov (*Vospominaniia*, Vol. I, p. 309) includes this question in a list of matters which were left to be decided in the future.
28 Miliukov, *Vospominaniia*, Vol. I, p. 309 admits that the programme's vagueness was based upon failure to agree.
29 This does not mean that they were the only element difficult to assimilate. Certain zemstvo men on the right of the party – E.N. Trubetskoi, N.N. L'vov and M. Kovalevskii – were to leave the party in the near future.
30 For the viewpoint of this group, see E.D. Kuskova, "Kto my", *Bez zaglaviia*, No. 3, 1906.
31 Gessen, "V dvukh vekakh", *A.R.R.*, Vol. XXII, p. 212.
32 Miliukov, *Vospominaniia*, Vol. I, pp. 269, 294.
33 Miliukov, *Vospominaniia*, Vol. I, p. 306.
34 Miliukov, *Vospominaniia*, Vol. I, pp. 276–84.
35 For Miliukov's growing realization of Bolshevism's significance, see "Raskol v russkoi sotsial-demokratii", *Osvobozhdenie*, No. 72, 8 June 1905.
36 Miliukov, *God bor'by*, SPB 1907, pp. 97–101.
37 E.D. Kuskova in *Bez zaglaviia*, No. 3, 1906, p. 81.
38 A.A. Chuprov, *Konstitutsionno-demokraticheskaia partiia i sotsializm*, Moscow 1905.
39 For a list of those elected see, *OTCHËT*, p. 3. For personal details of the Committee's members see in particular: *Russkie vedomosti 1863–1913 (sbornik statei)*, Moscow 1913, for the "Who's who" at the end of the book; *Pervye narodnye predstaviteli*, S.P.B. 1907; *Chleny 2-oi Gosudarstvennoi Dumy*, S.P.B. 1907; *Chleny 1-oi Gosudarstvennoi Dumy*, S.P.B. 1906; *Entsiklopedicheskii slovar' Brokgauz-Efron*, A.A. Andreevskii and K.K. Arseniev (eds), S.P.B. 1890–1907 and the *Bolshaia Sovetskaia entsiklopedia*, 1st edn, Moscow 1926; M. Vinaver, *Nedavnee*, Paris 1926; *Gosudarstvennaia Duma pervogo prizyva*, Moscow 1906.
40 This figure does not include the advocate V.A. Maklakov. Although he was not strictly speaking a member of the zemstvo "Second Element" he had very strong links with the organs of local self-government. He had for some time been permanent secretary to *Beseda* (Symposium), a society founded in 1899 to discuss the problems of zemstvo boards. The society was finally wound up in 1905.
41 I.V.Gessen, A.A. Kornilov, M.M. Vinaver, V.A. Maklakov, A.N. Maksimov, M.L. Mandelshtam, P.N. Miliukov, P.A. Petrovskii, N.N. Chernenkov, N.V. Teslenko, M.A. Sabashnikov.
42 He had lost his position as "Gentleman of His Majesty's Bedchamber" because of his political opinions. He was the son of a former Minister of Justice.
43 Even Chernenkov cannot really be said to have been a member of the lower intelligentsia. He was an economist and one of the most eminent statisticians in Russia. Prince D.I. Shakhovskoi had also served in the Third Element (in the administration

of zemstvo schools), but he was simultaneously a member of the zemstvo "Second" Element.
44 See, e.g., *Konstitutsionno-demokraticheskaia partiia – S''ezd 12–18 oktiabria 1905*, Moscow 1905, pp. 20–3 (GARF. f. 523, op. 1, d.42).
45 V.A. Maklakov, *Iz vospominanii*, New York 1954, p. 345.
46 Miliukov, *Vospominaniia*, Vol. I, p. 309.
47 For the text see: A.A. Kizevetter (ed.), *Polnyi sbornik platform vsekh russkikh politicheskikh partii*, Moscow 1906, pp. 5–7. See also pp. 8–12 for Witte's accompanying report which the Tsar ordered to be taken for guidance. See also Savich, *Novyi gosudarstvennyi stroi*, pp. 24–7.
48 Miliukov, *Vospominaniia*, Vol. I, p. 312. For Miliukov's views of the manifesto at the time see: *God bor'by*, pp. 72–8.
49 "Konstitutsionno-demokraticheskaia partiia", *S''ezd 12–18 oktiabria 1905*, pp. 25–6. For a full account of this congress, see also: "Pervyi s''ezd konstitutsionno-demokraticheskoi partii, 12–18 oktiabria 1905 goda", in V.V. Shelokhaev (ed.), *S''ezdy i konferentsii konstitutsionno-demokraticheskoi partii 1905–1920 gg*, ROSSPEN, Vol. I, (1905–7), 1997, pp. 18–45.
50 Maklakov, *Iz vospominanii*, pp. 342–8.
51 *Samoderzhavie i zemstvo, konfidentsial'naia zapiska ministra finansov S.Iu.Vitte*, P.B. Struve (ed.), Stuttgart 1901; Witte's memorandum had argued that zemstvo self-government was fundamentally incompatible with the autocratic system. The memo had been conceived chiefly as a political weapon to undermine the position of D.S. Sipiagin, the Minister of the Interior.
52 T.H. Von Laue, "Count Witte and the Russian Revolution of 1905", *ASEER*, Vol. XVII, No. 1, pp. 25–41.
53 See, e.g., "Manifest 17 oktiabria", in *Krasnyi Arkhiv*, No. 10–11, p. 61. Report to Tsar dated 12 October.
54 But see Von Laue, "Count Witte", p. 36.
55 S.Iu. Vitte, *Vospominaniia*, Berlin 1922, Vol. II, p. 8 (hereafter referred to as Vitte).
56 Vitte, p. 10.
57 See, e.g., J. Bing (ed.), *Letters of Tsar Nicholas and Empress Marie*, London 1937, pp. 185–9.
58 Savich, *Novyi gosudarstvennyi stroi Rossii*, pp. 28–31.
59 Von Laue, "Count Witte", p. 32.
60 Although Witte later received evidence of the participation of officials in pogromist actvity he failed to make an issue of this (see: Vitte, pp. 73–6). He apparently wished to avoid a conflict with the Tsar who on 23 December accepted badges of the pogromist Union of the Russian People for himself and his son (see *Dnevnik*, 23 December 1905, p. 229).
61 "Novyi poriadok", *Pravo*, No. 41, 25 October 1905.
62 Savich, *Novyi gosudarstvennyi stroi Rossii*, pp. 192, 224–7.
63 Savich, *Novyi gosudarstvennyi stroi Rossii*, pp. 438–44, 479–82 for the rules relating to the press and assemblies.
64 According to S. Kryzhanovskii, *Vospominaniia*, Berlin 1938, p. 60, Witte was out of touch with public opinion and supposed that the moderate right expressed the real desires of the people and were its "spiritual representatives".
65 For Shipov's account of this meeting, see Shipov, pp. 334–6.
66 Miliukov, "Rokovye gody", *Russkie Zapiski*, 1938–39, No. 14, p. 124.
67 Miliukov, "Rokovye gody", p. 125; Miliukov, *Vospominaniia*, Vol. I, p. 321.
68 Miliukov, *Tri popytki*, Paris 1921, p. 11.
69 Miliukov, *Vospominaniia*, Vol. I, p. 321.
70 See "Priëm S.Iu. Vitte predstavitelei biuro s''ezdov zemtsev", *Pravo*, No. 42, 1905.
71 Miliukov, *Tri popytki*, p. 12. Miliukov argued that the real dividing line lay on the very idea of a constitution.

72 Miliukov, *Tri popytki*, pp. 22–5; "Rokovye gody", *R.Z.*, No. 14, pp. 128–30.
73 Miliukov, *Vospominaniia*, Vol. I, p. 327.
74 The Bulgarian constitution had always been admired by Miliukov, who had been a professor at Sofia during a period of political exile. For details of the constitution see: *Constitution du Royaume de Bulgarie*, Sofia 1911.
75 It is significant that a few days earlier (24 October) the Kadet Vladimir Gessen, the editor of *Pravo*, also advised Witte to proclaim a constitution. See Gessen, "V dvukh vekakh", *Archiv russkoi revoiutsii*, Vol. XX, Berlin 1937, pp. 208–10.
76 Miliukov, *Tri popytki*, p. 24.
77 Miliukov, *Vospominaniia*, Vol. I, p. 328.
78 See also Howard D. Mehlinger and John M. Thompson, *Count Witte and the Tsarist Government in the 1905 Revolution*, Bloomington, IN 1972, p. 97. Mehlinger and Thompson are basically sympathetic to Witte and are often severely critical of the liberals. But they admit that if any substantial body of public men had been included in the cabinet this might only have served to deepen the suspicions of the Tsar and his reactionary advisers about Witte's government and its policies. And they conclude that if the liberal ministres had gone too far the Tsar would unquestionably have dismissed them.
79 Shipov, *Vospominaniia*, p. 339.
80 Vitte, Vol. II, Berlin 1922, p. 59.
81 Simultaneously Witte tried to persuade the right-wing Kadet E.N. Trubetskoi (who was later to leave the party) to accept the post of Minister of Education (see Vitte, Vol. II, p. 59). However, the party leadership compelled him to back down in the interests of party unity (see Miliukov, *Tri popytki*, p. 13).
82 Vitte, Vol. II, pp. 64–6.
83 Shipov, pp. 343–4.
84 Vitte, Vol. II, p. 62. See also V.I. Gurko, *Features and Figures from the Past*, Stanford 1939, pp. 403–4. Gurko suggests that the appointment was made because Witte was influenced by "some mysterious dependence upon Durnovo". The implication was that Witte was being blackmailed by Durnovo. See also Mehlinger and Thompson, *Count Witte*, p. 79.
85 Vitte, Vol. II, p. 66.
86 See Von Laue, "Count Witte", p. 35. Although sympathetic to Witte, Von Laue admits that "if he invited certain liberals into the Government he did so on the Government's own terms".
87 Shipov, p. 345.
88 Miliukov, *Vospominaniia*, Vol. I, p. 331.
89 A report of the congress's proceedings can be found in *Pravo*, No. 44–45/46. Miliukov's speech is in No. 44, pp. 3619–20.
90 *Pravo*, No. 44, p. 3619.
91 *Pravo*, No. 45/46, pp. 3701–3.
92 See also "Pervyi kabinet", *Pravo*, No. 42.
93 See "S''ezd zemskikh i gorodskikh deiatelei", *Pravo*, No. 45/46 (Editorial) for confirmation of this.
94 Another factor which may have encouraged the Foundation Congress to adopt radical attitudes was the presence of the revisionist socialists who were now (for the most part) no longer associated with the party.
95 See *Pravo*, No. 47, 1905, pp. 3812–13, for their declaration.
96 This strike – against Polish Martial Law, to prevent the execution of the Kronshtadt ringleaders, and for an eight-hour day – began on 12 November.
97 "S''ezd zemskikh i gorodskikh deiatelei", *Pravo*, No. 45.
98 Witte had sent a telegram to Petrunkevich asking the congress to display its patriotism in this crisis.
99 A Social Democratic delegation called on the congress to denounce its actions: "The

attempts of the Congress to enter into negotiations with Government" was, it proclaimed, "an auction and deal by the bourgeoisie concerning the rights of the people". *Pravo*, No. 44, 1905, p. 3617.
100 *Pravo*, No. 45/46, p. 3727. See also Galai, "The Tragic Dilemma of Russian Liberalism as Reflected in Ivan Il'iĉ Petrunkeviĉ's Letters to His Son", *Jahrbücher für Geschichte Osteuropas*, Vol. 29, 1981, pp. 1–29.
101 "Vtoraia zabastovka", *Pravo*, No. 44, 1905.
102 "Smuta", *Pravo*, No. 47, 27 November.
103 Editorial, *Svobodnyi Narod*, No. 1.
104 "Svoevremenna li vseobshchaia politicheskaia zabastovka?", in Miliukov, *God bor'by*, pp. 170–1.
105 "Kto vinovat v vseobshchei zabastovke?", in Miliukov, *God bor'by*, SPB 1907, pp. 172–4.
106 "Vosstanie v Moskve", in Miliukov, *God bor'by*, pp. 175–6; "Provokatsiia ili ne provokatsiia", *Rech'*, No. 4, 26 February 1906.
107 Editorial by Miliukov in *Narodnaia Svoboda*, No. 2, 16 December 1905.
108 P.B. Struve, "Eshchë ne pozdno", *Narodnaia Svoboda*, No. 2.
109 Struve's absence led to a decline in his personal influence.
110 "Ot redaktsii", *Poliarnaia Zvezda*, No. 1, 1905.
111 See for example: Struve, "My Contacts with Rodichev", *S.E.E.R.*, Vol. XII, 1934, p. 365.
112 See (for example), Struve, "Dve Rossii", *Poliarnaia Zvezda*, No. 6, 19 January 1906.
113 S. Frank, "Politika i ideia – o programme Poliarnoi Zvezdy", *Poliarnaia Zvezda*, No. 2.
114 Struve, "Revoliutsiia", *Poliarnaia Zvezda*, No. 1.
115 "Russkaia ideinaia intelligentsiia na rasput''e", *Poliarnaia Zvezda*, No. 7, p. 446.
116 Sef, *Burzhuaziia v 1905 godu"*, Moscow 1926, p. 110.
117 See, *Polnoe sobranie zakonov*, S.P.B. 1908. Ukaz to the Senate, No. 27029, p. 887. The new law was essentially a revision of the earlier Bulygin proposals. The latter had divided the electorate into three main curiae – for the landowners, peasants and townspeople. These were retained, but a new curia was set up for the workers, who had not previously been enfranchised. However, their representation was so inadequate that they were to have very little electoral weight. The peasantry and the nobility retained the favourable treatment which they had been given by the Bulygin proposals. The peasants were to have almost universal suffrage, and the greatest electoral weight in the elections to the Duma. In the towns the vote was now extended to a very wide spectrum of householders and taxpayers and came fairly close to universality. However, the poorest classes were excluded, and the workers' franchise was very restricted and indirect. Indeed, in all the curiae elections were multi-stage. In the case of the workers and peasants, there were as many as four electoral instances. With the exception of a number of large towns with separate representation, and the election of a limited number of peasant deputies, who were elected solely by the peasants, the last stage of the elections took place in provincial (guberniia) assemblies composed of the "electors" of all the different curiae voting together. The main lines of the electoral law were agreed at a Special Conference at Tsarskoe Selo, which included not only ministers and other bureaucrats, but also Shipov and other members of the moderate opposition. However, the Tsar decided against universal suffrage, which was supported by Shipov and Guchkov, in favour of the more conservative approach finally adopted. Witte's arguments, in particular, seem to have had a strong influence upon the Tsar's decision to reject the idea of universal suffrage.
118 "Izbiratel'nyi zakon 11 dekabria", *Narodnaia Svoboda*, 1905, No. 2.
119 "Vtoroi vserossiiskii delegatskii s''ezd", *Pravo*, No. 4, 1906, Supplement pp. 3–5 (Kornilov's report).

120 "Vtoroi vserossiiskii delegatskii s''ezd", pp. 4–5; *OTCHËT*, pp. 14–15.
121 *OTCHËT*, pp. 14–15.
122 Konstitutsionno-demokraticheskaia partiia, *S''ezd 12–18 oktiabria 1905*, pp. 13–14.
123 *OTCHËT*, p. 19.
124 See "D.Sh", "Zametka ob ustave partii", *Vestnik Partii Svobody*, No. 1, 1906. The author of this article argued that the Party Statute should be amended to take this situation into account.
125 *OTCHËT*, p. 12.
126 *OTCHËT*, p. 13.
127 *OTCHËT*, p. 22.
128 *OTCHËT*, pp. 19–20.
129 "Kadety v 1905–1906 gg", *K.A.*, No. 46, 1905, pp. 45–52.
130 *OTCHËT*, p. 20.
131 *OTCHËT*, p. 22. It also gives a list of further groups formed in December. There were eight provincial groups and seven more in the towns.
132 For some reason this group is left out of the official figures. For its foundation see: "Konstitutsionno-demokraticheskaia partiia, *Vtoroi vserossiiskii s''ezd*", Bulletin No. 2. Zernov's report. (Also available in ROSSPEN, 1997, *S''ezdy i konferentsii K.-d. Partii*, Vol. I, pp. 59–61).
133 "Konstitutsionno-demokraticheskaia partiia, *Vtoroi vserossiiskii s''ezd*", No. 5, pp. 1–2. Kornilov's report. (See also V.V. Shelokhaev (ed.), *S''ezdy i konferentsii K.-d. Partii*, 1997, Vol. I, pp. 47–58.)
134 "Konstitutsionno-demokraticheskaia partiia, *Vtoroi vserossiiskii s''ezd*", No. 5, pp. 1–2, pp. 1–2; *OTCHËT*, p. 4.
135 *OTCHËT*, p. 4.
136 "Vtoroi vserossiiskii delegatskii s''ezd", *Pravo*, No. 4, 1906, Supplement, p. 5. The important rôle played by Moscow is underlined in *OTCHËT*, p. 21.
137 *OTCHËT*, p. 6.
138 See *OTCHËT*, pp. 79–83 for a list of party publications.
139 "Vtoroi vserossiiskii delegatskii s''ezd", *Pravo*, No. 4, Supplement, p. 7.
140 "Vtoroi vserossiiskii delegatskii s''ezd", p. 7. Kornilov also mentions support for a time from Sablin's *Zhizn'* (Moscow).
141 Gessen, "V dvukh vekakh", *A.R.R.*, Berlin 1937, Vol. XXII, pp. 218–21; Miliukov, "Rokovye gody", *R.Z.*, 1938–39, No. 16, pp. 130–2.
142 The appeal had called for a financial boycott of the government.
143 As a result of "press offences" committed at this time the editors were prosecuted. This resulted in their being ineligible for election to the Duma.
144 "Vtoroi vserossiiskii delegatskii s''ezd", *Pravo*, No. 4, 1906, Supplement, pp. 8–9 (exchange between Polnov and Iakushkin).
145 "Vtoroi vserossiiskii delegatskii s''ezd", p. 8.
146 *OTCHËT*, p. 22.
147 *OTCHËT*, Supplement to *Pravo*, No. 7, p. 33. See Smagin's speech.
148 "Iz derevni", *Vestnik Partii Narodnoi Svobody*, No. 1, 22 February 1906.

4 The run-up to the First Duma

By the end of the year 1905 the balance of power within Russia was rapidly changing in favour of the government. The defeat of the December uprising both reflected and accelerated this great change. The forces of the revolution were on the wane, while those of the old regime were in the ascendant. The correlation of forces which had existed in October had vanished and this inevitably had important political consequences. The October Manifesto was the result of a combination of opposition pressure and government weakness. In the autumn the great bulk of the Russian army was still in the Far East or at the frontier, and it was sown with the dragons' teeth of discontent and rebellion. It had been these circumstances which had compelled Witte to recommend a programme of constitutional reform. However, he had done so with misgivings, because there had seemed no other way out.[1] Emotionally and habitually he still remained a supporter of autocracy. It is true that he had long desired a more efficient and reforming autocracy. He was aware, at least in theory, of the need for a greater respect for the rule of law, and increased co-operation with influential circles of public opinion. Moreover, he now seems to have felt that some form of constitutional limitation of the monarch's authority was inevitable. But there is no evidence that he was ever willing to meet the chief demands of the liberal opposition. He was certainly not prepared to concede a parliamentary constitution. This does not mean that he was not prepared to be flexible and grant some liberal reforms, but it does mean that "how far he would actually bend depended entirely on the needs of the moment".[2]

The situation had now been transformed since the October days, and Witte was in a position to take a stronger line with the liberals. Punitive expeditions were helping to restore discipline in the Far Eastern forces, and they were now gradually returning to Russia. This enormously strengthened the hand of the ministry in dealing with the revolution. After the crushing of the December uprising the government carried out savage reprisals against the instigators of revolution and disorder, and by the beginning of 1906 it once again held the upper hand – although it still had ample reason to fear further outbreaks. A further installment of revolution in the near future could by no means be ruled out.

Now that the political situation had changed, Witte found it increasingly difficult to resist the temptation to whittle away the earlier concessions to the opposition. However, he did not move into the camp of outright reaction – indeed, he seems to have been unable to hold fast to any firm or consistent line. The December crisis had had a traumatic effect upon Witte, and his physical and mental health had seriously deteriorated. This appears to have profoundly affected his political judgement and the stability of his views. His policy became increasingly contradictory, veering from moments of relative liberalism to periods of reaction. All this aroused the distrust, not only of the left, but also of the right, the bureaucracy, and the Court itself. As the Tsar commented in a letter to his mother (12 January 1906):

> As for Witte, since the happenings in Moscow he has radically changed his views, now he wants to hang and shoot everybody. I have never seen such a chameleon of a man. That is why no-one believes in him any more. He is absolutely discredited with everybody, except perhaps the Jews abroad.[3]

As the revolution receded, the more conservative sections of the establishment, including the Tsar himself, began bitterly to resent the promises of 17 October. Witte, who was regarded as their chief architect, came increasingly under attack. The Minister of the Interior, Durnovo, became the centre of a web of intrigues which found ready support from court circles – especially from General Trepov, who was now the Palace Commandant at Peterhof. Meanwhile, the Tsar was increasingly coming under the influence of the extreme right, including the pogromist Union of the Russian People. Witte's authority over the government had always been far from absolute, and as a consequence of the growing reaction at Court, he now began to lose control over wide fields of policy. As the influence of the right grew, Witte's position as "Premier" became increasingly hollow.

The Kadets' Second Congress (5–11 January 1906)

By the time the Kadets' Second Congress met in Petersburg in the early days of the new year, the political situation was rapidly changing in favour of the forces of reaction. By now the ultra-radical pose which the Kadets had adopted at their First Congress was something of an embarrassment to the party leadership. Ever since the October days they had been gradually moving towards a more realistic standpoint. And now, in view of the growing strength of reaction, they once again hastened to abandon the inflexible position which they had assumed in October. As Miliukov later explained, the Kadet leaders believed that it was essential "to bring the [party] programme closer to the actual conditions of the struggle".[4]

Ever since October 1905 the Kadets had been planning to hold a Second Party Congress. All sections of the party were unanimous in regarding this as a matter of the first importance. Another congress was urgently needed both to prepare for the election campaign and to complete the work of the original gathering in Moscow, which was still officially regarded as provisional. Because of this, the assembly which met at the Tenishevskii School in Petersburg on 5 January had good reasons for considering itself a second foundation congress. This was apparently Miliukov's own view. According to Miliukov, it was at the January Congress that the party first began to be conscious of its "collective will ... began to live with its own special life – became *itself*".[5]

This does not mean that the congress owed nothing to its predecessors. Indeed, the existing membership of the Central Committee was left largely intact,[6] and only a few alterations were made in the party programme. In his report on matters of programme, I.V. Gessen pointed out that few changes had been prepared, owing to the committee's preoccupation with organizational and tactical matters.[7]

One of the few changes which were made was opposed by the party leadership. Miliukov and the majority of the Central Committee wished to permit freedom of opinion on the question of female suffrage. However, following a speech by A.V. Tyrkova, the congress decided to include votes for women in the party's official platform.[8]

The most important modification to the programme concerned the constitutional position of the Tsar. The original Kadet programme had not even mentioned this question, but the Central Committee now urged the congress to accept an amendment to point 13 of the programme which explicitly stated that "Russia should be a constitutional and parliamentary monarchy".[9] Defending the committee's recommendation, I.V. Gessen said that for many Kadets the question of whether Russia should be a republic or a monarchy was a matter of secondary importance. The delegates should avoid approaching this issue from the standpoint of their personal convictions and should regard it as primarily a matter of practical politics. The fundamental question to be considered was whether a republic was possible in present circumstances. The party should clarify its position in this matter if it wished to avoid being suspected of subterfuge and dishonesty.[10] A minority of provincial delegates vigorously opposed any changes to this part of the party programme and argued that this question should be left open. However, the congress ultimately gave overwhelming support (77–13, with five abstentions) to the Central Committee's amendment.[11] This decision did not represent any real departure from party tradition – republicanism had never been part of the official platform of either the Kadets or the liberationists.

However, it did mark a *final* break with republicanism, and with the threatening leftist phraseology of the First Congress. The recognition of the monarchy implicitly endorsed the November Zemstvo Congress's resolution, which had made it clear that the party did not aim at a "Jacobin" constituent assembly with absolute power. If republicanism was not a practical proposition, then clearly, such an assembly – unlimited by any imperial veto – was still more impracticable. The Kadet leaders now hastened to abandon the ambiguous term "constituent assembly", since it left them open to charges of covert republicanism. However, they had not dropped their demand for some kind of constituent body. On behalf of the Central Committee, Miliukov explained that:

> in refusing to use the term "constituent assembly" the Party is not repudiating it in principle. In the (election) manifesto each word must be (carefully)

weighed up, while the term *constituent assembly* used without qualification may arouse misunderstandings: therefore it is not used in the manifesto.[12]

Although the Kadet leaders still favoured some kind of constituent body they no longer proposed that the forthcoming Duma should assume constituent functions. In a report on tactics in the Duma,[13] I.V. Gessen told the congress that "The Duma of (the Electoral Law) of 11 December seems to us to be extremely irregular and contradicts our fundamental demands". Both he and Kokoshkin argued that because of this the Duma could not be regarded as a satisfactory legislative body. Its activity should therefore be chiefly confined to passing laws on universal suffrage and civil liberty. As far as possible its rôle should be limited to preparing the ground for genuine popular representation. However, both speakers agreed that given the present state of the country the Duma would be unable to avoid taking urgent measures in the fields of agrarian reform and regional autonomy. At the same time the representatives would have to strive to obtain a ministry responsible to the Duma. However, Kokoshkin stressed that once its tasks were completed the Duma should be replaced by an assembly, "which must be constituent in fact, if not in name".[14]

Although the party leaders had now explicitly rejected a constituent assembly on "Leninist" or "Jacobin" lines, they had retained their commitment to some kind of constituent body. Moreover, they had officially refused to recognize the forthcoming Duma as a genuine legislature. However, by advocating that it should carry out a programme of social reforms, they had, in fact, come close to giving it a form of practical recognition.

Despite their formal reservations, the leadership in fact centred their entire tactics around the Duma and the election campaign. In his official report to the congress on behalf of the Central Committee, Miliukov firmly opposed any idea of boycotting the elections because of the Duma's imperfections.[15]

> We are not Blanquists and not Jacobins.... Our party is predominantly a parliamentary Party; its character, the means of political action available to it – all this makes the period of the electoral campaign especially important for it in the party sense.

In the course of his speech Miliukov emphasized considerations of practical politics rather than matters of principle. According to Miliukov the electoral campaign would have a vital rôle to play in strengthening the party organization in the country. Moreover, it was by no means certain that the Kadets would be defeated in the elections. Even if they were, the party could look forward to playing a vital rôle in opposition. In order to placate some of the more left-wing elements in the party Miliukov suggested that if necessary a final decision on whether the party should boycott the Duma could be made when the election results were known. However, the whole trend of his argument was in favour of entry.

The Central Committee's arguments were heavily endorsed by the congress. The delegates voted overwhelmingly in favour of entering both the elections and the Duma, and gave general approval to the line which had been laid down by the Central Committee.[16] The congress agreed that although the Duma was not a satisfactory representative body it could not limit its activity to passing bills on universal suffrage and civil liberty (passed by "a majority of all against 6, with 10 abstentions"). The Duma should not participate in "organic work" (i.e. ordinary day-to-day legislative activity), but it would be bound to concern itself with matters of an "unconditionally urgent character". At first the congress refrained from enumerating these measures, but Struve finally persuaded the delegates that it would be impossible to appear before the electorate without a positive commitment to a programme of reform. Although the congress avoided setting exact limits to the Duma's activity it now recommended that the Duma should concern itself with land and labour reform and "the satisfaction of just national needs". At the same time, the congress accepted a resolution from Fedor Kokoshkin which stressed that once these essential tasks were complete, the party should aim at the replacement of the Duma by an assembly based upon universal and direct suffrage.

The committee's tactical line had received strong support at the congress. However, serious opposition did arise over the proposal to drop the term "constituent assembly". When it came to a vote a large minority (80 as against 137)[17] opposed the leadership. Indeed the opposition was so great that the committee agreed that local groups should be allowed to use the *term* if they wished. In his *Memoirs*, Miliukov suggests that the opposition wanted "to return to the demand of a Constitutional Assembly *instead* of the Duma".[18] However, the facts do not seem to bear out this statement. The sweeping victories of the platform on tactical matters, especially on the decision to enter the Duma, show that very few members favoured a boycott, although there was an undercurrent of boycottist feeling among a minority of provincial delegates. The majority of the opposition apparently wished to emphasize the party's ultimate commitment to some kind of consituent body. But this does not mean that they were against entering the Duma; and certainly it does not mean that they favoured an assembly with absolute powers. True, this does seem to have been the standpoint of the small minority who had voted against recognizing the monarchy at this stage. The Vil'na delegate Rom, for example, opposed making any decision on the fate of the monarchy in advance of a constituent assembly. Some delegates had clearly interpreted the October resolution in the orthodox leftist sense. But to a large extent it appears that the opposition sprang from a deep dislike of retreating from earlier *slogans* and *terminology*. The demand for a "constituent assembly" had been the slogan of the entire opposition and several delegates feared that a decision to abandon it might confuse the people.[19]

In the months which followed their Foundation Congress the Kadets had been gradually drifting away from their "allies on the left". The decisions of the Second Congress formalized the breach. The Kadets had now officially disassociated themselves from the more extreme slogans of the socialist parties – from their demands for a "democratic republic" and an all-powerful constituent assembly. It is true that the congress still made friendly noises to the left; for example it condemned government atrocities in Moscow[20] and commemorated the anniversary of Bloody Sunday by suspending its debates. At the same time the congress passed a resolution called for the unity of the opposition on the "chief tasks" they had in common.[21] However, in view of its explicit break with the tactics and slogans of the left, this appeal had little chance of success. In reality the two wings of the opposition movement were now following divergent paths. Towards the end of the congress (on 11 January) the breach finally became irreparable when the party decided formally to renounce the use of force as a means of obtaining its objectives. In an official report to the congress, M.M. Vinaver pinned all the party's hopes on parliamentary methods and the peaceful organization of public opinion.[22] The congress expressed its complete agreement with Vinaver's report and decided that the party should direct all its efforts to securing "the widest (possible) organisation of social consciousness, using all methods with the exception of an armed uprising". The party would recognize all forms of political demonstrations against the government, including the general strike. "But the Party considers, and should consider, the chief field of its activities to be an organised representative assembly, while outside such an assembly its work should consist of agitation and propaganda."[23] Although the resolution went on to stress the need for the unity of the opposition, in the circumstances this had little practical significance.

The election campaign

At the party's Second Congress the Kadets had rejected the socialist parties' demands for a boycott of the Duma and the convocation of a constituent assembly. It had decided instead to adopt essentially peaceful, parliamentary tactics. This meant that during the next stage of its existence the party's attention would be focused primarily on the election campaign. However, the circumstances in which the campaign were held were in many ways unfavourable. The peaceful, Westernized methods which the party favoured required, ideally, a peaceful society with solid guarantees of the fundamental civil liberties. However, many areas of the country were in the grip of exceptional laws and police repression, which made open political activity difficult and sometimes impossible. In February the Central Committee felt compelled to protest against the persecution of the party: "In many localities of Russia", it complained, "the administration contrives to regard the Constitutional-Democratic Party as a sort of conspiratorial organisation, and persecutes the committees of the Party, its members, and its press merely because they belong to the Party".[24] The columns of the Kadet press in this period overflowed with reports of the persecution of the party and bureaucratic interference in the course of the elections. The administration deprived a number of Kadets – including Miliukov – of electoral rights, and brought pressure to bear upon the peasants to make them vote for conservative candidates.[25]

In fact, government interference was neither very systematic nor effective. According to S.E. Kryzhanovskii, the government made only half-hearted and belated attempts to manage the elections, mainly at the instigation of Durnovo.[26] However, bureaucratic pressure was most serious in the countryside and in the more remote parts of the provinces – where the Kadet organization was already at its weakest. In these circumstances, the party seems to have made little headway in bringing its influence to bear directly upon the peasantry and small landowners – at least at the primary stages of the indirect electoral system. The party openly admitted that outside the big cities work was very difficult and active supporters few.[27] In "out-of the-way corners", like provincial ("uezd") towns and villages, it admitted that things were difficult, and that "the initiative of individuals is hampered not only by a mass of police obstacles, but also by the inertness of the surrounding milieu and the powerlessness of individual activists". The shortage of party workers in the countryside was largely the result of the fact that the great mass of the rural population had little of no experience of political activity. But it also appears to have had a deeper significance for a party which had so many of its historical roots in the countryside. We have already seen that the party had almost from the outset lost the sympathy of part of the zemstvo "Third Element". And now, as the reactionary movement in the zemstvo grew it was increasingly losing support among the more moderate liberal gentry. Soon after the Second Congress the eminent Zemstvo Constitutionalist, E.N. Trubetskoi, left the party, complaining of its alleged failure to disassociate itself from the left. With the departure of Trubetskoi, said Miliukov, "a whole layer of Russian society fell away from us".[28]

Party organization

The shortage of party workers in the countryside and the hostile attitude of large sections of the bureaucracy, inevitably had an adverse effect upon the Kadets' attempts to build up their party organization in the provinces. Moreover, the Central Committee was so busy with electoral propaganda that organizational questions were neglected. As the committee itself later admitted:[29]

> the electoral campaign in this period became the chief task of the moment, pushing all others into the background. The organisation of the Party in the localities continued, but it was accomplished incidentally together with the organisation of the electoral campaign and often specifically for the sake of the elections. The number of constituted groups scarcely increased at all at this time, and if committees of the Party [...] did arise in many places, then these were, for the most part, simply electoral committees, the activity of which ceased with the end of the elections to the Duma.

Communications with the provinces remained irregular.[30]

Before the Central Committee got down to the task of organizing the electoral campaign, it set about reforming its own organization and functions.[31] For the first time it elected a permanent president – the wealthy zemstvo leader, Prince Pavel Dolgorukov, who claimed descent from the legendary Rurik. V.D.

Nabokov, father of the celebrated writer Vladimir Nabokov, and N.V. Teslenko, a Moscow lawyer, were chosen as his deputies.[32] At the same time, the committee decided that in future its regular meetings would take place twice monthly and would be held alternatively in Moscow and St. Petersburg. A special section of the Central Committee would be set up in the Baltic capital, together with a section of the secretariat. However, for the moment, Moscow still remained the chief party headquarters. All exceptional sessions of the committee continued to be held there, as were the meetings of various party commissions set up by the Second Congress. Moreover, for a long time the composition of the Petersburg section of the secretariat seems to have remained ill-defined – until March it even appears to have had no regular secretary.[33] The secretariat which sent out the instructions during the electoral campaign remained that of Moscow under Kornilov and Prince D.I. Shakhovskoi.[34] Moscow also continued to play a leading rôle in the field of party propaganda. This period witnessed a particularly rapid development of Maklakov's courses for party speakers and agitators.[35] Petersburg also developed courses of a similar type, and during the election campaign the "lecture-agitation bureaux" in the capitals sent out dozens of lecturers and orators and distributed large quantities of party literature.

The party press

Following the Second Congress the party leadership made a determined effort to extend the Kadet press. The congress had decided that it was essential to "publish a weekly journal devoted to questions of Party life".[36] The journal would be directed at the party "faithful" rather than the general public. It would be mainly concerned with keeping the provinces and the rank and file members in touch with the Central Committee. It was hoped that it would have an important rôle to play in strengthening party organization in the country and in coordinating the Kadets' activity during the election campaign.

In February 1906, the first number of the proposed weekly, the *Vestnik Partii Narodnoi Svobody* (*The Herald of the Party of the Freedom of the People*) appeared, edited and financed by Nabokov.[37] The *Vestnik*, which was the party's only official journal, printed editorials and articles by leading party spokesmen, together with election news and accounts of meetings of the Central Committee. At the same time, it regularly contained a section on the situation of the party in the provinces. However, the *Vestnik* experienced considerable difficulty in gaining the support of the provincials. The Central Committee later admitted that despite repeated appeals to provincial groups, "local party institutions assisted the *Vestnik* very little", not only in the matter of contributing material, but also in the matter of increasing the subscription to this publication, which was the sole party organ in print ("literaturnyi").[38] In 1906 the circulation did not exceed 3,000 copies, and the paper made a loss of nearly 18,000 rubles. This figure was regarded as extremely disappointing in view of the fact that the official estimate of the party's registered membership in this period was from 70–100,000, leaving out of account mere party sympathizers.[39]

However, even if the *Vestnik* had enjoyed wider success it could not have provided the basis of an adequate party press during the election campaign. It was, after all, directed at a relatively small group of political activists, rather than at the general public. The party was in urgent need of newspapers aimed at a much wider section of the electorate. Miliukov and I.V. Gessen therefore set to work to create a successor to *Svobodnyi Narod* (*The Free People*) and *Narodnaia Svoboda* (*Freedom of the People*).[40] Their chief difficulty was financial, but this was overcome with the support of the rich Jewish contractor and industrialist Yurii Bak. The first number of the new paper, which was entitled *Rech'* (*Speech*), appeared on 23 February in St. Petersburg. Although it was not, strictly speaking, official, it soon became the Kadet's chief voice in the Russian press. However, although it was distributed outside the capital, it seems to have been primarily directed at the public of St. Petersburg. Moreover, its style and content made it unsuitable for the great majority of the population; it was clearly attuned to a rather intellectual audience. There was, in fact, no truly popular Kadet paper. *Narodnoe Delo* (*The People's Cause*), a Moscow-based paper published by Komissarov and edited by Iakushkin, seems to have made some attempt to fill this rôle. But apparently it too was insufficiently adapted to the needs of the masses.[41]

Despite all the obstacles which the administration placed in its path, the Kadet Party was attempting to conduct a Western-style election campaign on the lines suggested at the Second Congress. Although the conditions were often unfavourable, it sought to carry on agitation in an open, peaceful manner by means of public meetings, party literature and the press. As we have seen, it was not a party which took readily to underground, illegal methods. Accordingly, when, on 4 March, the government promulgated a temporary law on unions and assemblies, which provided for the legalization of political parties,[42] the Central Committee seriously examined its possibilities. Although the Kadet leaders criticized the shortcomings of the new law,[43] the Central Committee decided to apply for legalization in order to prevent further persecution of the party.[44] However, the Petersburg authorities delayed the application on technical grounds, and this proved to be the first of a series of delays and obstructions which were to leave the party for years as an illegal, or at least non-legal organization.[45]

The Kadets and the left

The hostility of the administration proved a severe impediment to the Kadets in their efforts to conduct their electoral campaign. However, this was by no means the only obstacle which the Kadets had to surmount. The party also had to overcome severe antagonism from the left. The socialist parties – the Mensheviks, Bolsheviks and Socialist Revolutionaries – did everything in their power to spread the idea of boycotting the elections. They were still hoping for a new wave of revolution, and they did not want the public to be distracted by "parliamentary illusions". They believed that the revolutionary movement should fight for a constituent assembly, and should not let itself be deflected by the Duma.

They bitterly attacked the Kadets for breaking the common front against the government, for betraying the liberation movement, and for allegedly concealing their true nature – that of the class enemy of the revolution – behind a democratic facade. Writing about the Petersburg elections, Nabokov admitted that the party had suffered far more denigration from the socialists than from parties on the right.[46] It is true that the attitude of the socialists provided the Kadets with one great advantage: their boycott removed their electoral competition, and the Kadets were therefore the only major opposition party contending for seats. But on the other hand, the Party was planning to use the elections to mobilize public opinion behind the Duma and a programme of radical reform. Boycottist propaganda was bound to undermine these tactics. Moreover, the influence of the socialists was especially strong among the urban working class which, as the October strike had shown, had an importance out of all proportion to its numbers.

At the Second Congress the Kadets had continued to call for a united front of the entire opposition.[47] They apparently still hoped that the socialist parties might be persuaded to drop the extremist tactics which had led to the Moscow defeat, and to agree to limit their immediate objectives to the establishment of civil liberties and a parliamentary régime. In the course of the next three months the Kadets repeatedly called upon the socialists to adopt a more moderate attitude, and to abandon their boycott of the Duma. At the samt time the Kadets attempted to build up the party's support among the working class and to counteract the harmful effects of left-wing propaganda. At the Second Congress the party had decided to set up a commission to work out proposals of labour reform and publicize them among the working class.[48] On Struve's advice it also recommended that local party branches should consider forming professional groups of Kadets from a variety of occupations, including peasants, workers, artisans and shop assistants.[49] Struve laid special emphasis on the importance of obtaining the support of the workers. He even persuaded the congress that because of the inadequacy of the workers' franchise, the Central Committee should be authorized to negotiate with other parties with a view to presenting a certain number of seats in the Duma to workers' representatives.[50] Struve appears to have hoped that this would earn the gratitude of the working class and help to persuade the socialists to adopt a more moderate attitude.[51] Accordingly, Struve was appointed as head of the labour commission with authority to put these plans into effect.[52] On 16 January the committee agreed to subscribe 50 rubles to a "circle of workers organising the professional workers' movement",[53] and in February it approved a proclamation to the proletariat.[54]

The party's manifesto to the workers recognized the leading rôle that they had played in the fight for freedom. At the same time it reminded them that the main reason why the struggle had not yet resulted in complete victory was the continued existence of divisions within the opposition. The most effective way for the workers to defend their interests was to unite their efforts with those of other social classes within a single democratic party. The proclamation strongly denied that the Kadets were a "gentlemen's" party and urged them to join the movement as full and equal members. If they did so they could still retain a great deal of autonomy; the party would support the formation of independent non-party trade unions. The manifesto also explained the party's proposals for advanced labour legislation and educational reform and, recognizing the continuing links of many workers with the land, outlined the Kadets' agrarian programme. The workers should give their full support to efforts to achieve these reforms by parliamentary means, and should reject a boycott of the Duma.[55]

However, the party's efforts to win over the workers met with little success. On 13 March, *Rech'* admitted that: "factory and workshop workers ... have refused, in a large number of instances, to take part in the elections to the Duma; in places, as in Petersburg, they have done so in very decisive fashion". On 28 March,[56] *Rech'* noted that in several of Moscow's proletarian districts, "the elections from the workers went off, in general, sluggishly. Obviously the workers of these districts are still adhering to the decision to boycott the Duma".[57] As a conciliatory gesture to the left, the Moscow Kadets decided to present one of the city's seats to a representative of the workers.[58] However, this evoked little response from the socialist parties. It is true that for their own reasons the Mensheviks later changed their minds about the desirability of the boycott. As their expectations of revolution faded they too began to feel that the Duma could be utilized as a means of struggle against the government. These signs of a change of heart were welcomed by the Kadets,[59] but although the Mensheviks' new tactics gave them an electoral victory in the Caucasus, they came too late to affect the election campaign as a whole. Moreover, the Bolsheviks and S.R.s (Socialist Revolutionaries) continued to support the boycott.

Meanwhile, the Kadets' plan of forming trade union groups seems to have scarcely got off the ground in this period. The discussions of the Third Congress make it clear that with the possible exception of Moscow,[60] this undertaking was still in its infancy.

In the virtual absence of the socialists from the struggle for seats in the Duma, the Kadets found their strongest organized competitors to their right – in the Union of 17 October and its allies, all of which enjoyed either the support or benevolent neutrality of the bureaucracy. The Octobrist Party had largely grown up from the "Slavophile" minority of the zemstvo movement which had originally favoured a purely consultative representative assembly. These men had rather reluctantly accepted the October Manifesto, but they continued to oppose a parliamentary régime and the decentralization of Russia. The new party also contained convinced constitutionalists like Count Geiden, who were alienated by the radical position adopted by the Kadets. At first the party had been dominated by Shipov and other public men with a genuinely liberal outlook. However, the Octobrists were already being infiltrated by large numbers of "backwoodsmen" – landowners and businessmen with more reactionary opinions. The drift to the right eventually led to a walk-out by the party's more liberal members, and effective leadership increasingly devolved upon the more conservative Alexander Guchkov.

In the course of their struggle with the Octobrists and their allies, the Kadets decided to seek electoral support from political groups which had an outlook broadly similar to their own. At a meeting of the Central Committee with party representatives from 28 provinces it was decided that temporary electoral blocs were possible only with political parties, which "demand a constitutional state system based upon universal suffrage". If it should prove impossible to secure the victory of a Kadet or coalition candidate, preference should be given to "persons of the most progressive direction".[61] This was only a very general directive, and in practice it gave local Kadet groups wide discretion in making electoral agreements. In Petersburg the Kadets obtained the backing of the city's Jewish and Polish national groups.[62] In Moscow they had the support of Polish, Jewish, Moslem and Estonian groups and formed an alliance with a "non-party group of left elements".[63] In Kiev they entered a bloc with the United Polish Parties, the United Jewish organizations and the Ukrainian Democrats.[64] At times local party branches seem to have made more unusual alliances. In Tula there was even a case of a bloc with the Octobrists,[65] although there is no evidence that this met with the approval of the Central Committee.

In the main urban centres the Kadets appear to have enjoyed considerable success in organizing their electoral campaign. However, in the countryside, where their party organization was much weaker, and where there was more administrative interference, the Kadets found it far more difficult to make progress. At the primary stages of the voting they often found it almost impossible to exert much influence, especially among the peasants and small landowners. Because of this, the party had to concentrate upon the secondary stages of the elections.[66] But even here the Kadets appear to have been in a much less influential position than in the towns. As a result, their efforts seem to have been directed chiefly to securing the election of candidates with generally progressive views. The Kadets appear to have commonly come to electoral agreements with individual non-party socialists and members of the Peasant Union. The Kadets felt sure that once they arrived in the Duma, many of these representatives would decide to give the party their support.

The election results

The Kadet leaders had never regarded the outcome of the elections as hopeless. But they had always been cautious in evaluating their chances, especially in view of the government interference in the election campaign. In the provinces the Kadet mood had sometimes been openly pessimistic. In Iaroslavl', for example, repression was so severe that its Kadet group began to lose heart and even considered a boycott.[67] However, in general, administrative interference was not severe enough to guarantee victory for the right. Indeed, according to Miliukov, it had only served to rally the electors behind the Kadets.[68]

For a long time the actual result of the voting remained obscure. The elections were multi-stage, and were held on different dates in different parts of the Empire. Beginning in late February they were largely completed by mid-April. But in the more far-flung parts of the Empire they often continued well into the period of the First Duma. Therefore, the party had to be cautious in evaluating the early results. But as early as 7 March A. Smirnov, writing about the elections among the peasants, detected a considerable majority in favour of progressive candidates.[69] A week later, *Rech'* was already able to report Kadet victories in several large towns.[70] But it was only after a massive victory in Petersburg, where all 160 "electors"[71] were chosen from the Kadet list, that the party really gained confidence in an opposition victory. Later, as news of Kadet triumphs came in from more big towns, and of a new Kadet landslide in Moscow, the party began to feel that it would probably be able to group a Duma majority around its members. In the towns the Kadet victory was overwhelming.[72] On the other hand their fortunes were more mixed in elections among the landowners and peasants, and a very large number of peasant deputies had no clear party colour even on the eve of the Duma. However, the Kadets remained confident of attracting many of the latter to their banner. Any government plan to woo this group was doomed to failure, said *Rech'*. The peasants would soon realize that their true community of interests lay with the Kadets. The party would be able to count on agreement with the peasants and this would "determine the whole tactical position of the Party in the Duma".[73]

As the election results came in the Kadets experienced a growing wave of confidence. However, they realized that their victory was partly the result of the boycott by the socialist parties. The party leadership was fully aware that many votes had been cast for the Kadets because they were the only major opposition party confronting the government and the conservative right. Because of this they looked upon their success at the polls as a triumph for the opposition as a whole, rather than as purely "party" victory. They saw it as primarily an expression of no confidence in the government, and only secondarily as a vote for the Kadets. Commenting on the Petersburg landslide *Rech'* admitted that: "for the people of Petersburg our Party was only a well-prepared channel into which, with irrepressible force, poured a mighty wave of popular opinion, of popular indignation, of popular faith in the construction of the motherland on new principles".[74]

The elections to the Duma had resulted in a massive vote against the status quo, against the government and the régime. It was not a vote which encouraged the Kadets to water down the radicalism of their programme and come to terms with the government. If they had attempted to do so they would have run a grave risk of becoming completely discredited in the eyes of the public. Moreover, there was no real evidence that the government was prepared to go even halfway to meeting the Kadets' demands. There was still an almost unbridgeable gap between what the government was willing to concede and what the Kadets might have been prepared to accept. It is true that neither the Tsar nor the government intended completely to abrogate the promises which had been given in the manifesto, but they were determined to interpret them as narrowly as possible and limit their effect. The government had made its intentions crystal clear at the very outset of the elections, by taking concrete steps to limit the powers of the Duma. On 20 February the authorities at last did what Miliukov had advised in the Autumn: they promulgated a "constitution".[75] However, this was very different from the constitution which Miliukov had favoured, and it led to a chorus of protests from the opposition.

The laws of 20 February

From the point of view of the Kadets one of the most objectionable aspects of the new measures was their provision for an upper chamber. Witte's report accompanying the October Manifesto had hinted that the State Council (the existing, purely bureaucratic legislative body) would be retained but would be reformed. In itself this was not necessarily in sharp conflict with the Kadet programme since the party had not categorically rejected the ideal of a democratic second chamber. However, the "constitution" of 20 Feburary failed to reorganize the council on democratic lines. Half of its members were to continue to be nominated by the Crown (including its president and his deputy). The remainder were to be chosen by restricted electoral colleges from the zemstvos, the universities, the nobility and the business community. Members from the Church would be nominated by the purely bureaucratic Holy Synod. All this meant that the council was bound to be dominated by conservative elements.[76] Despite the unrepresentative nature of its membership the upper chamber was awarded formal equality with the Duma. It would have the right of legislative initiative, and would have power to reject bills proposed by the lower house. Only bills approved by both chambers would be forwarded to the Tsar for confirmation.

The existence of a conservative upper house was bound to limit the power and authority of the Duma. Moreover, the constitution imposed a number of other restrictions upon the rights of the popular representatives. The Crown was given the authority to determine the length of the sessions of both houses, and even the Duma's right to initiate legislation was hemmed in by restrictions. Any legislative proposal had to be signed by at least 30 members, and had to be accompanied by an outline of its fundamental propositions. The initial drafting of a detailed bill was entrusted to the ministry instead of the Duma. The appropriate minister would be given a month to decide whether he was prepared to draft a law on these lines and the Duma would have the right to form a committee to work out a bill only if the minister refused to do so. The ministry was granted a similar right of a month's delay in responding to parliamentary interpellations concerning the illegal activities of the bureaucracy. Once again, every question to a minister had to be signed by 30 deputies, and little redress was granted if the House was dissatisfied with ministerial replies. Furthermore, the representatives were not permitted to put down questions concerning the advisibility of government policies. There was no way of making the ministers genuinely accountable to the Duma; in reality they remained responsible only to the Tsar. Under the terms of the new "constitution" the Tsar retained very great power. He still had the right to propose new legislation, and could veto bills which had been approved by both chambers. The Crown was also authorized to promulgate emergency legislation when the Duma was in recess, although this was supposed to lapse if it failed to receive the approval of the chambers within two months of the beginning of a new session. Moreover, when the deputies entered the Duma they would have to take an oath to "His Imperial Majesty, the Sovereign Emperor and all-Russian *Autocrat*" (author's emphasis).

Less than a fortnight after the promulgation of the Laws of 20 February the government took further steps to limit the authority of the Duma. At the beginning of March the government enacted a set of Budgetary Rules which severely restricted the chambers' control of public taxation and expenditure.[77] They were explicitly forbidden to review the expenditures of the Court, the Imperial Family and the Imperial Chancery provided they remained within certain limits, and they were to have no power to reduce assignations upon state debts. Moreover, the budget rules also stipulated that if the chambers failed to agree a new budget, the estimates of the previous year would remain in force. At the same time, the Duma's powers were once again limited by the authority of the State Council, and the ministry was granted a right of exceptional expenditure similar to the Crown's emergency legislative powers.

Not surprisingly, these measures were met with cries of outrage from the Kadets. In a detailed attack upon the "constitution" of 20 February, I.I. Lazarevskii[78] laid especial stress upon the limitations which fettered the Duma's legislative initiative. According to Lazarevskii the proposals to entrust the drafting of bills primarily to the ministers were an open invitation to the ministry to bury unwelcome legislation by the processes of administrative delay. Miliukov declared that the government had betrayed the manifesto. The composition of the reformed State Council was utterly unsatisfactory,[79] wrote Miliukov. To grant it equal rights with the Duma was "an insult to the Duma, and it is impossible to doubt that the struggle against the very existence of the Council will become a new slogan of the liberation movement". Miliukov admitted that there had been some improvements – such as publicity for Duma sessions – over the provisions of the old Bulygin Duma. Moreover, the revision of the acts of 20 February still remained within the competence of the Duma. But he vigorously attacked the inclusion of the word "Autocrat" in the deputies' oath to the Crown, and the Tsar's power to enact exceptional legislation. According to Miliukov this power was far too wide, especially in view of the Crown's control over the length of Duma sessions. Because of this, wrote Miliukov:

> in calling the Duma annually for a session of no more than two months the Government receives the complete possibility, without infringing the Russian "constitution" to rule for the rest of the time with the help of whatever exceptional, "temporary", or perpetual laws and measures it likes.

At the same time, he bitterly attacked the restrictions on the Duma's legislative powers. The Budget Rules came under equally withering fire. On 4 March, *Rech'* proclaimed that their object was to give as much power as possible to the bureaucracy and as little as possible to the Duma.[80]

The reaction of the Kadet leadership was not surprising. The effect of the government measures was to create a constitution in which the balance of power was tilted heavily on the side of the representatives of the old régime. The acts of 20 February stopped far short of establishing the more or less parliamentary system desired by the Kadets; instead they had established a limited monarchy. This was perhaps something which the Kadet leadership might have been prepared to welcome in 1904 at least as an interim settlement, although even this is problematical. However, by 1906 their demands, and those of the opposition in general, had moved so far to the left that this constitution no longer represented the basis for a compromise agreement with the government. With the benefit of hindsight it might, perhaps, be argued that in view of the fact that the revolutionary movement was on the wane, the Kadets would have been wise to come to terms with the government upon the basis of this highly limited constitution. However, at the time it was still not clear whether the balance of forces in the country might not alter again. Moreover, if the Kadets had been willing to retreat so precipitately from their radical demands it seems likely that they would have lost much of their support among the public. Indeed, it seems very doubtful whether the Kadet leadership could have gained the support of their party as a whole for such a course. Among the Kadet rank and file the government's actions seem to have sparked off a storm of violent hostility to the administration, leading in some cases to demands for a boycott of the Duma.[81] Given this mood of extreme hostility to the government it seems highly unlikely that the leadership could have persuaded the party as a whole to adopt a more compromising attitude to the administration, even if they had wanted to. Moreover, the leadership's own hostility to the government had not diminished during this period. Following the publication of the laws of 20 February their attacks upon Witte became more bitter than ever.

The Kadets' antagonism to Witte was not wholly justified. Strictly speaking the "constitution" of 20 February was not the work of the government; it had been decided upon by a Crown Council under the chairmanship of Count Solskii, of which Witte was merely an important member.[82] However, although it is true that during the proceedings of the council, Witte adopted a more liberal position than extreme reactionaries like Stishinskii, his attitudes were far from radical. The height of his "liberalism" was his rather Slavophile proposal that Duma bills rejected by the State Council should be communicated to the Tsar purely for information purposes so that the voice of the people should be heard by the sovereign. On the other hand, he strenuously opposed publicity for Duma sessions, and even denied that the conference's proposals amounted to a real constitution. According to Witte the reform had established, "only an apparatus, of the highest stage of importance, by which the Sovereign Emperor wishes to rule". There seems, in fact, to be little evidence that Witte would have been prepared to make concessions of a type which might have been sufficient to build a bridge between himself and the Kadets. Moreover, as "Premier" he was bound to take responsibility for the actions of the government so it is only natural that Kadet hostility to the "constitution" was reflected in enmity to Witte.

The loan which "saved Russia"

The Kadet's animosity towards Witte was increased still further by recurring and justified rumours that he was negotiating with the French government for a massive loan to shore up the state finances, pay for the repression of the revolution, and weaken any financial pressure the Duma might bring to bear on the administration. From the first, the Kadet leaders spoke out against the loan, arguing that it would be used merely to keep the old régime in power. In the second half of March, the rumours became increasingly concrete and Kadet protests about the conclusion of the loan without the sanction of the Duma became more and more vocal. However, although the Central Committee opposed the loan, it baulked at the idea of officially trying to prevent it.[83] On the face of it, this seems to justify the rather scornful allegation of B. Grave that Kadet tactics never went beyond the rather English bounds of "His Majesty's Opposition".[84] However, the evidence suggests that the committee's decision on this question was motivated primarily by caution: it did not wish to give Witte a stick to beat them with – the charge of lack of patriotism – if it officially approached foreigners to try to prevent the loan. But its decision did not exclude unofficial attempts to influence the West, whether via the press or the actions of "individuals". In an editorial on 24 March, *Rech'* warned that the government intended to use the loan to free itself from the influence of the Duma. Only a constitutional government could ensure the proper conditions for Russian credit, claimed *Rech'*. And it went on specifically to address the West:

> We say to our Western friends: – "Do not prevent us creating these conditions as quickly as possible." We say to them honestly as good managers (khoziaeva): "Those who act for us do not enjoy our confidence – and we will come to an agreement with you on conditions becoming the dignity and wealth of Russia".

On 30 March, in another editorial clearly meant for French consumption, *Rech'* adopted an almost threatening tone – stressing the dangers to France if it alienated Russian public opinion: "How the first Russian parliament will regard Franco-Russian relations", warned *Rech'*, "and how the future parliamentary majority will determine its line of conduct in foreign policy – this cannot be a matter of indifference to the French public".

Meanwhile, two members of the Central Committee went still further in their opposition to the loan. At the beginning of April V.A. Maklakov and Pavel Dolgorukov participated in conversations in Paris with members of the French government – with Clemenceau (Interior) and Poincaré (Finance) – on the subject of the loan. In the course of these discussions Maklakov presented the French with a memorandum on the reasons for Kadet opposition to the proposed transaction.[85] In it he denied that the Russian government genuinely desired constitutional reform, severely attacked Witte, and announced that the young Russian democracy would regard the conclusion of the loan without its agreement as a disservice. He also informed the ministers that revolution was almost inevitable and suggested that the French money would be lost in the struggle with it. In expressing these opinions, he made it clear that these were also the views of his party, but he at no point said that he was acting on direct instructions from the Central Committee. Maklakov later claimed that his own presence (and that of Dolgorukov) in Paris was purely coincidental – he himself made frequent trips to the French capital, and Dolgurukov was there on holiday.[86] According to Maklakov his meetings with the ministers had been arranged by a non-party committee of left-wing Russian emigrés – although at first he had believed that the initiative came from the French government. He was not conducting a campaign against the loan, but he saw no reason why he should co-operate in obtaining it or refuse to explain the party's opinion. However, he denied having any official party backing.

The Central Committee's public statements at the time tend to confirm Maklakov's version of this episode – it explicitly refuted rumours that the party had approached France about the loan.[87] There is, in fact, no real evidence that the committee had given its prior blessing, official or unofficial, to the Paris talks. If it had, Maklakov, who later did everything possible to portray his political rôle in a right-wing light,[88] would surely have used this to excuse his leftist behaviour on this question. However, although the party does not appear to have been directly implicated in this affair, the indignation with which it later rejected rumours connecting it with the talks seems rather feigned. The editorials of *Rech'* make it clear that it was not only Maklakov and Dolgorukov who were prepared to appeal to the West. Moreover, the Kadets who had taken parts in the talks were not simply private individuals, but members of the Central Committee – indeed, Dolgorukov was its president. They were far from being a mere left-wing fringe. Furthermore, they do not seem to have suffered for their actions – in fact, Dolgorukov was chosen as president of the first session of the party's Third Congress in April. All this supports Maklakov's own statement that even if he did not have the party's prior blessing for the talks, he later had its covert sympathy.

Although the party officially disclaimed all responsibility for the Paris talks, this episode clearly illustrates the Kadets' hostility to the government. Their antipathy for Witte was in no way diminished by growing indications that the "premier" was softening his attitude to the opposition. As the election results came in, Witte's newspaper *Russkoe Gosudarstvo* (*The Russian State*) began to assume a relatively liberal posture. It began to suggest that the government was prepared to make concessions, providing that the Duma was willing to accept a subordinate rôle, and occupy itself with work on Witte's own programme of reforms rather than its own. It outlined a scheme of legislative activity centred around reforms of the Civil Code and the passport laws, together with an agrarian reform largely directed at the abolition of the commune.[89] However, the time had passed when the Kadets might have been prepared to have any confidence in Witte. Moreover, his proposals of reform fell far short of anything the Kadets were willing to accept. *Rech'* condemned Witte's programme of work for the Duma out of hand,[90] claiming that it consisted mostly of matters of secondary importance which had for a long time been under consideration in the bureaucratic machine. There was nothing on the question of civil liberties, universal suffrage or Witte's own temporary legislation. No one believed, said *Pravo (Law)*,[91] that the Duma could be kept within the limits of the government programme – the only course open to Witte was to resign.

The Fundamental Laws

The Kadets' attitude to the Witte government was hardened by rumours that it was preparing a new code of "Fundamental Laws", primarily designed to remove the review of the "constitution" of 20 February from the competence of the Duma. Miliukov[92] hastened to warn the authorities against taking such a step. *Russkoe Gosudarstvo* deceived no one with its blandishments, said Miliukov, the past could not be forgotten and the struggle would continue. However Miliukov's article was directed not so much at the government, in which the Kadets had by now lost all hope, as at the "ruling spheres" upon which the administration's authority rested. And towards these "spheres", which presumably included not only high officials of the Court and the bureaucracy, but also the Tsar himself, Miliukov adopted a more conciliatory attitude than towards Witte. Miliukov said that following the Kadets' election successes, "a moment has set in when the possibility has appeared, if not of coming to an agreement, then at least of understanding each other". The struggle with the old régime would continue, but the ruling group could keep it within "civilized limits", by leaving the path of peaceful reform open. At the moment, even the laws of 20 February could be changed by legislative activity. However, if the government were to shackle the representatives by means of new "Fundamental Laws" peaceful change might become impossible, and a new conflict might arise. If the ruling circles wished for a peaceful outcome they would drop such plans. In the meantime the present government must resign. This was essential to pacify public opinion.

However, neither the government nor the "ruling spheres" seem to have been greatly influenced by the arguments of the liberals. Despite the protests of the opposition, the Council of Ministers pressed ahead with the work of drafting a new code of Fundamental Laws which would define the rights of the Crown, the chambers and the Russian citizen. Once these laws were promulgated they would be subject to amendment only on the initiative of the Emperor. As the liberals had suspected, their chief effect would be to remove the general lines of the "constitution" of 20 February from the Duma's field of legislative competence. At the same time they were designed to protect the prerogatives of the monarch, by emphasizing his control of the executive, the armed forces and foreign affairs. At a Crown Council held at Tsarskoe Selo[93] to consider the Fundamental Laws, there was strong support for the idea of preventing the Duma from proposing changes to the constitution. Witte warned that unless this was done, the Duma would turn into a constituent assembly. In general, the "Premier's" rôle at the conference was not a liberal one: indeed he was one of the most ardent champions of the Tsar's prerogatives and of his right to take exceptional measures on his own initiative. He even came out strongly against the principle of the irremovability of judges, fearing that they might give revolutionary judgements and be supported by the Duma. In fact, Witte seems by now to have become obsessed with the danger of revolution. The conference as a whole tended to be more restrained than Witte, but for the most part it shared his desire to put limits upon the Duma. However, it was not simply reactionary – it did not intend to repudiate the promises of the manifesto; indeed, the Tsar explicitly rejected this idea. But, like the conference which had been held in February, it was determined to give the Tsar's promises their narrowest possible interpretation. Moreover, many of those who took part were disinclined to face up to the full implications of the manifesto. The Emperor, himself, showed great reluctance formally to concede that, following 17 October, he was no longer entitled to call his powers "unlimited". He admitted that for a long time he had been tormented by the question of "whether I have the right before my ancestors to change the limits of the power which I have received from them".[94] In the end he accepted that his powers were no longer absolute but he clearly did so with grave misgivings.

As the time drew nearer to the opening of the Duma, rumours of the impending publication of the "Fundamental Laws" grew. *Rech'* even obtained and published a draft copy of them.[95] Meanwhile, Miliukov once again warned the authorities about the dire consequences of enacting such measures: "Even the effect of the laws of 20 February will pale before the outburst of indignation which will await us."[96] At the same time several Kadet leaders seem to have taken some part in an initiative designed not so much to prevent the publication of the Fundamental Laws, as to remove some of their worst features and make them more liberal. With the encouragement of General Trepov, who had considerable influence upon the Tsar, the moderate liberal V.I. Kovalevskii, a former Assistant Minister of Finance, drew up a memorandum criticizing the Fundamental Laws as they stood, and proposing a more liberal draft. According to Witte,[97] on 18 April this was sent to Trepov who in turn communicated it to the Tsar.

Kovalevskii's draft[98] did not attempt to sweep away all the features which the Kadet leadership had publicly condemned, for example, it broadly approved the government's proposals for a reformed State Council. At the same time it recognized the Tsar's special prerogatives in relation to the executive, the armed forces, foreign affairs, the Court and the Church. And although it sought to limit the Tsar's power to issue ukases, it acknowledged his right to veto legislation. On the other hand, it proposed to widen the chambers' control over state finances and the budget. They were to have the right to agree all taxes, credits and obligations, and would even have to approve international commercial treaties and conventions.[99] The draft accepted that if the budget were not agreed by a given date the existing budget should remain in force. But it stipulated that this arrangement would not be permitted to continue for more than one financial year.

At the same time, Kovalevskii's draft attempted to establish a greater degree of ministerial responsibility to the Duma. Although the ministers would still be formally responsible only to the Tsar, the houses were to have the right to make representations to the Crown about the damaging effects of ministerial policies. The chambers were to have similar rights if they were dissatisfied with ministerial replies to their interpolations. Furthermore, the Tsar would not be able to prevent the Duma or the State Council prosecuting the ministers in the Senate for illegal activities. Formally speaking, only the Tsar would have the right to initiate changes to the Fundamental Laws. However, if two-thirds of a united sitting of both houses agreed that a change was essential they would have the right to present their considerations to the Tsar, although he was not bound to take action, nor need he do so in the case of representations regarding interpellations or government policies.

On the face of it, these proposals would have left the Crown with very considerable power. However, the evidence suggests that Kovalevskii intended this power to be more formal than real. Article 5 of his draft of the Fundamental Laws stated that "the person of the Sovereign Emperor is sacred, inviolable, and [constitutionally speaking] not responsible (neotvetstvennyi)", that is, not answerable to any other body for his actions. In his memorandum Kovalevskii made the radical implications of this article clear. He argued that only the ministers should bear the responsibility for their actions – the Tsar should be "irresponsible", a figure standing above and, implicitly, outside politics: "Standing above changeable moods and parties and outside the policies pursued by them, the Tsar must be the embodiment of the idea of the unity and greatness of the Empire, of truth and welfare ('blago') in this land."[100] The memorandum went on to link all this with the English doctrine of the constitutional monarchy.

Although Kovalevskii's proposals contained many concessions to conservative opinion, in practice they might well have led to radical constitutional change. If the Tsar had been expected to keep out of factional politics, the chambers' right of petitioning the Crown would have been immensely important. The Tsar could not consistently have rejected the representations of the chambers without prejudicing his essentially non-partisan position. It is true that he would have retained his prerogatives in such fields as foreign policy and the armed forces, and that he could have exercised considerable authority by means of ministerial appointments and nominations to the State Council. However, his influence would have been weakened by his withdrawal from direct involvement in the political arena. And given the chambers' increased authority over the budget and over the supervision of the ministry, it seems probable that the constitutional balance of power would ultimately have tilted in their favour. In the long run Kovalevskii's proposals might well have paved the way for a Western-style parliamentary system. However, they remained considerably more moderate than the published aims of the Kadets.

Nevertheless, the evidence of Witte's memoirs, together with the evidence found in his archives, indicates that leading Kadets took some part in the preparation of V.I. Kovalevskii's proposals. According to both sources the memorandum and the draft of alternative Fundamental Laws were drawn up in a meeting with the participation of V.I. Kovalevskii, Miliukov, I.V. Gessen and M.M. Kovalevskii (Party of Democratic Reform).[101] Witte's note on the original documents also mentions F.A. Golovin, N.I. Lazarevskii and Muromtsev. However, Witte obtained these documents only in 1907 and seems to have taken little part in Kovalevskii's original initiative. Because of this, it is difficult to know just how great Kadet participation really was. It is quite possible that Kovalevskii consulted the Kadets relatively informally. However, although V.I. Kovalevskii's proposals fell short of the Kadets' public demands, it is clear that leading Kadets were consulted to some extent. For their part they may well have felt that even if they could not prevent the publication of the Fundamental Laws they could at least try to mitigate their worst effects and attempt to ensure that peaceful progress towards a parliamentary system remained possible. It is arguable that Kovalevskii's proposals, and especially his recommendation that the Chambers should retain a limited right of suggesting changes to the Fundamental Laws, were broadly within the spirit of Miliukov's article directed at the ruling spheres. This had argued that the review of the constitution should not be removed from the Duma's sphere of competence, and that the path of peaceful legislative reform should be left open.

The fall of Witte

At the height of the Kadets' campaign against the official draft of the Fundamental Laws, their attention was suddenly captivated by sweeping changes in the government. The party leaders had long been aware that Witte's authority had been rapidly declining, and on 16 April the Tsar finally accepted his resignation. The Kadets' reaction was emotional rather than rational. Their initial impulse was to attribute Witte's fall to opposition pressure. *Pravo* was overjoyed. It saw Witte's resignation as a great victory, connected primarily with the exposure of the Fundamental Laws in the press. "The resignation of Count Witte", exulted *Pravo*, "is a new great victory of the KD.Party, irrespective of who takes his place".[102] Miliukov, also, saw Witte's fall as an opposition triumph. Even the news that Witte was to be replaced by the ageing and reputedly reactionary bureaucrat, Goremykin, did not immediately alter his evaluation. But unlike *Pravo* he sounded a note of caution. He clearly felt that this appointment *might* mean war with the Duma, even though there was not enough evidence for this yet. But he did feel that Witte's fall meant that his double-faced policies were at an end, and that society would now know where it stood. Moreover, he argued that the feeble and colourless Goremykin would be much easier to dislodge than Witte.[103]

In retrospect the Kadets' attitudes to Witte's fall – particularly their assumption that it was due to opposition pressure – seems highly unrealistic. If their vision had not been clouded by hatred for Witte, they would have realized that his resignation was more easily explicable as a victory for the right – especially when it became clear that Goremykin would be the new premier. The reactionary forces were now in a better position than at any time since the revolution began – the bulk of the army had now returned from the Far East and Witte had finally succeeded in shoring up the state finances with a massive 2.25 billion franc French loan. Witte's fall was largely due to the fact that now that the loan had been concluded he was no longer needed to provide a liberal facade for the régime. Moreover, his failure to ensure an election victory for conservative elements, together with his erratic and ambiguous policies, had undermined any remaining support for his government in ruling circles. Meanwhile the confidence of the right had been strengthened by the fact that the countryside remained relatively tranquil. The agrarian disturbances which had been expected to break out in the spring had failed to materialize on the anticipated scale. Although further disturbances could not be ruled out, and prominent officials remained in constant danger of assassination, the authorities were continuing to consolidate their position.

The Kadets' Third Congress (21–25 April 1906)

It was in these circumstances that the Third Kadet Congress met in Petersburg on 21 April, to consider the tactics and policies to be pursued by the party in the Duma. The delegates, who included the new Kadet deputies, met in an atmosphere of elation engendered by the party's success in the elections and by the fall of Witte. The attitude of the rank and file seems to have been one of confidence – they believed that they had received a mandate from the people, and they felt that this was no time to compromise. However, the confidence of the Central Committee was tempered by caution. It is clear from Miliukov's opening report on tactics[104] that the Kadet leaders were aware that the situation was not as favourable as many rank and file delegates supposed. At the very outset Miliukov struck this note of caution: "Tactics must always depend on circumstances", said Miliukov, "we will always undoubtedly, strive for the same thing, but we must act in completely different ways, taking into account whether we are strong or weak, what circumstances we are acting in, and what forces our opponents have at their disposal". Miliukov rejected any attempt to create a showdown with the government immediately; this might lead to a premature conflict, and "it is difficult to foretell how far we will be in a condition to go upon this route".[105] Instead the party should adhere broadly to the tactics laid down by the Second Congress. The party should concentrate on peaceful legislative activity, and endeavour to pass bills on universal suffrage, civil liberties and urgent measures such as agrarian reform and the satisfaction of "just national demands". It should also introduce bills on a political amnesty, the abolition of capital punishment and the criminal responsibility of officials.[106] If the Kadets were to implement this programme they would have to remain in the Duma "for a more or less prolonged period". These tactics were essential if the deputies wished to secure popular support for the Duma. Miliukov refused to be carried away by the idea that the election victory necessarily meant that the masses would unreservedly support the deputies. Just how radical the people were was open to question but:

> it is scarcely possible to dispute the fact that it is necessary to give into the hands of the people some kind of more or less tangible evidence upon which

it can form its own opinion about the conduct of its representatives.... We must do something tangible, important and useful for the people before our opponents risk entering upon a conflict.

Once the Duma had obtained the support of the public, it would be very difficult to dissolve. The Kadets' proposals for land reform would have a central rôle to play in securing popular support for the Duma. Miliukov told the Congress that "absolutely everything else" might "depend on a successful solution to this task". The party should strive to achieve its objectives even if this led to a conflict with the government. However, a showdown should be put off to the most favourable moment and the responsibility for it should be seen to fall upon the government. The immediate tasks facing the Duma-legislation on universal suffrage, civil liberties and agrarian reform, still lay within the competence of the representatives. Moreover, it was precisely in these fields that Miliukov expected least resistance from the government.[107]

On the other hand, Miliukov warned the Congress that the party should avoid conflict over the laws of 20 February. Although the latter were unconditionally unacceptable to the Kadets, the party must try to work within them: "directly to ignore them", said Miliukov, "seems possible only at a distance". Although a clash might arise over these measures, their revision was, strictly speaking, a matter for an assembly based on universal suffrage, since this question lay in the field of constituent activity. According to Miliukov, the government itself would attempt to avoid a collision with the Duma. The fall of Witte and the apparent shelving of the Fundamental Laws suggested that "the Supreme Authority has shown ... that conflict between the Duma and the Ministry is considered dangerous and undesirable". Therefore, Miliukov advised a wait-and-see attitude to the new ministry. It did not deserve the party's confidence and the Kadets should seek a ministry responsible to the Duma. But the party should not take any definite resolutions concerning the new ministers – this would be premature until the government had declared its policy in the Speech from the Throne.

Despite Miliukov's cautious optimism about the implications of the change of government, the tactics which he proposed were clearly predicated upon the realization that the administration was now in a much stronger position than many people assumed. However, Miliukov denied that he was suggesting that the revolution was over. He argued that the very existence of the Duma would be a mighty factor capable of altering the entire course of events. This appears to have been the key to the leadership's tactical proposals. They hoped that the Duma's programme would attract such overwhelming support that the authorities would be forced to capitulate to the opposition.[108] However, reading between the lines of Miliukov's official report, it is possible to discern the outlines of an alternative strategy which could be adopted if circumstances turned out to be less favourable than the Kadets hoped. In view of Miliukov's reservations about the extent of popular support for the Duma, and his realization that the government was stronger than many people believed, it seems unlikely that either he himself, or the Central Committee for which he was the spokesman, thought that a capitulation by the old régime was inevitable. And if the establishment refused to give way, the Kadets' cautious tactics would have been well suited to making the best of this situation. By stressing the need to keep as far as possible within legal limits, and by emphasizing the importance of remaining in the Duma for a more or less protracted period, Miliukov had gone a long way to proposing de facto recognition of normal legislative work in the Duma, at least for the time being. And if the Kadets' more sanguine expectations failed to materialize, the way would have been paved for a longer-term acceptance of the "Duma of the electoral law of 11 December" as a legal means of struggle against the régime. When it later became evident that Goremykin had no intention of capitulating to the Duma, Miliukov made it clear that if necessary he was prepared for a very long siege of the government indeed, making use of gradual, legal parliamentary pressure.

In retrospect it is clear that Miliukov's report was based upon a relatively realistic appreciation of the balance of power between the Duma and the government: indeed, if it erred, it was on the side of optimism. Nevertheless, a series of delegates at the Congress hotly denounced this approach as over-cautious, and demanded more decisive action. They had clearly been convinced by the election triumph and by widespread demonstrations in favour of the new deputies, that the people were already solidly behind the Duma, and that the national mood of opposition was now at fever pitch. Veisman (Tomsk) insisted that the country *was* revolutionary: "It is not inclined peacefully to decide questions of legislation after unheard-of atrocities and and an agony of tyranny. It is not inclined to see its deputies as diplomats." The deputies must remember that they were the moral victors, and boldly proclaim the people's demands to the government. If their conditions were not met, they must turn to the country for support, and even (though his demand was not taken up by other speakers) to "those extreme elements of which there are many".[109] Applause greeted the remarks of the Moscow student Ovchinikov, when he too attacked Miliukov's report: "I think", declaimed Ovchinikov, "that we should take for guidance not Kuropatkin's wise rule – patience, patience and more patience; we should take a bold and threatening initiative against the knights of darkness and violence".[110] The proposal not to directly challenge the laws of 20 February came in for especially bitter criticism, and Durnovo (Kostroma) even resurrected the ghosts of the Second Congress when he claimed that the words "constituent assembly" should have been in Miliukov's report.[111] Nevertheless, in the end the arguments of the leadership gained the support of the congress and Miliukov's general theses were accepted with relatively minor changes.[112]

However, following strong pressure from a large number of delegates the platform agreed to draft a resolution emphasizing the need for decisiveness in implementing the party programme, and reaffirming the Kadets' confidence that the Duma would receive overwhelming popular support. The resolution proclaimed that:

> Having heard the communications of the delegates about that mood of the country which created the victory of the Party ... at the elections, and

having recognized in the tactical resolution that it is the duty of the people's representatives to defend the popular demands formulated by the Party with all possible energy and firmness, without retreating before an open breach with the Government – the Congress at the same time declares its complete confidence that the resoluteness of the deputies in striving for the implementation of popular demands will meet a lively response in the broad masses of the people, and that in the most grave minutes of the forthcoming struggle, unanimous support will be rendered them not only by our Party, but also by the whole country.[113]

However, this resolution clearly did not go far enough to satisfy many delegates and it was approved by only 119 votes to 79.[114] The opposition to the leadership's policies was not confined to the question of tactics in the Duma. A large number of delegates also attacked the Central Committee's decision to seek legal status for the party. Many Kadets believed that the party should have refused to have any dealings with an administration which had proved that it was not to be trusted.[115] The undercurrent of discontent among the delegates even overflowed into criticism of the composition of the Central Committee; there were complaints that it no longer represented the true feelings of the party, and that it insufficiently represented provinces and minority nationalities. After pressure from Professor Luchitskii (a Duma deputy from Minsk), and from Goldberg (Pinsk), a Moslem delegate formally requested the committee to consider a change in its composition. To the Central Committee's surprise, when the question was put to the vote, the congress supported this proposal.[116] However, following representations from the party leadership the congress agreed not to re-elect the entire committee and decided to limit the elections to the choice of ten new members.[117] Moreover, there was no great victory for the left, in the ensuing elections. The largest number of votes went to the moderate Moscow zemstvo man F.A. Golovin, while one of the leaders of the left, E.N. Shchepkin, received the lowest vote of all the successful candidates.[118]

In fact, despite the clamour from the opposition the party leadership remained in control of the congress. The relatively cautious, diplomatic line of the committee seemed to have triumphed. However, at the end of the congress, the actions of the government obliged even Miliukov to adopt a much more militant tone. On 25 April, it became known that the original draft of the Fundamental Laws had been officially promulgated after all, with only a few relatively minor concessions to liberal opinion. When the congress heard the news, Miliukov found it impossible to maintain his earlier restraint:

"The Central Committee proposed to you that we should be restrained in our tactics, and the Congress agreed with us. After this decree we have obtained the right to be severe ("rezkie"). What we have read today is a deception, the people have been deceived, and we must reply to this deception immediately."

98 The run-up to the First Duma

The congress then proceeded to condemn the government's actions:

> On the eve of the opening of the State Duma, the Government has decided to throw down a new challenge to the Russian people. Fundamental Laws have been published, and the right of reviewing them has been taken away from the people; the ruling bureaucracy has been given back the plenitude of power which belonged to it. They are trying to reduce the State Duma, the focus of the hopes of a country worn out by suffering, to the role of a servant of the bureaucratic Government.... The Party of the Freedom of the People and its representatives in the State Duma ... proclaim that they regard this move of the Government as an open and sharp infringement of the rights of the people solemnly recognized in the Manifesto of 17 October and that no obstacles created by the Government will prevent the people's representatives from fulfilling the tasks entrusted to them by the people.[119]

However, even this resolution did not satisfy all the delegates. According to *Pravo*, "Amidst the continuous hum of the indignant auditorium, voices were heard: Too weak! This does not express all the significance of what has been done!"

In the face of the proclamation of the Fundamental Laws, it is not surprising that Miliukov and the leadership reacted violently and rather emotionally, adopting a much more hostile tone towards the government. However, they must rationally have been aware that the balance of power upon which their relatively restrained tactics had been based had not changed. Indeed, it was now clear that the government was less concerned to avoid a clash than Miliukov had supposed. The objective situation gave them in fact, no real grounds for adopting a more bellicose tactical line. On the other hand, the Fundamental Laws were bound to increase the Duma opposition's hostility to the government. They were scarcely likely to encourage the deputies to adopt an attitude of restraint, whatever the objective balance of power. It was now clear that if the Kadet leaders wished to adhere to the tactical line laid down by Miliukov they would have to tread a very precarious tightrope in the Duma. Nevertheless, it was along this political tightrope that the leadership was now preparing to tread.

Notes

1. For Witte's motives in the autumn of 1905 see Von Laue, "Count Witte", pp. 25–47.
2. Von Laue, "Count Witte", p. 31.
3. Nicholas II (Emperor), *The Letters of Tsar Nicholas II to the Empress Maria Fedorovna*, J. Bing (ed.), London 1937, p. 212.
4. Miliukov, "Rokovye gody", *Russkie Zapiski*, 1938–39, No. 17, p. 111.
5. Miliukov, "K itogam pervogo s''ezda", *Pravo*, No. 3, 1906.
6. See *OTCHËT*, p. 5. Only two of its members were replaced – Kablukov, a Moscow professor and zemstvo man, and Petrovsky, a lawyer and journalist, while Iakushkin, an academic historian and zemstvo leader took temporary leave of absence. However, there was a fairly large influx of newcomers – V.M. Gessen and L.I. Petrazhitskii, both academic jurists on the editorial board of *Pravo*, A.A. Kizevetter,

history academic and publicist, F.I. Rodichev (formerly a prominent zemstvo liberal, now an advocate), P.B. Struve, G.F. Shershenevich (another academic jurist) and A.A. Mukhanov, formerly a "gentleman of His Majesty's Bedchamber". This list marks something of a shift away from the zemstvo gentry. Of seven new members only two – Rodichev and Mukhanov – had links with the zemstvo.

7 Konstitutsionno-demokraticheskaia partiia – *Vtoroi vserossiiskii s''ezd*, S.P.B. 1906, Bulletin No. 6, p. 3. For proceedings of the Second Congress, see also "Vtoroi s''ezd K.-d. Partii 5–11 Ianvaria 1906", in V.V Shelokhai (ed.), *S''ezdy i konferentsii K.-d. Partii*, Vol. I, ROSSPEN 1997 (hereafter referred to as Shelokhaiev), pp. 46–198.
8 The party also clarified its agrarian policy with regard to the compensation to be paid for alienated land. See: "Rezoliutsii priniatye vtorym s''ezdom", *Pravo*, No. 2, 1906. See also: Shelokhai, Vol. I, pp. 178–9, Resolution 1. This question will be dealt with more fully later. Another important change concerned the party's official title. The congress decided to adopt another name for the party to be used as an alternative to its present title, which sounded rather foreign to the Russian ear. The title decided upon was the "Partiia Narodnoi Svobody" ("The Party of the Freedom of the People").
9 Shelokhai, Resolution I, point 1.
10 *Vtoroi vserossiiskii s''ezd*, Bulletin No. 6, p. 3.
11 *Vtoroi vserossiiskii s''ezd*, Bulletin No. 6, p. 4.
12 *Vtoroi vserossiiskii s''ezd*, Bulletin No. 4, p. 2.
13 *Vtoroi vserossiiskii s''ezd*, session of 5 January, Gessen's report on tactics.
14 "Vtoroi vserossiiskii s''ezd", *Pravo*, No. 7, 1906 Supplement, p. 28.
15 "Doklad II s''ezdu", Miliukov, *God bor'by*, pp. 102–10.
16 See *Vtoroi vserossiiskii s''ezd*, Bulletin No. 4, p. 1 for the resolutions and the voting figures. There was only one vote against entering the elections and only two in favour of boycotting the Duma.
17 *Vtoroi vserossiiskii s''ezd*, Bulletin No. 4, p. 2.
18 Miliukov, *Vospominaniia*, p. 355.
19 *Vtoroi vserossiiskii s''ezd*, Bulletin No. 4, p. 2. See the remarks of the "Kostroma delegate", and the following speakers.
20 "Rezoliutsii priniatye vtorym s''ezdom", *Pravo*, No. 2, 1906, Resolution VI.
21 "Rezoliutsii priniatye vtorym s''ezdom", Resolution I.
22 *Vtoroi vserossiiskii s''ezd*, Bulletin No. 8; Shelokhai, Vol. I, pp. 167–70 (Vinaver's report).
23 "Rezoliutsii priniatye vtorym s''ezdom", Resolution X.
24 "Ot tsentral'nogo komiteta", *Pravo*, No. 7, 1906.
25 For an account of government interference (from an opposition viewpoint), see: M.A. Kr–1, *Kak proshli vybory v Gosudarstvennuiu Dumu*, S.P.B. 1906.
26 S.E. Kryzhanovskii, *Vospominaniia*, Berlin (1938), pp. 76–9. Kryzhanovskii was the bureaucrat chiefly responsible for the conduct of the elections. See also: Mehlinger and Thompson, *Count Witte*, pp. 241–88.
27 "V chëm dolzhna zakliuchitsia deiatel'nost' otdelnykh chlehov partii i melkikh raënnykh grupp", *Vestnik Partii Narodnoi Svobody* (hereafter referred to as *Vestnik*), No. 2, 1906.
28 Miliukov, "Rokovye gody", *R.Z.*, 1938–39, No. 17, p. 114.
29 *OTCHËT*, p. 23.
30 See "Kratkii otchët o deiatel'nosti ts.komiteta", *Vestnik*, No. 1, 1906, pp. 30–1.
31 Ibid.
32 It should be emphasized that the election of Dolgorukov, Nabokov and Teslenko was in no sense an election of party *leaders*.
33 *OTCHËT*, p. 6.
34 Maksimov had now left the Secretariat. *OTCHËT*, p. 4.

35 *OTCHËT*, p. 6. (For reports on these courses in the two capitals see *Vestnik*, No. 1, pp. 33–4).
36 "Rezoliutsii priniatye vtorym s''ezdom", *Pravo*, No. 2, Resolution No. XII.
37 For an account of the history of this paper see *OTCHËT*, pp. 71–4.
38 *OTCHËT*, p. 73.
39 *OTCHËT*, p. 74.
40 Miliukov, "Rokovye gody", *R.Z.*, 1938–39, No. 17, pp. 115–16; *Vospominaniia*, Vol. I, pp. 357–8. Gessen, "V dvukh vekakh", pp. 115–16.
41 *OTCHËT*, pp. 26, 90.
42 Savich, *Novyi gosudarstvennyi stroi*, S.P.B. 1907, pp. 482–6.
43 See, e.g., Miliukov, *God bor'by*, pp. 92–6.
44 See: "Kadety v 1905–06 gg", *Krasnyi arkhiv*, entries for 19/III/1906 and 29/III/1906. See also D.B. Pavlov (ed.), *Protokoly Tsentral'nogo komiteta 19 and 29 March 1906*, Vol. I, No. 17 and 18 (GARF. f. 523, op. 1, d.33v, ll.1406–18, and ll.1706–21).
45 *OTCHËT*, pp. 10–12.
46 V.D. Nabokov, "Peterburgskie itogi", *Vestnik partii narodnoi svobody*, No. 4.
47 For example, Struve, who unequivocally rejected violent revolutionary tactics, had still found it "impossible to separate the interests of the Social Democrats and the Constitutional Democrats". See "Vtoroi vserossiiskii s''ezd", S.P.B. 1906, Bulletin No. 8, pp. 2–3.
48 "Rezoliutsii priniatye vtorym s''ezdom", *Pravo*, No. 2, 1906, Resolution No. IX.
49 "Rezoliutsii priniatye vtorym s''ezdom", Resolution No. IV.
50 "Rezoliutsii priniatye vtorym s''ezdom", Resolution No. III.
51 The Petersburg group was meanwhile spending considerable sums – nearly 15,000 roubles by 1 May – helping to feed unemployed workers in the capital. This had begun in the period of the general strikes, but in the electoral period these were replaced by lockouts by the employers to get back earlier concessions.
52 "Kadety v 1905–06 gg", *K.A.*, Vol. 46, p. 54, 12/1/1906, Nos 16, 18.
53 *K.A.*, 16/1/1906, Vol. 46, p. 55, No. 27.
54 *K.A.*, 19–20/II/1906, No. 81, Vol. 46, p. 56.
55 Konstitutsionno-Demokraticheskaia Partiia, *K rabochim*, Moscow 1906.
56 Editorial, *Rech'*, No. 19, 1906.
57 "Vybory ot rabochikh", *Rech'*, No. 33.
58 *Vestnik partii narodnoi svobody*, No. 5, p. 291.
59 See, e.g., "P.N. Miliukov" – "Plekhanov i boikot", *Rech'*, 20 March.
60 In Moscow a "bureau for assistance to professional labour" seems to have had some significance in the electoral campaign. See Rozhdestvenskii's speech in "III s''ezd delegatov", *Pravo*, No. 18, 1906, p. 1683.
61 "Zasedanie ts.k. pri uchastii delegatov mestnykh komitetov", *Vestnik*, No. 2.
62 V.D. Nabokov, "Peterburgskie itogi", *Vestnik*, No. 4.
63 "Moskovskaia gorodskaia gruppa – vybory v Moskve", *Vestnik*, No. 6.
64 "Obshchee sobranie chlenov Partii Narodnoi Svobody gub.Kieva", *Vestnik*, No. 8.
65 "Tula 15 marta", *Vestnik*, No. 4, p. 219.
66 "Ot sekretariata ts.k-a", *Vestnik*, No. 7, pp. 497–9.
67 *Vestnik*, No. 2, p. 117.
68 "Pochemu pobedili kadety", in Miliukov, *God bor'by*, pp. 230–2.
69 A. Smirnov, "Vybory v derevne", *Vestnik*, 7 March.
70 "Vybornaia kompaniia", *Rech'*, 15 March.
71 The first stage of the elections in St. Petersburg was devoted to the election of 160 electors who would later be responsible for choosing deputies to the Duma. The first stage of the elections took place on 20 March.
72 See for example *Vestnik*, No. 7, p. 540 for evidence of the size of the Kadet victory in a group of large towns with independent representation in the Duma. Of a total of 1761 "electors" chosen at the first stage of the elections 1,468 were Kadets.

73 Miliukov, "Krest''iane i taktika k.d. bol'shinstva", in *God bor'by*, pp. 239–42 (*Rech'*, 31 March).
74 "Solntse nas ne obmanulo?", *Rech'*, 22 March.
75 For these measures see: Savich, *Novyi gosudarstvennyi stroi*, pp. 66–8, 84–92, 96–113. The measures of 20 February were not formally speaking a "constitution", and certainly the government would not have accepted this description. But they did in fact lay down the outlines of the extremely conservative constitutional system, which were later incorporated into the Fundamental Laws of the Empire in April 1906.
76 See "Tsarskosel'skie soveshchaniia", *Byloe*, No. 5–6, 1917, p. 293, for Witte's comment that: "In general it may be affirmed with confidence that the State Council will be deeply conservative".
77 Savich, *Novyi gosudarstvennyi stroi*, pp. 119–22.
78 I.I. Lazarevskii, "Vtoroe uchrezhdenie Gosudarstvennoi Dumy", *Pravo*, No. 8–9, 1906.
79 Miliukov, "Novoe uchrezhdenie Gosudarstvennoi Dumy", *God bor'by*, pp. 86–90.
80 "Biudzhetnye prava russkogo predstavitel'stva", *Rech'*, 4 March.
81 The party leadership continued to oppose a boycott. Miliukov declared that "the imperfection of the Duma does not make struggle within it impossible: it is necessary to enter it, since the struggle must be carried on both in the Duma itself and outside it" ("Sobranie k.d.p.", *Rech'*, 27 February). However, some concessions were made to the mood of the time. After consulting party opinion, the leadership decided not to participate officially in the elections to the State Council. It was argued that they would distract attention from the main electoral struggle. Moreover, the small electoral colleges were unsuited to a real election campaign. However, the party did not recommend *individual* members to boycott the elections.
82 See "Tsarskosel'skie soveshchaniia", *Byloe*, S.P.B, No. 5–6, 1917, pp. 289–311.
83 "Kadety v 1905–06 gg", *K.A.*, Vol. 46, p. 58, 29/III/1906, No. 112.
84 *K.A.*, Vol. 46, p. 41.
85 The memorandum is reprinted in O. Crisp, "The Russian Liberals and the 1906 Anglo-French Loan to Russia", *S.E.E.R.*, June 1961, pp. 508–11.
86 See V.A. Maklakov, *Vlast' i obshchestvennost'*, Paris 1936, Vol. II, pp. 525–42, for Maklakov's account of this episode.
87 "Kadety v 1905–06 gg", *K.A.*, No. 46, p. 60, 5/IV/1906, No. 134.
88 Incidentally this incident casts doubt upon whether Maklakov was on the right-wing of the party at this time. See Crisp, "The Russian Liberals", p. 498. For the attitude of the Central Committee to Dolgorukov's participation, see: D.B. Pavlov (ed.), *Protokoly tsentral'nogo komiteta*, 8–9 April 1906 goda, No. 21, para 141.3. (GARF, F.523,op. 1, d.33v, ll.24ob.-29).
89 See A. Gurko, *Features and Figures from the Past*, Stanford 1939, p. 452; *Russkoe gosudarstvo*, 5 April 1906.
90 "Plan zaniatii dumy", *Rech'*, 6 April.
91 "Neobchodimyi shag", *Pravo*, 8 April.
92 "Elementy konflikta", *Rech'*, 24 and 30 March.
93 "Tsarskosel'skie soveshchaniia", *Byloe*, No. 4, 1917, pp. 184–245.
94 "Tsarskosel'skie soveshchaniia", p. 204.
95 "Proekt osnovnykh gosudarstvennykh zakonov", *Rech'*, 11 April.
96 "Chto dume zapreshcheno", Miliukov, *God bor'by*, pp. 284–6 (*Rech'*, 10 April).
97 Vitte, Vol. II, p. 267 (1922 Berlin edition).
98 "Iz arkhiva S.Iu.Vitte", *K.A.*, No. 11–12, pp. 121–42, Kovalevskii's memorandum is on pp. 116–20.
99 However, the State Council's rights in budgetary matters were to be more restricted than those of the Duma. It would have power only to accept or reject the budget as a whole.

100 "Iz arkhiva S.Iu.Vitte", *K.A.*, No. 11–12, p. 118.
101 "Iz arkhiva S.Iu.Vitte", *K.A.*, No. 11–12, pp. 107, 116; Witte, *Vospominaniia*, Berlin 1922, Vol. II, p. 267. For Witte and the Fundamental Laws, see also: *Iz arkhiva S.Iu. Vitte, Vospominaniia*, S.P.B. 2003, Vol. II, pp. 460–70.
102 "Otstavka gr.Vitte", *Pravo*, 25 April.
103 Miliukov, "Novoe ministerstvo", *Rech'*, 19–20 April (*God bor'by*, pp. 307–11). See also Miliukov, "Otstavka grafa Vitte", *Rech'*, 19–20 April (*God bor'by*, pp. 303–6).
104 Miliukov, *God bor'by*, pp. 317–35. The Central Committee had approved Miliukov's moderate tactics only after a heated debate: *Protokoly Tsentral'nogo komiteta*, No. 22, 19/IV/1906, para. 8 (GARF. f. 523, op. 1, d.27, ll.41–43 ob.).
105 Miliukov, *God bor'by*, p. 332.
106 Miliukov, *God bor'by*, pp. 334–35, Theses I–IV.
107 Miliukov, *God bor'by*, p. 331.
108 Although Miliukov's report failed to make this explicit, the evidence suggests that the leadership hoped that their relatively restrained tactics would increase the likelihood of a capitulation by the establishment. They probably believed that by casting themselves in the rôle of a responsible, if determined, opposition they would reduce the "ruling spheres" opposition to a parliamentary ministry. The leadership certainly made considerable use of this stratagem in the Duma. They displayed a strong tendency to appeal to the Tsar and the Court over the heads of the ministry, and to portray themselves as a civilized alternative to an otherwise inevitable revolution.
109 "III s''ezd delegatov", *Pravo*, No. 18, 1906, p. 1671. For the protocols of the Third Congress, see also Shelokhai, Vol. I, pp. 200–354.
110 Konstitutsionno-demokraticheskaia partiia, *Protokoly III s''ezda*, S.P.B. 1906, pp. 25–6.
111 Konstitutsionno-demokraticheskaia partiia, *Protokoly III s''ezda*, pp. 22–3.
112 For the theses see "Postanovleniia III-ego s''ezda", *Pravo*, No. 18.
113 "III s''ezd delegatov", *Pravo*, No. 18, p. 1684.
114 Konstitutsionno-demokraticheskaia partiia, *Protokoly III s''ezda*, p. 94.
115 See Konstitutsionno-demokraticheskaia partiia, *Protokoly III s''ezda*, pp. 163–70 for the debates on legalization. There was also a strong criticism of the official proposals of agrarian reform. This will be dealt with in a later chapter.
116 *Pravo*, No. 18, pp. 1680–1.
117 *Pravo*, No. 18, p. 1685.
118 At the first ballot Golovin obtained 122 votes and A.S. Izgoev, an Odessa moderate, 113. The highest vote for a clearly identifiable member of the "left" opposition was D.V. Vasil'ev's 61. Only three of the ten members who were elected had taken a *clearly* oppositionist stand at the congress and they came seventh, eighth and tenth in the list of those chosen. (See "Postanovleniia III s''ezda", *Pravo*, No. 9, 1906).
119 *Pravo*, No. 18, p. 1694.

5   The First Duma
   (27 April–9 July 1906)

Kadet tactics and policies in the Duma

Throughout the First Duma the Kadets were to be subject to strong leftward pressures. Inside the chamber the leftist parties repeatedly clamoured for the adoption of a more aggressive tactical line. Meanwhile, from outside the walls of the Tauride Palace,[1] other factors encouraged the Kadets to take a decisive stand against the government. From the people, especially from the peasants, the deputies received a stream of *nakazy* ("instructions") demanding land and liberty. At the same time, the Kadets had to suffer repeated attacks from the boycottist left, who accused them of preparing to do a deal with the government, and betray the people.

But despite these pressures from the left, the Kadet leadership was aware that the old régime was continuing to consolidate its position at the expense of the revolutionary movement. Although there were sporadic agrarian disturbances and mutinies in the armed forces the authorities were by now gaining the upper hand. This inevitably strengthened the government's political position. It is true that there was no guarantee that this situation would last forever, and the constant rumblings from below were still enough to unnerve large segments of the bureaucracy. But, for the moment, the objective circumstances dictated relative caution, as the Kadet leaders had recognized at the Third Congress. The congress had not, at first, been unequivocally hostile to the new government – indeed, its appointment had been seen as a positive (though inadequate) step. On Miliukov's advice, the Kadets had refrained from condemning the new ministry's members, at least until it had announced its programme. If the ministry had shown itself to be more accommodating, it is possible that the Kadets' tactics would have moderated still further.[2]

However, the Fundamental Laws were the first sign that the government had no intention of giving ground to opposition pressure. And as the true nature of the ministry became clear, Kadet attacks upon it became as severe as their assaults upon Witte. At first, *Rech'* (*Speech*) was inclined to see the Fundamental Laws as less an act of government malice than a result of government's stupidity – of an organic inability to see the opposition's point of view – and it admitted that some improvements had been made compared with the original draft of these laws.³ However, it soon became clear that the Fundamental Laws were not an isolated action of the government. It became apparent that Goremykin, the leader of the new cabinet, was a convinced opponent of constitutional principles. His appointment as premier was singularly unfortunate. Almost all ministerial memoirs of the period unite in condemning him. Kokovtsov, the moderate bureaucrat who was Minister of Finance, asserts that he warned the Tsar beforehand against appointing Goremykin as premier. He severely criticized Goremykin for "his great indifference towards everything, his utter inability to compromise, and his outspoken unwillingness to meet the new elements in our state life". These traits "would not only fail to help us get acquainted with them, but would serve to increase the opposition".⁴ According to the Foreign Minister, A.P. Izvolskii, Goremykin

> resolved simply to ignore the Duma, affecting to consider it as a collection of tiresome persons who were of no real importance, and declaring publicly that he would not even do them the honour of arguing with them, but would act as if they did not exist.⁵

V.I. Gurko, the Assistant Minister of the Interior, and well to Izvolskii's right, asserts that Goremykin

> decided to ignore the Duma, to establish no relations with its chairman or its individual members. He had decided at the outset that no understanding with that body could be reached, and concluded that all efforts in this direction would be fruitless, even harmful, since they might be construed as a capitulation of the Government.⁶

Moreover, Goremykin's views were shared by other members of the ministry which included confirmed reactionaries like Stishinskii (Agriculture), and Shirinskii-Shakhmatov at the Holy Synod. It is true that there were also men sympathetic to moderate constitutionalist principles – Izvolskii and Stolypin, the new Minister of the Interior, but Izvolskii's influence was limited, while Stolypin lacked experience and was unable to make his weight felt at the outset. The Tsar himself retained his essentially conservative outlook. By conviction a believer in absolutism, who considered that his powers were a sacred trust to hand on to his son, he now regretted the manifesto, which he felt Witte had exacted from him under duress. Indeed, his chief motive in choosing Goremykin appears to have been a reaction against Witte: "What is most important to me", he told Kokovtsov, "is that Goremykin will not act behind my back, making concessions and agreements, to damage my authority".⁷ However, the appointment of Goremykin does not mean that the Tsar intended to go back upon his promises. If he had been determined to do this, he could have done so fairly easily in later years by means of the complete abolition of the Duma. But he had no intention of making any further concessions to the opposition, and he meant to give the manifesto an essentially limited, conservative interpretation. Moreover, his appointment of the reactionary Goremykin as premier suggests that he failed to comprehend the full significance of the profound changes which were taking place in Russian political life. According to General A.A. Mosolov, who was the head of the Court Chancellory, "the idea never entered the Tsar's head that these few hundreds of men (the Duma members) could be accepted as legitimate representatives of his people – the people which had accustomed him to the spectacle of delirious acclamations".[8]

In later years V.A. Maklakov severely criticized his former party's record in the Duma. He alleged that the Kadets displayed undue intransigence towards the ministry and were far too inclined to flirt with the left. In his view the party should have realized that parliamentary government could only have developed gradually, "in proportion to the growth of the authority of the Duma in the country, and in the eyes of the Sovereign". It could have been obtained only if the representatives had succeeded in establishing "confidence in the seriousness and loyalty of the Duma and not by the Duma itself demanding it from the Supreme Power".[9] According to Maklakov the Kadets should have moderated their attacks on the government, and should have been more willing to cooperate with it.

Maklakov's argument has a certain superficial plausibility. However, it fails to take sufficient account of the negative rôle played by the Goremykin government. It is true that Maklakov admitted that the appointment of the Goremykin ministry was a "disaster".[10] But in general his criticisms of the government were far less severe than those made by the Duma's moderate right – whom Maklakov depicted as the true heroes of the Duma. In fact, although it is easy to be wise after the event, the conduct of Goremykin and his ministry gave the Kadet leaders little reason to believe that they could obtain their aims by the course suggested by Maklakov. They really had no good grounds for believing that the government would give way – if indeed it could be made to do so at all – before anything other than strong and sustained pressure from the Duma and the public. And in the circumstances they could not easily afford to ignore the value of a possible accommodation with the Duma left.

Before the Duma met, the Kadets had confidently expected to be in an absolute majority. They had expected that a large number of the radical peasant deputies from the countryside – who had often been elected in alliance with, or with the support of the Kadets – would adhere to their party group (or "faction") in the Duma. However, they were taken by surprise by the formation of a large "Trudovik" (or "Labour") group, which absorbed many of the deputies the Kadets had hoped to attract. It formed a large if unstable bloc of peasants, socialist intellectuals and workers. Despite the socialist, and especially populist, colouration of most of its members, it was not essentially a revolutionary group, even though it contained a number of extremists. Its only substantial programme difference from the Kadets was its more radical approach to the land question (it favoured more alienation and less compensation). But it had no clear or consistent tactical line, and although it did not deny the value of legislative work, it tended to be influenced by leftist pressure from outside the Duma. And it was far less concerned than the Kadets were to avoid a head-on collision with the government, and more inclined to appeal to the people.

The balance of parties within the Duma is not easy to determine with any finality. Throughout the existence of the Duma, deputies continued to arrive from the provinces, and party allegiances were changing. But by 15 May, according to the authoritative figures of Borodin,[11] the Kadet "faction" had 153 members (34.1 per cent of the total), and the Trudoviks 107 (23.8 per cent). The remainder of the house was composed chiefly of a large group of 63 national autonomists (14 per cent),[12] mainly from Poland, who were mostly of liberal sympathies, and a large group of uncommitted or "non-party" members, who were mostly peasants (105, 23.45 per cent). The right-wing of the Duma was very small – the Octobrists having only 13 members, while the Party of Democratic Reform (close to the Kadets in its programme, but rather more moderate, especially in tactics)[13] also constituted a small minority. However, the conservatives and moderates also enjoyed a certain amount of support from non-party members.

Although the Kadets did not have an absolute majority they were, undoubtedly, the dominant party in the Duma. They had a more well-defined programme, better-educated personnel, and a much better leadership than their only conceivable rivals – the Trudoviks. And in alliance with the latter they could form a large majority in the House. Even without such an alliance, they could still hope to obtain a majority by relying on support from the Autonomists and a large section of the non-party deputies,[14] or by a policy of playing off one political group against another.

However, as events were later to prove, without an accommodation with the Trudoviks, the Kadet majority would have been an unstable one. Moreover, without it there was a grave risk of a divided (and therefore weakened) opposition, something the Kadets were determined to avoid. The Kadet leaders realized that the Trudoviks were not basically violent revolutionaries, and they hoped that for the most part they could be induced to follow the Kadets' lead. In an article published in *Rech'* on 29 April, Miliukov turned his attention to the Trudovik group.[15] He came to the conclusion that, despite the Trudoviks' socialist tinge, they had an essentially cautious and reserved attitude to the ideas of the extreme left. Their views were in general close to those of the Kadets. Under the influence of practical work in the Duma their initial distrust of the party would soon disappear, said Miliukov, "and it seems to us that the natural place of both groups is side by side".

Even before the Duma was opened, the Kadets made strenuous efforts to take the radical peasant deputies under their wing. On 5 April the Kadet Central Committee had proposed to "organize a special bureau in Petersburg for finding suitable apartments" for peasant deputies, and to try to attract them to a democratic party club.[16] Later, after the formation of the Trudovik group the committee proposed joint sittings with it "for agreement (with it), and for joint consideration of day-to-day ('ocherednye') questions of parliamentary life". At the same time, it decided to bring further influence to bear upon the Trudoviks by means of the distribution of party literature among its members, and by holding lectures and discussions on current questions.[17] Throughout the life of the First Duma, the Kadets attempted to take the Trudovik group in tow, and to limit its rôle to that of a junior partner. At the same time, they never abandoned the hope that individual Trudovik deputies might be induced to join the Kadet faction. This was by no means an unrealistic prospect. Towards the end of the Duma's existence, the Trudovik group became increasingly weaker, and tended to split up into its constituent parts. This tendency first became evident when a number of working-class deputies joined a new Social-Democratic (Menshevik) group in the Duma. Later on, individual Trudoviks began to be attracted into the orbit of other parties, including the Kadets.[18] This process was even admitted by the prominent Trudovik T.V. Lokot', although he did his best to minimize its significance.[19]

Some writers, including Maklakov, have attacked the Kadets for their informal alliance with the Trudoviks, alleging that it prompted the liberals to adopt extreme attitudes. There may, perhaps, be a certain amount of truth in this argument, but it does appear to have been overstated. Certainly the Trudoviks did not succeed in persuading the Kadets to adopt tactics markedly more radical than those laid down by their Third Congress. However, it is true that the liberals could not have severely watered down their official tactics without arousing the opposition of the Trudoviks. On the other hand, there is no doubt that the Kadets continually made use of their friendship with the Trudoviks to restrain them from actions which might otherwise have endangered the existence of the Duma. Indeed, the first step of the Kadet "faction" (in the only joint meeting they actually succeeded in holding with the Trudoviks), was designed to avoid a premature conflict with the government and the Tsar. In a meeting on 26 April with the Trudoviks and members of other opposition groups the Kadets strove to prevent a clash over the content of the oath which had to be taken by all deputies, and which referred to the Tsar as an "Autocrat". To avoid a confrontation on this issue the Kadets persuaded the meeting to declare that it did not believe that in this context the word "Autocrat" implied an unlimited monarchy.[20]

Soon afterwards, the Kadets again found it necessary to restrain the Trudoviks. The chief task of the first week of Duma activity was the working-out of a reply to the Tsar's speech at the Winter Palace, when he had extended a formal welcome to the new Duma deputies (27 April). It had been generally anticipated that the "Reply to the Speech from the Throne"[21] would be presented to the Tsar by a deputation of Duma members. However, by 7 May, it became clear that the deputation would not be received, and that instead the Duma's considerations would be presented to the Crown by the President of the Council of Ministers. This was widely interpreted on the left as an insult and a provocation, and might well have led to a head-on collision with the government. However, Miliukov successfully persuaded the Trudoviks to avoid taking any rash steps, by convincing their parliamentary group that this was a question of secondary importance – merely a matter of Court etiquette,[22] an argument reiterated by Nabokov and Novgorodtsev in the Duma.[23] Even over the question of a political amnesty – the common demand of the entire opposition – the Kadets exercised a moderating influence. The Trudoviks had adopted a truculent attitude on this issue, which the Fundamental Laws had included within the sphere of the monarch's prerogatives. The Kadets wished to respect the constitutional rights of the Crown, and proposed that the Duma should limit itself to a *request* for an amnesty in the "Reply to the Speech from the Throne". F.I. Rodichev advocated that the Chamber's appeal should be couched in moderate and respectful language, and that the Duma should ask for an amnesty "as a guarantee that in the work which has begun the Monarch will go hand-in-hand with the people".[24] However, Aladin, the Trudovik leader, adopted a threatening attitude: "The country is behind us – both town and country will stand behind us and will follow us. Our brothers in the prisons, in exile, in penal servitude, may be assured that we ourselves will take them from there ... and if not..." – at this point Aladin was interrupted by shouts of "That's enough!" from the Kadets and the deputies to their right.[25] Later, the Trudovik Kornilev demanded that the Duma should express its will through an approach to the Tsar by the President of the Duma. However, the Kadets successfully resisted this proposal, arguing that it might be interpreted as an ultimatum. G.F. Shershenevich, supported by F.F. Kokoshkin and N.A. Gredeskul, warned that "if we single out this question especially, we face a conflict" ("idĕm na konflikt").[26]

In avoiding a show-down at this stage, the Kadets were, in fact, adhering closely to the line enunciated by Miliukov at the Third Congress. During the life of the Duma Miliukov remained the party's chief authority on matters of tactics. He was now strengthening his hold on the unofficial leadership of his party – a position which was partially recognized by his appointment as deputy president of the Central Committee.[27] Although the administration had deprived him of the right to stand for election to the Duma, as a member of the Central Committee Miliukov was entitled to take part in all meetings of the party's "parliamentary" group. Indeed, he was elected as a member of its Executive Committee. Moreover, as a representative of the press he was able to obtain constant access to the Duma sittings. Miliukov later denied that he had "directed the Duma from the buffet", but even he admitted that his rôle was a large one, and that his intercourse with the deputies from the journalists' lodge was constant.[28] Moreover, the parliamentary party as a whole was too large to keep abreast of events,[29] and this also seems to have applied to the 25-man Executive Committee. Miliukov claimed that in these circumstances, effective leadership devolved upon himself and three other main leaders – Petrunkevich, Vinaver and Kokoshkin, who were all linked with Miliukov by close personal friendship and understanding.[30]

Miliukov, the son of a prominent architect, had already distinguished himself as one of Russia's greatest historians. His *Outlines of Russian Culture*[31] remains a standard work on the history of Russian civilization, and Miliukov never ceased to look at political events through the eyes of a historian. He always retained many of the characteristics of the cool, detached academic. He was no popular orator; he dominated the Kadet Party by sheer force of intellect and by his great powers of reasoning and persuasion. As a university professor, his progressive views had more than once brought him into conflict with the authorities, and had led to a spell of exile in the Balkans and a short prison term. In common with many other Russian academics he had been heavily influenced by the ideas and example of Western Europe. He was particularly deeply impressed by the English constitutional system and by the writings of the positivists August Comte and Herbert Spencer. His historical scholarship had made him well acquainted with the peculiarities of Russian development. However, he believed that the process of political evolution in Russia was essentially similar to that in the West; it had merely been held back by Russian "backwardness" and the special nature of Russian conditions.[32] In true positivist fashion Miliukov was convinced that Russia's political development was now inexorably converging with that of West European states. However, although he believed that the ultimate triumph of constitutional principles was assured, he was not dogmatic about the timetable for achieving this or the tactics which his party should adopt on the path to victory. As Miliukov himself told the party on 21 April:

> We will always undoubtedly strive for the same thing, but we must act in completely different ways, taking into account whether we are strong or weak, what circumstances we are acting in, and what forces our opponents have at their disposal.[33]

Miliukov's flexibility in matters of tactics was closely allied to a talent for effecting compromises and reconciliation within the party. Describing his rôle during the First Duma, Miliukov himself observed that in general it fell to his lot "to divine the average thoughts of a meeting and to seek conciliatory formulae".[34] Given the size of the Kadet Party and the diversity of the elements within it, this proved to be one of the chief keys to Miliukov's very great influence. At times Miliukov has been criticized for this and has been attacked for his alleged failure to provide more positive leadership. However, given the diverse, and sometimes turbulent nature of the Kadet Party at this time, it is extremely doubtful whether this kind of leadership was really a practical proposition.

Maksim M. Vinaver was an eminent Jewish St. Petersburg advocate and something of a legal authority. He was a well-known writer on legal affairs and one of the editors of the journal *Vestnik Prava* (*The Legal Herald*). In 1905 he had become deeply involved in the professional movement, and had played a prominent rôle in the Advocates' Union and the Union for Full Rights for Russian Jews. He was one of the founders of the Kadet Party and had been elected as one of its deputies for St. Petersburg.[35] Fedor F. Kokoshkin[36] (born in Poland) was a distinguished jurist, and was a visiting lecturer in constitutional law at Moscow University. He had taken an active part in the zemstvo movement, especially in the Union of Zemstvo Constitutionalists. In 1904–5 he had played a leading rôle in drafting the Union of Liberation Constitution and the so-called "Muromtsev" Constitution, which had been accepted "at its first reading" by the Fourth Zemstvo Congress.

In the Duma Kokoshkin emerged as the party's chief constitutional expert, and as a great orator and parliamentarian in the English style. However, he was primarily concerned with matters of principle and with legislative activity rather than with tactical questions.[37] Moreover, Petrunkevich, the Grand Old Man of the movement, was by now unable to keep abreast of events,[38] although he continued to enjoy immense moral authority in the party. In these circumstances the management of day-to-day tactics in the Duma appears to have been left largely in the hands of Miliukov and Vinaver.[39] According to Miliukov it was Vinaver who effectively floor-managed the Kadets, and took the main part in inter-faction diplomacy – in restraining the Trudoviks from going beyond the Kadets' "parliamentary tactics".[40] But Miliukov admits that he himself was usually the originator of tactical decisions; Vinaver's main concern was to see that they were in accordance with the party faith. "Of the two of us", said Miliukov, "I represented the concept of relativity, and the working out of tactics was usually entrusted to me".[41] But even if Miliukov was by now the "unconstituted leader of the Kadet Party",[42] he was not the party dictator, and he could still be overruled in the Central Committee[43] or in the parliamentary group. In fact, the leadership of the party seems to have retained a strong collective element. However, even before the Duma opened, Miliukov and Vinaver had emerged as the party's chief spokesmen in matters of tactics, and they continued to enjoy special authority in this field.[44]

However, if the Kadets were to gain control of tactics in the Duma, it was essential first of all to secure the appointment of their nominees to a number of key offices in the chamber. They were, in fact, successful in obtaining the election of the moderate Kadet, S.A. Muromtsev, as President[45] of the Duma, Peter Dolgorukov and N.A. Gredskul' as his deputies, and Shakhovskoi as secretary.[46] Later on, the Kadets were elected to the chief offices in almost all the Duma's legislative committees. The Kadet hegemony in the Duma was reinforced by the relatively high degree of discipline exercised by the party caucus. It is true that in an article in *Rech'* Nabokov drew attention to a number of breaches of discipline, but these appear to have been exceptions to the rule.[47] In general the party held together well, despite the defection of two members – I.V. Galetskii, who joined the Trudoviks, and N.N. L'vov, who, after disagreements over agrarian policy, went over to the Party of Democratic Reform. There does seem to have been some discontent from the rank and file Kadets in the Duma – many of whom apparently felt that the party's tactical line was too restrained. But even A.M. Koliubakin, who had a leftist reputation, spoke publicly in favour of the party's tactics, and against oppositionist elements which demanded a more radical posture.[48] In fact, Miliukov appears to have been justified in saying that although there were shades of left and right within the party, "partly as a consequence of the quickly changing position, they did not succeed in forming a firm majority and minority of the 'parliamentary group' or 'wings' of the party". The party was too concerned with struggling with its opponents to have much time for quarrels within it.[49] This appears to have been true enough in the field of party *policy* (although the question of agrarian reform provides an exception to this rule); and although there were disagreements upon tactics, they were not publicized outside the faction. But as events would show, there *was* a difference of temperament within the parliamentary party although it cannot simply be described as one of the left versus right. According to N.F. Ezerskii, a rank and file Kadet, this clash of temperaments was between the leadership and its "parliamentary" tactics and the provincial deputies, who thought that legislative work, while important, was not always enough.[50] However, this seems to have been something of an over-simplification: even among the leadership there were some differences of temperament. And even among the provincials there was a great deal of support for the leadership's general tactical line. Indeed, when at the time of the Vyborg Manifesto Miliukov and the majority of the Central Committee transcended the boundaries of narrowly parliamentary activity, provincials like Ia.Ia. Tennison and V.V. Ianovskii were among the opposition to this step. It is true that the provincial members often exerted strong pressure in favour of a more radical tactical line. On occasion this even led to the defeat of the leadership, but it never resulted in the formation of a well-defined "left-wing" within the party. And although it is true that the leadership was in general more cautious and flexible in its tactics than many of the rank and file, this is a very general feature of political parties. In all parliamentary parties the leaders tend to be more moderate than their rank and file merely by virtue of the greater responsibility devolving upon them, and their possession of information of which their followers are ignorant.

The Kadets' first major task in the Duma was the drawing up of the Reply to the Speech from the Throne. Although the address was not, strictly speaking, a party document, it was essentially Kadet-inspired. The final text approved by Duma adopted a respectful, almost Slavophile, tone towards the monarch, attacking only the bureaucracy, which had allegedly separated the Tsar from the people. In order to preserve a united front, the Duma's demands were set out only in broad terms, without entering into detail. However, in general the address[51] followed the Kadet line. It demanded universal suffrage, a ministry enjoying the confidence of the Duma, and an end to all categories of exceptional law. The address asserted that creative work would become possible only when the State Council had ceased to exist in its present form, and when the Duma had obtained control of state finances. The address went on to state the Duma's intention of working out laws on the basic civil liberties, and on equality before the law. The Duma would strive to free the country from administrative oppression, and to make its citizens responsible only to the courts. In addition, the House pledged itself to take steps to abolish capital punishment, and appealed to the Tsar to suspend the death penalty until this was done. In the field of social reform, the Duma promised to work out laws on the compulsory alienation of private and state lands, on establishing the legal equality of the peasantry, and on the satisfaction of the needs of the working class. The Duma would also carry out work on educational and tax reform and "the urgent demands of individual nationalities". Finally, the address requested the Tsar to grant a complete political and religious amnesty.

The implications of the impressive legislative programme outlined in the address were clear. The Kadets and the remainder of the opposition were preparing to make the Duma the main source of legislative initiative. This was not in accordance with the modest rôle allotted to the chamber by the Fundamental Laws. The "constitution" had, in effect, given the Duma a subordinate position in a limited monarchy. However, the chamber's legislative programme made it clear that the Duma itself wished to be at the centre of the stage. This attitude was clearly expressed by Muromtsev in his opening speech to the Duma. Amidst applause, he called upon the deputies to labour not only upon the basis of "respect for the prerogatives of the Constitutional Monarch", but also "upon the basis of the implementation of the rights of the State Duma *which derive from the very nature of popular representation*"[52] (author's emphasis). In fact, the Kadets were determined to act as if they were in a parliamentary monarchy, and while avoiding conflict with the letter of the Fundamental Laws, they clashed radically with their spirit.

In the Duma the Kadets continually refused to recognize the credentials of the ministry, and behaved as if it were the usurper of the Duma's rightful authority. The Kadets' attitude was, perhaps, most clearly expressed by Nabokov's ringing words to Goremykin on 13 May: "Let the executive power submit itself to the legislative power!"[53] This was a travesty of the "constitution", which in fact made the ministry responsible only to the Crown, and not to the Duma. But it seems to have been Kadet policy to ignore this. Later, they were to express their indignation when the ministry chose to speak in the name of the Crown in the government communiqué on the agrarian question. The Kadet attitude – and that of the bulk of the opposition – was to attempt to reduce the ministry's constitutional rôle to that of a mere executive, and to deny its claim to "exclusive union with the Supreme Power" now that the Duma was in existence.[54] Kokoshkin underlined this in a speech on 4 July, in which he accused the "executive power" of misappropriating the authority of the Tsar, and attacked it for striving "to draw the Crown into the Party struggle, and to transfer the responsibility onto the Crown".[55] In the Duma, the Kadets continually attempted to keep the Crown out of politics, and to portray its rôle as essentially similar to that of the English parliamentary monarchy. The Kadets avoided direct confrontation with the monarch – all their fire was reserved for the ministry and the bureaucracy. They had avoided a clash with the Crown over the question of the parliamentary oath, and over the question of an amnesty. And they had refused to countenance proposals for a direct approach to the Tsar over the heads of the ministry.[56] Miliukov warned the ministry about the dangers of dragging the Crown into the political struggle. This would only fan the flames of revolution, and might well endanger the very existence of the monarchy.[57]

This policy of attempting to keep the Crown out of the direct political struggle harmonized with the Kadet tactics of treating the Duma as if it were a true parliament on the English model. At the same time, by keeping the Crown out of the political arena, and by denying the ministry's right to speak in its name, they hoped to weaken the government by stranding it in a constitutional no-man's land, where it would have no direct support either from Tsar or people. The Kadet leader also apparently hoped that so long as the Crown were kept out of direct involvement in the political battle, it might still be open to rational argument, and might be induced to favour a responsible ministry. The Kadets had adopted a respectful attitude to the Crown in the Reply to the Speech from the Throne, and they continually attempted to portray themselves as moderates and to depict their programme as the only peaceful way out of the crisis. While clashing with the ministry, they constantly denied that they were violent revolutionaries or that they supported violence. It is true that they refused to condemn revolutionary terror categorically[58] (as Stakhovich had proposed in the Duma), taking the view that the government's own use of force was primarily to blame for revolutionary violence. But Nabokov hotly denied that this meant that the Duma supported terror. This was the opposite of the truth. "In reality, is it not the whole sense of the Duma address to indicate those routes by which freedom and justice ('*pravo*') may be achieved peacefully and lawfully?"[59] Nabokov asked.

In fact, far from supporting violence, the Kadets continually attempted to suggest – primarily for the benefit of Russia's "ruling spheres" – that the fulfillment of their demands was the only way of avoiding a bloody revolution. This line of argument – which was fundamental to Kadet tactics in the Duma – was perhaps most clearly expressed by Miliukov in an article in *Rech'* on 10 May.[60] He began by attacking the "revolutionary illusions" of the Bolsheviks and the extreme left, and suggested that the absence of true parliamentarism was the chief accomplice of such illusions. More importantly, he openly accepted the comparison of the Kadets with the French Gironde, in so far as it was a moderate party threatened by two extremes. And he went on to make significant analogies with the English and French revolutions:

> If, at the time of the first English revolution absolutism "by God's grace" could have honestly put its signature to the demands of the parliamentary majority of that time for a constitutional monarchy, the logical development of the English Revolution would have stopped at the triumph of the Presbyterians; the affair would not have got as far as the victory of the republican tendencies of the Independents, nor the struggle of Cromwell with his "Saints", when the latter, by the sharpness of their "levelling" tendencies, filled the English man in the street with "bourgeois" fear for his property and called forth a military dictatorship with his passive support. In just the same way, at the time of the great French Revolution, the logical development of events would scarcely have led to the same results – to republicanism and military dictatorship – if an honest agreement had been possible between Louis XVI and the constitutional monarchists, if the relations of the Crown and the émigrés and their hopes of an internal conspiracy, supported by foreign help, had not brought the suspicious democrats of France to the highest stage of irritation and distrust.

This was a clear avowal by Miliukov that the Kadets were opposed to further revolutionary outbreaks, and desired a relatively moderate outcome of the struggle between government and opposition. At the same time it was a carefully calculated appeal to the ruling circles – and in particular to their instinct of self-preservation. Miliukov's message was clear – they must either make concessions to the Kadets, or run the risk of being swept away by a revolutionary tide. But this article was not an overture to the ministry, which it roundly condemned, and portrayed as mere puppets of leaders behind the scenes. It was an appeal over their heads to the monarch and the Court to come to terms with the Kadets before it was too late.

Although the Kadets' attitude towards the Crown was one of restraint, and even respect, their relations with the ministry swiftly worsened as its true nature became clearer. The virtual refusal of an amnesty, the continuation of government repression, and the ministry's initial failure to submit any serious legislative programme to the Duma engendered increasing resentment in the chamber. When, on 13 May, Goremykin finally condescended to visit the Duma for the first time, he did so only to underline that the government had no intention of giving way to the representatives' chief demands.[61] It is true that his speech did contain some crumbs of comfort. Goremykin proclaimed his willingness to consider a reform to establish civil equality for the peasantry, as well as a reform of local government. He announced that the ministry was currently working out bills on local justice, peasant passports, the legal responsibility of officials and tax reform. But the "Prime Minister" utterly outraged the opposition by his provocative statement on the land question: "The Council of Ministers", he said, "considers it its duty to proclaim that the solution of this question on the foundation proposed by the State Duma is unconditionally *impermissible*". And he haughtily reminded the Duma that such matters as a responsible ministry, the abolition of the State Council, the question of an amnesty and the use of the exceptional laws were outside the competence of the Duma. The latter part of Goremykin's statement was strictly speaking true, but the House was profoundly antagonized by the ministry's intransigence in the face of its demands. In particular, they were affronted by his categorical statement that compulsory alienation of agricultural land was "impermissible", a declaration which, certainly at this stage, he had no constitutional authority to make. Even Count Geiden, one of the leaders of the moderate right, found both the tone and content of this speech deplorable.[62] The vast majority of the Duma, including the Kadets, went further. By an overwhelming majority they passed a resolution of no confidence in the government, and demanded its resignation.

From this point on the relations between the ministry and the Duma deteriorated rapidly, and the left-wing deputies grew restive. Despite the vote of no confidence, the ministry refused to resign, and merely carried on as if nothing had happened, making no real concessions to Duma opinion. As time went on, rumours about the imminent dissolution of the Duma became more and more persistent.[63] Meanwhile, the government continued to strengthen its position in the country by savage punitive methods, which were sanctioned by the widespread use of exceptional laws. The representations of the Duma were ignored. For example, despite a Duma interpolation the government went ahead with a number of political executions in Riga. In the Duma, ministerial spokesmen agreed that the exceptional laws were imperfect, but they continued to defend them on the grounds that they were the only instrument available to them at present; the only alternative was revolution.[64] On 19 May Stishinskii and Gurko reiterated Goremykin's opposition to compulsory alienation and put forward alternative proposals based on the purchase of land by the existing Peasant Bank, the promotion of migration, and the building of a more individualistic agricultural system.[65]

Against this background it is not surprising that a mood of despair seems to have spread throughout the Duma. In the early days a note of relative confidence had been present in the Kadet press.[66] But now all this had changed. According to Vinaver, after the news of the Riga executions (17 May) many Kadet deputies began to feel like disbanding, returning to the provinces and explaining the impasse in the Duma to the electorate.[67] There was even talk of issuing a Duma communiqué to the people. However, at a meeting of the Kadet parliamentary party the idea of any such appeal to the nation was turned down:

> After careful consideration, the impossibility of a communication of the Duma to the population with manifestos of any kind was finally clarified, since this would have deprived the Duma of the possibility of making use of the much more powerful means of struggle which it has at its disposal, in the form of legislative activity. The faction therefore agreed that it should maintain contact with the general mood in the country by means of the introduction into the Duma of bills which meet the demands of the population, and which provide the possibility of responding to the critical questions troubling the country.[68]

Although the faction also decided that its members should make more of an effort to go out and propagandize in the country, the general import of its decisions is clear. It continued to support the basically parliamentary tactics of the leadership – tactics which continued to avoid a head-on constitutional confrontation, and strove to keep for as long as possible, within strictly legal channels. And although stress continued to be laid upon the importance of agitation in the country, it would later be admitted that this task had fallen into the background.

The Kadets' only answer to the deadlock after 13 May was to push on regardless with their legislative programme. A series of bills was presented to the Duma.[69] Only one of these – a bill for the abolition of the death penalty – actually completed all its stages in the Duma. However, several other bills – on the inviolability of the individual, civil equality and freedom of assembly – were introduced into the House, and were passed on to Duma committees for further consideration. A number of other legislative proposals were prepared for the Duma and, although formally introduced, did not find time for discussion (on the freedom of societies and unions, and the freedom of conscience and of the press). Meanwhile, bills on universal suffrage and zemstvo reform had either been worked out, or were being drafted, by the Central Committee or the parliamentary party. Moreover, a group of Kadets were responsible for introducing the "Memorandum of the 42", which outlined the fundamental propositions of a radical agrarian reform. This was subsequently forwarded to an agrarian committee for further consideration (it was not yet strictly speaking a bill nor even a formal draft of fundamental propositions).

The legislative work of the Duma proceeded rather slowly. The provisions of the Laws of 20 February were at least partly to blame for this. According to the law the ministry bore the primary responsibility for working out detailed legislative proposals. Properly speaking, the Duma was initially empowered to formulate only the fundamental propositions of a proposed law. The ministry was then given a month in which to decide whether it was willing to draft a detailed bill. The Duma could undertake this work only if the ministry refused to do so.[70] In fact, the Kadets did not adhere strictly to the spirit of this arrangement: their bills were passed straight into committee immediately after the completion of the debates in the Duma, and their fundamental propositions had been communicated to the ministry.

At first there was no formal challenge to the ministry's right to take the initiative in drafting detailed legislation. The Kadets argued that the ministry's prerogatives did not preclude the Duma from setting up committees merely for the preliminary examination of the fundamental propositions of proposed legislation.[71] But in reality they did not confine themselves to this limited task. In fact, if not in theory, they were almost indistinguishable from full-fledged legislative committees. There can be little doubt that this conflicted with the spirit of the laws of 20 February. However, the restrictions and delays prescribed by the "constitution" might well have led to the build up of dangerous tensions and frustrations in the Duma. In the circumstances the commissions acted as a valuable safety-valve by providing the Duma with a programme of constructive activity.[72]

The Laws of 20 February were not the only factor which slowed down the work of the Duma. The deputies themselves undoubtedly shared some of the responsibility for this. A large number of deputies – especially those from the Trudovik group – were unable to control their addiction to undue speechifying. At times this almost brought the Duma's activity to a full stop. The most notorious case was that of the debates on sending the "Memorandum of the 42" (regarding agrarian reform) into committee. Over 100 deputies demanded the right to speak, and these debates lasted a total of three weeks. The Kadets must accept their share of the blame for this, although many of their leaders realized the threat it posed to efficient legislative activity.[73] The work of the Duma was slowed down still further – especially in the second month of the chamber's existence – by a stream of interpellations to the ministry, mostly from the Trudoviks: 379 had been tabled by July, and these too unleashed a spate of oratory. However, in all fairness, it should be remembered that these were not normal times. Although the revolutionary movement was on the wane, the country was still suffering from the effects of recurrent disturbances and savage government reprisals. The atmosphere remained supercharged with tension. In the circumstances it was not surprising that it was difficult to carry on with calm effective legislative work. And although the Kadets cannot escape a share of the blame for the relatively slow pace of legislative work in the Duma they were not primarily responsible. Indeed, they constantly strove to make the Duma an effective legislative body by keeping it to the rules of parliamentary procedure. For example, they successfully persuaded the House to restrict the time available for interpellations to particular days and hours, thus leaving time for legislative activity.[74]

However, the Kadets' efforts to create a businesslike legislative assembly were increasingly undermined by the attitude of the Duma's left-wing. After 13 May, the Trudoviks became more difficult to restrain, and their informal alliance with the Kadets increasingly broke down. Their attacks upon the government grew more and more violent. The Kadets, also, severely attacked the ministry, repeatedly calling upon it to resign, but they kept within the bounds of "parliamentary" behaviour. However, the Trudoviks were now increasingly coming under the influence of the extreme left. Within the Duma a Menshevik faction of 17 had been formed, which constantly encouraged the Trudoviks to adopt more radical tactics. Meanwhile, from outside the chamber, the Bolsheviks were attempting to wean them away from Kadet influence, and convert them to the idea of an extra-parliamentary armed uprising. Because of all this the Trudoviks were becoming increasingly ready to challenge the limits set by the "constitution" and to turn to the people for support. For example, when the ministry refused to drop its right to a month's delay in the case of the bill to abolish the death penalty, the Trudovik Anikin demanded that the House should ignore the "constitution" and pass the bill immediately.[75] Only the Kadets' insistence that this would be a mere resolution and serve no purpose, prevented the chamber from taking this risky step. Meanwhile, the representatives of the government were subjected to increasing barracking and obstruction in the Duma. When the Chief Military Procurator, Pavlov, who bore special responsibility for the use of courts-martial under the exceptional laws, attempted to address the Duma on 19 June, he was silenced by aggressive shouts and hubbub.[76] On 22 June, after a deputy had been beaten up by the police, the Trudovik leader Aladin even went so far as to threaten the ministers with physical violence if the incident was repeated.[77]

The Kadet response to such behaviour was, on the whole, negative. Nabokov reacted to Aladin's threats by demanding respect for the Duma, and by deploring attempts to leave the constitutional path.[78] It is true that after 13 May, many rank and file deputies began to call for a tougher line with the government. However, the Kadet leadership refused to abandon their relatively restrained tactical approach. Despite their earlier criticism of the Duma, the Kadet leaders were increasingly coming to regard it as a real parliament and they resisted attempts to shift the centre of the struggle outside the Duma. When a large number of Trudoviks supported the Socialist-Revolutionary inspired "draft bill of the 35",[79] on the agrarian question – a project which suggested that the Duma was incompetent to work out an agrarian law, and transferred the centre of the work to local committees, the Kadet leaders hotly opposed this.[80] Miliukov, meanwhile, was toying with the idea of adopting a more cautious tactical line. In an article in *Rech'* on 30 May,[81] Miliukov said that although it might appear that government intransigence made legislative work hopeless, this was not his own view. It was wrong to expect from a month "what only *years* [author's emphasis] can give". A more or less protracted period of parliamentary work was needed to re-educate the public and the ruling circles. The very existence of the Duma would be the key factor in achieving this:

> It seems to us that the simple fact of the presence, here in the middle of Petersburg, of lawful representatives of the Russian people, is capable of producing a revolution in the conceptions of the Court and of the whole country.

As the weeks and months passed, the idea of the Duma as a force to be reckoned with would grow. The moderate tactics of the Duma majority were more dangerous to the government than revolutionary methods: "The Government has begun to fear the Duma only since it saw that it would not succeed in enticing it to extremes." He claimed that the government was already morally defeated, and that even conservative newspapers were beginning to favour a Kadet ministry – including *Novoe Vremia* (*New Times*), which was close to ruling circles. Miliukov had clearly not abandoned his hope of influencing the Court and the "ruling spheres". But at the same time, he now argued that parliamentary government could grow gradually of its own momentum – by the growth of the Duma's moral authority and by the increase of its powers upon the basis of precedent as in England. "There is no greater force", he said, "than the power of accomplished facts, and in the tactics of the Duma majority, each accomplished fact opens the way to the next". Moreover, in true nineteenth-century liberal-positivist fashion, Miliukov suggested that history was on the side of the Kadets:

> We know where the general course of life lies and are boldly directing our rudder into its chief fairwater. What we have already done, while moving by this route, guarantees our success in what still remains to be done. In this knowledge, in this assurance, lies the secret of our success.

These were not the words of the uncompromising radical Miliukov has sometimes been accused of being. Here he clearly contemplated an evolutionary solution of the crisis lasting months or even years – much longer than anything he had directly suggested at the Third Congress, and at the same time he had laid stress on the value of moderation. But as it turned out, the life of the Duma was already half-complete. The remainder of its existence would be measured not in years or even months, but in weeks. The dénoument of the crisis was already fast approaching.

Discussions on the formation of a new ministry

The month of June marked a temporary upswing in the fortunes of the revolutionary movement in the country. There were widespread agrarian disturbances, mutinies in the armed forces and a weakening of the position of Russian credit. The rising tide of revolution was not without its effect. Miliukov's attempts to appeal over the heads of the government to influential circles in the bureaucracy and at Court (and ultimately to the Tsar himself), now met a certain amount of tangible success. General D.F. Trepov, the Palace Commandant at Peterhof, a man very close to the Tsar, now began to make overtures to the Kadet leaders. Trepov had previously been one of the leaders of the reactionary party at Court, and the military strong man of the "Bulygin" ministry in 1905, when he had possessed very great influence. Moreover, it was rumoured, falsely as it turned out, that he still retained his earlier authority, acting as a kind of dictator behind the scenes. Trepov now seems to have lost his nerve, and to have come to see concessions to the opposition as the only way to avoid revolution – the very argument which the Kadet leaders were themselves putting forward. Izvolskii later suggested that Trepov's overtures to the Kadets were not sincere. In his view the Palace Commandant, "the soul of the reactionary party", was involved in a policy of provocation. His main concern was to thwart any attempt to get a moderate coalition ministry, and he calculated that the best way to do so was to support a Kadet ministry:

> He calculated with good reason that such a cabinet at the very outset could not fail to enter into a violent conflict with the Emperor. He would then be able to appeal to force, establish a military dictatorship, and abrogate the charter.[82]

However, it is difficult to accept Izvolskii's rather confused account of this affair:[83] other ministerial memoirs shed quite a different light upon it. Gurko depicts Trepov as having given up the idea of keeping power for the bureaucracy, and as being prepared to turn to the Kadets to save the royal family from the revolution.[84] When Trepov later heard of the dissolution of the Duma, his reaction was one of sheer panic. "This is terrible! We shall have all St.Petersburg here in the morning."[85] Again, after the dissolution had clearly succeeded, Trepov permanently lost favour at Court.[86] Other evidence points in the same direction. According to Kokovtsov, Trepov had, in the early days of the Duma, broached the idea of a responsible ministry to him – and received a negative response.[87] Moreover, during the period of "negotiations", Trepov's brother, A.F. Trepov, had warned Kokovtsov about the Palace Commandant's plans. According to A.F. Trepov, his brother had exclaimed, "All is lost, and we must save the Emperor and the dynasty from an inevitable catastrophe!"[88] Trepov's disposition to panic is confirmed by Witte, who records that much earlier, Trepov, having lost his nerve, advocated the alienation of private land to save the country from revolution.[89] He had also acted as an intermediary in Kovalevskii's attempts to obtain the modification of the Fundamental Laws,[90] which suggests that he continually toyed with the idea of making concessions to the liberals.

The thesis that Trepov was acting under the influence of panic gains still further support from Miliukov's account of his own dealings with Trepov. According to Miliukov, in the middle of June, he was approached by Lamarck, an American journalist acting as an intermediary for Trepov, and was invited to meet the Palace Commandant. Petrunkevich apparently received a similar invitation, but refused to take part in clandestine talks without the approval of the Kadet group. However, Miliukov decided to meet Trepov on his own initiative, without telling the faction. His encounter with Trepov took place on about 13–15 June,[91] in the "Kiuba" restaurant. Opening the conversation, Trepov stressed that he was not a politician:

> he was a plain soldier, but he was deeply devoted to the Sovereign, and the desire to disentangle the present difficulties had made him a politician against his will ... the difficulties, in his opinion, were exceptionally great. But that was why the measures for overcoming them must also be exceptional. When one's house was on fire then there could be only one choice: either to be burnt in it, or to risk a leap from the fifth storey, even at the risk of breaking one's legs. An appeal to the Kadets seemed to the General to be just such a risky but inevitable leap.[92]

Miliukov told Trepov that the root cause of the present crisis was "the belatedness and indecisiveness of the inevitable concessions".[93] He went on to explain the fears of the liberals, and their fundamental distrust in the sincerity of the concessions made so far. He reminded the General that "the very principle of the new régime remains undefined, and officially unrecognized". Trepov, however, insisted that the concessions which had been made were final. "But", he added, "it is necessary to take into consideration what difficulty we have in defending the line we have taken, the influential circles that insist on a rejection of the chosen route, and with what stubbornness they do so." "However that may be", responded Miliukov, "wide layers of society know nothing of this. They see only the consequences of the struggle behind the scenes, those constant zigzags which remove any possibility of trusting the firmness of the chosen course."

Miliukov insisted that public confidence in the government could not be restored by half-measures. If the authorities wanted a solution to the crisis, they should agree to a Kadet ministry[94] and accept its programme in full. As a first step there should be a general amnesty, abolition of the death penalty, and the removal of the exceptional laws, followed by a purge of higher officialdom and a radical reform of the State Council. Trepov made no objection to most of what Miliukov said, although he suggested that the State Council would, in any case, follow any government of the day, and that its reform was therefore not important. But on the question of an amnesty, he dug in his heels. A partial amnesty was possible, but "a complete amnesty, including bomb-throwers would meet the most decisive opposition. It is impossible to leave wild beasts at liberty". Concerning the remainder of the Kadets' demands, Trepov made no real objections.⁹⁵ He agreed with the Kadets' basic proposals on the question of land reform (although he wanted the difference between a "just" valuation and the market price of land to be made up by the state). But he insisted that the principle of the reform should be announced to the people by an imperial manifesto, "as a special act of (imperial) favour". Trepov went on to demand a list of possible candidates for the ministry. Despite Miliukov's reluctance to discuss this at this stage, the General jotted down his observations on certain candidates. At the same time he made a note of the Kadets' chief demands.

Miliukov was soon involved in further talks – this time with members of the cabinet – and he naturally assumed that they were a continuation of this earlier conversation. But in fact, the ministry had not even been directly informed of Trepov's initiative – and it certainly did not share his interest in a Kadet government. According to Kokovtsov, after 13 May the cabinet had decided in principle that the Duma would have to be dissolved; only Izvolskii had raised fundamental objections.⁹⁶

The Tsar had fully agreed with the cabinet, and constantly displayed his impatience at the government's failure to take any positive action in this matter. Support for a dissolution came even from the moderate ministers, "who thought that the Government should fall in line with the new trends provided these did not fundamentally contradict the newly published laws, and the prerogatives of the Tsar".⁹⁷ Both reactionaries and moderates were determined to resist compulsory alienation, the abolition of the Fundamental Laws in favour of a parliamentary régime, and the seizure of all power by the people. According to Kokovtsov, he first gained an inkling of Trepov's plans only between 15 and 20 June, when the Tsar told him that:

> I have heard from certain sources that matters are not so bad as one might gather from the Duma speeches, and that if we only wait patiently, and don't get nervous, the Duma is sure to get down to work, and see for itself that the state machine is not so simple as it first believed.⁹⁸

Although the Tsar went on to stress that his own opinion was different, Kokovtsov was alarmed. He immediately suspected Trepov, and warned Stolypin to watch him carefully. "The position held by Trepov", he told Stolypin, "is completely unclear to me, but the Sovereign trusts him absolutely, and he can be either an active ally, or a covert but dangerous opponent".⁹⁹ At about the same time (15–20 June) the Tsar showed Kokovtsov a "curious document" containing suggested candidates for a cabinet dominated by the Kadets and headed by the moderate Duma President, S.A. Muromtsev.¹⁰⁰ Kokovtsov warned the Tsar against accepting any such schemes – it would lead to a monarchy of the English type, for which Russia was not ready. Instead, he advocated a dissolution and a revision of the electoral law. However, the Tsar denied that he had decided upon such a cabinet, and said that until he did so decide, "do not believe it if you hear that I have already made this leap into the unknown".

During Kokovtsov's next audience with the Emperor (22–27 June) the Tsar set his doubts at rest:

> I can tell you now in perfect composure that I never intended to embark upon that distant and unknown journey which I have been so strongly advised to take. Now I can tell you that your opinion was supported by nearly everyone with whom I talked on this subject. I have no more misgivings, nor have I ever really had them, for I have no right to renounce that which was bequeathed to me by my forefathers, and which I must hand down to my son.[101]

It seems clear from all this that Trepov was acting on his own initiative without the support, or connivance, of the ministry as a whole. Indeed there is no evidence that he had the support of any of the ministers for his action. Izvolskii, the most liberal of the ministers, denied all knowledge of any negotiations at this time by Trepov.[102] Meanwhile, however, Izvolskii himself was making a separate attempt to come to terms with the Duma. He seems to have believed that the Kadets were, in essence, moderates, and seems to have been impressed by their claim that they were not violent revolutionaries. To this extent the Kadet leaders' policy of relative moderation seems to have enjoyed a certain degree of success, as it had already had in the case of Trepov.

In the second half of June the Kadets' "parliamentary" tactics were for the first time threatening seriously to inconvenience the government. When, on 19 June, Stolypin was compelled to ask the Duma to approve exceptional credits for famine relief, it soon became clear that the House would not be prepared to hand over the sum demanded by the government. Instead, it became clear that it would use its limited control over state finances to restrict the appropriations to a lower figure. According to Izvolskii, this deadlock was one of the factors which drove him to take action.[103] His first step was to sound out some moderate liberals, and the results convinced him that an understanding with the Duma was possible. Together with the former Kadet, N.N. L'vov, he drew up a memorandum to the Emperor, suggesting that the Duma was not essentially revolutionary, and that the Kadets were basically moderates driven to extremes by government intransigence. The memorandum[104] called for a coalition ministry, including both bureaucrats and public men, in order to end the present stalemate. Once again Muromtsev was proposed as premier, but in this list, Stolypin was kept at the Interior (otherwise Muromtsev should hold this office as well as the premiership). Shipov should be included, and V.D. Kuzmin-Karaiev (Party of Democratic Reform) should be Minister of Justice. Miliukov should also be brought in owing to his very great influence: "His entry into the Ministry might even be unavoidable, for he would become the most vigorous defender of the Government against the attacks of the extreme left", said the memorandum. This suggests that Miliukov's declarations of opposition to revolution had not been without their effect. Izvolskii's next step was to approach the Tsar,[105] who listened "with great benevolence" although he did make serious objections to the

Foreign Minister's arguments: "In his eyes, the Duma was entirely dominated by a most dangerous spirit, and resembled a revolutionary meeting rather than a parliamentary assembly." However, he did give his approval to exploratory talks with the individuals named by Izvolskii, with a view to the formation of a *coalition* cabinet. On the other hand he did not commit himself to any definite course of action. Izvolskii now went ahead with his plans, contacting both Muromtsev and Miliukov through A.S. Ermelov, the Minister of Agriculture.[106] Meanwhile, Stolypin, who had also associated himself with Izvolskii's initiative, was carrying on parallel talks, although it seems doubtful whether he was prepared to make as many concessions to the liberals as Izvolskii.[107]

According to Miliukov, between 19 and 24 June, he was invited to take part in conversations with Stolypin.[108] From Miliukov's earliest account of this meeting it is clear that he mistakenly considered it as a continuation of his earlier interview with Trepov. Miliukov relates that[109] he was first approached by a court official (i.e. Trepov) "to take part in the composition of a ministry.... After this preliminary conversation, my interview with P.A. Stolypin took place, proceeding in the presence of one other high official" (i.e. Izvolskii). "I was, of ourse, bound to suppose", wrote Miliukov, "that the Minister of Internal Affairs was informed about the preceding conversation I have referred to, and the continuation of the 'talks' on the same subject proceeded on the grounds of the proposal made to me earlier". Once again, he felt that the question being discussed was one of either a coalition or a K.D. cabinet. As before, Miliukov insisted on a Kadet ministry and the acceptance of its policies, but Stolypin skated over questions of programme, clearly finding Miliukov's demands unacceptable. According to Miliukov, Stolypin did not make it clear whether the issue being discussed was one of a Kadet cabinet or whether it was one of a coalition ministry. And Stolypin "finally lost interest in the conversation as soon as it became clear to him that he was not wanted".[110] Initially, Miliukov put Stolypin's attitude down to personal ambition,[111] and there may have been some degree of truth in this. But a more likely reason for Stolypin's attitude may have been Miliukov's categorical demand for a Kadet ministry, in the mistaken belief that this was the chief point at issue. But in fact, neither Stolypin nor Izvolskii had ever proposed such a cabinet: their project was for a coalition cabinet, and even this had not been definitely approved by the Tsar. Izvolskii denied that Stolypin was motivated by personal ambition, and claimed that his colleague was alienated by the Kadets' apparently doctrinaire position. According to the official government version of this incident, Miliukov's categorical demands were communicated directly to the Tsar, "with the conclusion of the Minister of Internal Affairs that the fulfulment of the desires of the Constitutional-Democratic Party could affect the interests of Russia only in the most disastrous fashion, which conclusion was immediately entirely approved by His Majesty".[112]

Events now began to move in a different direction. According to Shipov, an exceptionally reliable witness, on 25 June he received an invitation to take part in talks with Stolypin. N.N. L'vov told him that Stolypin was now thinking of dissolving the Duma, but he felt that it must be done by a government led by a public man enjoying wide confidence in society (i.e. Shipov). At first Shipov declined even to discuss this proposal, but when he received a summons to attend an audience with the Tsar, he decided to see Stolypin after all.[113] At this meeting with the minister (27 June) Shipov reiterated his opposition to a dissolution. Nevertheless, Stolypin proceeded to put forward proposals for a coalition cabinet which would include himself, Izvolskii and the present ministers of the Court, War and Marine. However, Shipov insisted that members of the Kadet Party must be brought in – otherwise a coalition cabinet would have no hope of gaining the confidence of the Duma. Stolypin strongly opposed this – only Izvolskii seemed prepared to countenance such a step.

Before his audience with the Tsar (28 June), Shipov asked Count Geiden to sound out Miliukov and discover his views on a coalition cabinet. According to Shipov, Miliukov rejected the idea, and insisted on an exclusively Kadet cabinet.[114] Meanwhile, Shipov contacted the President of the Duma and attempted to obtain his support for a cabinet led by Muromtsev himself, and composed of Kadets and members of the moderate parties to their right. Muromtsev's personal reaction to Shipov's proposals was favourable, but he did not feel that he could change the established policy of his party. Furthermore, said Muromtsev, "Miliukov already feels himself to be Premier". At the same time he expressed doubts about whether such a cabinet could last long given the present mood of the people. Revolutionary outbreaks were inevitable, and the government would have to repress them, thus losing popular support.[115]

At his audience with the Tsar on 28 June[116] Shipov once again opposed a dissolution. And presumably as a result of his approaches to the Kadets, he now attempted to persuade the Tsar that the only way out of the constitutional deadlock was a cabinet from the majority of the Duma – arguing that once in power the Kadets would be prepared to compromise on many of their policies, including those on an amnesty, the agrarian question and Polish autonomy. As the leader of the new government Shipov, once again, suggested Muromtsev, rather than Miliukov. According to Shipov the Tsar seemed favourably impressed by his arguments – an impression confirmed by Izvolskii on the following day.[117] However, Stolypin showed his displeasure, and Shipov became convinced that he would oppose the idea of such a cabinet. For the next week the Tsar's attitude to Shipov's proposals seems to have continued to be favourable, but according to Shipov Izvolskii later told him that by 5 July, the Emperor's mood had changed decisively.[118]

This date ties up with the fact than on 4 July, the government was given a pretext for dissolving the Duma. On 20 June, the ministry had published a "governmental communiqué" on the agrarian question, rejecting, as well as distorting, the Duma's demand for compulsory alienation of land, and outlining the government's own proposals.[119] On the initiative of Kuzmyn-Karaiev (Party of Democratic Reform), the Duma decided to issue its own counter-communiqué to the people. This question was originally raised in the Duma on 26 June, and came up for discussion on 4 July.[120] The communiqué, as drafted by the Duma's agrarian committee,[121] was by no means an inflammatory document. It outlined the work of the Duma on the agrarian question, and pointed out that no law could be passed without its consent. It insisted that the House would not retreat from the policy of compulsory alienation. However, it reminded the people that "only a carefully considered and properly worked out law can give the people the necessary land". And it went on to express the hope "that the people will peacefully and tranquilly await the conclusion of its work on the promulgation of such a law". In the Duma, the Kadets consistently portrayed the communiqué chiefly as a means of pacification – of preventing agrarian outbreaks in the face of government intransigence over the agrarian question – even though this aroused Trudovik opposition.[122] Of the Kadets, only Petrazhitskii felt that the communiqué was an act endangering the existence of the Duma.[123] Kokoshkin stressed that the promulgation of such a communication was in no sense a revolutionary action.[124] But nevertheless, as the Duma's first official communiqué to the people, it was something of a dangerous precedent from the government's point of view.

On the day of the debate Stolypin appeared in the ministerial lodge, and confined himself to taking down details of the proceedings.[125] According to Vinaver, until this point the Kadet leaders had paid little attention to the communiqué, and at first attributed no special significance to it.[126] Miliukov denied any knowledge of it until 5 July, when he heard of Stolypin's visit.[127] However, Stolypin's behaviour instantly made Miliukov sense danger. He quickly explained his fears to Petrunkevich, and insisted on measures to at least render the text harmless.[128] However, the Kadet faction refused to back down and rejected serious changes by a large majority.[129] Nevertheless, Petrunkevich stuck to his guns. On 6 July he introduced a revised text into the Duma, which was slightly more moderate in tone, and underlined the fact that the purpose of the communiqué was to pacify the people.[130] The Kadet rank and file followed Petrunkevich's lead, but the parties to their left refused to accept this climb-down. In the end, the communiqué was passed by Kadet votes alone – the Trudoviks abstained, and the Mensheviks and the extreme right opposed. The communiqué was, in fact, voted for by only a minority; the figures were 123 for, 101 abstentions, and 54 against. This, for the first time, made it clear to everyone that the Kadets' control of the Duma was by no means as absolute as had been generally believed. This was bound to weaken the Kadets' bargaining position vis-à-vis the government.[131]

However, if Shipov's account is to be credited, the apparently favourable mood at Peterhof had changed already. Moreover, according to Izvolskii, on about 4 July, Goremykin – who had never favoured overtures to the Kadets – told the Council of Ministers that the Duma was to be dissolved. A ukaz had already been prepared and only required the Tsar's signature. Izvolskii, the most ardent supporter of an agreement with the Duma, says that he felt there was nothing to be done but resign once the ukaz was signed and portrays Stolypin as also being prepared to resign.[132] The Tsar's approach to Stolypin, offering him the premiership, took Stolypin by surprise, according to Izvolskii. And he only accepted as a duty, and on condition that the reactionary ministers Stishinskii and Shirinskii-Shakhmatov were dismissed, and that he retained the right to add members from the chambers according to his earlier plan. Gurko confirms that Goremykin was primarily responsible for the decision to dissolve the Duma, whereas Stolypin would have preferred to have continued as before, having replaced the two reactionaries by Duma members. However, he did not try to stop the dissolution.[133] Izvolskii's assertion that Stolypin was an opponent of dissolution does, in fact, seem to be too categorical. We have already seen that he had earlier supported it provided it was carried out by a coalition cabinet. Moreover, his appearance in the Chamber on the crucial day of 4 July does suggest that he was building up a case against the Duma. But his desire to remove the most reactionary cabinet ministers (which he later put into effect), and his negotiations with the moderate right immediately after dissolution, suggest that his approach was different to that of Goremykin. It suggests that he would still have preferred to have seen the dissolution carried out by a coalition cabinet. And it also explains why he may have had severe doubts about Goremykin's proposal for a dissolution, since there is no evidence for believing that the latter ever supported bringing public men into the cabinet.

When the Tsar asked Stolypin to accept the premiership on 7 July, the dissolution had apparently already been decided upon,[134] and Stolypin probably fell in with this, while hoping to mitigate its effect by pressing on with plans for a mixed ministry immediately afterwards, thus making the best of the situation. And whatever his misgivings, he was never a man to flinch from grasping unpleasant nettles. On the night of Saturday/Sunday 8–9 July, while the deputies were absent on their weekend recess, the Duma was surrounded by troops and police, and the dissolution was proclaimed.

The bubble of the Kadets' expectations had burst. For a time, a Kadet ministry had seemed a real possibility, but now any such prospects had vanished. Miliukov portrays himself as having been sceptical about the Kadets' chances of forming a ministry, but admits that following the Duma President's conversation with Shipov, Muromtsev confidently awaited a call to Peterhof. He claimed that the President of the Duma asked to see him, and demanded point-blank: "Which of us shall be Premier?"[135] Miliukov says that he did not take the chances of a Kadet cabinet seriously, and replied, "In my opinion neither of us will be" ("po-moemu nikto ne budet"). In any event, said Miliukov, if the question should arise, it would be for the party to decide, and he knew, although he did not say so to Muromtsev, that the party would not have chosen the Duma's President. But to placate Muromtsev, he said half-jokingly, "for my part, I renounce the premiership with pleasure, and present it to you". Muromtsev was transported with delight. "In those days he, obviously completely seriously, awaited an invitation from Peterhof." On the other hand, Miliukov denied Muromtsev's assertion to Shipov that "Miliukov already feels himself to be Premier". However, the evidence indicates that Miliukov did in fact, take the chances of a Kadet ministry seriously, and he must have known that he would be an obvious choice to lead it. Gessen, his close collaborator in *Rech'*, asserts that at this period, "the hope that the alternative which stood to the fore – the dissolution of the Duma or a Kadet ministry – would be decided against a dissolution, passed with Miliukov into a direct certainty".[136] On 3 July, Miliukov even called an extraordinary meeting of the Kadet group to inform it about the course of the negotiations and to obtain its instructions.[137] This apparently was regarded as so urgent that it could not wait even until the next regular meeting on 5 July.[138] Miliukov later claimed that this meeting was held primarily to allay rumours about a Kadet ministry, and said that the faction was more concerned about the dangers of dissolution than the possibility of a Kadet ministry, which was regarded as less probable.[139] However, N.F. Ezerskii, a rank-and-file Kadet deputy, evaluates the affair differently. According to Ezerskii there were growing rumours about the imminent appointment of a Kadet cabinet: "The question was brought up for discussion in the Duma faction of the K.D. Party; the summons of Muromtsev was expected from day to day."[140] The foreign press, meanwhile, reported the confidence of the Kadets, and also generally believed that a Kadet ministry was on the way. On 3 July the *Times* correspondent reported that, "I must say that the facts compel me to infer that the formation of a Constitutional Democrat cabinet is a question of hours".[141] Miliukov's *Rech'* also gives the impression that he himself took the prospects seriously. He continually made use of the paper to lay down his terms and to reject the idea of a coalition ministry. After the issue of the agrarian communiqué came to the fore Miliukov did become seriously agitated over the possibility of a dissolution.[142] However, he hoped that the unfavourable attitude at Court would prove to be temporary, and he admitted that the prospects of a Kadet ministry had earlier been regarded as tangible. In an article published in *Rech'* on 9 July, Miliukov wrote that, "the swings of the political pendulum at Peterhof continue to take place at an angle of 180 degrees. Not so long ago, the pendulum swung to the left, and all but reached the point against which is written: a ministry from the majority".[143]

There can be little doubt that Miliukov and at least a large part of his party believed that they had a real chance of coming to power. However, in fact their prospects were probably poor. In the final analysis, the crucial factor was bound to be the attitude of the Tsar, and there is little solid evidence that he would have been willing to accept a parliamentary régime, unless he had been compelled to do so by overwhelming public pressure. At most he may have been prepared to contemplate a mixed ministry of bureaucrats and public men. The only real evidence to the contrary is his apparently favourable response to the ideas of Shipov. And even this was based upon the latter's arguments that the Kadets would have been prepared at this juncture seriously to compromise on their policies – an assertion which Miliukov,[144] and the balance of evidence, contradicts. Moreover, the Tsar's apparently favourable attitude to Shipov's arguments does not prove that the Emperor was prepared to agree to them all. Shipov may well have exaggerated the warmth of his reception. One of the Tsar's characteristics was to give those he received this kind of impression, whatever his own ideas. He consistently avoided unpleasantness at his audiences. Miliukov relates that the Tsar told Kliuchevskii: "Now they say Shipov is a clever man. But I pumped him the whole time and told him nothing."[145] Shipov may well have misinterpreted the Tsar's response. Although he is usually a reliable witness, at times his judgement was affected by a tendency to ingenuousness and naiveté, which is clearly discernible in his *Memoirs*. These weaknesses were shared by his informant, Izvolskii, who also seems to have suffered from a certain degree of credulity.[146] In fact, Shipov may merely have set off another bout of the Tsar's chronic indecisiveness about fixing a final date for dissolving the Duma. The Tsar's diary clearly reflects the apprehension at Court about the possible consequences of a dissolution. On 9 July the Tsar wrote: "It is done! Today the Duma was closed. At lunch after Mass many strained faces were noticeable."

It is of course, possible that if the dangers had been much greater, the Tsar's indecision might have resolved itself by capitulation to the Kadets; but given his basically reactionary sympathies, it seems unlikely that he would have done so except under the most overwhelming pressure. It is true that Trepov had considerable influence upon the Tsar, but even he failed to persuade him of the desirability of a Kadet ministry. Moreover, like Shipov, Trepov seems to have imagined that the Kadets could be persuaded to water down their programme. In an interview given to Reuters (25 June),[147] in which he reiterated his support for a Kadet ministry, Trepov again opposed a complete amnesty, and this time he also rejected expropriation of land. He even suggested that if a Kadet ministry failed, force could be resorted to and this casts doubt upon the consistency of his support for such a government.

Moreover, the serious plans of Stolypin and Izvolskii never went beyond a mixed ministry of bureaucrats and public men. Although it seems possible that Izvolskii was prepared to go further,[148] his views were certainly not shared by his more influential colleague. Stolypin was no mere reactionary, and would probably have liked to have come to an agreement with the Duma on his own terms; but he was not prepared to give in to what he considered to be the Kadets' extreme demands. Indeed, his arguments were not entirely unreasonable. According to Sir Donald Mackenzie Wallace, Stolypin told Sir Arthur Nicholson of his conversation with Miliukov during the discussions about a new cabinet.

> In the course of the conversation, he (Stolypin), perceived that he (Miliukov), was inordinately ambitious, and anxious to become Prime Minister, but that what he demanded would never be accepted by the Emperor. Among these conditions was the adoption of the Kadet programme as a whole, including a general amnesty, the abolition of a capital punishment, etc. Besides this, an Imperial Manifesto should be published, clearly declaring that the old régime was at an end, and an entirely new order of things introduced.
>
> M. Stolypin, who believes himself to be pretty well acquainted with the views of the revolutionary Socialists, explained that these gentlemen were waiting for such a state of things as M.Miliukov recommended, and as soon as they found it, they would make desperate efforts to overthrow all existing institutions and establish in their place the Socialist republic. What could M.Miliukov do as Prime Minister at that most critical moment when words would be of little avail? M.Miliukov had his answer ready, he would shoot

down the anarchists freely, more freely than Stolypin himself. To this, Stolypin replied that a bureaucrat might employ measures of this type, but that a leader of the Kadet Party, who had insisted on a general amnesty, the abolition of capital punishment, and who professed to be a humanitarian liberal in the widest sense of the term, could not use such energetic measures without completely discrediting himself and his party. Within a month he would be compelled to resign, and would disappear in a deluge of execration launched at him by his former admirers.[149]

There was much justice in this argument. It is probably true that, whether Miliukov was prepared to put down the revolutionaries or not, he would have found it difficult to justify repression. And, indeed, in 1917 the Kadets were in fact swept away by the revolutionary tide – although so, for that matter, was the Tsarist régime. But on the other hand, 1906 was not 1917 and the threat from the left was less acute. Moreover, there was a great deal in the Kadets' arguments that only reform could really pacify the country. Here the crucial factor was the agrarian question. In 1906–8 the Kadets insisted that without expropriation of land, the revolution could not be stopped. And although they were proved wrong in the short term, 1917 proved their arguments to be correct. The peasants' land-hunger was probably the greatest single factor in the success of the Bolshevik Revolution. If it could have been assuaged in 1906, it is possible that the Revolution might never have succeeded;[150] the peasantry might well have become a basically conservative class. This was, of course, also to be Stolypin's own objective in his reforms aimed at the dissolution of the commune. But this was essentially a gradualist solution, and unknown to Stolypin, the time was already too short for success. However, Stolypin was probably correct in feeling that a Kadet ministry was a risk. The Kadets' legislative solution of the land problem would have taken some time, during which the masses might have grown restive, and repression might have become inevitable. It seems, therefore, probable that, given the circumstances of the time, the Kadets were too categorical in their demands for the immediate establishment of civil liberty on Western lines.

If the government was not prepared to meet the Kadets' unabridged demands, and if the Kadet proposals were not entirely realistic in a revolutionary situation, can their leaders be blamed for the impasse which resulted from this situation? Should they have been prepared to agree to a coalition ministry and a compromise policy? It would, of course, be easy to simply condemn Miliukov for undue dogmatism in his "negotiations" with the bureaucracy, but it should be remembered that these negotiations were not merely between individuals. Miliukov's general political conduct and his articles in the press do not identify him as a dogmatist: indeed, they suggest that he was one of the most realistic of the Kadet leaders. But it is very doubtful whether, if he had been prepared to seriously compromise on his party's policies, he could have carried the Duma with him, especially the left. It is even doubtful whether he could have obtained the support of the whole of his own party. Indeed, according to Miliukov, there were many in the party who, when informed of his negotiations, looked upon them as "a dangerous political adventure connected with compromise of a shady character".[151] This does not necessarily mean that they had lost hope of influencing the Crown by appeals to the monarchy's enlightened self-interest. But they probably envisaged a capitulation by the Tsar as a result of overwhelming public pressure rather than secret negotiations with a ministry they had condemned. Even Petrunkevich shared this distaste for such secret negotiations and refused to meet Trepov.[152] However, although Miliukov felt it inadvisable to tell the Duma faction beforehand,[153] it subsequently, somewhat grudgingly, approved his actions.[154] But at the same time they reaffirmed his demand for the unconditional acceptance of the entire party programme.[155] "Given the mood of the faction", said Miliukov, "the question of the permissibility of a cabinet of mixed composition could not even be raised".

It is equally doubtful whether, if the Kadets had entered the cabinet as junior partners, they could have kept their popular support. Unless a coalition government had adopted the chief planks of the Kadet policy, the party might well have been discredited. Miliukov made this clear in his interview with Trepov:

> If it is impossible to do without serious compromises, then an appeal to my political group is useless. It will bring no benefit to the Government, for in these conditions we would be unable to lead the country behind us, while for the group taking such an equivocal role upon itself, this would be political suicide.[156]

Moreover, Stolypin never gave any indication that a coalition cabinet would have gone very far to meet the opposition's demands. Miliukov records that during his interview with Stolypin the latter seemed disinclined to discuss programmes. The moderate right later gained the same impression in their own negotiations with Stolypin. After the dissolution, Stolypin continued to negotiate with public men – with Geiden, Stakhovich, N.N. L'vov and Shipov.[157] However, they reluctantly came to the conclusion that the government only wanted new *personnel* and was not interested in their programme. Count Geiden complained that they had been invited to fulfil "the role of hired children with ladies of easy virtue".[158] While affirming his support for Stolypin's plan for bringing public men into the ministry, the Tsar told the Premier that he "was against a whole group of persons coming forward with some kind of programme".[159] On the other hand, the public men were not prepared to enter the cabinet taking its programme on trust. And if this was true of the parties to the right of the Kadets, it is hardly surprising that the latter felt unable to trust the government.

The truth was that the opposing sides were too far apart to come to an agreement. Society distrusted the government to such a degree that it felt that only a ministry responsible to the Duma could be trusted to carry out radical reform. On the other hand, although the Tsar and Stolypin might have agreed to include public men in the ministry in a subordinate position, they were unwilling to concede a government dominated by representatives of the Duma majority.

Quite apart from their other objections, they feared that a Duma ministry might be the prelude to a violent revolution led by the extreme left. Only two things could have ended the impasse which had been created by the mutually exclusive positions taken up by the two sides, and made possible the development of a genuinely liberal régime in Russia. On the one hand, much greater popular pressure upon the Tsar and the bureaucracy might have compelled them to accept a Kadet ministry whether they wanted it or not. Although such a ministry might have had severe difficulty in maintaining order, it is not impossible that it might have succeeded in doing so. On the other hand, the government itself could have taken the initiative in inaugurating an era of reforms, without releasing its grip on the maintenance of order. Now, for a long time, the Kadet Party's predecessor, the Union of Liberation, had looked for reform from above, and only the frustration of this hope, and with it, a growing distrust of the government, had driven it, and the Kadets into a posture of radical opposition. It is therefore probable that a sincere programme of liberal reform from above would have gradually moderated the Kadets' distrust of the government, and made some form of co-operation with it feasible in the future. This concept, indeed, probably lay, initially, at the root of Stolypin's own subsequent reforms, but unfortunately they did not go far enough to restore the liberals' confidence. And although he initiated a programme of radical agrarian reform, his rejection of compulsory alienation of land condemned him to adopt the rigorous repressive measures which earned him the enmity of the opposition. What was needed was a man prepared to follow in the footsteps of Alexander II. But even if Stolypin had been such a man, he could not have obtained the support of Nicholas II, who had neither the vision nor the inclination to stand at the head of a revolution from above. Stolypin instead, tried to stand at the head of an *evolution* from above, but this was now too little and too late.

The Kadets and the left

If public pressure upon the old régime had been great enough in 1905–6, the bureaucracy might have been forced to capitulate, and this might, perhaps, have happened provided all opposition parties had been united behind the Duma and the demand for a responsible ministry. But unfortunately this was not to be. The extreme left – the Bolsheviks and Socialist-Revolutionaries – were still hoping for a revolution in the immediate future, and feared that the Duma might lead the people away from revolutionary paths in favour of "parliamentary illusions". However, following the decisions of the Stockholm Social-Democratic Congress, the Mensheviks dropped their earlier boycottism, and belatedly entered the Duma as a means of struggle with the old régime. There they caused considerable embarrassment to the Kadets by infiltrating the Trudovik group and inciting them to move to the extreme left. But as time passed their initial distrust of the Kadets diminished. Plekhanov, in an article in *Kurier*, opposed extremist attacks upon the Kadets: "while calling for using the Duma as an instrument for influencing the masses, he argued against strenghthening the position of the

Reaction by rash attacks on the liberal opposition".[160] Moreover, the Menshevik-dominated Central Committee of the Social-Democratic Party passed a resolution calling for the mobilization of the workers behind the Duma, and supporting the demand for a responsible ministry, as the first stage in disarming the Reaction. The Mensheviks were, then, increasingly coming to favour the idea of a revolution around, and in support of, the Duma.

However, the Bolsheviks refused to be bound by the Stockholm decisions, and continued to hope for a revolution over the head of, and independent of the Duma. Although, in theory, they still argued that the forthcoming revolution would be a "bourgeois" one, they were already stretching this concept to its limits. They were determined to accept nothing less than the "democratic dictatorship of the proletariat and the peasantry" – a completely democratic republican régime under their own leadership. They hoped that this would shorten the path to the socialist revolution. The last thing they wanted was that the bourgeois revolution should stop halfway, leading to a conventional Western-type bourgeois régime, followed by a long trek towards the socialist revolution. Moreover, they already hoped that their own brand of revolution might spark off a proletarian rising in the West, making possible an early socialist revolution in Russia. Accordingly, their main concern during the Duma was to attack Kadet "treachery": the supposed willingness of the liberals to do a deal with the autocracy, and stop the revolution halfway. At the same time, they were afraid that Kadet "parliamentary" methods might distract the attention of the public – and especially that of the peasantry – away from the idea of a violent revolution. Consequently, their chief concern during the sittings of the Duma came to centre around attempts to detach the radical peasant deputies – the Trudoviks – from Kadet influence. They felt that the Trudoviks should be encouraged to struggle against the conciliatory policies of the liberals and to link up with the revolutionary forces outside the Duma.

Although the Kadets disagreed with the Mensheviks' belief in violent revolution, they welcomed their increasing signs of moderation. They welcomed Plekhanov's article in *Kurier*,[161] and felt that in so far as the Menshevik line supported the Duma, it to a certain extent coincided with their own. But they realized that the Bolsheviks were dividing the opposition, and undermining the Duma's authority. The Kadets consistently tried to wean the Bolsheviks away from "Blanquism". Miliukov warned them that "a face to face struggle of the revolutionaries with the Government is hopeless and utopian if it poses itself the task of the direct victory of the revolution", and stressed the value of parliamentary methods.[162] *Rech'* claimed that Bolshevik policies would lead to a military dictatorship. The Kadets would not help them to bring this about: "The Duma will be an instrument for the pacification of the country, or it will be nothing, but it will not be an instrument for the establishment of chaos."[163] Miliukov said that the Menshevik attitude made a united opposition front a real possibility and it was very important that it should defeat Bolshevik arguments: "The success of the whole liberation movement may, in certain conditions, depend on a timely solution [of this dispute]", he claimed.[164] These words were to prove prophetic. Despite the arguments of the Kadets and the Mensheviks, the Bolsheviks retained considerable influence. Most important of all, their support was particularly strong among the workers of the capital, where the Bolsheviks had a majority on the Social-Democrats' City Committee. The Duma was therefore largely deprived of the backing of the St. Petersburg proletariat, which was in a position to exert uniquely powerful and immediate pressures upon the government. Instead of encouraging the workers to support the Duma, the Bolsheviks continually warned them against falling a prey to "parliamentary illusions". At political meetings in the capital they consistently showered the Duma "majority" with abuse,[165] and when the dissolution took place the proletariat remained silent.

The grassroots

This absence of adequate public support was accentuated by the Kadets' failure properly to organize their own support. At the Third Congress the party had fully recognized the need to develop their agitational and organizational work, in order to obtain support for the Duma, and to prepare the ground for future electoral activity.[166] The Kadets had decided to strengthen their cadres of lecturers and propagandists, increase their publishing activity, and improve party organization. They had proposed to establish closer co-operation between the pro-Kadet press, and backed a demand for a popular Kadet newspaper. During the existence of the Duma, attempts were made to put these plans into effect. For example, the Central Committee founded a "Bureau of the Progressive Press" to distribute articles by prominent Kadets, and information about the Duma to the provincial newspapers. According to A.V. Tyrkova, within a month of its inauguration, 18 local papers had joined the scheme.[167] Although the chief headquarters of the Central Committee had now shifted to Petersburg, the centre of Duma activity,[168] a special section remained in Moscow. This continued to carry on party agitational work, sending out orators and lecturers to the countryside. At the same time, Moscow remained the chief centre of Kadet publishing activity, which was now largely directed at keeping the people informed of events in the Duma. Later the Kadet party group itself established a special committee to maintain the links between the Duma and the people.[169] Moreover, Kadet deputies repeatedly made trips into the provinces, in order to keep in touch with their constituents.[170] Pavel Dolgorukov, the president of the Central Committee, took the lead in stressing the need for agitational activity. In a report to the Moscow section of the committee,[171] he admitted that sending out speakers from the centre was inadequate, and proposed to establish eight regional centres for training party activists and directing them to the localities. Unfortunately, however, this scheme had little success – only the regions based upon the capitals obtained any real significance.[172] Moreover, although plans were made to improve local party organization by sending Central Committee members on a series of visits to the provinces, they were never put fully into effect.[173] Proposals for the publication of a popular daily newspaper also failed to get off the ground despite talk of transferring Moscow's *Narodnoe Delo* (*The People's Cause*) to the capital and using it for this purpose.[174] The fundamental reasons for this seem to have been the party's lack of sufficient financial resources, and the peasantry's inability to pay for newspapers.[175] Indeed, finances continued to be in their previous parlous state. In early May, a meeting between the Central Committee and representatives of local party groups[176] revealed the continuing weakness of Kadet organization and finances. Membership dues continued to be largely unpaid, and there was continuing fear of persecution in the countryside, despite partial recognition of the party by the government.[177]

But repression and lack of funds do not seem to have been the only considerations limiting the Kadets' extra-parliamentary activity. Perhaps still more crucial was the fact that once the Duma was in existence, the party's efforts were directed away from the work of agitation at the grassroots and towards legislative activity. The Central Committee itself later admitted that:

> During the period of strenuous activity in the First Duma, almost all the available energies of the Central Committee were concentrated on serving the Party faction in the Duma. As a consequence of this, the tasks of extra-parliamentary activity and agitational work moved willy-nilly into the background ("vtoroi plan").[178]

This once again illustrates the Kadets' tendency to gravitate towards narrowly parliamentary tactics. The party took no real steps to evolve a clear plan of extra-parliamentary action in the event of a head-on collision with the old régime. They certainly made no attempt to persuade the people to support the Duma by revolutionary methods: quite the reverse. As A. Smirnov noted with gratification in an article in the *Vestnik* (*The Herald*): "The deputies who have travelled observe that in many places their tour (of the countryside) has significantly pacified an agitated peasantry which was expecting agrarian disturbances."[179] But while the Kadets may have had some success in persuading the peasants not to use violent methods, there is no evidence that they proposed anything very concrete in their place, except for giving vague exhortations to the peasantry to support the Duma.

Now it is true that on 4 June, the Central Committee had considered what action to take if the Duma were dissolved or sent home on a premature recess.[180] The drawing up of a manifesto to the people was foreshadowed, and a majority of speakers decided in favour of refusing to leave the Duma if it was dissolved. But although this gained the support of Vinaver, and even Struve, it became clear that a substantial body of opinion was opposed to abandoning strictly parliamentary tactics. Miliukov, Nabokov and Petrazhitskii feared that such gestures had no hope of practical success, and argued that they would benefit the revolutionaries rather than the Kadets. Although the more radical viewpoint gained majority support and was apparently endorsed by the Kadet deputies,[181] it was clear that the leadership already entertained serious doubts about the idea of transcending the limits or purely parliamentary activity – even in the event of a dissolution. And it is significant that although the committee decided to draw up a manifesto to the people, this had not been done by the time of the Duma's demise. Vinaver's explanation is that since it was expected that a dissolution would take place while the House was in session, it was felt that it would not be difficult for the deputies to work out a manifesto on the spot. But in view of the fact that Miliukov was given the task of drawing up the appeal, it seems likely that the delay is partly explicable by the leadership's reservations about the proposed manifesto.

The Vyborg Manifesto

When the dissolution actually took place, the Kadets were completely unprepared for it. It came like a bolt from the blue, while the Duma was dispersed for the weekend, and the Tauride Palace was immediately surrounded by troops and police. Owing to police activity, the Kadets could not meet in the capital, and instead, together with the Trudoviks and Mensheviks, they proceeded to Vyborg in Finland. There they took the initiative in issuing a manifesto to the people, condemning the government's action and calling on the nation to adopt tactics of passive resistance against the authorities – to refuse to pay taxes or to provide recruits for the army. The Kadet leaders were conscious that their action might be construed as illegal and revolutionary, and might lead to their being deprived of electoral rights.[182] But on the basis of certain technical defects in the royal manifesto proclaiming the dissolution (the lack of a ministerial counter-signature and of a date for new elections) they argued that the document was itself illegal. Consequently, said Miliukov, "it was fully constitutional to construct a manifesto on the principle of passive resistance".[183] Moreover, the Kadets believed that the government action was an assault on the very principle of popular representation. The manifesto alleged that during the coming months the government would struggle against the popular movement in order to obtain a subservient Duma, and "if it is successful in completely crushing the popular movement it will not convoke any Duma whatsoever".[184]

Miliukov now cast aside his earlier doubts about an appeal to the people, and became a firm supporter of the manifesto – indeed, he himself composed the original draft.[185] It is true that Vinaver felt that his text was not strong enough,[186] but the fact remained that Miliukov spoke in favour of the manifesto and defended it in the parliamentary party.[187] Miliukov's reaction was probably partly due to a feeling that the party leaders had been deceived by Stolypin. Their fears of a dissolution had been put at rest by a special request from Stolypin to be permitted to address the Duma on Monday, 10 July.[188] The members had then peacefully dispersed to their homes for the weekend. The dissolution had then struck them like a thunderbolt, and probably threw the Kadets off balance, especially since it came after a period when hopes of a Kadet ministry had been high. Their reaction seems to have been an emotional one rather than a carefully thought out response. At first, at a preliminary meeting of Kadet leaders in Petersburg, Vinaver noted no disagreement about the need to take such measures: "This seemed – especially in the first minute – so elementarily simple and natural, a minimum, a sorry minimum, of the action remaining at our disposal."[189] But it is noteworthy that, in the evening of the 9 July, and also on the following day, the manifesto as it stood[190] met stubborn resistance from a large number of Kadets.[191] Indeed, at a poorly attended party meeting on the morning of 10 July, more than half the Kadet deputies spoke out for rejecting Part 2 of the manifesto – the section proposing passive resistance. They argued strongly that only the first part, which contained a protest against the dissolution, should be retained.[192] The dispute spilled over into the general sessions of the former Duma deputies, and again the Kadets split into two almost equal groups opposing or supporting Part 2. Both the Central Committee and the provincial deputies were divided on this issue. Kokoshkin, Vinaver and Dolgorukov led the defence of Part 2, while Petrazhitskii, Gertsenshtein and Mukhanov opposed.[193] It was clear that although the party had never officially preached legality at all costs, and had never rejected methods of passive resistance, the attitudes expressed in the Central Committee on 4 June were not dead. According to Vinaver, there were few Kadet deputies who opposed Part 2 in principle. Only Petrazhitskii, the prime exponent of purely legal tactics, had spoken against the proposed measures on the ground that they were unconstitutional. Vinaver claimed that the opposition centred around the alleged impracticability of the measures proposed.[194] And indeed, the records confirm that the opponents of passive resistance seriously doubted whether it would gain enough popular support. However, the evidence[195] suggests that they also had serious objections in principle against unconstitutional methods, and feared giving any assistance to the cause of the revolutionaries. Ia.Ia. Tennison (Lifland province) asserted that "the rejection of constitutional struggle signifies the downfall of constitutionalism in Russia". Gertsenshtein proclaimed that to accept the proposed measures "would for some of us mean betraying our previous convictions". V.V. Ianovskii, echoed by G.P. Iollos, opposed working out any joint measures with the left parties: "It is necessary to let each party retain the possibility of acting according to its own principles", he declared. And he joined with Medvedev in fearing that Part 2 might alienate the moderate right and the industrialists. Although the opponents of Part 2 also criticized the proposed measures as weak and ineffectual, this was no left-wing opposition demanding more radical methods. While advocating the dropping of Part 2, they did not propose stronger action. The extreme left was represented only by S.P. Frenkel', who alone seemed to look forward to a decisive, violent revolutionary struggle. And he strongly favoured the manifesto as a means of crippling the government.[196]

Later, however, Vinaver asserted that the defenders of Part 2 had never looked upon the proposed measures as a practical proposition. They too had doubted whether the measures could be implemented, and whether the people were ready to support them.[197] But they felt that they had a duty to show the people how their rights should be defended in principle. The manifesto was designed as:

> the best possible legacy of the Duma to future times, and the most effective warning to any governments, present and future, in the case of encroachments

on the rights of the people. The sword of Damocles – even when it had not fallen – was frightening.[198]

However, despite Vinaver's later rationalization of the Kadets' actions at Vyborg it is difficult to believe that the manifesto was meant to be merely a gesture of this type. Vinaver's account is weakened by, for example, Kokoshkin's assertion on 10 July that "the practical significance of the proposed measures is by no means as insignificant as many seem to think".[199] Furthermore, at the time, Vinaver had supported a political strike, and proposed that the deputies should deliberately court arrest in St. Petersburg. "The State Duma in prison", said Vinaver, "would serve as a good symbol and stimulus for social struggle".[200] This was not the tone of a man who felt that the organization of opposition was impracticable. This is not to say that the Kadet supporters of the manifesto were confident of the success of their efforts. While stressing the need to organize the people, Pavel Dolgorukov admitted that "the dimensions of the movement we will call forth ... are unknown".[201] But the evidence does suggest that they did hope to call forth a massive response among the people centred around the idea of passive resistance to the government.

However, the party could hardly enthusiastically implement a manifesto with which so many of its members disagreed. Indeed, it was only after a second faction meeting on 10 July, and a defence of Part 2 by Miliukov, that the faction was induced to accept it – a large minority having agreed to be bound by the decision.[202] Miliukov even suggests that it was only the intrusion of the Vyborg Governor-General, demanding that the sitting be closed, which induced the Kadet "opposition" to vote for the manifesto as it stood.[203] In the light of all this, it is not surprising that soon after the manifesto had been signed, the Kadets began to retreat from it. At first the Kadet press seems to have still hoped for a popular movement which might defeat the government. On 13 July, *Rech'* clearly looked forward to another October:

> The time is obviously drawing near when love for the motherland and a feeling of elementary self-preservation will force the whole country to act as one, as it did in those days when society went, in reality, from one victory to another: from the Ukaz of 12 December to the Rescript of the 18 February, and from this Rescript to the Manifesto of 17 October.

The apparent equanimity of the public to what had happened was misleading. The public had merely halted in contemplation, while "within it a force is building up which is already unconquerable".[204]

However, despite the use of such bold language the Kadets in fact took no concerted steps to put the manifesto into effect. Immediately after Vyborg they set off for a conference at Terioki in Finland (13–15 July), to discuss their tactics and the holding of a Fourth Party Congress.[205] Although the conference had no power formally to drop the call to passive resistance, according to Miliukov this was the actual outcome of the conference.[206] Vinaver denies that the conference's decisions were directly related to Vyborg. But he admitted that the distribution of the manifesto was not discussed – the general view was that it would be distributed anyway (by the press, etc.), without any great efforts on the part of the Kadets. Accordingly, it seems clear that, at the very least, no real attempt was to be made, in practice, to put the manifesto into effect. Meanwhile, the Kadets were carrying on discussions with the Trudoviks – who were also present at Terioki – on the question of setting up a Duma committee to take charge of organizational activity among the people. However, the Kadets opposed resurrecting Duma activity in the present circumstances, and held that the people themselves knew how to carry on the struggle. An organizing committee was unnecessary.[207] Any prospect of the manifesto being put into effect now depended primarily upon the appearance of more or less spontaneous public resistance. But despite isolated revolutionary outbreaks, including disturbances in the forces at Sveaborg and Kronshtadt, the people, for the most part, remained silent. The Bolsheviks continued to oppose any action in support of the Duma, and the nation as a whole seems to have grown weary of the continual struggle. In the circumstances it became increasingly clear that there was no longer any possibility of implementing the manifesto. On 2 August, the Central Committee convened a meeting with representatives of local party branches to discuss this matter.[208] Pavel Dolgorukov, earlier a supporter of the manifesto, now felt bound to propose a change of tactics. A few speakers, such as the leftist A.M. Koliubakin, were still prepared to attempt to carry out the Vyborg proposals. But the majority finally recognized that this was impossible given the present mood of the country. It became clear that the manifesto's reception, both in the party and in the country, had been so mixed that no concerted action was possible. Some of the delegates such as Golovin (Moscow), reported that the party's supporters were opposed to it in principle. Others revealed deep divisions of opinion in their localities.

But even if the party members had unequivocally supported the manifesto, they would have had great difficulty in putting it into effect. The delegates were forced to admit that local party organization was in a weak condition, and in no condition to organize a vast campagn of passive resistance. Despite the party's huge vote in the elections it became clear that the Kadet giant had feet of clay: "All our activity was only during the elections", admitted Koliubakin. "It was brilliant, but in all other cases – shameful inactivity." Other speakers confirmed this, and described the weakness of party cadres and their indadequate financial position. Doubts were also expressed about the extent to which Kadet voters were prepared consistently to support the party. Vasil'ev even admitted that "in the Samara province there is no Kadet Party in the proper sense ('chistyi vid')". It had been supported "only as a programme-minimum" in view of the boycott by the socialist parties. Against this background of disunity and disarray, it was impossible to give further support to the manifesto. Although the Fourth Party Congress in September approved the action which the Kadet deputies had taken, it recognized that the proposals of the manifesto were now impracticable. It is true that it simultaneously recognized passive resistance *in principle*, but this was merely blowing the bugles of advance to cover up the fact of retreat.[209] The party had already disassociated itself from violent revolutionary methods at its Second Congress in January 1906. Later, during the life of the Duma, it had gravitated towards exclusively parliamentary tactics. The tragicomedy at Vyborg pushed the Kadets still further along the path of moderation. Despite their defiant reaffirmation of the principle of passive resistance at their Fourth Congress, the Kadets henceforth adopted tactics of strict legality. Following the Vyborg fiasco they gradually lost faith in the people, and increasingly became a party of the electoral *pays légal*. In fact, they were fated to become the moderate, legal opposition party for which their temperament had always suited them.

During the Second Duma (February–June 1907) the Kadets sought to avoid confrontation with the government and became disenchanted with the provocative behaviour of the extreme left, which now included a Bolshevik faction. On 3 June the Stolypin government once again dissolved the Duma, while a new electoral law ensured that in future the chamber would be dominated by conservative and reactionary parties. During the Third Duma (1907–12) the Kadets became still more moderate and pragmatic, abandoning their remaining ties with their former "allies on the left". In the country as a whole, the party's grassroots activity declined, while the Kadet leadership gave priority to legislation and tactics in the State Duma.

Notes

1 The Duma sessions were held in the Tavricheskii Dvorets – the Tauride Palace in St. Petersburg.
2 It is noteworthy that when Stolypin adopted a firm but respectful approach to the Duma, the Kadets were much less extreme in their attacks upon him than upon other ministers. See, e.g., Gosudarstvennaia Duma, *Stenograficheskie otchëty*, Vol. II, pp. 1125–41, 8/VI/1906 (This publication will hereafter be referred to as *S.O.*).
3 "Rokovaia oshibka", *Rech'*, 26 April 1906.
4 V.N. Kokovtsov, *Out of My Past*, Stanford 1935, pp. 126–7.
5 A.P. Izwolsky (Izvolskii), *Memoirs of Alexander Izwolsky*, London 1920, pp. 170–1.
6 V.I. Gurko, *Features and Figures from the Past*, Stanford 1934, pp. 459–60 (hereafter referred to as "Gurko").
7 Kokovtsov, *Out of My Past*, p. 127.
8 A.A. Mosolov, *At the Court of the Last Tsar*, London 1935, p. 140.
9 V.A. Maklakov, *Pervaia duma*, Paris 1939, p. 73.
10 Maklakov, *Pervaia duma*, p. 33.
11 N.A. Borodin, "Lichnyi sostav pervoi gosudarsvennoi dumy", in A.A. Mukhanov and V.D. Nabokov (eds), *Pervaia Gosudarstvennaia Duma*, S.P.B. 1907, Vol. 1, pp. 23–4.
12 The figure for the autonomists does not include about 40 Kadets who belonged simultaneously to the group of autonomists. Borodin, "Lichnyi sostav pervoi gosudarsvennoi dumy", p. 24.
13 This basic pattern remained much the same throughout the Duma. But by 26 June (Borodin, "Lichnyi sostav pervoi gosudarsvennoi dumy", p. 27) the Kadet faction had grown to 179 (37.4 per cent). Meanwhile a small Social Democrat (Menshevik) fraction had been formed following the arrival of a solid phalanx of S.D.s from the Caucasus. These had been joined by a small number of former Trudoviks. In the same period some Octobrists had moved to the left and, after abandoning their

formal allegiance to their party formed the nucleus of a new "Party of Peaceful Renovation".

14 Borodin, "Lichnyi sostav pervoi gosudarsvennoi dumy", p. 25, says that 25 of the non-party deputies (10–15 May), proclaimed that they were "closest to the Kadets".
15 Miliukov, "Otnoshenie mezhdu dvumia glavnymi partiiami", *God bor'by*, pp. 384–9 (*Rech'*, 29 April).
16 "Kadety v 1905–1906 gg", *K.A.*, No. 46, p. 60, 5/IV/1906, No. 131. See also: *Protokoly Ts.komiteta*, No. 20, 5/IV/1906, pt.131.1.
17 *Protokoly Ts.k.*, No. 28, 10 May 1906, para. 1 (GARF. f. 523, op. 1, d.27, l. 76).
18 See, e.g., Editorial in *Rech'*, 25 June 1906.
19 T.V. Lokot', *Pervaia duma*, Moscow 1906, pp. 274–9. ("Partiinaia peregruppirovka").
20 Lokot', *Pervaia duma*, pp. 154–6; "Parlamentskaia fraktsiia", *Vestnik partii narodnoi svobody*, No. 9, pp. 615–18; M.M. Vinaver, *Konflikty v pervoi dume*, S.P.B. 1907, pp. 8–16.
21 As Vinaver had styled it in imitation of the English model.
22 Vinaver, *Konflikty*, p. 64; Lokot', *Pervaia duma*, pp. 182–3.
23 *S.O.*, Vol. I, pp. 245–7, 8/V/1906.
24 *S.O.*, p. 25, 29 April 1906.
25 *S.O.*, p. 25, 29 April 1906.
26 *S.O.*, p. 34; 30 April.
27 "Kadety v 1905–06 gg", *K.A. (Krasnyi arkhiv)*, No. 46, pp. 60–1, 6/V/1906. See also: *Protokoly Ts.komiteta*, No. 26, 6/5, 1906, para. 1.
28 Miliukov, *Vospominaniia*, Vol. I, p. 366.
29 Miliukov, "Rokovye gody", *Russkie Zapiski*, Paris 1938–39, No. 18, p. 113; see also, "Parlamentskaia fraktsiia", *Vestnik*, No. 19, 1906, col. 1162.
30 Miliukov, "M.M.Vinaver kak politik", in *M.M.Vinaver i russkaia obshchesvennost' v nachale XX veka*, Paris 1937, p. 19. The official leadership was vested in the Administrative Section of the Committee – Petrunkevich, Nabokov, Vinaver and Kokoshkin. See: "Parlamentskaia Fraktsiia", *Vestnik*, No. 11, p. 373.
31 Miliukov, *Ocherki po istorii russkoi kul'tury*, 3 Vols, S.P.B. 1896–1901.
32 See, e.g., Miliukov, *Russia and its Crisis*, p. 550.
33 Miliukov, *God bor'by*, pp. 317–35.
34 Miliukov, "M.M.Vinaver kak politik", p. 21.
35 Miliukov, "M.M.Vinaver kak politik", pp. 5–50.
36 See M.M. Vinaver, "Tragediia russkogo parlamentariia (F.F.Kokoshkin)", in M.M.Vinaver, *Nedavnee*, Paris 1926, pp. 134–64; A.A. Kizevetter, "Fedor Fedorovich Kokoshkin", in N.I. Astrov, *K pamiati pogibshikh*, Paris 1929, pp. 9–24.
37 Miliukov, "Rokovye gody", *R.Z.*, No. 18, p. 115. Kokoshkin played a prominent part in a number of legislative commissions in the Duma. He was also a member of the party's special committee for drafting legislation.
38 Miliukov, "Rokovye gody", *R.Z.*, No. 18, p. 113. See also "IV s''ezd Partii Narodnoi Svobody", *Rech'*, 26 September 1906. The account of the afternoon sitting of 24 September during the party's Fourth Congress provides evidence that Petrunkevich's health had been poor for at least part of 1906.
39 Miliukov, "M.M.Vinaver kak politik", pp. 19–21. Although Miliukov says that he and Vinaver always stood shoulder to shoulder on the same course, in fact Vinaver tended to favour a rather bolder tactical line.
40 Miliukov, "M.M.Vinaver kak politik", p. 24; Miliukov, *Vospominaniia*, Vol. I, p. 367. Vinaver later wrote a book describing this task. See: *Konflikty v pervoi Gosudarstvennoi Dume*, S.P.B. 1907.
41 Miliukov, "M.M.Vinaver kak politik", p. 21.
42 F.J. Piotrow, *Pavel Miliukov and the Constitutional-Democratic Party* (PhD thesis, Oxford, 1958), p. 149.
43 See, e.g., "Kadety v 1905–06 gg", *K.A.*, No. 46, pp. 63–6, 4/VI/1906.

44 Miliukov had been responsible for laying down the official tactical line at the Third Congress, while earlier, in the Central Committee, Vinaver had been the chief proponent of the programme of Duma activity on which the party's tactics were based. See *OTCHËT*, pp. 51–2.
45 *S.O.*, Vol. I, p. 2. Sergei Muromtsev, a professor of constitutional law at Moscow University, carried out his duties with a dignified parliamentary style reminiscent of the democracies of Western Europe. He was mainly responsible for working out the instructions which governed the activity and procedure of the Duma.
46 *S.O.*, Vol. I, pp. 17–19, 27/IV/1906.
47 V.D. Nabokov, "K voprosu o parlamentskoi distsipline", *Rech'*, 30 May.
48 "Iz zhizni partii", *Rech'*, 19 May.
49 Miliukov, "M.M.Vinaver kak politik", p. 22. It is perhaps significant that when the parliamentary "faction" elected its committee the party "establishment" – Nabokov, Petrunkevich, etc. – triumphed while the leftist E.N. Schepkin was only narrowly elected (*Vestnik*, No. 11, p. 735).
50 N.F. Ezerskii, *Duma pervogo sozyva*, Penza 1907, pp. 106–8.
51 *S.O.*, Vol. I, pp. 239–41, 5/V/1906.
52 *S.O.*, Vol. I, p. 3, 27/IV/1906.
53 *S.O.*, Vol. I, p. 325, 13/V/1906.
54 See *S.O.*, Vol. II, pp. 1754–6, 26/6/1906, for an interpolation supported by the entire opposition and endorsed by Vinaver, Kokoshkin and other leading Kadets. See also D.D. Protopopov, "Po povodu pravitel'stvennogo soobshcheniia", *Rech'*, 24 June 1906.
55 *S.O.*, Vol. II, pp. 2000–2, 4/VII/1906.
56 We have already noted Kadet resistance to one such proposal – see p. 107. The Kadet leadership also resisted a similar proposal from M.M. Kovalevskii. See *S.O.*, Vol. I, p. 42. Later, on 26 May, two Kadets, A.G. Sipiyagin and N.A. Ogorodnikov (*S.O.*, Vol. I, pp. 661, 665) demanded an approach to the Tsar by Muromtsev to request the suspension of the death penalty. Again, on 9 June, another Kadet, I.P. Aleksinskii, made a similar proposal as a means of breaking the constitutional deadlock (*S.O.*, Vol. II, p. 1164). However, the Kadet leadership firmly resisted all such proposals.
57 Miliukov, "Duma v narodnom soznanii", *God bor'by*, pp. 372–75 (*Rech'*, 8 June).
58 *S.O.*, Vol. I, pp. 226–35, 4/V/1906.
59 "Parlamentskaia nedelia", *Vestnik*, No. 10, 11 May, p. 641.
60 "Glavnoe delo dumy", in Miliukov, *God bor'by*, pp. 347–51 (*Rech'*, 10 May).
61 *S.O.*, Vol. I, pp. 321–4.
62 *S.O.*, Vol. I, pp. 349–51.
63 See: Editorial, *Rech'*, 20 May; Miliukov, "Podgotovka gosudarstvennogo perevorota", *God bor'by*, pp. 369–72 (*Rech'*, 6 June). "Kadety v 1905–06 gg", *K.A.*, No. 45, pp. 63–6, 4/VI/1906. Also: Pavlov, *Protokoly Ts.k.*, Vol. I, No. 32, 4 June 1906 (GARF. f. 523, op. 1, d.27, ll.80–2; d.33v, ll.44–6).
64 See Stolypin's speech to the Duma on 8 June in: *S.O.*, Vol. II, pp. 1125–9.
65 *S.O.*, Vol. I, pp. 509–23.
66 For example, there had been widespread confidence that a complete amnesty would be granted. See: "Pervye shagi", *Vestnik*, No. 9, 4 May, p. 602. For Miliukov's initially relatively sanguine mood see: "Dva neprimirnykh shaga", *God bor'by*, pp. 342–4 (*Rech'*, 30 April).
67 Vinaver, *Konflikty*, p. 100. The Trudoviks were meanwhile reacting very similarly. See: Lokot', *Pervaia duma*, pp. 203–11.
68 "Parlamentskaia fraktsiia", 17 May, *Vestnik*, No. 12, col.783.
69 *OTCHËT*, pp. 56–7.
70 Savich, *Novyi gosudarstvennyi stroi*, S.P.B. 1907, pp. 84–96, Articles 55–57.
71 P.I. Novgorodtsev proposed the first commission of this type on 12 May. See: *S.O.*,

142 The First Duma

pp. 295–8. See p. 302 for Muromtsev's formal justification of the commission. He argued that Articles 5 and 6 of the Duma Statute had given the House the right of preliminary work on bills.

72 Later (on 23 May) Vinaver introduced a bill to amend the provisions of Articles 55–57 of the Laws of 20 February when he realized that they had not been incorporated in the Fundamental Laws. See *S.O.*, Vol. I, pp. 553–5.
73 See, e.g., V.D. Nabokov, "Parlamentskaia fraktsiia", *Vestnik*, No. 10, 11 May, pp. 644–5. N. Kareev, "Dumskie Rechi", *Rech'*, 2 July.
74 *S.O.*, Vol. II, pp. 1369–70, 1372–4, 15/V/1906.
75 *S.O.*, Vol. I, p. 644, 26/IV/1906.
76 *S.O.*, Vol. II, p. 1481.
77 *S.O.*, Vol. II, p. 1576. Aladin threatened to "decline all responsibility for the safety of the ministers".
78 *S.O.*, Vol. II, p. 1576–7. See also: *Rech'*, 24 May for opposition to the barracking of Gurko in the Duma.
79 *S.O.*, Vol. II, p. 672, 26/V/1906.
80 See *S.O.*, Vol. II, pp. 672–84 for the debates.
81 "Pervyi mesiats dumskoi raboty", *God bor'by*, pp. 356–62 (*Rech'*, 30 May).
82 A. Izwolsky (Izvolskii), *Memoirs of Alexander Izwolsky*, pp. 211–13.
83 Izvolskii was apparently unaware of Trepov's initiative at the time. *Memoirs*, p. 211.
84 Gurko, pp. 482–3. Izvolskii also stresses Trepov's devotion to the royal family – see Izwolsky, *Memoirs*, p. 214.
85 Gurko, p. 486.
86 Gurko, p. 493.
87 Kokovtsov, *Iz moego proshlogo*, Paris 1933, Vol. I, p. 196.
88 Kokovtsov, *Out of My Past*, pp. 448–9.
89 Vitte, *Vospominaniia*, II (Berlin edition, 1922), p. 172.
90 "Iz arkhiva S.Iu.Witte", *Vospominaniia*, Vol. II, S.P.B. 2003, pp. 460–70. See also: *Krasnyi Arkhiv*, Vol. 11–12.
91 See Miliukov, "Moe svidanie s generalom Trepovym", *Rech'*, 13 February 1909. Miliukov puts it at one-and-a-half weeks before he heard of Trepov's later interview with the press (circa 27 June). Miliukov's article in *Rech'*, 16 June 1906, makes it clear that his meeting with Trepov had already taken place by this date. See Miliukov "Rokovye gody", *R.Z.*, 1938–39, No. 19, p. 109.
92 Miliukov, "Rokovye gody", *R.Z.*, No. 19, p. 108.
93 "Moë svidanie s generalom Trepovym", *Rech'*, 17 February 1909.
94 The choice of the Ministers of the Court, War and Marine, were, however, assigned by Miliukov to the sphere of the royal prerogative.
95 This may, of course, have been partly because Trepov seems to have seen his rôle as that of an intermediary between the Kadets and the Tsar.
96 Kokovtsov, *Iz moego proshlogo*, Vol. I, p. 182.
97 Kokovtsov, *Out of My Past*, p. 138.
98 Kokovtsov, *Out of My Past*, p. 146.
99 Kokovtsov, *Iz moego proshlogo*, Vol. I, p. 196.
100 Kokovtsov, *Iz moego proshlogo*, Vol. I, pp. 196–7.
101 Kokovtsov, *Out of My Past*, pp. 148–9.
102 Izvolskii, *The Memoirs of Alexander Izwolsky*, p. 211.
103 Izvolskii is inaccurate here in saying that the Duma was supported by the State Council at this stage. In fact this only became clear towards the end of the month. Izvolskii may be exaggerating the influence of this question, since the attitude of the Duma itself became clear only on 23 June – clearly after Izvolskii's plans were already in motion. (Miliukov was interviewed at the latest on 24 June).
104 Izvolskii, *The Memoirs of Alexander Izwolsky*, pp. 181–7.
105 For Izvolskii's interview with the Tsar, see: Izvolskii, *The Memoirs of Alexander*

Izwolsky, pp. 187–90. Izvolskii dates his interview on 8 July (25 June Old Style), but his dates are, as usual, confused, and do not tie up with those from other sources.
106 Izvolskii, *The Memoirs of Alexander Izwolsky*, p. 190; Miliukov, "Rokovye gody", *R.Z.*, No. 19, p. 111.
107 According to Stolypin he took part in the talks only on the instructions of the Tsar. See *Foreign Office General Correspondence*, Series 371, Vol. 127, Document 27544.
108 Miliukov, "Rokovye gody", *R.Z.* 1938–39, No. 19, p. 115.
109 "Peregovory o k.d.kabinete", *Rech'*, 15 February 1909.
110 Miliukov, "Rokovye gody", *R.Z.*, 1938–39, No. 19, p. 116.
111 Miliukov, *Tri popytki*, p. 27. However, later in "Rokovye gody", *R.Z.*, No. 19, p. 117, he admitted that it was probably not simply egotism – Stolypin had seen himself as the indispensable saviour of the Fatherland.
112 See the communication from the "Information Bureau" in "Vecherniaia khronika", *Novoe Vremia*, 15 February 1909.
113 Shipov, Vospomonaniia, Moscow 1918, p. 446.
114 Shipov, pp. 447–8.
115 Shipov, p. 449.
116 Shipov, pp. 451–7.
117 Shipov, pp. 459–60.
118 Shipov, pp. 459–60.
119 Printed in: *Novoe Vremia (New Times)*, 20 June 1906.
120 *S.O.*, Vol. II, pp. 1953–7, 1954–2002.
121 *S.O.*, Vol. II, pp. 1955–6.
122 See, e.g., *S.O.*, Vol. II, pp. 1974–5 (Zhilkin's speech).
123 *S.O.*, Vol. II, pp. 1956–68.
124 *S.O.*, Vol. II, p. 2001.
125 Vinaver, *Konflikty*, p. 164.
126 Vinaver, *Konflikty*, p. 162. See also "Parlamentskaia fraktsiia", *Vestnik*, No. 19–20, for evening sitting of 5 July. This states that this was the first time the faction had dealt with the question of the communiqué.
127 Miliukov, "Rokovye gody", *Russkie Zapiski (R.Z.)*, 1938–39,No. 21/22, p. 103.
128 Ibid., p. 104.
129 *Vestnik*, No. 19/20, cols.1235–6.
130 "Gosudarstvennaia Duma", Supplement to *Rech'*, 7 July, p. 1.
131 "Gosudarstvennaia Duma", p. 4. See also Shmuel Galai, "The Kadet Domination of the First Duma and its Limits", in Jon Smele, *The Russian Revolution of 1905*, London and New York 2005, pp. 211–21.
132 *Memoirs of Alexander Izwolsky*, p. 192.
133 Gurko, pp. 487–90.
134 Kokovtsov, *Out of My Past*, p. 155.
135 Miliukov, *Vospominaniia*, Vol. I, pp. 394–5.
136 Gessen, "V dvukh vekakh", *A.R.R.*, Vol. XXII, Berlin 1937, p. 230.
137 Miliukov, "Rokovye gody", *R.Z.*, 1938–39, No. 20/21, p. 102; "Parlamentskaia fraktsiia", *Vestnik*, No. 18, pp. 1165–7.
138 Vinaver, *Konflikty*, p. 162.
139 Miliukov, *Vospominaniia*, Vol. I, 366.
140 N.F. Ezerskii, *Duma pervogo sozyva*, Pensa 1907, p. 74.
141 *The Times*, London, 16 July (New Style). See also: *The Times*, 10 July (N.S.), p. 5, "The Position of the Ministry".
142 See, e.g., "Priblizhenie razviazki", Miliukov, *God bor'by*, pp. 378–81 (*Rech'*, 6 July).
143 "Mezhdu 'verkhom' i 'nizom'", *Rech'*, 9 July.
144 Miliukov, *Tri popytki*, pp. 46–7.

145 Miliukov, *Vospominaniia*, Vol. I, p. 394. Stolypin's own account of this episode confirms Kliuchevskii's story. See *Foreign Office General Correspondence*, Series 371, Vol. 127, Doc. No. 27544, 13 August 1906.
146 This was later apparent in (for example) his later dealings with the Austrians over Bosnia-Hercegovina.
147 Published in *Novoe Vremia*, 25 June 1906.
148 See, e.g., "Peregovory o k.d.kabinete", *Rech'*, 15 February 1909.
149 *Foreign Office General Correspondence*, Series 371, Vol. 127, Doc. No. 27544, 13 August 1906.
150 Although it is possible that land reform would have helped prevent a Bolshevik Revolution, this does not mean that it would necessarily have made Russia safe for constitutional democracy. If, in particular, it is assumed that the Great War would have taken place even under constitutional government – and this is a matter of conjecture rather than history – then it is quite possible to argue that some form of dictatorship, although not necessarily on the *left* was its almost inevitable outcome. But more of this later.
151 Miliukov, *Vospominaniia*, Vol. I, p. 396.
152 Miliukov, "Rokovye gody", *R.Z.*, No. 19, p. 107.
153 Miliukov, "Rokovye gody", *R.Z.*, No. 19, p. 107.
154 Miliukov, *Vospominaniia*, Vol. I, p. 396.
155 Miliukov, *Vospominaniia*, Vol. I; "Parlamentskaia fraktsiia", *Vestnik*, No. 18, pp. 116–67.
156 Miliukov, "Moë svidanie s Generalom Trepovym", *Rech'*, 17 February 1909.
157 Shipov, pp. 461–79.
158 Quoted from Miliukov, *Tri popytki*, p. 68.
159 "Perepiska N.A.Romanova i P.A. Stolypina", *K.A.*, No. 5, p. 103, letter dated "July".
160 M. Martov, "Sotsialdemokratiia 1905–07 gg" in L. Martov, P. Maslov and A. Potresov (eds), *Obshchestvennoe dvizhenie*, S.P.B. 1909, Vol. III, p. 622.
161 *Rech'*, Editorial, 21 May.
162 *Rech'*, Editorial, 10 May.
163 *Rech'*, Editorial, 24 June.
164 *Rech'*, Editorial, 28 May.
165 See, For example, *Rech'*, Editorial, 11 May.
166 "III s''ezd delegatov", *Pravo*, No. 18, 1906, pp. 1682–4.
167 A.Tyrkova, "Biuro progressivnoi pechati", *Vestnik*, No. 13, 1906. Tyrkova and A.S. Izgoiev were responsible for running the bureau. For a detailed account, see: *OTCHËT*, pp. 75–7.
168 *OTCHËT*, pp. 6–7.
169 *OTCHËT*, p. 29; "Parlamentskaia fraktsiia", *Vestnik*, No. 18, p. 1163.
170 See, e.g., A. Smirnov, "Poezdki deputatov v provintsiiu", *Vestnik*, No. 18.
171 "Tsentral'nyi komitet 16 May", *Vestnik*, No. 12.
172 *OTCHËT*, p. 27.
173 *OTCHËT*, p. 26.
174 *OTCHËT*, pp. 26, 89–94 (see also "Kadety v 1905–06 gg", *K.A.*, No. 46, p. 63, 4/6/1906).
175 *OTCHËT*, pp. 90–1.
176 "Tsentral'nyi komitet", *Vestnik*, No. 10.
177 "K voprosu o legalizatsii partii", *Vestnik*, No. 15.
178 *OTCHËT*, p. 7.
179 A. Smirnov, "Poezdki deputatov v provintsiiu", *Vestnik*, No. 18, 1906.
180 "Kadety v 1905–06 gg", *K.A.*, No. 46, pp. 63–6, 4/VI/1906. See also: Pavlov (ed.), *Protokoly Tsentral'nogo komiteta 1905–11 gg*, Vol. I, No. 32, 4 June 1906, para. 7 and M.M. Vinaver, *Istoriia Vyborgskogo vozzvaniia*, Petrograd 1917, pp. 6–8 (GARF. f. 523, op. 1, d.27, ll.80–2; d.33v, ll.44–6).

181 Vinaver, *Istoriia Vyborgskogo vozzvaniia*, Petrograd 1917, p. 8.
182 Vinaver, *Istoriia Vyborgskogo vozzvaniia*, p. 10; Miliukov, "Rokovye gody", *R.Z.*, No. 20/21, p. 109.
183 Miliukov, "Rokovye gody", *R.Z.*, 1938–39, No. 20/21, p. 108.
184 "Pervaia Gosudarstvennaia Duma v Vyborge", *K.A.*, No. 57, p. 98.
185 Miliukov, "Rokovye gody", *R.Z.*, No. 20/21, p. 108.
186 Vinaver, *Istoriia Vyborgskogo vozzvaniia*, pp. 10–11; Miliukov, "Rokovye gody", *R.Z.*, No. 20/21, p. 109.
187 Vinaver, *Istoriia Vyborgskogo vozzvaniia*, p. 33.
188 Vinaver, *Istoriia Vyborgskogo vozzvaniia*, p. 9; Miliukov, "Rokovye gody", *R.Z.*, No. 20/21, p. 106.
189 Vinaver, *Istoriia Vyborgskogo vozzvaniia*, p. 11.
190 By 10 July this had been amended by a joint commission including Kokoshkin, Vinaver, two Mensheviks and two Trudoviks, although according to Vinaver (*Istoriia Vyborgskogo vozzvaniia*, p. 27) it was basically only a revised draft of the original. However, there had been some changes. For example, a call to "abstain from violence" had been dropped (see "Pervaia gosudarstvennaia Duma v Vyborge", *K.A.*, No. 57, p. 89).
191 Vinaver, *Istoriia Vyborgskogo vozzvaniia*, pp. 20–1, 29.
192 Miliukov, "Rokovye gody", *R.Z.*, No. 20–21, p. 110; Vinaver, *Istoriia Vyborgskogo vozzvaniia*, p. 29.
193 "Pervaia Gosudarstvennaia Duma v Vyborge", *K.A.*, No. 57, pp. 89–97.
194 Vinaver, *Istoriia Vyborgskogo vozzvaniia*, p. 23.
195 "Pervaia Gosudarstvennaia Duma v Vyborge", *K.A.*, No. 57, pp. 89–97.
196 "Pervaia Gosudarstvennaia Duma v Vyborge", *K.A.*, No. 57, p. 94.
197 Vinaver, *Istoriia Vyborgskogo vozzvaniia*, p. 24.
198 Vinaver, *Istoriia Vyborgskogo vozzvaniia*, p. 24.
199 "Pervaia Gosudarstvennaia Duma v Vyborge", *K.A.*, No. 57, p. 92.
200 "Pervaia Gosudarstvennaia Duma v Vyborge", *K.A.*, No. 57, pp. 87–8. Deputies who signed the manifesto served short prison sentences. They were also deprived of electoral rights and ceased to be eligible for election to the Duma.
201 "Pervaia Gosudarstvennaia Duma v Vyborge", *K.A.*, No. 57, p. 92.
202 Vinaver, *Istoriia Vyborgskogo vozzvaniia*, pp. 32–3.
203 Miliukov, "Rokovye gody", *R.Z.*, No. 20/21, p. 111. Vinaver's version is probably to be preferred since it is something of a party-authorized version of the affair. Moreover, Miliukov, who was not a member of this Duma, was not present at the general sitting of the Vyborgists.
204 "K momentu", *Rech'*, 13 July. See also: Editorial, *Rech'*, 16 July.
205 Vinaver, *Istoriia Vyborgskogo vozzvaniia*, p. 46.
206 Miliukov, *Vospominaniia*, Vol. I, p. 417.
207 Lokot', *Pervaia duma*, pp. 310–11.
208 For these discussions, see: "Kadety v 1905–1906 gg", *K.A.*, No. 47–48, pp. 112–28 and "Protokoly soveshchaniia 2–3 avgusta s predstaviteliami gubernskikh komitetov", in Pavlov (ed.), *Protokoly Tsentral'nogo komiteta*, No. 43, pp. 92–106. (GARF. f. 523, op. 1, d.27, ll.148–85, 192–6 ob.).
209 "Postanovleniia IV-ogo s''ezda partii Narodnoi Svobody" (Section II), *Vestnik*, No. 30, 1906 (1 October 1906).

6 Kadet Party policy

The constitution and civil rights

The policies of the Kadet Party have already been dealt with in some detail. Nevertheless, some aspects of party policy do need further discussion or evaluation, although owing to limitations of space several will be considered only briefly. It will not always be possible to say *exactly* where the Kadets stood upon any particular issue; they were not a rigidly doctrinaire party, and some aspects of party policy never obtained very exact or final formulation.

This is particularly true of some of the most fundamental questions confronting the party: what kind of constitution were they aiming at, what powers should the popular representatives enjoy, and what should be the rôle of the monarchy? In the Duma the Kadets had continually demanded an essentially parliamentary régime. Even in his secret conversations with Trepov and Stolypin, Miliukov had insisted on a ministry from the majority of the Duma. Moreover, the Kadets had consistently demanded that the monarch should be above the political arena, and that he should take no part in party or factional politics. This seems to imply a Crown of the English type, retaining relatively little power, although in his interview with Stolypin Miliukov was apparently willing to leave a restricted sphere of authority to the Tsar:

> Stolypin dwelt very superficially upon questions of programme, but he took an interest in, for example, whether I included the ministers of war, marine, and the Court in the number of ministers subject to K.D. nomination. I answered him, as I had answered Trepov, that we did not intend to interfere in the field of the Monarch's prerogative.[1]

This suggests that the monarch would have been more than a mere cipher, but the fact remains that, in common with the rest of the party, Miliukov insisted that political power in Russia should lie primarily in the hands of the popular representatives.

However, it should be remembered that the Kadets adopted this apparently unequivocal, democratic attitude only after a long period of disillusionment with the government and the bureaucracy. During the history of the Union of Liberation, the men who were later to play a dominant part in the Kadet leadership had associated themselves with relatively moderate constitutional proposals. The "Union of Liberation Constitution" and the essentially similar document accepted at its "first reading" by the July 1905 Zemstvo/Town Duma congress had both left wide powers to the monarchy. It is true that neither of these "constitutions" can be regarded as a statement of the Union's ultimate objectives; they were primarily aimed at influencing moderate opinion in the zemstvo and respectable society towards their own viewpoint. But the fact that the liberal leaders were prepared to support such proposals does suggest that they were willing, at least for the moment, to accept a relatively moderate constitutional settlement. The same impression is given by the essentially moderate attitude of the deputation to the Tsar on 6 June 1905, which included Petrunkevich, Pavel Dolgurukov, Rodichev and Shakhovskoi.

It is true that in the highly charged atmosphere of October 1905, the Kadets adopted an uncompromising attitude. They had responded to the promises of the October Manifesto by insisting on a "constituent assembly" and demanding a "cabinet of the representatives of the majority".[2] However, in the weeks and months which followed they gradually retreated to a more flexible position and abandoned their commitment to a constituent assembly. In his private conversation with Witte, Miliukov suggested that in the final analysis his party would probably be prepared to accept a published constitution similar to that of Bulgaria. This constitution had many radical features. Bulgaria had a unicameral legislature elected by universal suffrage, and the constitution gave the representatives extensive legislative powers, including authority over the budget. But it had also left the Crown considerable authority over the armed forces, the executive, the appointment of ministers, foreign affairs, and the dissolution of the representative assembly. Miliukov's reference to Bulgaria was not a chance one. He had already, in *Russia and its Crisis*,[3] suggested the Bulgarian constitution as a possible model for Russia. Moreover, he had recently published a monograph on it.[4] This had not simply idealized the constitution: Miliukov admitted that it had been open to considerable abuse and manipulation. He was aware that in Bulgarian conditions the prince's rights to choose ministers had given him a very great influence. However, he felt that the Bulgarian régime was a real improvement upon autocracy, and that it was having a valuable effect in providing greater freedom for public opinion, and in educating the nation in constitutional principles. Miliukov did not necessarily want an exact replica of the Bulgarian constitution, but he clearly believed that his party would have been prepared to accept something like it if the government had demonstrated its good faith. Miliukov's awareness of the failings of this constitution is significant. He had admitted that his study of Bulgaria was meant to cast light upon whether a constitution was workable in Russia, since both countries were underdeveloped compared with Western Europe. And his open admission that the Balkan constitution had been abused suggests that he did not necessarily expect a similar Russian constitution to work perfectly. Moreover, since he admitted that in practice the Bulgarian Crown had very considerable power, he was presumably willing to countenance a somewhat similar position in Russia.

The Kadet leadership continued to display signs of flexibility right up to the inauguration of the Duma. Miliukov's overtures to the "ruling spheres" in March, and the apparent association of several prominent Kadets with Kovalevskii's initiative in April, suggest that at times the Kadets were prepared to countenance a relatively moderate, gradualist solution to the crisis. And even the Kadet-inspired "Reply to the Speech from the Throne" did not unequivocally demand a ministry from the majority of the Duma − it had limited itself to a demand for a ministry responsible to, and enjoying the confidence of, the Duma.[5] In fact, the evidence suggests that if the government had shown that it sincerely intended to introduce a genuine constitutional régime, the Kadets would have been more prepared to compromise. This does not mean that they would have dropped their demands for a basically parliamentary system. But they might well have agreed to wider powers for the Crown, and might not have insisted immediately upon a purely Kadet ministry. They adopted an apparently uncompromising attitude only after Goremykin's behaviour had finally disillusioned them with the government. Moreover, the evidence suggests that, even then, the Kadet leaders continued to toy with the idea of achieving their aims by gradualist, evolutionary means.

However, although at times the Kadet leaders were prepared to be flexible, they never wavered in their commitment to a consistently democratic electoral system. They had always insisted that the chamber of popular representatives should be elected by universal, direct, secret and equal suffrage. This demand had been put forward by both the Union of Liberation and the Kadet Party. The Kadets' Second Congress had even proposed the extension of the suffrage to women. In the Duma, the Kadet faction had given the question high priority, and had immediately formed a committee for drafting an appropriate bill. However, the dissolution prevented its introduction, and a bill on this subject was introduced only in the Second Duma.[6] The Kadets' attachment to democratic principles even led a large selection of the party to oppose the establishment of an upper chamber. The "Union of Liberation Constitution" and the "Muromtsev Constitution" of July 1905 had both provided for an upper chamber elected by reformed zemstvo institutions. Moreover, the party programme had laid down that if a second house were established it should be based on these lines. However, the party as a whole never finally committed itself to bicameralism. The question remained a source of disagreement, although all sections of the party united in condemning the State Council in its existing form. Miliukov strongly opposed a second house, seeing it as a restriction of the principle of direct suffrage, and argued that it would only serve to create further resentment on the left.[7] On the other hand, Kokoshkin believed that the two houses were essential in order to guarantee that legislation would be properly thought out, and to ensure the effective representation of the interests of the localities and minority nationalities.[8] A.I. Kaminka outlined very similar arguments in an article in the *Vestnik* (*The Herald*), and pointed out that an upper house would help to prevent head-on collisions with the Crown.[9] The question remained a matter of controversy in the Duma. In the debates on the "Reply to the Speech from the Throne", S.A. Kotlarevsky supported a bicameral system, while V.E. Iakushkin and Peter Dolgorukov strongly opposed it.[10] This aspect of Kadet demands received, then, no further definition in the Duma.

However, the parliamentary faction did attempt to work out some sections of party policy more fully and drafted a number of bills for the consideration of the House. The majority of these were aimed at creating the preconditions of a constitutional régime, by establishing the principles of civil liberty and equality and the rule of law. Of these bills, some (on the inviolability of the individual, civil equality, and freedom of assembly) were considered by the Duma, and were submitted to parliamentary committees for further working out, while others (on the freedom of societies and unions, liberty of conscience, freedom of the press, and judicial reforms) were presented to the Chamber but not discussed.

This group of bills represented a consistent development of the party programme. The bill on the inviolability of the individual,[11] as worked out by a Kadet-dominated committee of 15[12] laid down that no one should undergo punishment save by order of the regular courts, and forbade the practice of trying civilians by military justice. No one should be detained unless this was in accordance with the provisions of the law, and on the orders of the judiciary. The individual's dwelling and correspondence should in future be inviolable, and officials guilty of breaches of the law were to be responsible to the general courts for their actions. These principles were clearly designed to end the system of administrative justice so widely employed in Russia, and to eliminate the large measures of legal immunity enjoyed by the bureaucracy. They would also have outlawed the use of extraordinary courts as a means of repressing popular disturbances.

The bill on civil equality[13] also strove to eliminate the abuses of the old régime. The "fundamental propositions" of the bill were divided into four sections. The first aimed at giving the peasantry legal equality with other classes, and freeing them from their subjection to special jurisdictions such as the arbitrary authority of the land captain ("zemskii nachal'nik"). The second was directed at abolishing the legal disabilities suffered by religious minorities and non-Russian nationalities. The third proclaimed the abolition of all privileges of the nobility in state service, local self-government, and the ownership of immovable property, while the fourth proposed the ending of all restrictions on the civil rights of women. The only other bill of this group which actually entered into a Duma commission, that on the freedom of assembly,[14] sought to establish wide liberty of assembly without preliminary permission from the police. Of these three bills only one, that on the inviolability of the individual, completed its passage through the appropriate committee. And owing to the dissolution, even this bill failed to receive any further consideration in the Duma as a whole.

The remaining bills did not undergo even preliminary discussion in the Chamber. The proposed law on the freedom of conscience[15] laid down that civil and political rights should not depend on the individual's religion or faith. All Russian citizens were to be free to leave one faith and join another. A government measure of 17 April had already gone some way to meeting demands for religious liberty, but not as far as this Kadet proposal. It had failed to extend the principle of toleration to the Jews, and had left Orthodoxy with the sole right of proselytizing those of other faiths. The provisions of the Kadet bill were designed to rectify these deficiencies. Of the other two bills dealing directly with individual liberty, one proposed to grant the public very wide freedom to form societies and unions, and to endow them with wide juridical rights,[16] while the second, concerning the freedom of the press, provided for the abolition of the censorship, and proposed to strictly limit the number of offences for which the press could be indicted.[17] The final bill in this group was not, strictly speaking, on civil liberty, but in fact it was indissolubly linked to this issue. Rodichev made it clear[18] that the bill on inviolability depended on the reform of the judiciary, if it was to be fully effective, since the provisions of the bill were to be guaranteed principally by the judges. The Kadets therefore introduced an interim measure on this question into the Duma. It was not designed to be an exhaustive reform of the entire system, but it did seek to abolish all illiberal accretions to the judicial reform of 1864, and to obtain an independent judiciary and equal justice for all by means of the amendment of the existing law.

Local government and regional autonomy

All these bills had something of a constituent character, in that they were aimed at laying down the foundations on which a liberal régime would have been based. The same is true of the party's work on local government reform, in that it sought to limit the power of the central bureaucracy, and establish an administrative system permitting much more scope for local initiative. According to Kokoshkin,[19] the Kadets set themselves six main aims in the field of zemstvo and town Duma reform:

1 to reorganize and democratize local government on the basis of universal suffrage;
2 to liberate it from administrative tutelage;
3 to widen the sphere of affairs subject to its authority, "with the exception only of those administrative tasks which by their very nature demand centralisation";
4 to reform local taxation;
5 to establish a small zemstvo unit to replace the present volost' self-government, which was confined entirely to the peasants and subject to strong bureaucratic pressure; and,
6 to extend the zemstvo to those parts of the Empire which were still without it.

In the Duma, a Kadet Committee set to work to draft legislative proposals on this subject,[20] although none of them reached the stage of being introduced to the Duma. However, three bills were worked out by subcommittees, two of them on the zemstvo, and the third on the reform of town dumas. The aim of one of these bills was to base zemstvo elections on the principle of universal suffrage.[21]

However, the subcommittee did not consistently put the "four tails" into effect. In particular, the old system of electing the higher zemstvo bodies by the lower ones was kept in force, thus retaining an element of indirect election.[22] This was justified by the subcommittee on the grounds that it was desirable to maintain a personal link between different levels of local government.[23] But it is difficult not to suspect a conservative element in another provision of the bill. The majority of the subcommission argued that it was essential to exclude outsiders without a real interest in a locality from the right to vote. They therefore insisted on a residence qualification longer than the period needed to draw up the electoral register,[24] and fixed its duration at one year. The minority opposed this, pointing out that this would effectively disenfranchise a great number of migratory workers, who played an exceptionally large part in the economy of Russia.[25] The arguments of the majority would have been more convincing if they had not adopted a double standard. The same bill would have given the vote to those paying zemstvo taxes irrespective of whether they resided in the area. This suggests that property owners were looked on with more favour than those who merely contributed labour to a given locality. It also implies that property-owners would have been entitled to more than one vote, provided they paid zemstvo taxes in several different areas.

The commission would, ideally, have liked the second bill on the zemstvo to have been a completely exhaustive reform redefining the powers and functions of the zemstvo. However, the commission decided that this would take too long, and directed its subcommission to draft a bill composed merely of amendments to the existing law.[26] The resulting bill[27] was chiefly designed to free the zemstvo from bureaucratic tutelage, and eliminate the restrictions laid upon the zemstvo by the 1890 Zemstvo Statute. The First Chapter, for example, amended the 1890 Act to permit free intercourse between the zemstvos. They should enjoy freedom of action save as laid down by law; and the district court was to decide on the legality of the zemstvo's actions (Chapter II). The Third Chapter was largely aimed at eliminating the provincial governor's wide powers of interference in zemstvo affairs. The governor's right of confirming the appointment of members and presidents of zemstvo boards and zemstvo servants was to be removed, and zemstvo officials were no longer to be answerable to government institutions in matters of discipline. The government's powers of interference over the dates for the convocation of zemstvo assemblies were to be abolished. The limits on zemstvo taxation were removed, and zemstvo accounts and reports were to be freely published. All stipulations of the existing law which gave the zemstvo the character of a class institution were to be annulled. For example, all citizens were to have the right to stand in elections, and the marshal of the nobility was no longer to be the obligatory president of zemstvo assemblies. At the same time, the governor should no longer have the right to give a ruling on the advisability of zemstvo decisions. Such supervision was to be exercised only by the central government and was to be,

> strictly limited to those cases where local interests are so directly and inseparably connected with those of the state as a whole that the exact demarcation of

the competence of the organs of local self government and the central authority seems impossible.

The right of the Ministry of the Interior to confirm zemstvo decisions should be limited to issues where non-local interests were affected. However, since the bill was only an interim measure, it did not attempt to delineate the fields in which the Kadets would have granted the zemstvo effective autonomy.

The proposed law on the reform of town dumas,[28] on the other hand, was meant to be more comprehensive and this makes it possible to obtain some idea of the powers the Kadets wished to confer upon local self-government. This bill, which in general adhered closely to the principles and provisions laid down by the two proposals on the zemstvo, outlined a wide sphere of duma authority within which decisions would not be subject to government confirmation. The objects of duma competence included: control of town finances, education, public health, the police and fire services, and the care of squares, bridges and public gardens. Furthermore, the reformed dumas were empowered to take "in general all measures" which they "recognised to be necessary in the interests of the inhabitants of the town". The state's sanction would be needed only over the introduction of new types of taxes, and for certain loans. The administration would be allowed to appeal only against the legality of a duma's actions. This principle did not exclude the state from all interference in education, for example, since the legislature could still have laid down general laws which local authorities would have to observe. But by largely excluding administrative interference in local self-government (even, it appears, by means of financial pressures), the bill would have granted an unusually great degree of autonomy to the town duma. The Kadets clearly intended to apply similar principles in the case of the zemstvos.

The question of local self-determination was closely related to the issue of Kadet policies towards the nationalities. Now it is true that, in the Duma, the party did give some attention to the national problem. We have already noted that the bill on civil equality had aimed at eliminating the legal disabilities of non-Russian minorities. Moreover, the Kadets had repeatedly attempted to defend the Jews from pogroms, and had exposed the involvement of government officials in anti-Jewish violence.[29] However, Kadet proposals for national autonomy received no further development in the Duma. These proposals had achieved prominence only in the latter half of 1905, and never obtained very close definition. The party programme had been specific about national autonomy only in the case of Poland.[30] Because of its high cultural level and its past experience of statehood, Poland held a special position in K.D. schemes of autonomy.[31] Concerning other areas the programme was less concrete. It merely proclaimed that:

> a lawful route must be opened up, in accordance with the procedure of general state legislation, for the establishment of local autonomy and regional representative assemblies, possessing the right of participation in

the implementation of legislative authority in particular fields *according to the needs of the population* [author's emphasis].

The reference to "the needs of the population" makes it clear that the Kadets were not considering a uniform solution to this question. Whereas Poland would have been granted a wide degree of autonomy, smaller, less "advanced" nationalities would not have enjoyed the same level of self-government. It is not, in fact, clear how far the Kadets would have gone in these cases beyond their programme demand for cultural self-determination.[32] And on one issue the Kadets were clear: regional autonomy was not meant to undermine the unity of the Empire. Quite the reverse: they hoped that by granting concessions to the nationalities they would weaken separatism, and strengthen the forces working for unity.[F1,33] Kokoshkin, the party's chief spokesman on this question, emphasized the need to preserve the unity of the Empire and stressed that the party was not demanding a federal system in which each unit would enjoy absolute sovereignty in its own field. The limits of local jurisdiction would be laid down by the Imperial legislature, and could be revised by the same authority, and autonomous regions would continue to elect members to the central representative body. And in all cases the state would remain in control of the armed forces, foreign affairs and general state finances. The Kadets did not, then, take the principle of decentralization to its extreme limits and adopt the federal principle. In the final analysis the central legislature was to be supreme, and the party was never very specific about the powers autonomous regions would enjoy.

On the other hand, in the field of strictly *local* government, the Kadets proposed severely to limit central interference in the zemstvos' (and town dumas') sphere of competence. However, in an underdeveloped, culturally heterogeneous state it would be difficult to guarantee that all areas would be able to display sufficient initiative to be trusted with such wide autonomous powers. Moreover, the Kadets were not believers in laissez-faire but in a state which would take the lead in wide, radical social reforms and the redistribution of wealth. It is not easy to reconcile this with the degree of independence local authorities would have enjoyed. Underdeveloped states in the twentieth century tended to become increasingly centralized, having found that comprehensive social and economic planning were necessary for their development. Even modern advanced states have been reluctant to restrict interference in this sphere of administration to the passing of general laws. They have often felt it necessary to limit local and regional government by, for example, the central government's power of the purse, and its ultimate control over regional and

---

F1 In the light of subsequent events, such hopes may seem unrealistic. The Kadets may well have underestimated the force of national separatism, which was later to fissure both Russia and the USSR.

   In the final analysis the multi-national Russian Empire had been held together primarily by coercion, by an autocratic centralized state, rather than by the bonds of a common citizenship. In this context a liberal, decentralized régime was perhaps more likely to stimulate separatism than to defuse it.

local planning. It is, therefore, difficult to see how Russia could successfully have implemented such wide local autonomy, given its relative backwardness. A question like education, for example, was not just a local matter: it was bound up with the need of the state rapidly to modernize itself in an era of fierce international competition. It could not safely have been left to local authorities guided only by the provisions of a general law. The Kadets should, at least, have provided for some further degree of governmental interference in such matters, if only by partial control of local finances in order to guarantee greater uniformity of policy.

Social reform

The workers

With the notable exception of the agrarian question, the Kadets devoted little attention to social problems during the life of the First Duma. For example, they did almost nothing to satisfy the needs of the working class. This was subsequently admitted by an authoritative article in the *Vestnik*, which explained that the Central Committee had been absorbed in other matters.[34] The writer (almost certainly N.I. Iordansky, the chief spokesman on this subject at the Fourth Congress) proposed that the party should form "bureaux of assistance to the unification of labour".[35] These would be open to all workers, regardless of party, and would provide legal help to unions, and premises for meetings, lectures and labour exchanges. This would help wean the workers away from the influence of the extreme parties, and would promote the formation of "non-party" unions free from the domination of any one sectarian faction. Iordansky believed that the problems of the working class would only be solved by advanced labour legislation and by Western-style trade unionism. And he went on to argue that only non-party unions could avoid the weakening of the power of labour by its division into narrow factional groups. Moreover, unions of this type would be open to wider liberal influence and might well lead to the formation of a broad workers' party emancipated from the control of the extreme left. These arguments were reiterated by Iordansky at the Fourth Congress (24–28 September 1906),[36] which officially endorsed his proposals.[37]

Agrarian policy

Unlike their proposals in the field of labour reform, the Kadets' agrarian demands received very close attention, both before and during the Duma. We have already seen that the First Congress had remained rather vague when laying down the party programme in this field. The programme's proposals had centred on a demand for the expropriation of state, monastery and private lands, which would constitute a state land fund for distribution to the poor and landless.[38] However, the programme had remained indefinite on the question of how much private land should be alienated, and what compensation should be paid. Article

36 merely stated that the land should be alienated "in the dimensions required", "with the compensation of the present owners at a just valuation". The programme also failed to define which categories of private land would be subject to expropriation. Article 37 was equally unclear about the nature of the state land fund, although according to Chernenkov[39] it was not based upon the principle of land nationalization. The Kadets had merely wished to underline the fact that the peasants would receive the land from the state, and not from their individual pomeshchik, as in 1861. The programme also remained rather vague on the question of how the land would be distributed. The programme laid down that whether the land should be granted out to (for example), the obshchina, or into personal possession ("vladenie") would depend on local custom. However, according to Chernenkov the word "possession" was used rather than the word "property" in order to avoid predetermining the issue of whether land could be distributed on the basis of absolute rights of ownership.[40] This was apparently largely in deference to a large body of opinion in the party which favoured land nationalization, and probably also to a more general feeling that absolute property rights would lead to a new mobilization of landed property and its renewed concentration in a few hands.

The Kadet Central Committee was fully aware that the party's agrarian programme was inadequate as it stood. At the Second Congress it therefore set up an agrarian committee which was given the task of working out a more detailed programme and submitting its proposals to congress. The committee made a determined effort to define which lands should be subject to alienation. It proposed that only leased lands, and land which was already worked by a peasant inventory should be unconditionally expropriated, while recommending limitations on the alienation of estates worked by their owners, especially where farming was of an exceptionally high cultural level. At the same time, Prince Pavel Dolgorukov presented the congress with a set of theses which would have made it possible to distribute the land to the peasantry upon the basis of limited private property in regions where the local population demanded it, and which more closely defined the means by which a "just valuation" would be determined for expropriated estates. It would be determined "according to the normal profitability (of land) in a given locality under the conditions of independent husbandry, without taking into attention leasehold rents created by shortage of land".[41] The proposals of the committee came in for fierce criticism from the congress. They satisfied neither a strong body of opinion which opposed private property in land in any form, and supported the principle of nationalization, nor those who wished to keep alienation within more modest limits. While Iakushkin, for example, wanted extensive expropriation, Usov demanded further safeguards to protect the smaller landowner.[42] Rodichev even opposed compulsory alienation altogether, and called instead for a progressive land tax.[43] Eventually, Miliukov recognized that the committee's formulation of the agrarian question had not secured the support of the congress, and he called upon the delegates to refrain from taking categorical decisions of a kind which would be "unacceptable to a section of the Party, and which would lead to its disintegration".[44]

In the end, the majority of the committe's proposals were withdrawn. Only Dolgorukov's thesis defining a "just evaluation" for expropriated land was accepted and incorporated into the party programme. At the same time a permanent "commission" attached to the Central Committee was set up to carry out further work on the agrarian question.[45]

Immediately after the congress, the commission got down to the task of collecting relevant materials and preparing an agrarian bill for the Duma. The prime responsibility for drafting the project was laid upon Professor M.Ia. Gertsenshtein,[46] an agrarian expert (and, according to A.A. Kornilov,[47] also Professors N.A. Kablukov and A.A. Manuilov). However, owing to the shortage of time available before the Duma, the commission was unable to prepare a detailed bill, and had to content itself with drafting only the fundamental propositions of the reform.[48]

Before being presented to the Third Congress, the resulting draft was reviewed by a conference of the Central Committee with representatives of local party branches (17–19 April). At the congress itself it underwent further amendment by a special "section" of the assembly before being submitted to the gathering as a whole.[49] The document that emerged[50] provided for far-reaching alienation of private land. The right to a new allotment was to be granted not only to farming families which were short of land, but also to landless agricultural labourers and even (according to special rules), to families which had been compelled to give up farming, if they wished to return to agriculture. According to Chernenkov,[51] an earlier proposal by the commission to bring peasant plots up to the level of the higher norms granted in 1861 had been rejected in case it narrowed the scope of the proposed redistribution. Instead it was proposed in principle to bring small landholdings up to a "consumption norm", that is, up to an amount "sufficient for covering average needs in provisions, clothing and housing and for bearing state obligations". However, the rigours of this norm were mitigated by the stipulations of Article 5, which defined which lands should be subject to alienation and which should not. Once again the chief assault was upon lands under the lease system (Section l) or worked by a chiefly peasant inventory. These were to be alienated unconditionally, as were lands exceeding a maximum size of holding which would be laid down by law for each locality – a provision which would have struck hard at the latifundia of the upper nobility. However, in the case of other private lands (i.e. estates of moderate size farmed by their owners), alienation was to take place only where this was necessary to eliminate an inconvenient mingling of peasant and private land; where the population lacked certain essential types of land; and to satisfy purely local needs when these could be met from no other source. They would not be available to migrants from other localities, although this was provided for in the case of other expropriated estates. This was not the only restriction on alienation: indeed, a wide category of other lands were to be completely exempted from it. Many of the exemptions were of a purely practical, common-sense nature, such as those for lands under homesteads and gardens, or under factories, workshops and agricultural undertakings (buildings, warehouses, etc.). However, regard was also paid to the interests of the small property owner, in that all lands within the dimensions of a "labour norm" were to be exempted.[52] At the same time steps were taken to protect high levels of agrarian culture, and the interests of the model capitalist farmer. Article 5, III(b) exempted "estates or parts of estates, the preservation of which shall be recognised to be necessary, from the point of view of their important social significance, owing to their being exceptionally intensive, providing a model for others, etc.". There were also to be exemptions for lands of special cultures, such as vineyards, and nurseries, while lands used to supply industrial undertakings closely related to agriculture were to be alienated only by a special procedure.

A fairly considerable number of exceptions to the principle of alienation were, then, laid down by this project. According to Chernenkov, the commission had originally proposed that in no case should moderate-sized estates farmed by their owners lose more than about half their land.[53] However, this had been withdrawn by the Moscow conference, as a concession to radical opinion. The party programme had left the question of whether land might be granted out as private property open, and had failed to determine whether the state land fund should be permanent or temporary. But Article 6 now seemed to rule out private property, and to give the land fund a permanent regulating rôle. It provided that "lands from the state land fund are given into long-term use for a date laid down by the appropriate organs. The subsequent transfer of the said lands to others is not permitted". This point (related Kornilov) "was then interpreted by many as the first step on the route to the nationalisation of all land in Russia".[54] In fact, however, the swing to the left was by no means as categorical as Article 6 appears to indicate. An appendix to the proposals made it clear that they were meant to apply chiefly to "the agricultural belt of Russia", where the principles of redistribution of land, and of use rather than property, were already dominant. It provided that, "for regions which differ sharply in their economic relations and conditions of life, correspondingly amended theses must be worked out, with the direct participation of the organs of local self-government reformed on democratic principles". In the case of these areas, then, the issue of the principles of land-use and redistribution had still not been decided on with absolute finality.[55] Not even the eventual granting of land into private property can be said to have been ruled out.

The remaining articles of the project were rather less controversial, and dealt primarily with the financial side of the reform. Article 8 provided for the compensation of landowners, while Article 9 laid down that at least part of the cost of the land would be met by those who received it. It provided that a payment would be "collected from all lands allotted to cultivators from the state land fund". Its size would be determined "in accordance with the profitability of the land, and in compliance with a general plan of land taxation".

Despite its concessions to opinion on the left, at the Third Congress, the projected reform met a series of objections from those, mostly provincial, delegates who wanted it to be based explicitly on the principle of nationalization. This concept never obtained any exact connotation among the Kadets. But it certainly did not imply that the state itself would take over the task of farming the land. What was wanted was a recognition that the land belonged to the entire nation and that, in principle, all had an equal right to work it. Taken to its logical conclusion this would have meant absolute equality of individual landholdings and the abolition of all private property in land. According to the Kadet "nationalizers" this would be achieved by the state leasing out the land to obshchinas and individual farmers and carrying out periodic redistributions. They saw Point 6 as a first step towards this, but they themselves did not, in practice, call for immediate, consistent nationalization. For example, Engel'mieer (Riazan') asked the congress: "How can one conceive of the future, if not in the form of a *constant drawing nearer* to the system of relations given by the socialist ideal?"[56] It is clear that the party was, in this question, still influenced by socialist ideas. But it is also apparent that this was a socialism of a reformist, gradualist nature. As Chernenkov put it:[57]

> With individual exceptions, (the principle of nationalisation) was proposed, namely, only in the quality of a guiding principle illuminating a route of gradual reform of the land system. Its immediate application, however, was regarded as possible only within those limits and forms proposed in the project.

This was something of an overstatement in view of the fact that many delegates were in favour of a wider degree of alienation, but in general it is justified. Primarily the opposition wanted the recognition of the *principle* of nationalization, rather than its immediate implementation. And as a concession to this important body of opinion the party leadership proposed a compromise formula which was duly accepted by the congress. The "guiding principle of the Party" was to be "the transfer of the land into the hands of the toilers",[58] a form of words which committed the party to nothing very definite. In fact, the congress made few concrete proposals on the question of agrarian reform. Because of the shortness of time available for discussion, and probably also in view of continued disagreements, it did not ratify the project in detail. It merely endorsed its "general propositions", and transferred it to the Duma faction for further working out.[59]

In the Duma a committee of the Kadet faction decided to introduce the proposals which had been considered by the Third Congress with only one substantial change. A new Point 10 provided for the setting up of local and central institutions to take part in the preparation and execution of the agrarian reform.[60] Once the "general theses" of the reform had been laid down by law, they would collect all the relevant information needed to draft exhaustive legislation on these lines, and to put it into effect. However, the committee's proposals did not receive the unanimous endorsement of the party in the Duma. According to Chernenkov the chief source of disagreement once again arose from Point 6, and the question of whether the land should be granted to the peasantry on the basis of use or private property.[61] Because of this it was decided to introduce the project in the name of a certain number of Kadets rather than from the party as a whole. Moreover, it would be introduced not as the fundamental propositions of a new law, but merely as material for the consideration of a Duma agrarian committee.[62] The result was the so-called "Memorandum of the 42", introduced to the Duma on 8 May, which was not binding on the Kadet deputies. Indeed, its members were specifically granted freedom of criticism with regard to the memorandum.[63]

The agrarian debates were long and formless, but on 6 June, the Duma finally chose a committee to work out an agrarian reform. The Kadets provided 41 of its 88 members, its president and secretary and the heads of all its subcommittees.[64] Gertsenshtein, the chief Kadet spokesman on agrarian policy, was chosen as chairman of the subcommittee on general questions, on which the committee's work concentrated. The subcommittee recommended that the first tasks of the committee should be the drafting of a law laying down the general principles of the reform. Following this it should work out a law on local land institutions, which would clarify the position of the land question in the localities. When this was done it would be possible to work out all the details of the agrarian reform and incorporate them in the law.[65] Once the law was confirmed, it would be put into effect by a different set of local land institutions with wide executive authority.[66]

In addition to working out a general strategy for the preparation of an agrarian reform, Gertsenshtein's subcommittee[67] itself also took on the major rôle in drafting its general principles. By the time the Duma was dissolved, the subcommittee had succeeded in working out most of the propositions of the bill, and had obtained the committe's approval for much of its work. The main outlines of their proposals were broadly similar to those of the "42".[68] Once again, certain categories of land were to be exempted from alienation. In general the exemptions were in line with the provisions of the Kadet memorandum, but there were some modifications. For example, the limitations on the expropriation of lands which were needed by industrial and agricultural enterprises were now more narrowly defined, to include only acreages under buildings and other structures.[69] The restrictions of the memorandum in relation to exceptionally well-farmed estates were, on the other hand, retained: "Estates or sections of land ... recognised by the land institutions as having a socially useful character" ("obshchepoleznoe znachenie") were to be inviolable. However, this formula was undoubtedly less concrete than that of the "42", and the commission stressed that it should apply only to exceptional cases.[70]

The subcommittee also attempted to delineate those categories of land which should be unconditionally expropriated. Once again it was decided that leased lands and those worked mainly with a peasant inventory should form the basis of this category. The fate of estates farmed by their owners was to be determined only after the local land committees had carried out their investigations.[71] The question of whether the land should be granted to the population as property, or merely leased out, was also put off until a later stage. It was agreed that this issue could be decided only "in accordance with local conditions of landownership and land use".[72] The subcommittee also failed finally to decide on the amount of land the peasantry should be granted, although according to Iakushkin the majority of its members had come down on the side of the higher norm of 1861.[73] Moreover, the subcommittee had still not made up its mind what price should be paid for the land, and had still not decided how compulsory purchase would be financed.[74]

When the dissolution of the Duma came, the work of the agrarian committee was broken off. The theses of the agrarian bill remained incomplete, and its work had not been ratified neither by the Duma in general nor the Kadet Party in particular. Indeed, the Kadets had never given their definite approval to any detailed proposals for agrarian reform. Although it is probable that in the final analysis the majority would have been prepared to accept something close to the theses of the "42", it is impossible to say precisely where the party stood on this issue.

The Kadets' agrarian policies have often been severely criticized by academics. For example, D.W. Treadgold has attacked the party for seeking a solution to the problems of the peasantry in the expropriation of private land. He points out that in this period private estates were already undergoing a process of rapid liquidation, and that by 1916, 90 per cent of the land was already worked by the peasants.[75] According to Treadgold, there was not a great deal of land to be redistributed, and when private estates were eventually seized in 1917, the peasants soon found that this was no solution to their problems.[76] In Treadgold's view, the intelligentsia should, like Stolypin, have concentrated on the creation of an individualistic, Western-style peasant class, and on such measures as the abolition of the commune and migration to Siberia. During the First Duma the representatives of the government expressed, in some ways, similar views. Stishinskii, for example, also argued that there was not enough private land to solve the peasants' problems. What the latter really wanted was to be granted their land as private property, and the establishment of consolidated farms in place of their scattered strips. He rejected compulsory alienation as an assault upon the rights of property, and proposed instead the purchase of land by the existing Peasant Bank, and measures to improve land use and to promote migration to Siberia. Gurko reiterated these arguments, laying special stress on the virtues of private property, and on the need to grant the peasantry economic freedom. In the long term he saw the solution of the agrarian problem in the industrialization of Russia. This would both siphon off excess rural population, and provide agriculture with a lucrative market. And both he and Stishinskii felt that by subverting private estates, compulsory alienation would damage the national economy. They feared not only that peasant farming would be less productive, but also that it would be less adapted to the task of producing for export and for feeding the towns.[77]

The government's arguments were in some ways far-sighted, and even courageous. They were, in particular, making a serious attempt to tackle the question of the commune and the system of landholding in general. And Gurko was almost certainly correct in seeing the long-term solution of the problem largely in the growth of industrialization and the towns. The ministry was, in fact, right when it argued that compulsory alienation was not the ultimate solution to the peasantry's problems. However, the Kadets themselves at no time argued that expropriation was the complete answer to the agrarian question; they saw it, rather, as a short-term emergency measure. The true solution, Gertsenshtein told the Duma, was the intensification of farming, the provision of abundant credit facilities, and other measures to help the small cultivator. However, alienation was essential if the peasantry were to be pacified. The agrarian disturbances were a fire which must be put out and it could be extinguished only by increasing the peasant's allotment.[78] On the other hand, the Kadets' arguments were not solely political. They consistently and convincingly argued that although improvements in peasant farming were the ultimate solution to the crisis, the plots of many peasants were too small to make this possible. They could not generate the necessary capital, nor could they support effective systems of crop rotation.[79]

Furthermore, the Kadets undoubtedly had a strong case in demanding the alienation of a least one category of private lands: those that were already on lease to the peasantry. According to Pavlovskii,[80] in 1905 the peasantry had 160 million desiatins of land, the gentry had 46 million and other private owners 18 million. Of the 64 million falling into the last two categories, 20–25 million were cultivated by the peasants on lease. These figures cannot but support Treadgold's thesis that the peasantry was already farming the vast majority of the land, and that only a relatively small amount was available to add to it. But although this assessment is statistically impeccable, it ignores the baneful role that leaseholding played in the lives of the peasantry. While it is true that the peasants were already farming such lands, this does not mean there was no need for radical reform. Leases were commonly on a very short-term basis and at very high rents owing to the shortage of land. Moreover, as Pavlovskii rightly points out,[81] short leases had a damaging effect on agriculture. Without the guarantee of any security on the land a cultivator was loath to make any improvements. The entire Duma, including not only the Kadets, but also parties to their right, united in condemning the leasehold system as a grave agrarian abuse. It seems clear that the alienation of these lands could have brought little but benefit, both to agriculture and to the peasantry. Moreover, it seems unlikely that the alienation of other private lands would have inflicted such great damage to agriculture as some people feared. Both Pavlovskii and Robinson have a low opinion of the agricultural level of the great majority of private land.[82] Pavlovskii admits that although large, efficient capitalist farming was on the increase there was, in general, little scientific cultivation. According to the figures of the Bank of the Nobility (1896–1900), 51 per cent of gentry land was leased, 29 per cent was cultivated by its owners, and 20 per cent was in some kind of transition between the first two categories.[83] Quite apart from the very wide extent of the lease system, a great deal of gentry land was contained in small estates whose owners were often more concerned with professional work than with agriculture. The number of estates of advanced capitalist farming was, then, relatively small. And as we have seen, the mainstream of Kadet opinion were willing to exclude at least the best of these lands from alienation. It seems doubtful, therefore, whether compulsory expropriation would have done much serious damage to agriculture.

However, in one respect Gurko and Stishinskii were probably correct. If the agrarian reform had gone through as planned, there might have been some difficulty in feeding the towns and keeping up the level of agricultural exports. Unlike the private estates, peasant plots tended to produce for the subsistence of their cultivators rather than for the market. It is true that they did provide a large amount for sale, but this was only because of their need for ready cash. And if they had obtained the gentry's land at terms more favourable than they had formerly enjoyed, their need for money would have declined, and with it their need to produce for the market. It is, moreover, doubtful whether the peasants' desire for consumer goods and industrial products would have provided a sufficient stimulus to production for sale. According to Pavlovskii, many peasants had produced for the market only under very severe pressure of their need for cash, even at the expense of undermining their own diet.[84] And it seems likely that if their need for money had diminished they would first have satisfied some of their own needs, and only then have concerned themselves with the question of purchasing more industrial products. The only mechanism which might have persuaded the peasantry to produce for the market on the former scale would have been heavy taxation. And this ran counter to the declared Kadet policy of reducing the tax burden borne by the masses. However, as we shall see, the party was beginning to have reservations about this.

It is clear, then, that the Kadets' proposals were not without their limitations. The party's most serious weakness in this field of policy was undoubtedly their failure to evolve any adequate long-term view of the future of Russian agriculture. We have already seen that the party as a whole had failed to tackle the fundamental questions which were posed by the continued existence of the obshchina. Could Russian agriculture thrive in the long term under a widespread system of land tenure which weakened individual initiative and divided peasant plots into scattered strips? Did not the principle of the equalization of peasant holdings help to preserve the inefficient farmer and prevent the emergence of Western-style peasant proprietorship?

It is true that some Kadets did face up to these questions. L.I. Petrazhitskii, in particular, opposed the communal principle of the periodic redistribution of the land, which he felt the proposals of the "42" could only encourage. He saw the long-term solution to the agrarian problem not in terms of the continued equalization of plots, but in a régime of free competition based upon individual ownership of the land. Petrazhitskii argued that the chief solution to rural overpopulation was the absorption of surplus labour by industry and the towns. However, if the peasant was not free to sell his plot he would have no incentive to leave; he would simply lose his land without the hope of compensation. What was needed in the countryside was "the possibility of (social) differentiation" and the freedom for "those who find it better in the town ... to sell their plot and go to the town".[85]

Petrazhitskii's arguments gained little support from the party leadership. But on the issue of private property a large body of Kadet deputies, primarily from regions with no strong communalist tradition, opposed the idea of a permanent, redistributive land fund. O.I. Ryutli and I.Kh. Kreitzberg, for example,[86] both demanded that the land should be granted to the peasantry of the Baltic regions upon the basis of private property. However, for the most part these deputies were not trying to argue about the merits of private property for Russia as a whole. They were merely asking for respect for local traditions of land-use. In general the Kadets either did not face up to the question of the obshchina squarely, or even defended it. Gertsenshtein, for example, admitted that when the state land fund distributed land to individual communes, this would probably give the signal for a new redistribution of allotments within the obshchina. But, he asked, "Why be horrified? This is the most appropriate and desirable outcome".[87] Moreover, he even cast doubts on the value of consolidated holdings (or "khutors"), compared with the existing system of scattered strips.[88] And he denied that large-scale farming had great advantages over smaller farms, quoting Denmark as a case to prove his point.[89] However, he failed to mention that even though Danish farming made effective use of cooperatives, it was based on private property. Moreover, it certainly did not make use of the archaic three-field system, which had long become outmoded in the advanced agricultural countries of the West. It is, in fact, surprising that Gertsenshtein, the chief Kadet agrarian spokesman, was so uncritical of the commune, and made no real attempt to face the very real problems which its existence posed. Even some Kadets who had in the past expressed severe reservations about the commune,[90] now made little attempt to publicize their doubts. It seems probable that they were content to let sleeping dogs lie for fear of splitting the opposition in its struggle against the government by raising such a potentially divisive issue.

However, to be fair to the Kadets, it must be remembered that they were not putting forward a long-term solution to the agrarian question, but rather an emergency measure designed to meet the immediate crisis on the land. Because of this it might indeed have been impolitic to have caused unnecessary splits by prematurely raising such questions. Moreover, not even Article 6 of the Memorandum of the "42" completely ruled out a future agrarian system based on private ownership. On the face of it, this article appeared to firmly establish the principle of redistribution of the lands upon the basis of long lease rather than property. However, at the Third Congress Kaufman gave the impression that this implied very long lease indeed, upon the model of the perpetual leasehold system of Siberia.[91] With its very great degree of security of tenure this system was closer to being a form of limited property than to traditional leases. Struve stressed that if delegates voted in favour of long lease the possibility of granting land to the peasants as private property would remain open. It would not be difficult to effect the transition from one to the other.[92] Moreover, it is probable that the party would have had to make concessions to the strong body of opinion which demanded private property in regions where it was already the rule, especially since the Memorandum of the 42 had provided for alterations to its theses in accordance with local custom.

In the Second Duma the party did, in fact, move in this direction, and away from the principle of Article 6 of the memorandum. In the bill then put forward by the party there was no provision for a permanent state land fund. This was not completely excluded as a temporary redistributive instance,[93] but it would no longer have had a permanent regulating rôle. It would merely have transferred the land to the obshchinas as well as to other peasant communities and to individual farming families. Moreover, the land would have been made available for "permanent use" in accordance with local traditions of land tenure. It is true that this would have left the redistributive principle intact in areas of communal ownership. But in view of the fact that the Kadets' proposals no longer provided for continual repartitions by the state land fund, they were now less likely to promote recurrent equalizations of land within the commune. Moreover, by this time the Kadets' attachment to the obshchina was already beginning to decline. At first they strongly opposed Stolypin's measures of 19 November 1906, which provided for peasants to leave the commune and claim their allotment as private property. However, by the time of the Second Duma they had modified their position, and they themselves drafted a bill permitting separation from the commune, although they sought to eliminate some of the more inequitable features of Stolypin's legislation.[94] It seems likely, then, that despite the party's initial failure to face up to the problems posed by the continued existence of the commune, it might in time have evolved towards a position of support for Western-style individual peasant proprietorship.

For a party containing such a large number of landowners the policy of expropriation of private land was in many ways a remarkable one. However, we have already observed that many of the Kadet gentry were already moving away from exclusive dependence on agriculture and were merging with the professional classes. Moreover, the mainstream of Kadet opinion had repeatedly called for safeguards for exceptionally well-cultivated estates and for lands farmed by their owners. Kadet proposals for alienation had always concentrated primarily on leased lands and on the broad acres of the great latifundia. Both these categories of land tended to a large extent to belong to the upper nobility who by tradition worked in the central bureaucracy, and who were, more often than not, absentee landlords. The Kadets had never had a great deal of sympathy for this class. They had always shown more consideration for the provincial "gentry", especially where they still worked the land.[95]

Moreover, it was never very clear just how much private land the Kadets were prepared to alienate. In 1905 the Union of Liberation had at first demanded the expropriation of private estates only where no other land was available. However, with the course of time and under the influence of leftward pressures the Kadets had grown increasingly more radical. Gertsenshtein, in common with, for example, Kaufman, felt that this had gone too far. He himself was a moderate and wanted greater safeguards for private agriculture. He felt that the adoption of a consumption norm or the higher norm of 1861 would make this impossible. Moreover, he doubted whether there was enough land to satisfy either of the proposed norms.[96] However, not all the party's agrarian experts agreed with him. Both Manuilov and Chuprov believed that provided the 1861 norm was adopted, very substantial acreages would have remained in private hands.[97]

Nevertheless, it is clear that the party's agrarian proposals would have been bound to damage the interests of the Kadet landlords to a considerable extent. Despite the fact that they would have been compensated for their land, this would have been at a rate below the market price. However, one overriding factor seems to have made them willing to make concessions – the continual outbreaks of agrarian disturbances. At the April 1905 agrarian congress, Pavel Dolgorukov argued that "from the point of view of intelligent self-interest, it is better for landowners to look reality squarely in the face than to remain motionless, and risk losing everything in some kind of catastrophe". It was "better to liquidate farming completely and look upon one's country seat as a dacha" than to live amidst a hostile population.[98] During the agrarian debates in the Duma, the Kadet deputy, Katsenelson, told the house that many landlords in Kurland were willing to sell their estates because of their fear of disturbances.[99] And both inside and outside the Duma the Kadets repeatedly argued that social peace could only be guaranteed by radical land reform. Petrunkevich argued that repressive measures would not stop the agrarian disturbances. What was necessary was a policy of social reconciliation: "The state order must rest on a wider foundation, upon the agreement of conflicting class interests with higher state interests. Only on this basis can the labours and property both of individuals and of whole classes be safeguarded."[100] To some extent, therefore, it could be argued that the Kadet agrarian programme was in the intelligent self-interest of a large part of the landowning classes. Nevertheless, the Kadet gentry deserve great credit for refusing to act like many other landowners, who were determined to keep everything they possessed, even if this meant supporting a policy of repression. Moreover, it was not merely self-interest which deterred the Kadets from this course, but also a strong vein of humanitarian idealism. They genuinely shrank back in horror from the idea of employing large-scale violence against the peasantry.

In the field of agrarian reform, the Kadets consistently argued in favour of concessions to the masses in order to allay class hatreds and to prevent anarchy. This line of argument was not restricted to the agrarian question. The Kadet leaders repeated similar arguments to justify their other proposals of radical reform. Kokoshkin, for example, opposed granting electoral privileges to the nobility on the grounds that this was against their own interests. It could "arouse only animosity and hostility in the other classes of society" and weaken the nobility's authority and moral credit.[101] The peasantry could be persuaded to achieve its ends by legal, non-violent means only if it was granted the right to vote.[102] Kokoshkin saw class hatred as "the chief evil of contemporary Russia"[103] and felt that the state system should attempt to weaken its influence. It should "teach classes to restrain their selfish aspirations and subordinate them to the principle of the general good", and should make the authority of the state "a power standing above classes and their mutual struggle, capable of evaluating the special interests of classes from the point of view of the whole state and of bringing them into agreement and reconciling them from the same point of view".[104] Miliukov also argued that any restrictions upon democratic principles would sow the seeds of further political and social struggle. And he went on to hope that "the actual practice of general suffrage" would "do more than anything else to disillusion the socialists and to free them from one or more of those utopias preserved by their theoreticians from the earlier stages of their political education".[105]

Notes

1 P.N. Miliukov, *Vospominaniia*, Vol. I, New York 1935, p. 385.
2 These demands were made in a resolution passed on 18 October when the Kadets appear to have been under the influence of a wave of revolutionary enthusiasm. However, the party programme approved by the Congress had been less dogmatic, and had been indefinite about the exact balance of power in a future constitutional régime. It had merely demanded that popular representatives should "participate" in legislation and in control over the budget, and that no law should be promulgated without their agreement. The representatives should also participate in control over the actions of the executive.
3 P.N. Miliukov, *Russia and its Crisis*, Chicago/London 1905, pp. 563–4.
4 P.N. Miliukov, "Bolgarskaia konstitutsiia", in P.D. Dolgorukov and I.I. Petrunkevich (eds), *Gosudarstvennyi stroi sovremennykh stran*, S.P.B. 1905, pp. 545–652 (in the Bulgarian language it was published in book form).
5 *S.O.*, Vol. I, p. 240, 5/IV/1906.
6 N.I. Astrov, *Zakonodatel'nye proekty i predpolozheniia Partii Narodnoi Svobody 1905–07*, S.P.B. 1907, pp. 79–83. The actual bill is published on pp. 100–12, together with an explanatory memorandum (see pp. 83–99).
7 Miliukov, *Russia and its Crisis*, pp. 520–3.
8 F.F. Kokoshkin, *Ob osnovaniiakh zhelatel'noi organizatsii narodnogo predstavitel'stva v Rossii*, Moscow 1906, pp. 82–94.
9 A.I. Kaminka, "Gosudarstvennyi sovet 20 feb.", *Vestnik partii narodnoi svobody*, No. 7, 1906.
10 *S.O.*, Vol. I, pp. 166–70, 4/V/1906.
11 "Zakon o neprikosnovennosti lichnosti", in A.A. Mukhanov and V.D. Nabokov (eds), *Pervaia Gosudarstvennaia Duma (P.G.D.)*, S.P.B. 1907, Vol. 2, pp. 191–4 (this book will hereafter be referred to as *P.G.D.*).
12 Eight of 15 members were Kadets. See: *S.O.*, Vol. I, pp. 387–8, 15/V/1906.
13 "Proekt osnovnykh polozhenii zakona o grazhdanskom ravenstve", in *P.G.D.*, Vol. 2, pp. 222–3.
14 "Zakonoproekt o sobraniiakh", *S.O.*, Vol. II, 16/VI/1906, pp. 1446–7.
15 "Proekt zakona o svobode sovesti", *P.G.D.*, Vol. 2, pp. 223–4.
16 "Proekt zakona o soiuzakh", *P.G.D.*, Vol. 2, pp. 219–21.
17 "Proekt zakona o pechati", *P.G.D.*, Vol. 2, pp. 225–9.
18 "Zaiavlenie ob izmenenii zakona o sudoustroistve i sudoproizvodstve", in Astrov, *Zakonodatel'nye proekty*, pp. 243–53.
19 F.F. Kokoshkin, "Proekt reformy zemskogo samoupravleniia", *P.G.D.*, Vol. 2, pp. 25–6.
20 Kokoshkin, "Proekt reformy zemskogo samoupravleniia", p. 27.
21 "Proekt polozheniia o vyborakh v gubernskie i uezdnye zemskie uchrezhdeniia", *P.G.D.*, Vol. 2, pp. 194–9.
22 Kokoshkin, "Proekt reformy zemskogo samoupravleniia", p. 30.
23 Kokoshkin, "Proekt reformy zemskogo samoupravleniia", p. 43.
24 Kokoshkin, "Proekt reformy zemskogo samoupravleniia", p. 43.
25 Kokoshkin, "Proekt reformy zemskogo samoupravleniia", p. 43.

26 Kokoshkin, "Proekt reformy zemskogo samoupravleniia", pp. 28–9.
27 "Proekt zakona ob izmenenii polozheniia o gubernskikh i uezdnykh zemskikh uchrezhdeniiakh", *P.G.D.*, Vol. 2, pp. 199–205.
28 "Proekt gorodskogo polozheniia", *P.G.D.*, Vol. 2, pp. 206–17. See also M.I. Petrunkevich, "K proektu gorodskogo polozheniia", *P.G.D.*, Vol. 2, pp. 67–74.
29 See A.R. Lednitsky, "Natzional'nyi vopros v pervoi Gosudarstvennoi Dume", *P.G.D.*, Vol. 1, pp. 154–67.
30 "Programma K.D.P." (Art. 25) *Pravo*, No. 41, 1905. The programme had also called for the restoration of the Finnish constitution, but this had been granted by the government itself in late 1905.
31 See, e.g., A.A. Kizevetter (ed.), *Napadki na Partiiu Narodnoi Svobody*, Moscow 1906, pp. 51–2.
32 "Programma K.D.P." (Arts 11–12), *Pravo*, No. 41, 1905. The party programme specified the complete freedom to use minority languages and dialects in public life and education. Although Article 12 laid down that Russian should remain the language of the armed forces and central administration it also demanded the right of elementary and, if possible, further education in one's own language.
33 See F.F. Kokoshkin, *Oblastnaia avtonomiia i edinstvo Rossii*, Moscow 1906. See also, Kizevetter, *Napadki na Partiiu Narodnoi Svobody*, pp. 50ff.
34 N.I., "O formakh sodeistviia professional'nomu dvizheniiu", *Vestnik*, No. 29, 21 September 1906.
35 The establishment of bureaux of this type had already been proposed by Rozhdestvenskii at the Third Congress but nothing had been done to implement this proposal. A bureau was already operating in Moscow, and it had been intended that it would provide the model for a much wider network.
36 "S chetvĕrtogo s''ezda ... Zasedanie professional'noi kommissii", *Rech'*, 30 September 1906.
37 "Postanovleniia IV-ogo s''ezda" (Sect. IV), *Vestnik partii narodnoi svobody*, No. 30, 1906.
38 "Programma K.D.P.", *Pravo*, No. 41, 1905. See in particular Articles 36–7.
39 N.N. Chernenkov, *Agrarnaia programma partii Narodnoi Svobody*, S.P.B. 1907 (hereafter referred to as Chernenkov), pp. 16–17.
40 Chernenkov, pp. 6–7.
41 "S''ezdy i konferentsii k.d. partii" Vol. I, ROSSPEN 1997. Evening session 7 January, pp. 131 and 139.
42 "S''ezdy i konferentsii k.d. partii" Vol. I, ROSSPEN 1997. Evening session 7 January, p. 135.
43 "S''ezdy i konferentsii k.d. partii" Vol. I, ROSSPEN 1997. Evening session 7 January, p. 140.
44 "S''ezdy i konferentsii k.d. partii" Vol. I, ROSSPEN 1997. Evening session 8 January, pp. 146–7.
45 "S''ezdy i konferentsii", Resolution X, p. 185.
46 A. Kaufman, "Agrarnyi vopros", in *P.G.D.*, Vol. 3, p. 1 (this article will hereafter be referred to as Kaufman).
47 A.A. Kornilov, "Agrarnye zakonoproekty partii Narodnoi Svobody", in N.I. Astrov, *Zakonodatel'nye proekty i predpolozheniia partii Narodnoi Svobody*, 1907, pp. 369f (this article will hereafter be referred to as Kornilov).
48 Chernenkov, pp. 23–4.
49 Kornilov, pp. 369–70.
50 *OTCHĔT*, pp. 123–44.
51 Chernenkov, pp. 28–9.
52 The "labour norm" was the name given to the amount of land a family could cultivate by its own labour without outside help.
53 Chernenkov, p. 37.

54 Kornilov, p. 372.
55 Indeed, they cannot be said to have been worked out for any part of Russia. Chernenkov (pp. 31–3) admits that the text of point 6 gave some reaon to believe that the project favoured a permanent state land fund dealing with individual land users over the head of the obshchina and other collective associations. But Chernenkov denies that this was the intention of the compilers of the project. They had originally proposed a formula directly referring to the granting of land in the first place to "obshchinas, and groups of householders and hereditary proprietors" which were deemed to be short of land. The latter would then take upon themselves the task of distributing the land to individuals. Those who had drafted the project had not wished to disregard local methods of land use, and had realized that to grant land over the head of the obshchina, for example, would have led to its break-up, which was not their intention. However, the reference to collective units had been removed by the Moscow conference, and replaced by a vague reference to the distribution of land to "agriculturists". According to Chernenkov this was largely the result of the adoption of very general and vague terminology as a whole. And the adoption of such terminology in this case was largely conditioned by the fact that "the whole practical organisation ('postanovka') of this side of the reform had still not succeeded in receiving sufficient definition and concreteness".
56 "III s''ezd delegatov...", *Pravo*, No. 18, 1906, p. 1690.
57 N.N. Chernenkov, "Agrarnyi vopros na III s''ezd", *Vestnik*, No. 10, 1906.
58 *Pravo*, No. 18, 1906, p. 1694.
59 *Pravo*, No. 18, 1906, p. 1694.
60 *S.O.*, Vol. I, p. 250, 8/V/1906.
61 Chernenkov, p. 41.a.
62 Chernenkov, p. 41; Kornilov, p. 373; *S.O.*, Vol. I, p. 250.
63 "Parlamentskaia fraktsiia", *Vestnik*, No. 11, p. 735. For the Memorandum of the 42, see also: GARF. f. 523, op. 2, d.76 and 77.
64 Kaufman, p. 23; V.E. Iakushkin, "K polozheniiu agrarnogo voprosa", *Vestnik*, Nos. 21–22, p. 1287 (hereafter referred to as Iakushkin).
65 Kaufman, pp. 25–8; Iakushkin, pp. 1287–8.
66 Kaufman, pp. 25–8; Iakushkin, pp. 1287–8.
67 Kaufman (p. 23) lists the membership of the subcommittee as six Kadets, four Trudoviks, two non-party and one each for the party of Democratic Reform, the Polish "Kolo" and the "Progressists".
68 See D.D. Protopopov, *Chto sdelala pervaia Gosudarstvennaia Duma*, Moscow 1906, pp. 11–14.
69 Kaufman, p. 107.
70 Iakushkin, p. 1291.
71 Kaufman, pp. 103–4.
72 Iakushkin, p. 1291.
73 Iakushkin, p. 1291.
74 Iakushkin, p. 1291.
75 D.W. Treadgold, *The Great Siberian Migration*, Princeton 1957, p. 41.
76 Treadgold, *The Great Siberian Migration*, pp. 249–51.
77 *S.O.*, Vol. I, pp. 509–23, 13/V/1906.
78 *S.O.*, Vol. I, p. 529, 19/V/1906.
79 See, e.g., M.Ia. Gersenshtein, *Natsionalizatsiia zemli*, S.P.B. 1905.
80 G. Pavlovskii, *Agricultural Russia on the Eve of the Revolution*, London 1930, p. 96.
81 Pavlovskii, *Agricultural Russia on the Eve of the Revolution*, pp. 104–8.
82 Pavlovskii, *Agricultural Russia on the Eve of the Revolution*, pp. 190–221. G.T. Robinson, *Rural Russia under the Old Regime*, New York 1949, pp. 129–30.
83 Pavlovskii, *Agricultural Russia on the Eve of the Revolution*, p. 191.
84 Pavlovskii, *Agricultural Russia on the Eve of the Revolution*, pp. 250–1.

85 *S.O.*, Vol. I, pp. 451–8, 18/V/1906.
86 *S.O.*, Vol. I, pp. 496–500, 19/V/1906.
87 *S.O.*, Vol. I, pp. 527–8, 19/V/1906.
88 *S.O.*, Vol. I, p. 577, 23/V/1906.
89 *S.O*, Vol. I, p. 466, 18/V/1906.
90 See, e.g., Miliukov, *Russia and its Crisis*, pp. 347–53.
91 Konstitutsionno-Demokraticheskaia Partiia, "Protokoly III s''ezda", S.P.B. 1906, p. 128. (See also Gertsenshtein's similar views, in *S.O.*, Vol. I, p. 524, 19/V/1906).
92 Konstitutsionno-Demokraticheskaia Partiia, "Protokoly III s''ezda", pp. 123–4.
93 Kornilov, pp. 379–80. See also: "Proekt glavnykh osnovanii zakona o zemel'nom obezpechenii", in *OTCHËT*, pp. 123–44.
94 Kornilov, pp. 384–6.
95 See, e.g., F.F. Kokoshkin, *Ob osnovaniiakh zhelatel'noi organizatsii narodnogo predstavitel'stva v Rossii*, Moscow 1906, pp. 8–10. Kokoshkin adopted a sympathetic attitude to the owners of moderate-sized estates, maintaining that this section of the nobility played an active and valuable part in the life of their localities. "This class has put forth from its midst the leaders of self-government, the councillors of zemstvo assemblies, the presidents and members of the boards, the mediators and justices of the peace", said Kokoshkin. However, he attacked "the upper layer of the nobility belonging to the highest official and aristocratic circle" as "completely divorced from the land". They played no part in provincial life, and held aloof from the local nobility. They were mostly absentees, using their land purely as a source of revenue, and concerning themselves mainly with government service.
96 M.Ia. Gertsenshtein, *Zemel'naia reforma v programme partii Narodnoi Svobody*, Moscow 1906, pp. 26–39.
97 See A.A. Manuilov, "Pozemel'nyi vopros", and A.A. Chuprov, "K voprosu o dopolnitel'nom nadelenii", in *Agrarnyi vopros*, Vol. I, pp. 62–71, 225–31.
98 "Agrarnyi vopros s tochki zreniia krupnogo zemlevladeniia", in P.D. Dolgorukov and I.I. Petrunkevich (eds), *Agrarnyi vopros*, Vol. I, pp. 6, 8.
99 *S.O.*, Vol. I, pp. 817–18, 30/V/1906.
100 I.I. Petrunkevich, "K agrarnomu voprosu", *Agrarnyi vopros*, Vol. I, p. XVY.
101 Kokoshkin, *Ob osnovaniiakh*, p. 12.
102 Kokoshkin, *Ob osnovaniiakh*, p. 52.
103 Kokoshkin, *Ob osnovaniiakh*, p. 51.
104 Kokoshkin, *Ob osnovaniiakh*, p. 27.
105 Miliukov, *Russia and its Crisis*, p. 522.

7 Who were the Kadets?

One of the chief reasons for the Kadets' attempts to reduce class conflicts was their determination to rescue Russia from the turmoil into which it had fallen. At the same time they were also motivated partly by enlightened self-interest: by their desire to protect the more prosperous and cultivated members of society from the threat from below. This once again raises the question of which social classes made up the bulk of Kadet support, and what social interests they represented.

It may therefore be useful to make a further examination of this question, beginning with a brief evaluation of the social position and interests of the Kadet deputies in the Duma. The information on this subject is limited and often unsystematic but it is adequate to enable the investigator to make a number of important generalizations.

The first thing worth noting about the Kadet group in the Duma is the continued influence of the zemstvo. Of 168 Kadet deputies for whom information is available,[1] 89 had taken part in the affairs of the zemstvo Second Element as zemstvo councillors or as presidents or members of zemstvo or town duma boards. However, only 33 appear to have been gentry landowners with purely agricultural interests. All the remaining zemstvo gentry also had important occupations, primarily in the field of professional work. Moreover, not all of the zemstvo men were nobles: at least 18 can be identified as belonging to other social estates. Twelve were peasants, three were "merchants" ("kuptsy"), one was a Cossack, one was a petty-bourgeois ("meshchanin") and one came from a clerical family.[2] Of this group of 18 zemstvo men, one was an industrialist and big landowner, one had banking interests, five (all peasants) were in trade, one was a zemstvo insurance agent, one managed an estate, one was a peasant volost' official, and one (the "petty-bourgeois") had his own estate. One of the "merchants" was also a big farmer. Apart from this, one was a worker and the remainder were professional men.

The professions were, in fact, exceptionally well-represented among the Kadet deputies. Ninety out of 168 had some kind of profession. Sixteen either were, or had been, academics, 27 were lawyers, 15 were doctors, 10 were teachers and 6 were editors or journalists. There were also four engineers or technologists, and smaller numbers of agronomists, statisticians, priests and other professional men.

A feature of special interest is the large number of Kadet deputies from the higher professions and those most favoured by the nobility: in particular the academic profession and the law. The substantial number of academics in the Kadet ranks once again underlines the strong influence of the universities in the party. The importance of the universities is also confirmed by the researches of Borodin, who found that 67 per cent of Kadet deputies had been educated at universities or similar establishments.[3] The influence of the legal profession is at least equally striking, especially when it is taken into account that out of 168 deputies, 61 had received a specialist legal education, even though they did not all enter the legal profession. The significance of these facts will be considered later.

The fact that such a large number of deputies had professional occupations does not, of course, mean that they had no other interests. We have already noted that many of them were also members of the zemstvo Second Element. Clearly then, a substantial number of professional men also depended partly on land or other property. The extent of landownership among the Kadets was, in fact, very considerable. According to the figures of N.A. Borodin, which relate to a total of 153 Kadet deputies, 63 owned more than 100 desiatinas[F1] of land. Of these, three had between 5,000 and 10,000 desiatinas, eight had 2,000–3,000, eight had 1,000–2,000, 30 possessed 500–1,000 and 14 had 100–500. In addition there were ten deputies with between 10 and 100 desiatinas.[4] As Borodin points out, the majority of these fell into the category of middle-sized landowners who possessed zemstvo voting qualifications and tended to dominate local self-government.

The Kadet landowning interest, then, remained strongly represented in the Duma. However, far fewer of the Kadets had connections with the world of industry and commerce. Only three Kadet deputies can be identified as owning industrial establishments. One of these, M.G. Komissarov, was the proprietor of a glass factory, but he was also a big landowner. Another owned a sugar factory and another (E.E. Rameev) possessed gold mines. Owing to the strong connections of sugar refining with the land, only the mine-owner can be said to have represented purely industrial interests. The same close connection with the land is also discernible in a small group of six members holding important posts in financial institutions. They were mostly involved in savings associations and banks designed to provide small credit to agriculturalists. Gertsenshtein had been the secretary of the Moscow land bank, which was clearly concerned with agricultural rather than industrial credit. Nor can a small group of six publishers be unequivocally described as businessmen since this was an occupation closely allied to the professions (one of them, however, was Komissarov, publisher of the Kadet *Narodnoe Delo* (*The People's Cause*), whose important business interests have just been noted). Apart from these groups there were ten deputies involved in trade. But with the exception of one big trader, the rest were mostly involved in commerce of a very rudimentary kind. Eight were small peasant traders mostly dealing in the products of handicrafts or the wood trade, and

---

F1 desiatina = 2.7 acres.

combining trade with farming. At the other end of the scale, that of industrial and commercial employees, six either were or had been white-collar or professional workers in private service. Only two railway workers could be described as proletarians and then only with reservations. They were both legally peasants and at least one of them still farmed his own land.

The fact that deputies often had interests and occupations inconsistent with their nominal social status makes it very difficult to place them into hard and fast social categories. Russia was in a period of transition in which the old social order based upon estates with well-defined status and interests was breaking down. One of the features of this transitional period was a tendency for individuals to have more than one occupation or interest. We have just noted than a man could be a peasant farmer and simultaneously be engaged as a worker in industry. Similarly, a deputy might well be a landowner, a professional man, have business interests, and have worked in private or state service. Because of this it would be misleading to attempt to place individual deputies into only one occupational or social category. Instead it has been found preferable simply to calculate the total number of deputies connected with various occupations and interests, and there is bound to be a degree of overlap between the figures.

The case of deputies who had worked in the Zemstvo Third Element is a case in point. At least 16 of the Kadets had been employed in this kind of work. These men were of very mixed social composition: seven can be identified as nobles, five as peasants and one as a "merchant". Of the total of 16 deputies, nine[5] were also members of the zemstvo Second Element; altogether five had been members of zemstvo or town Duma boards, including one marshal of the nobility. Thirteen of this group were professional men, including all seven nobles and two peasants, while the "merchant" by social class was actually a zemstvo doctor. Two deputies had also worked in private service and one had been employed in the service of the state.

The number of Kadet deputies who had served the state as regular members of the bureaucracy was, however, not large. Nine had held relatively minor official posts in various ministries, including three who had worked as tax inspectors and four professional men who had used their specialist knowledge in government service. Two Kadet deputies, Mukhanov and Nabokov, were both connected to the upper circles of the bureaucracy, having both been "gentlemen of His Majesty's bedchamber". Vladimir Nabokov was the son of a former minister of justice.

Apart from this, three Kadets had worked as land captains, four had worked at their local office for peasant affairs, and a similar number were retired military officers with significant military service. This was not the limit of the Kadets' connection with public or state service: for example, 27 Kadets had been Justices of the Peace. However, this was typically an occupation of the Kadet zemstvo gentry as, indeed, was service in offices for peasant affairs. These positions do not justify describing their holders as regular members of the bureaucracy. The same is true of another group of eight Kadets, who were working or had worked in posts connected with the machinery of justice as members of district courts or assistant procurators. They were all professional men – lawyers – and were working in a public institution still influenced by the ideal of the independence of the judiciary from the administration. In general, then, the Kadet deputies clearly did not have very strong links with the bureaucracy, especially with its upper layers. But a very large number, whether in the zemstvo, the administration of justice or in the lower levels of the bureaucracy, were in fact doing a great deal of the day-to-day humdrum unglamorous work necessary for the proper functioning of Russia. This conclusion is reinforced by the fact that nine peasants had held office as "starshina" (headman, elder) in the lowest organ of (theoretically) local self-government, the "volost'".

This group tended to be drawn from the better-off layers of the peasantry, and in general the Kadet deputies who were legally peasants do not appear to have been typical of their class. Out of 28 "peasant" deputies for whom biographical details are readily available, only two appear to have been solely concerned with agriculture. Eight were small traders, and ten had professions: there were four lawyers, two teachers, one agronomist, one mullah, one zemstvo doctor and one editor/publisher. Of the remainder two had worked in zemstvo service and one in private service. One was the manager of an estate, two were rail workers, one was as shop assistant ("prikazchik") and one combined husbandry with joinery work. Like many of the Kadet gentry, the majority of the party's peasant deputies were clearly moving away from exclusive dependence on the soil.[6] Moreover, for the most part they were clearly more prosperous and better educated than the majority of the peasantry. The small number of rank and file peasants among the Kadet deputies, together with the very limited number of industrial workers, once again suggests that the party's appeal was not primarily to the poorest sections of society.

However, parliamentary deputies are normally of a higher social class than the people they represent. It may, therefore, be useful to see where the party's support came from among the people at large. Which sections of the population had elected the Kadets? This is difficult to determine accurately, since the majority of deputies were elected to the Duma by provincial congresses of electors chosen by all social classes. However, it is possible to discover which class curiae initially chose the Kadets, making use of Borodin's statistics on 448 deputies, including 153 Kadets.[7] Once again the Kadets' relative weakness among the peasants and workers is clear. Even in conditions of boycott by the extreme left, the party contained only two deputies chosen by the workers out of a total of 17 (13 went to the Trudoviks, some later joining the Menshevik group). And of 169 members from the peasant curia, only 24 were members of the Kadet parliamentary group. The majority were either Trudoviks or non-party, although after Borodin's investigations were completed there was something of a drift of peasant members towards the Kadets. In the curia of larger landowners the Kadets did considerably better. Of 74 members elected by this category of voter, 29 were Kadets, the largest number from any party. But even here they did not have a majority. The party had a similar proportion of the members chosen by the small landowners – (those possessing one-tenth of the property qualification necessary to vote in the other landowning category). Out of a total of 15 deputies, five entered the K.D. Duma group. This curia included not only the poorest gentry but also some more prosperous peasants.

Since these curiae did not themselves elect the deputies, they can, of course, only give a very general idea of the courses of Kadet support, but they cannot be discounted, especially as they tend generally to coincide with findings from other evidence. However, one feature is rather unexpected for a party which had so many of its roots in the countryside. This was the exceptionally large number of Kadets chosen by the town and city voters. More than half of the 153 Kadets had been chosen by urban voters, 83 out of a total of a possible 115. Moreover, out of 24 cities which enjoyed the right to elect deputies directly to the Duma, the Kadets gained 29 out of a possible 35 seats.[8] And in both capitals the party gained all 160 of the electors chosen at the first stage of the voting. The electoral law had enfranchised a very wide section of the urban population. It had given the vote to all those owning taxed immovable property, holding industrial certificates, paying business taxes, or household tax, and to those occupying separate dwellings for more than a year. However, the working class had been granted only very limited representation. The predominant power in the urban elections thus lay in the hands of the lower salariat and the small property owners, the petty officials and the professional men, in broad terms the middle classes. To achieve their success, therefore, the Kadets must have enjoyed very considerable support in this section of the electorate. This analysis is confirmed by the available evidence on the composition of local Kadet groups. According to the *Vestnik* (*The Herald*) in February,[9] the Moscow city membership was made up as follows: commercial and industrial salaried employees, 20 per cent; members of the free professions, 18.7 per cent; salaried employees of the state and social institutions, 9.6 per cent; merchants, 7.4 per cent; students, 7.2 per cent; those without paid employment, 5.1 per cent; artisans, 4 per cent; workers, 4 per cent; domestic servants, 0.7 per cent; clergy, 0.5 per cent. Of course, Moscow was something of a special case, owing to its unusual degree of urbanization, but even in the provincial and uezd (district) groups the professional and white-collar influence was very strong. The Vladimir provincial group, for example,[10] reported that at first it had been composed entirely of intelligentsia, especially members of the Third Element and other zemstvo men. But by February 1906 it also included a fair number of government officials and teachers. Recruiting the lower classes had proved more difficult, though it had not been entirely unsuccessful. In March the Ekaterinograd regional group gave a basically similar description of its own composition: "The predominant element in the party membership is the intelligentsia of every possible kind of profession and employment."[11] Like the Muscovites, the Novotorzhskii Uezd group (Tver' province) went beyond generalizations and actually published figures relating to its members' occupations and status. It had ten peasants, eight landowners, nine professional men, six "petty bourgeois", four merchants, two shop assistants and two artisans.[12]

All these accounts of the composition of local groups make it clear that professional men played a very important rôle not only among the Kadet deputies, but also among the party rank and file. Moreover, in the case of Moscow, there was a sizeable number of students and an active university Kadet group. If most of the students are considered to be professional men in training, this emphasizes the rôle of this class even further. Looked at in another way, the amount of student support once again stresses the importance of the universities for the Kadets. Even when the professional men are not taken into account, it is once again clear that the Kadet rank and file came primarily from elements which were better educated and rather higher up the social scale than the mass of peasants and workers. It is true that there were ten peasant members in the Novotorzhskii uezd group but there is no evidence that they were ordinary run-of-the-mill peasants. Like the K.D. peasant deputies, they may well have been from the better-off layers of their class.

It is particularly interesting to note the very important rôle played in Moscow by the commercial and industrial employees, compared with the low figure for small independent producers, the artisans. This reflects the fact that the Russian urban petty bourgeoisie, in the Marxist sense, never attained the degree of development it had in the West, and that it had been overtaken by the international growth of large-scale industry and commerce. Because of this the Kadets already found themselves, like the liberal parties of the advanced Western countries, considerably dependent for support upon a white-collar salariat. Their rôle was indeed so important that at the Third Congress the party decided that it was essential to place the question of the legal protection of commercial and industrial employees of this category on the agenda for the First Duma.[13] Moreover, in the Second Duma priority was given in the field of labour legislation to bills on this question.[14] Another section of the salariat which appears to have given the Kadets considerable support were the government officials. Their rôle is almost certainly understated in the statistics relating to the membership of local groups. They were officially discouraged from joining the party, and a report from the Vladimir group suggests that they were hesitant about becoming members.[15] Nevertheless, their support for the party was so great that at a meeting of the Central Committee in August 1906 Fedorov attacked "the bureaucratic opportunism reigning in the Party in Petersburg". At the same time he cast doubt upon the genuineness of party support among the city's electorate. Of the votes gained by the party, claimed Fedorov: "only 25% belonged to members of the Party. 75% were non-party, (officials, shop-assistants, latent Kadets)".[16] Such doubts were not entirely new. At the time of the elections the K.D.s had seen the large vote for the party as probably more a general vote of opposition to the government rather than a vote specifically for the Kadets. One reason for this had been the boycott of the elections by the extreme left. However, the support for the Kadets among the urban electorate proved to be quite solid in the elections to the next Duma, when the boycott by the left had been abandoned.

The overwhelming weight of evidence indicates that support for the Kadet Party came primarily from the middle layers of Russian society. At one end of the spectrum the party attracted the moderately prosperous gentry, while at the other it appealed to the poorer white collar salariat and the better-off members of the peasantry. But although it was a "middle-class" party, it was not the party of the "bourgeoisie" in the classic Marxist sense. It had only relatively weak connections with the world of financial and industrial capitalism, and it even contained few artisans. It is true that in Moscow, 7.4 per cent of the membership were classified as "merchants", but Moscow was socially very different from Russia as a whole. Moreover, it is not clear how far the classification of "merchant" actually refers to occupation, and how far it merely describes legal status.

Now it is true that the party finances were heavily dependent on donations from wealthy supporters. Throughout this period, the Kadets' finances were in a state of chronic weakness. Largely as a result of the shortcomings of party organization in the country it proved almost impossible to secure adequate funds via subscriptions from local Kadet groups: "In such circumstances" (the Central Committee later admitted), "the Central Committee had to act chiefly on funds subscribed by a few better-off members of the Party".[17] On 6 May 1906 the Central Committee set up a special Finance Committee composed of Prince Peter Dolgurukov, Nabokov and A.I. Kaminka.[18] This was primarily concerned with obtaining money from rich sympathizers. One of the party's benefactors was M.K. Morozova, a member of the wealthy Morozov textile and merchant family.[19] However, Miliukov represents her interest in the Kadets as only half-serious dilettantism.[20] For the most part financial support for the party came from rich landowners rather than from business people. The records of meetings of the party's Central Committee mention, for example, Count Orlov-Davydov, one of the richest landowners in Russia, and Countess Panina, the wife of Ivan Petrunkevich.[21] In the period up to 20 October 1906 the *Vestnik* listed donations to the party totalling over 21,000 rubles; the bulk of which was in the form of large sums from rich supporters. These included big donations from one industrialist-cum-landowner, Komissarov (2,000 rubles), from Prince Pavel Dolgorukov, and the rich landowner Orlov-Davydov (both 1,000 rubles). There were also large anonymous gifts, some of which may have come from businessmen, but on the face of it, the majority of donations appear to have come from non-industrial sources.

The dependence of the Kadets upon the aid of their wealthier supporters was, of course, made much of by Soviet historians who tended to see it as proof that the party was a front for rich capitalist/pomeshchik paymasters.[22] However, the receipt of such donations was not peculiar to the Kadets. The Bolsheviks themselves depended heavily upon donations from bourgeois sympathizers, including the Moscow industrialist Savva Morozov. This was, in fact, a chronic feature of political life in a country where the organization of parties was in its infancy, and political repression was still the order of the day. The Kadets' dependence upon funds from rich supporters does not prove that the party was the creature of either business of pomeshchik (i.e. landowner) interests. It is true that its policies were, perhaps, in the enlightened self-interest of many of the Kadet gentry, but as we have seen, they also appealed to a much wider range of social classes. Moreover, Kadet policies were not in accord with the interests of the owners of the great latifundia, of whom Orlov-Davydov was one of the richest.[23] Although some business people were prepared to help finance the Kadets, the party's policies were not unduly favourable to the interests of commerce and industry; if anything the reverse was true. Their support for labour reform, including the legal protection of commercial and industrial employees, shows that they were not concerned to protect the narrow self-interest of the employers. It is true that to a considerable extent the Kadets did come from the better-off social strata, and that many of their leaders were convinced that only a programme of radical reform could avert the threat of a bitter class war.

Moreover, it must be admitted that the growth of the liberal movement was partly a result of the damage done to landowning interests by the government. Witte's policies had severely weakened the bonds between the landed gentry and the government and had helped to create the strong oppositionist movement out of which the Kadet Party had been born. However, although the number of gentry in the party remained high, they were increasingly merging with the growing professional classes. Increasingly, it was the professional element in the party which came to hold a dominant position. The very readiness of the Kadet gentry to countenance large-scale expropriation of private land suggests that many of them were willing to liquidate their connections with agriculture and follow those who were already exclusively or mostly dependent on the professions or other occupations of a non-agricultural type. If the Kadet land reform had gone through, it seems inevitable that the Kadets would more than ever have been dominated by men of the free professions rather than by the interests of landowners. Moreover, as we have seen, the party had increasingly gained support among the middle and lower-middle layers of society, especially among white-collar elements in the towns. Landowning interests remained important in the party, but by 1906 the liberals had come to depend much less on the support of aristocratic frondeurs and more on social elements of a more modern type.

One of the most striking characteristics of this influential body of support for the Kadets is its very high degree of Westernization. The elections had revealed that the greatest concentration of K.D. voters lay in the towns, which in general were much more Europeanized than the countryside. The party had had one of its greatest electoral successes in the most Westernized of Russian cities, St. Petersburg. Moreover, within the towns a great part of its support came from classes of a very Westernized type. In particular the influence of a European-style salariat was making itself felt. But the strongest Europeanizing influence came from the professional men. The very basis of their professional knowledge was derived largely from the West, and the universities, the main training ground for the professions, were therefore the chief source of Western influence in Russia. Quite evidently, it was difficult for professional men in close contact with Western ideas not to be influenced by European political concepts. This was even more true when, as frequently happened among the Kadets, knowledge of European ideas was supplemented by travel and study abroad. According to Miliukov, who was himself a striking example of a "Russian European", S.A. Muromtsev, the Duma President, had initially become a Westernist at university, under the influence of Solov'ev's interpretation of Russian history.[24] His views had later been confirmed by his studies at Göttingen University.²⁵ A similar period of study at a German university had also been instrumental in converting Kokoshkin from conservatism to liberalism.²⁶ The influence of the universities in spreading Western political ideas and in particular liberalism, the dominant political creed of the West, is mirrored in the extraordinarily large number of academics in the Kadet Party, especially in its leadership. It is also reflected in the very high proportion of Kadet deputies who had received a university education.

The influence of the universities and of professional men with a Western-style education in the Kadet Party is very significant, as is the weakness of the representation of the business classes in their ranks. It underlines the fact that liberalism in Russia did not grow up in response to the development of a large industrial and commercial bourgeoisie. The Russian industrial bourgeoisie was still, numerically speaking, a very small class, under the shelter of government protection, and it did not offer a very favourable soil for opposition to the régime. The domination of the Kadet Party by the professional intelligentsia, a class which was influenced by Western ideas more than any other social group, suggests that liberalism in Russia was not so much the home-grown product of a still backward society, as an intellectual import from Europe. It should not be forgotten that the Russian professional classes largely owed their very existence to the artificial transfusions of Westernization effected by different Tsars, who had seen that if Russia was to survive it needed to adopt much of the professional and technical expertise of Europe. The autocracy itself had therefore promoted, willy-nilly, the growth of a large class of professional men strongly influenced by Western modes of thought. The Great Reforms of the 1860s had given a particularly powerful impetus in this direction. Hitherto the lower layers of administration had been left in the hands of the arbitrary patriarchal class authority of the pomeshchik. However, Alexander II had replaced this by a much more efficient and complex administrative machine consisting of an enlarged bureaucracy, the zemstvo institutions and a reformed legal system. All of these increased the demand for professional men. The zemstvo provided an increasing number of openings in its "Third Element", the legal system needed a greater number of lawyers, and the growing complexity of the bureaucracy necessitated the employment of larger numbers of professional experts.²⁷

Except for the academics, who had perhaps a natural affinity with liberalism, owing to their overriding concern for academic freedom – an ideal which also probably strongly influenced other professional men in the course of their own academic education – it was perhaps the lawyers who had the strongest natural tendency towards liberalism. In 1864, the autocracy itself had attempted to reform the legal system upon the basis of the liberal concepts of the rule of law, the independence of the judiciary, and equality before the law. Although these principles had subsequently been increasingly undermined, they had become something like the "Ark of the Covenant", in the eyes of the increasingly influential legal profession. And in so far as the lawyers were deeply attached to the principle of the rule of law and the independence of the judiciary, this fostered a belief in putting at least some limitation on the power of the autocracy, and tended to make the profession a natural centre of constitutionalist thought. Just as the establishment of the zemstvos had been bound in the long run to foster Western-style beliefs in self-government, in much the same way the legal reforms had created a large body of men devoted to liberal legal ideas, and, indirectly, to the principles of constitutionalism. This probably goes a long way to explaining the extraordinarily great influence of the legal profession in the Kadet Party.

The Great Reforms, then, were largely responsible for opening up Russia to Western ideological influence, and facilitating the growth of liberalism. The government had done its best to prevent this happening. It had striven to prevent the spread of Western political influences in the universities, and to restrict their activities to the narrowly academic sphere. With this end in view it had carried on a policy of repression in the universities, subjecting the students to strict discipline and banning their societies. It had also conducted a series of purges against elements regarded as politically unreliable: students had been conscripted into the army, and members of teaching staffs had been dismissed. Both Miliukov and Muromtsev (for example) had lost their posts for political reasons. However, if anything, the policy of repression had merely intensified the intelligentsia's opposition to the government and had vested the victims of reaction with the halo of martyrdom. The intolerance of the government had only increased the intellectual appeal of Western liberal ideas among the educated classes. The old régime had failed in its attempt to introduce Europeanization by retail. From the universities and other contacts with the West, European liberal ideas streamed out, affecting all the more literate classes, especially the professional intelligentsia, the white-collar workers, the progressive gentry, and even members of the bureaucracy.

Liberalism was not an indigenous creed in Russia. It did not grow up in response to the needs of a Western-style industrial bourgeoisie. It was instead centred around the intelligentsia, a section of the population which by virtue of its liberal Western education regarded the reactionary nature of the Tsarist régime with unmitigated horror. And it is only natural that in seeking to reform the system, the intelligentsia turned for its inspiration to Western political ideas. However, it must not be forgotten that intellectual influence of the West did not foster the spread of liberalism alone. It also resulted in the attraction of a large section of the intelligentsia towards other European political doctrines, especially Marxism. In analysing exactly why the Kadet intelligentsia adopted liberalism rather than Marxism, it is difficult to give an explanation based entirely on their disinterested intellectual preference for liberal thought. It is true that the intelligentsia were men of ideas, but they were not without their own self-interest. It has already become apparent that on the whole the Kadet Party drew its support from a rather higher social spectrum than that of the left parties. Kadet support among the intelligentsia was no exception to this rule. There was a strong tendency for the Kadet professional men to be drawn from the higher professions and simultaneously to possess land or other property. In particular, they overlapped heavily with the landowning zemstvo gentry. Given the relatively high social status and prosperity of the

Kadets, it is not surprising that their Westernism did not take the form of revolutionary socialism, with its hatred for property, the bourgeoisie and the nobility, but instead drew them towards the more moderate doctrines of liberalism. This was primarily a party of respectable men who naturally eschewed extremes. And in borrowing their political ideas from the West, they quite naturally turned to the latest brand of liberalism in the West which preached social reconciliation rather than class war. This harmonized not only with their humane ideals but also with their desire to assuage the growing threat to the better-off and more cultivated classes stemming from the growing unrest among the masses.

The Kadet leaders were not ashamed to admit that they had, as it were, taken Western liberalism "off the peg" in an effort to solve Russia's severe social and political problems. In the Duma, G.F. Shershenevich, introducing the bill on freedom of assembly, proclaimed[28] that there was no peculiarly Russian solution to this question: "I do not think we have our own arbitrary distinctive method of solving this problem. I think that the models of Western political life will serve as our models for a long time to come." And he freely admitted that the bill he was presenting was based on the French law of 1881. Similar heavy use of German and French legislation was made in drafting the bills on the press and on the unions.[29] On the face of it, the Kadets' willingness to borrow from the West appears to be the reverse of nationalism, but paradoxically it contained a strong nationalistic undercurrent. The Kadets were fully aware that Russia was lagging behind compared with other major powers. And they tended to see the adoption of advanced Western political forms as an essential prerequisite to rebuilding their country's power and prestige in the world, and as vital to the modernization of Russia. N.A. Gredskul', for example, argued that the lack of civil equality inevitably bred social and national antagonisms within the state which were bound to weaken it vis-à-vis other countries.[30] The result could be that it would be "incapable of sustaining the struggle with other powerful states". Gredskul' asked:

> Is there any need to prove that if (Russia) had abolished serfdom in the beginning of the 19th Century, and had introduced a constitution at the end of its first half, then it would never have reached the stage of state weakness revealed by the Japanese War? Is there any need to prove that until we have absolutely firmly established a constitution with the freedom and civil liberties which accompany it, we cannot rest easy about our historical fate?

Kokoshkin also saw freedom and democracy as prerequisites of the modernization of Russia, just as essential as railways or industry. It was essential in an age of mass politics to harness the energies of the whole people:

> Now, when the popular masses have actively come forward onto the political scene, when they have appeared as active participants in world events, only a country where the consciousness of the full and equal rights of the individual as a citizen has taken root in the masses of the people can be prepared for wide development. A government having only administrative

means in its hands, is in no condition to compete with one which draws forth all the living forces from the depths of the people.

If the energies of the people were to be harnessed, it was essential to establish not only political freedom but also equal civil rights and universal suffrage. No one should be thrown overboard from the ship of state. This was the only way to soften class enmities and to achieve the unity and organization of society.[31] Like Gredskul' and Kokoshkin, Rodichev also expressed concern about the divisive effects of the lack of civil equality. And his language took on a definitely nationalist ring when he declaimed in the Duma: "Every Russian subject, however modest his lot ('sushchestvovanie'), must have the right to call Russia his fatherland." A.I. Kaminka employed similar arguments in the debates on civil equality. In a speech on 6 June he told the House that: "We have no people, no nation, in the political sense of this word. The nation is the essential foundation of the contemporary constitutional state." And until civil equality was established a nation could not exist.

Notes

1 Biographical details of the Kadet deputies has been obtained primarily from the following sources: "Spisok chlenov parlamentskoi fraktsii partii Narodnoi Svobody", *Vestnik narodnoi svobody*, No. 17, 29 June, cols. 1107–16; *Pervye narodnye predstaviteli*, S.P.B. 1907; *Chleny 1-oi Gosudarstvennoi Dumy*, S.P.B. 1906; *Chleny 2-oi Gosudarstvennoi Dumy*, S.P.B. 1907; *Russkie Vedomosti 1863–1913* (sbornik statei). See the biographical section at the end of the book. The most important single source employed is *Gosudarstvennaia Duma pervogo sozyva*, Moscow 1906.
2 These descriptions refer purely to legal status and not necessarily to occupation. According to the figures of Borodin, the status of 153 Kadet deputies was as follows: nobles – 92 (60.1 per cent); "honourable citizens" ("pochëtnye grazhdane") – 1 (0.6 per cent); spiritual calling – 5 (3.2 per cent); merchants – 7 (4.5 per cent); Cossacks – 1 (0.6 per cent); petty bourgeois – 6 (3.9 per cent); peasants – 36 (28.5 per cent); no indication – 5 (3.2 per cent) (see N. Borodin, "Lichnyi sostav pervoi Gosudarstvennoi dumy", in *P.G.D.*, Vol. I, p. 29).
3 Borodin, "Lichnyi sostav pervoi Gosudarstvennoi dumy", p. 28.
4 Borodin, "Lichnyi sostav pervoi Gosudarstvennoi dumy", pp. 29–30.
5 Of the nine members of the Second Element, five were nobles, two were peasants and one was a "merchant".
6 According to Borodin ("Lichnyi sostav pervoi Gosudarstvennoi dumy", p. 30), of a total of 36 Kadet nominally "peasant" deputies, 26 had no land.
7 Borodin, "Lichnyi sostav pervoi Gosudarstvennoi dumy", pp. 37–9.
8 Calculated upon the basis of the list of Duma members and their constituencies printed in: Gosudarstvennaia Duma, *Ukazatel' k stenograficheskim otchëtam*, S.P.B. 1906.
9 *Vestnik*, No. 1, p. 39.
10 *Vestnik*, No. 1, pp. 45–6.
11 *Vestnik*, No. 5, p. 293.
12 *Vestnik*, No. 9, pp. 619–21.
13 "Postanovleniia III s''ezda" (Section III), *Vestnik*, No. 9, 1906. See also Gubar'ev's speech in "III s''ezd delegatov", *Pravo*, No. 18, 1906, p. 1683 and *S''ezdy i konferentsii K.-d.partii*, Vol. I, pp. 272 and 349 (ROSSPEN 1997).

14 See Astrov, *Zakonodatel'nye proekty i predpolozheniia Partii narodnoi svobody*, pp. 326–38.
15 *Vestnik*, No. 1, 1906, pp. 45–6.
16 "Kadety v 1905–06 gg", *Krasnyi arkhiv* (*K.A.*) No. 47–8, 2/VIII/1906.
17 For the Kadets' financial position, see: *OTCHËT tsentral'nogo komiteta konstitutsionno-demokraticheskoi partii za dva goda 18 oktiabria 1905 po oktiabr' 1907 g.*, S.P.B. 1907, pp. 12–13.
18 "Kadety v 1905–1906 gg", *K.A.*, No. 46, p. 61, 6/V/1906.
19 "Kadety v 1905–1906 gg", *K.A.*, No. 46, p. 63, 4/VI/1906.
20 Miliukov, *Vospominaniia*, New York 1955, Vol. I, p. 229.
21 "Kadety v 1905–1906 gg", *K.A.*, No. 46, p. 63, 4/VI/1906.
22 See, e.g., B. Grave in *K.A.*, No. 46, p. 42.
23 B. Grave in *K.A.*, No. 46, p. 42. According to Grave, Orlov-Davydov was also subsidizing the progromist Union of the Russian People which casts doubts upon the consistency of his support for the Kadets. If Grave is correct, he may well have been hedging his political bets in an effort to be on the winning side of the political battle in any event.
24 P.N. Miliukov, "Sergei Andreevich Muromtsev: biograficheskii ocherk", in D.I. Shakhovskoi (ed.), *Sergei Andreevich Muromtsev*, Moscow 1911, p. 10.
25 Miliukov, "Sergei Andreevich Muromtsev: biograficheskii ocherk", pp. 22–4.
26 A.A. Kizevetter, "Fedor Fedorovich Kokoshkin", in N.I. Astrov (ed.), *K pamiati pogibshikh*, Paris 1929, pp. 197–8.
27 See, *inter alia*, Fischer, *Russian Liberalism*, pp. 46–52.
28 *S.O.*, Vol. II, 20/6/1906, p. 1548.
29 See, e.g., A.I. Kaminka, "Proekt zakona o soiuzakh" and G.B. Iollos, "Zakonoproekt o pechati", in *P.G.D.*, Vol. 2, pp. 103, 189.
30 N.A.Gredskul', "Proekt zakona o ravnopravii", *P.G.D.*, Vol. 2, p. 113.
31 *S.O.*, Vol. II, p. 1066, 6/VI/1906.

8 Some conclusions

The Kadets believed that the only solution to Russia's chronic ills was the establishment of a democratic, constitutional régime. However, Russia was still a much less advanced country than France, Britain or the United States. Its level of literacy was low, its national composition was heterogeneous, and its economy relatively undeveloped. Was it really possible for such a country successfully to adopt an advanced liberal political system? During the last hundred years, attempts to graft advanced Western constitutionalism onto less developed countries have met with only limited successs. State after state in Asia and Africa have rejected forms of political democracy, and have succumbed to various types of authoritarianism.

However, this does not prove that liberal, democratic régimes can never survive in developing countries. India, a state sharing many of the problems of early twentieth-century Russia, has contrived, for almost 70 years of its independent existence, to maintain its democratic constitutional system. It has shown that political democracy is possible in an initially underdeveloped country even more nationally heterogeneous than Russia. It must, of course, be admitted that India has had special advantages. In the first place its educated classes had thoroughly absorbed constitutional ideas from the British. Moreover, the struggle for independence helped to unite the people behind a single party, thus imparting an initial stability to Indian politics. These advantages were not enjoyed by Russia. On the other hand the Kadets, the dominant party in the First Duma, were exceptionally well-versed in the forms and practice of Western constitutionalism, and the emergence of such a large, highly cultured liberal party, well schooled in the procedures of political democracy, provides in itself strong evidence that Russia was not totally unprepared for the adoption of a representative form of government. Moreover, Russia was not without a tradition of self-government at the local level. Quite apart from the experience gained via the zemstvos, the peasantry had long made use of democratic procedures in the commune and in "volost'" (cantonal) self-government.

Now it is true that if the Kadets had come to power in 1906 they would have faced special difficulties stemming from the continued existence of the danger of revolution. And in these circumstances their demands for the ending of all exceptional laws, and the immediate introduction of all the Western civil liberties, did represent something of a risk. But if it was a risk, it was a calculated one. The Kadets consistently argued that the revolution could not permanently be stopped by repression, but only by a policy of reform, and in particular by the redistribution of the land. And indeed, if the Kadets had managed to carry out their grandiose plans of agrarian reform, it seems likely they would have gained the support of a large part of the peasantry for a constitutional régime. However, the Kadets' agrarian proposals would undoubtedly have taken a considerable time to put into effect. And in the meantime, a liberal government might have found it increasingly difficult to maintain order. However, 1906 was not 1917, and it is possible that popular unrest might have been held in check. A Kadet government would not necessarily have proved unworkable in the conditions of the time. True, if the Kadets had been liberals of the Manchester type it seems very doubtful whether their policies would have been viable in a country with such grave social problems. But, in fact, like the most advanced Western liberals, their ideas were strongly influenced by the concept of social justice, and they were prepared to contemplate state intervention in order to obtain it. This alone might have helped to defuse the dangerous class and national tensions in Russia, and to make a liberal constitutional system workable. However, it is true that in Russian conditions a liberal régime might not have worked as well as in the West. Miliukov was clearly aware that this was a real possibility.[1] Nevertheless, this does not mean that a constitution would not have worked at all in Russian conditions, at least for a time. On the other hand, it is more problematic whether a constitutional system could have survived for long in Russia, or whether a Kadet government could have solved the country's most deep-seated problems.

These problems were, to a great extent, rooted in the economic backwardness of the Empire. Could Kadet policies have succeeded in eliminating this fundamental weakness? It has already been observed that in the field of agriculture they were disinclined to face up squarely to the problems posed by the continued existence of the commune, and did not have an adequate long-term view of the future of this branch of the economy. However, in time, they might well have faced up to this problem.

In the opinion of T.H. Von Laue, a much more serious liberal weakness was their opposition to Witte's programme of forced industrialization. In Von Laue's view the rapid state-sponsored development of industry was essential if Russia was to survive and hold its own in a period dominated by the arms race and fierce international competition. However, he admitted that Witte's policies imposed very severe burdens on the people, in the form of increased taxes and import duties, together with excessive exports of grain. Indirect taxes, for example, had increased no less than 108 per cent between 1880 and 1901.[2] In Von Laue's view no democratic government would have been able to impose such hardships on the people, and certainly the liberals would not have done so: "Russian liberalism", he argued, "was largely agrarian in orientation and opposed to foisting economic sacrifices on the population". According to Von Laue, "Russians had to choose between freedom and power".[3]

Now it cannot be denied that the Kadets had, in fact, always opposed the Witte system, and the heavy burdens it placed upon the agricultural classes. And it is also true that, in general, they did not fully realize Russia's urgent need for rapid industrialization and that they did indeed have an "agrarian orientation". Petrazhitskii was almost alone in seeing industrialization as the chief solution to Russia's economic problems. Indeed, some Kadets showed a definite antipathy to the process of urbanization and industrialization. For example, V.P. Obninskii, the chairman of one of the Duma subcommissions on agrarian reform, refused to accept Petrazhitskii's arguments concerning the desirability of drawing off excess agricultural labour into the towns.[4] On the contrary, he hoped that the agrarian reform would start a reverse movement of workers into the countryside. If the factories required labour they should move to the villages. And he even advised the academics in the Duma to follow suit: "Come to us out of these repositories of stone", Obninskii declared, "come to our provincial and uezd backwoods, onto all the spaciousness of the fields of our motherland". The position of the Kadets as a whole was by no means so extreme, but their programme demands for the lowering of import duties and the "gradual abolition of indirect taxation on articles consumed by the popular masses" struck at the very basis of the Witte system. Miliukov, for example, fiercely attacked the misery caused to the peasantry by the crushing weight of taxation.[5] He pointed out that under the policy of the protection of industry the people had had to pay severely increased prices for imported goods. The taxpayers had also, in effect, to support all the dividends of the new enterprises. Industry was largely underpinned by government orders, and the people had also been compelled to pay for the construction of government railways designed to serve industrial needs.[6] Witte's financial policy also came under withering fire. Miliukov admitted that the gold standard had had the virtue of stabilizing the currency. But one of its results had been to cast Russia "into the fast-tightening folds of the contracting money supply". And he went on to attack Witte's heavy borrowing abroad, which had led to a vast increase in the public debt, and a concomitant increase in interest charges. He even referred to Witte as the "Russian Calonne" because of his heavy borrowing, and deplored his policy of obtaining a free surplus in the budget at the expense of a starving population.[7]

However, Miliukov did not oppose forced industrialization purely on humanitarian grounds. He was writing in the aftermath of the severe industrial and financial crisis of the turn of the century, and argued that this demonstrated the failure of attempts to foster industry by artificial means. According to Miliukov, this had proved disastrous even for industry itself. Industry had been developed only at the cost of imposing heavy burdens upon the people, and this had undermined its ability to pay the taxes which underpinned the system, or to provide an effective home market for industrial products: "Just then, at the close of the nineties", Miliukov argued, "the 'paying' and the 'purchasing power' of the population proved to be so exhausted that the protected industries themselves began sorely to feel the consequences. The crisis had come; industry had to face (relative) over production". The peasant taxpayer had been ruined, and in this situation the government could no longer keep up the flow of state orders for rails, rolling stock and the rest. "Under these conditions, the government found it difficult to support, on the former scale, metallurgic enterprises started under its auspices." Not surprisingly, Russian manufacturers were dissatisfied with this turn of events. However, the only solution was to improve the condition of the mass of the people in order to provide a market for industry; it could not continue to rely on government orders.[8]

In the Duma, Gertsenshtein launched a similar attack on the policy of forced industrialization. In his view "all our attempts to create capitalism and big industry have led to nought".[9] And he returned to the attack while dealing with the arguments of Gurko, who had stressed the crucial rôle of industrialization in solving the agrarian crisis:

> You say that in other countries there is industry. But, you know, it cannot be created artificially. You have, you see, already made attempts of this sort and, as a result, a series of factories have been obtained at state expense. Take a closer look at the accounts of the State Bank, and you will see what consequences the artificial propagation of industry has had. Many hundreds of millions of Belgian and French money has been lost on it. Until we have a prosperous (syty) peasantry we shall have no industry. At the Nizhnii Novgorod fair the trade in cotton goes well only when the country has had a (good) harvest.[10]

The Kadets' arguments were not entirely without foundation, but it must be admitted that they failed to do justice to the great achievements of Witte's policies. Largely as a result of Witte's management of the economy, Russia had witnessed a remarkable development of industry in the 1890s. And despite the recession which had set in at the turn of the century, the basis had been laid for a further period of advance in the years immediately before the Great War. However, as Von Laue rightly points out, the Kadets were inclined to see only the hardships incurred by the Witte system. They did not take proper account of Russia's need for rapid industrialization in view of the international arms race, nor did they realize that given Russia's economic "backwardness" and its urgent need to catch up with Western Europe, industrialization might take a path radically different from that of more advanced countries.

The Kadets, in fact, seemed to believe that the industrialization of Russia should follow a similar route to that taken by industry in England. In this, as in so much else, they were thorough Westernists. What they wanted was the gradual, organic development of industry in response to the demands of the market, rather than forced industrialization based on protectionism and state orders. However, as Alexander Gershchenkron has pointed out,[11] development of the English type is ill-suited to the needs of "backward" countries, entering industrialization at a much later date than the pioneer industrial nation. He makes it clear that, certainly after the mid nineteenth century, different branches of industry had become so interdependent, that if industry was to develop effectively there had to be a concerted movement forward simultaneously over a wide field, in several different "development blocs". This meant that there had to be, in effect, some kind of planning mechanism capable of stimulating growth over a wide area of the economy, and of concentrating and centralizing the meagre resources of capital available in a backward country. This was all the more essential in view of the large sums of capital required to build and operate the most modern types of plant, which were tending to increase in size and complexity. It was also essential to centralize the scarce resources of entrepreneurial talent available in order to compensate for the lack of initiative from below. In France and Germany, which had been more advanced than Russia when entering upon their industrial revolutions, the rôle of concerting economic development had devolved upon the banks. Their promotion of industry had acted as a substitute for the more organic processes of English industrial growth. However, Russia entered upon industrialization later, and its economic problems were more acute. The shortage of capital and private initiative was more serious than in either France or Germany. In this situation it was necessary to substitute government action for that of the banks in order to concentrate scarce resources still further, and to guarantee a concerted forward movement in industry. In Russia, writes Gershchenkron, "The supply of capital for the needs of industrialization required the compulsory machinery of the government, which through its taxation policies succeeded in directing incomes from consumption to investment".[12] The state could not afford to wait for the possible development of industry in response to the demands of the market. In Russian conditions, effective industrial growth could not be guaranteed upon this basis. Instead the government found it necessary to implement its own industrial policies instead of promoting development in response to consumer demand. The state itself provided the effective industrial market by placing government orders for capital goods. It protected Russian manufacturers and encouraged an inflow of foreign capital by means of tariff barriers and its financial policies. The result was the brilliant industrial flowering of the 1890s.[F1]

This rapid spurt of industrial growth could not have been obtained under K.D. policies, and the Kadets were undoubtedly unjust in not recognizing the achievements of Witte's economic management. However, this does not necessarily mean that Kadet policies would have had disastrous consequences for industry if the party had come to power in 1906. Even Witte himself was aware that his policy of forced industrialization could not go on for ever; he recognized that there would eventually have to be a transition to more conventional modes of economic development.[13] Moreover, by 1904–6 the Witte system had effectively broken down. Agriculture was in a deplorable condition, and the industrial life of the country was still suffering from the effects of the severe crisis which had

---

F1 By contrast with the theses of Gershenkron and Von Laue, Paul R. Gregory plays down the importance of state intervention in promoting economic development in late imperial Russia, emphasizing instead the rôle of market forces. While this is an indispensable contribution to the debate and is in line with current economic precepts, it understates the rôle of the government and the significance of the Witte system (see Further Reading).

set in at the end of the 1890s. The chief reason for the industrial recession was undoubtedly an international financial crisis, but both Gershchenkron and Von Laue agree that this was not the whole story. They admit that in Russia the crisis was intensified by the widespread ruination of the peasantry. Largely as a result of the crushing burdens laid upon it by the Witte system, the peasantry was no longer able to meet the costs of the programme of forced industrialization. According to Gershchenkron, "It is fairly clear ... that beneath the surface phenomena (of the crisis) lay the exhaustion of the tax-paying power of the rural population".[14] Von Laue confirms this analysis. The Witte system had, he acknowledges, come up against "the exhaustion of the paying powers of the population". The conclusion was inescapable: "Unless he (Witte) could satisfy the clamor of the agrarian population he could not continue his policy of rapid industrialization."[15] Witte himself recognized this when in 1902 he set up his "Special Conference on the Needs of the Agricultural Industry". Now it is true that Witte himself did not wish to improve the lot of the peasantry by abandoning his policy of forced industrialization. He was not prepared to lower taxes or tariff barriers. His solution lay in promoting prosperity by granting the peasants economic freedom and independence.[16] However, this was really a long-term answer to the question: it would not have made it possible for the peasants to bear their state burdens in the near future. The fact was that the taxpayer was no longer able to meet the burdens imposed by industrialization, and against this background some relaxation of the Witte system was probably inevitable. The Kadets were not, then, being entirely unrealistic in demanding that the burden upon the peasantry should be eased. Indeed, after the fall of Witte, the government itself hastened to abandon the rigours of the Witte system. Kokovtsov, who dominated Russian finances in the years between 1906 and the war, carried on a financial régime of relative thrift, although government orders for industry did not entirely dry up.[17] Moreover, under Stolypin's premiership government policies were more concerned with agriculture than industry. However, all this did not severely retard Russia's industrial growth. According to Gershchenkron, the industrial growth rate in the years 1905–14 was no less than 6 per cent per annum, slower than in the 1890s it is true, but still a very rapid rate of development. The conclusion to be drawn from this, writes Gershchenkron,[18] is that, by now, "Russian industry had reached a stage where it could throw away the crutches of government support, and begin to walk independently". Industry was still unable to stand entirely on its own feet, but "at least to some extent the role of the retreating government was taken over by the banks".

Given the growing independence of industry, the Kadets' desire to lighten the burdens on agriculture and to end the system of forced industrial development need not have had severely damaging results, at least in the short term. The government's own rejection of the Witte system had not prevented industrial expansion. It is, of course, true that the party had demanded a more radical break with previous policies than that made by Kokovtsov. However, if the Kadets had taken office, it is probable that they would have modified their policies to some extent. It seems likely that, faced with the exigencies of great power politics and the international arms race before the First World War, they would have become more conscious of the need for rapid industrialization. This is all the more probable in view of the fact that, as later events were to confirm, the Kadets were not complacent about Russia's position in the world and their party had a definite nationalist tinge. Even in opposition, the Kadets indicated that they were becoming aware of the critical nature of the international situation. For example, a Kadet publication issued soon after the demise of the First Duma explicitly rejected socialist proposals to reduce indirect taxation by replacing the standing army with a militia. Russia, (it was argued) could not do without an army in a world of mighty armed states.[19] Given their basic realization of the dangers of a militarily weak Russia, it seems more than likely that once in power, the party would have gradually adopted a more sympathetic attitude towards the need for industrial growth. And even if they had not, it is not clear how far their policies would have severely damaged industry now that it was gaining increasing independence from the state. Indeed, since industry was now evolving towards a position where it could begin to rely on the market it seems possible that the Kadets' proposals for increased mass purchasing power might have had at least some beneficial results for the manufacturing sector of the economy.

Moreover, by 1906 the party was already moving away from one of its most extreme financial demands – its proposal for the gradual abolition of indirect taxation on articles consumed by the mass of the people. It has already been observed that if this had been done and the financial burdens on the peasantry had been greatly eased, the pressure upon this class to produce for the market would have severely diminished. Consequently, the towns and industrial centers might have found great difficulty in guaranteeing their supplies of food. However, soon after the dissolution of the First Duma the Kadets began to adopt a far less inflexible position on the question of indirect taxation. In a booklet containing a comprehensive explanation of party policies, it was admitted that direct taxes alone could not provide an adequate source of revenue in Russia: an income tax would yield at most one-sixth of the present receipts from indirect taxation. It would therefore be unrealistic to expect any serious decrease in the general level of taxation. All that could be promised was that in future the state revenues would be devoted to increasing the prosperity of the people and to meeting essential state needs.[20] In the Second Duma the party adopted a similar position. While proposing a shift from indirect to direct taxation, it was now recognized that its abolition was impossible. It was necessary to avoid exaggerated expectation of the results of financial reform.[21]

In view of all this, it does not necessarily follow that the Kadets' economic policies would have proved as disastrous as some commentators have assumed. Given a prolonged period without major wars, it is possible that under the Kadets, industry would have continued to develop an independent momentum of its own, and that Russia might gradually have succeeded in escaping from its economic backwardness. Moreover, it is probable that some degree of relaxation of Witte's programme of forced industrialization was inevitable in the years immediately following the First Russian Revolution. However, in the long term twentieth-century conditions were to prove highly unfavourable for the implementation of the gradualist, orthodox economic policies favoured by the Kadets. The early twentieth century proved to be a period of unprecedented international conflict and war. Time and again armed conflict shattered the Russian economy and endangered the very existence of the nation. In these circumstances the need for rapid industrialization re-emerged as the overriding priority for the Russian state. Without an all-out drive to develop a powerful industrial base Russia could not have survived in a hostile international environment.

It is true that the Kadets were not unaware of the need to maintain Russia's military and industrial strength; but it is extremely doubtful whether a programme of economic growth based upon popular consent and organic development would have continued to be viable, given the damage and disruption to industry wrought by the consequences of military catastrophe in the First World War. Moreover, it is clear that in an economy adapted to the needs of the market, heavy industry – which provided the basis of the Empire's military strength – would have lost some ground to the production of consumer goods and the manufacture of agricultural capital equipment. And it is certain that under a liberal régime, industrial development would not have been as rapid as it had been under Witte. Von Laue is undoubtedly correct in saying that a democratic government could not have carried out a massive programme of industrialization matching that of Stalin.

Now it may well be true that the forced development of heavy industry was essential to protect Russia in an age of savage international rivalry and unprecedented wars. If, in fact, it is assumed that Russia was inevitably fated to face the disasters of the First World War, together with all the other crises and conflicts which it brought in its wake, it is difficult to believe that liberalism had any real chance of survival in the Russia of the first half of the twentieth century.

Quite apart from narrowly economic considerations, the period ushered in by the First World War was singularly unfavourable for the development of political democracy in Europe in general. Indeed, it came under continual attack from both the right and the left. It even failed to survive in large parts of Western Europe, where it had much deeper roots than in Russia. Even Bulgaria, which Miliukov had felt offered proof that a constitution was viable in a relatively "backward" country, suffered a right-wing coup in 1923, which established an authoritarian régime. Parliamentary democracy can prosper only where political passions do not go to extremes, where there is a certain amount of common ground between the major opposing factions, and where social and political tensions are not so great that they cannot be assuaged by peaceful constitutional means and by rational argument.

These conditions did not exist in the period of European history which commenced in 1914. The economic hardships bred by the war, together with the national humiliation suffered by the defeated countries, engendered fear and despair. And these, in their turn, led to the growth of violent national and class hatreds. This situation was later aggravated by the international economic recession of the 1930s, and the inexorable slide towards the Second World War. In

Russia, conditions were even more unsuitable for the flowering of democracy than they were in the West. No other great power had suffered such humiliating military defeats, and no country had suffered greater economic dislocation. Moreover, these disasters struck a country without any deep-rooted tradition of constitutional government. Against this background it seems hardly surprising that Russia succumbed to dictatorship in 1917. Now it is true that if the Kadets had been able to provide the peasants with land in 1906 or even in 1917, the Bolsheviks might have had less opportunity to mobilize peasant discontent in their own favour. It is, in fact, possible that the Bolshevik dictatorship might have been avoided. However, it is difficult not to feel that some kind of authoritarian régime was probably inevitable in Russia given the conditions of the time, although it need not have been guided by Lenin. It might perhaps instead have taken the form of a right-wing military régime.

However, all this presupposes that the First World War, and the events which followed it, were inevitable – and it is impossible categorically to assert that this was the case. If a Kadet government had emerged from the First Russian Revolution, this would undoubtedly have altered the international situation existing in the years before 1914. And it is very difficult to say what the results of this might have been. True, the war might still have taken place (although it might not have been conducted in quite the same way, nor need it have had precisely the same outcome), but even this cannot be stated with any assurance. The establishment of a liberal régime in Russia would have been bound to have an effect upon the conduct of the country's foreign policy, and might perhaps have helped to avert or postpone a war.

It is perhaps noteworthy that before the outbreak of war in 1914 the Kadets were not inclined to give unequivocal support to Serbia. Miliukov, the Kadets' chief authority on foreign affairs and the Duma's greatest expert on the Balkans, had long been aware of the excesses of aggressive Serbian nationalism and continually counselled policies of restraint. If Miliukov and the Kadets had shared power and influence in a constitutional government, war with Austria and Germany might perhaps have been avoided in 1914.

And if, in fact, a war had not occurred until many years later, it is conceivable that by that time Russia might have succeeded in resolving its economic problems by means of the relatively organic development favoured by the Kadets. Moreover, in the meantime, Russia might have built up a tradition of constitutional government strong enough to have a chance of surviving the shocks of war.[22]

However, the history of Russian liberalism is full of conjecture and "might have beens". In reality the Kadets did not come to power in 1906, and the First World War did, in fact, take place. And given the grave international and internal disasters which then beset the country, liberalism and political democracy had little chance of flowering in Russia. Although the Kadets did not realize it in 1905–6, the immediate future, as in many other European countries, lay with the adherents of dictatorship.

Notes

1 Miliukov, *Russia and its Crisis*, pp. 563–4.
2 T.H. Von Laue, *Sergei Witte and the Industrialisation of Russia*, New York; London 1963, p. 101.
3 Von Laue, *Sergei Witte*, p. 306.
4 *S.O.*, Vol. I, p. 503, 19/V/1906.
5 Miliukov, *Russia and its Crisis*, pp. 442–7.
6 Miliukov, *Russia and its Crisis*, pp. 461–2.
7 Miliukov, *Russia and its Crisis*, pp. 466–7, 472–3.
8 Miliukov, *Russia and its Crisis*, pp. 462–5.
9 *S.O.*, Vol. I, p. 466, 18/V/1906.
10 *S.O.*, Vol. I, p. 529, 19/5/1906.
11 Alexander Gershchenkron, *Economic Backwardness in Historical Perspective*, New York 1962; see especially the following chapters: "Economic Backwardness in Historical Perspective", pp. 5–29. "Russia: Patterns and Problems of Development 1861–1958", pp. 119–42.
12 Gershchenkron, *Economic Backwardness in Historical Perspective*, p. 20.
13 Von Laue, *Sergei Witte*, pp. 76–7.
14 Gershchenkron, *Economic Backwardness in Historical Perspective*, p. 132.
15 Von Laue, *Sergei Witte*, p. 222.
16 Von Laue, *Sergei Witte*, p. 224.
17 Gershchenkron, *Economic Backwardness in Historical Perspective*, p. 133. See also pp. 21–2.
18 Gershchenkron, *Economic Backwardness in Historical Perspective*, p. 22.
19 A.A. Kizevetter (ed.), *Napadki na Partiiu Narodnoi Svobody*, Moscow 1906, p. 20.
20 Kizevetter, *Napadki na Partiiu Narodnoi Svobody*, pp. 18–21.
21 N.I. Astrov, "Finansovaia i ekonomicheskaia politika", in N.I. Astrov (ed.), *Zakonodatel'nye proekty i predpolozheniia partii narodnoi svobody 1905–07*, S.P.B. 1907, pp. 292–300. See also Kutler's speech in *S.O.*, Vol. I, 1907, 20/3/1907, pp. 809–32.
22 See Melissa K. Stockdale, *Paul Miliukov and the Quest for a Liberal Russia*, Ithaca and London 1996, pp. xiv–xv, 82–5, 210–18 and Wayne Dowler, *Russia in 1913*, DeKalb 2010, p. 197.

For the causes of the Great War, see Christopher Clark, *The Sleepwalkers*, London and New York 2013, and Sean McMeekin, *The Russian Origins of the First World War*, Cambridge, MA, 2012.

Glossary

Russian	English translation
Birzhevye vedomosti	*The Bourse Gazette* (newspaper)
guberniia	province; provincial
narod	people; nation
Narodnaia svoboda	*Freedom of the People* (newspaper)
narodniki	populists (agrarian socialists)
Narodnoe delo	*The People's Cause* (newspaper)
Narodnoe pravo	*The People's Right* (newspaper)
Novoe vremia	*New Times* (newspaper)
Obshchina/mir	village commune
Osvobozhenie	*Liberation* (newspaper)
Poliarnaia zvezda	*Pole Star* (newspaper)
pomeshchik	(noble) landowner
Pravitel'stvennyi vestnik	*The Government Herald* (newspaper)
Pravo	*Law* (legal journal)
Rech'	*Speech* (newspaper)
Russkie vedomosti	*The Russian Gazette* (newspaper)
Russkoe gosudarstvo	*The Russian State* (newspaper)
soiuz	union
Soiuz osvobozhdeniia	Union of Liberation
Soiuz soiuzov	Union of Unions
soslovie	(official) social estate
starosta	village/commune elder
starshina	volost' (canton) elder
svoboda	freedom, liberty
Svobodnyi Narod	*The Free People* (newspaper)
Trudovik Group	Labour Group
uezd	(historical) district
ukaz	decree, edict, ukase
Vestnik partii narodnoi svobody	*The Herald of the Party of the Freedom of the People* (newspaper)
volost'	canton (peasant administrative and judicial unit covering several village communes); cantonal
vospominaniia	memoirs
zemskii nachal'nik	land captain (an official, usually a landowner, with power to discipline the peasantry)
zemstvo	unit of provincial/uezd self-government

Further reading

Ascher, A. *The Revolution of 1905*, Stanford, 2 Vols, 1988–92.
Bradley, Joseph *Voluntary Associations in Tsarist Russia: Science, Patriotism, and Civil Society*, Cambridge, MA 2009.
Dowler, Wayne *Russia in 1913*, DeKalb 2010.
Emmons, T. *The Formation of Political Parties and the First National Elections in Russia*, Cambridge, MA 1983.
Emmons, T. "Liberation or Liberalism?", *Kritika*, Vol. 5, Issue 1, 2004, pp. 107–12.
Fediashin, Anton *Liberals under Autocracy: Modernisation and Civil Society in Russia 1866–1904*, Madison 2012.
Figes, O. *A People's Tragedy. The Russian Revolution 1891–1924*, London 1996.
Fischer, George *Russian Liberalism*, Cambridge, MA 1958.
Freeze, G.L. "A National Liberation Movement and the Shift in Russian Liberalism 1901–1903", *Slavic Review*, Vol. 28, No. 1, March 1969.
Frölich, K. *The Emergence of Russian Constitutionalism 1900–1904*, The Hague 1981.
Galai, S. *The Liberation Movement in Russia, 1900–1905*, Cambridge 1973.
Galai, S. "The Tragic Dilemma of Russian Liberalism as Reflected in Ivan Il'ic Petrunkevic's Letters to His Son", *Jahrbücher für Geschichte Osteuropas*, Vol. 29, 1981, pp. 1–29.
Galai, S. "The True Nature of Octobrism", *Kritika*, Vol. 5, 2004, pp. 137–42.
Galai, S. "The Kadet Domination of the First Duma and its Limits", in Jon Smele (ed.), *The Revolution of 1905*, pp. 196–217, London and New York 2005.
Gregory, Paul R. "The Role of the State in Promoting Economic Development: The Russian Case and Its General Implications", in Richard Sylla and Gianni Toniolo (eds), *Patterns of European Industrialization: The Nineteenth Centrury*, pp. 64–79, London and New York 1991.
Gregory, Paul R. *Before Command: An Economic History of Russia from Emancipation to the First Five-Year Plan*, pp. 14–101, Princeton 1994.
Haimson, Leopold "The Problem of Social Stability in Urban Russia 1905–1917 (Part 1)", *Slavic Review*, Vol. 23, No. 4, December 1964, pp. 619–42.
Haimson, Leopold "The Problem of Social Stability in Urban Russia 1905–1917 (Part 2)", *Slavic Review*, Vol. 24, No. 1, March 1965, pp. 1–22.
Hoch, Steven L. *Essays in Russian Social and Economic History*, Boston 2015, pp. 7–83.
Hosking, Geoffrey A. *The Russian Constitutional Experiment: Government and Duma, 1907–1914*, Cambridge 1973.
Kroner, A. "The Influence of Miliukov and Maklakov on Current Views of Russian Liberalism", *Revolutionary Russia*, Vol. 9, 1996, pp. 143–63.

Lieven, D.C.B. "Bureaucratic Liberalism in Late Imperial Russia: The Personality, Career and Opinions of A.N. Kulomzin", *S.E.E.R.*, Vol. 60, 1982, pp. 413–32.

McKean, Robert B. *"*Constitutional Russia", *Revolutionary Russia*, Vol. 9, No. 1, June 1996, pp. 33–42.

Mehlinger, H.D. and Thompson, J.M. *Count Witte and the Tsarist Government in the 1905 Revolution*, Bloomington 1972.

Moon, David "Peasants into Russian Citizens: A Comparative Perspective", *Revolutionary Russia*, Vol. 9, No. 1, June 1996, pp. 43–81.

Pipes, R. *Struve: Liberal on the Left, 1870–1905*, Cambridge, MA 1970.

Pipes, R. *Struve: Liberal on the Right, 1905–1944*, Cambridge, MA 1980.

Raeff, Marc "Some Reflections on Russian Liberalism", *Russian Review*, Vol. 18, 1959, pp. 218–320.

Riha, Thomas *A Russian European: Paul Miliukov in Russian Politics*, Notre Dame, IN 1969.

Smele, Jon and Haywood, Anthony *The Russian Revolution of 1905, Centenary Perspectives*, London and New York 2005.

Stockdale, Melissa K. "Politics, Morality and Violence: Kadet Liberals and the Question of Terror 1902–11", *Russian History*, Vol. 22, 1995, pp. 455–80.

Stockdale, Melissa K. *Paul Miliukov and the Quest for a Liberal Russia 1880–1918*, Ithaca, NY 1996.

Thatcher, Ian D. (ed.) *Late Imperial Russia, Problems and Prospects: Essays in Honour of R.B. McKean*, Manchester 2005.

Zimmerman, J.E. "Russian Liberal Theory, 1900–17", *Canadian-American Slavic Studies*, Vol. 14, Issue 1, 1980, pp. 1–20.

Bibliography

The following list includes the sources, both primary and secondary, consulted by the author but it is not intended to be exhaustive.

Agrarnoe dvizhenie "Agrarnoe dvizhenie v Rossii v 1905–1906", Pub. Imperatorskoe Volnoe Ekonomicheskoe Obshchestvo, 2 Vols, S.P.B. 1908.
Agrarnyi vopros Kn.P.D. Dolgorukov and I.I. Petrunkevich (eds), Moscow, Vol. I, 1905, Vol. II, 1906.
Astrov, N.I. (ed.) *Zakonodatel'nye proekty i predpolozheniia partii Narodnoi Svobody 1905–07*, S.P.B. 1907.
Astrov, N.I. *K pamiati pogibshikh*, Paris 1941.
Astrov, N.I. *Vospominaniia*, Paris 1941.
Belokonskii, I.P. *Zemskoe dvizhenie*, 2nd edn, Moscow 1914.
Bez Zaglaviia (S.P.B. Journal) No. 3, 1906.
Borodin, N.A. "Lichnyi sostav pervoi Gosudarstvennoi Dumy", in *Pervaia Gosudarstvennaia Duma*, 1, pp. 1–39 (listed separately).
Byloe Nos 3, 4 and 5/6, S.P.B. 1917, on the "Tsarskosel'skie soveshchaniia" of December 1905, and February and April 1906.
Chernenkov, N.N. *Agrarnaia programma partii narodnoi svobody i eë posleduiushchaia razrabotka*, S.P.B. 1907.
Chuprov, A.I. *K.d.p. i sotsializm*, Moscow 1906.
Constitution du Royaume de Bulgarie, Sofia 1911.
Crisp, O. "The Russian Liberals and the 106 Anglo-French Loan to Russia", *S.E.E.R.*, Vol. 39 (June 1961).
Dolgorukov, Prince Pavel D. and Petrunkevich, I.I. *Agrarnyi vopros* (listed separately above).
Dolgorukov, Prince Pavel D. and Petrunkevich, I.I. *Politicheskii stroi sovremennykh gosudarstv*, S.P.B. 1905.
Dolgorukov, Prince Pavel D. and Petrunkevich, I.I. *Voprosy gosudarstvennogo khoziaistva*, S.P.B. 1907.
Dolgurukov, Prince Pavel D. and Shakhovskoi, Prince D.I. *Melkaia zemskaia edinitsa*, S.P.B. 1903.
Emmons, T. *The Russian Landed Gentry and the Peasant Emancipation of 1861*, Cambridge 1968.
Ezersky, N.F. *Gosudarstvennaia Duma pervogo sozyva*, Penza 1907.
Frank, S. *Biografiia P.B. Struve*, New York 1966.
GARF *Gosudarstvennyi Arkhiv Russkoi Federatsii*, Moscow. Fond 523 (Partiia Narodnoi

Svobody (Kadety)) and 579 (P.N. Miliukov). (On Internet: www.statearchive.ru). See also under Shelokhaev, V.V. (ed.) (cited below) and Pavlov D.B. (ed.) for GARF and other relevant materials. See also TsGAOR (cited below).
Ger''e, V. *Pervaia russkaia Gosudarstvennaia Duma*, Moscow 1906.
Gershchenkron, Alexander *Economic Backwardness in Historical Perspective*, New York 1962.
Gertsenshtein, M.Ia. *Agrarnyi vopros: natsionalizatsiia zemli*, Moscow 1905.
Gertsenshtein, M.Ia. *Agrarnyi vopros v programmakh razlichnykh partii*, Moscow 1906.
Gertsenshtein, M.Ia. *Nuzhna li krest''anam zemlia – Rechi deputata M.Ia. Gertsenshteina v Gos. Dume*, Moscow 1906.
Gertsenshtein, M.Ia. *Zemel'naia reforma v programme partii Narodnoi Svobody*, Moscow 1906.
Gessen, I.V. "V dvukh vekakh", Berlin 1937 (Vol. XXII of *Arkhiv russkoi revolyutsii*).
Goldenweiser E.A. "The Russian Duma", *Political Science Quarterly*, Vol. 29, 1914.
Gosudarstvennaia Duma *Gosudarstvennaia Duma, Stenograficheskie otchëty*, 2 Vols, S.P.B. 1906.
Gosudarstvennaia Duma *Ukazatel' k stenograficheskim otchëtam*, S.P.B. 1906.
Gosudarstvennaia Duma (Biographies of deputies):
Gosudarstvennaia Duma *Chleny 1-oy Gosudarstvennoi Dumy*, Moscow 1906.
Gosudarstvennaia Duma *Gosudarstvennaia Duma pervogo prizyva*, Moscow 1906.
Gosudarstvennaia Duma *Chleny 2-oi Gosudarstvennoi Dumy*, S.P.B. 1907.
Gosudarstvennaia Duma *Pervye narodnye predstaviteli*, S.P.B. 1907.
Gurko, V.I. *Features and Figures from the Past*, Stanford 1939.
Iakushkin, V.E. *V Gosudarstvennoi Dume o zemle*, Moscow 1906.
Iakushkin, V.E. "K polozheniiu agrarnogo voprosa", in *Vestnik Partii Narodnoi Svobody*, No. 21–22, 3/7/1906.
Izvolskii, A.P. (Izwolsky, A.) *Memoirs of Alexander Izwolsky*, London 1920.
Izvolskii, A.P. *Vospominaniia*, Moscow 1924.
Kaminka, A.I. and Nabokov, V.D. *Vtoraia Gosudarstvennaia Duma*, S.P.B. 1907.
Karelin, A.E. "Deviatoe ianvaria i Gapon. Vospominaniia (Zapisano so slov A.E. Karelina)", *Krasnaia Letopis'*, 1922, No. 1.
Karpovich, Michael "Two Types of Russian Liberalism: Maklakov and Miliukov", in E.J. Simmons (ed.) *Continuity and Change in Russian Thought*, Cambridge 1955.
Kaufman, A. "Agrarnyi vopros", in *Pervaia gosudarstvennaia Duma* (listed separately), Vol. 3, pp. 1–117.
Kiriukhina, E. "Vserossiiskii krest''ianskii soiuz v 1905g", *Istoricheskie zapiski*, Vol. I, 1955, pp. 95–141.
Kizevetter, A.A. (ed.) *Napadki na partii Narodnoi Svobody i vozrazheniia na nikh*, Moscow 1906.
Kizevetter, A.A. *Na rubezhe dvukh stoletii – vospominaniia 1881–1914*, Prague 1929.
Kochan, L. "Kadet Policy in 1917 and the Constituent Assembly", *S.E.E.R.*, Vol. 45, January 1967, No. 104.
Kokoshkin, F.F. *Ob osnovaniakh zhelatel'noi organizatsii narodnogo predstavitel'stva v Rossii*, Moscow 1906.
Kokoshkin, F.F. *O pravakh natsional'nostei i detsentralizatsii*, Moscow 1906.
Kokoshkin, F.F. *Oblastnaia avtonomia i edinstvo Rossii*, Moscow 1906.
Kokovtsov, V.N. *Out of My Past*, Stanford U.P., 1935.
Konstitutsionno-demokraticheskaia partiia (Agrarnaia kommissiia) *Krest''anam*, Nizhnii Novgorod 1905.

198 Bibliography

Konstitutsionno-demokraticheskaia partiia *Chego khochet konstitutsionno-demokraticheskaia partiia*, Moscow 1906.
Konstitutsionno-demokraticheskaia partiia *Krest''anam o konstitutsionno-demokraticheskoi partii*, Moscow 1906.
Konstitutsionno-demokraticheskaia partiia *K rabochim*, Moscow 1906. Also published in No. 2 of *Vestnik Partii Narodnoi Svobody* (listed separately).
Konstitutsionno-demokraticheskaia partiia *Novaia Duma – platforma partii Narodnoi Svobody*, S.P.B. 1906.
Konstitutsionno-demokraticheskaia partiia *O manifeste 17 oktiabria*, Moscow 1906.
Konstitutsionno-demokraticheskaia partiia *Tronnaia Rech' i otvetnyi adres Gosudarstvennoi Dumy*, S.P.B. 1906.
Konstitutsionno-demokraticheskaia partiia *Vestnik Partii Narodnoi Svobody* – the official weekly of the K.D. Party (Nos for 1906).
Konstitutsionno-demokraticheskaia partiia, *Agrarnyi vopros na IV delegatskom s''ezde partii Narodnoi Svobody*, S.P.B. 1907.
Konstitutsionno-demokraticheskaia partiia *Oblastnoe soveshchanie po agrarnomu voprosu po 8 gub, tsentralnoi promyshlennoi polosy*. (Moskva, noyabr' 1906), S.P.B. 1907.
Konstitutsionno-demokraticheskaia partiia *otchët tsentral'nogo komiteta konstitutsionno-demokraticheskoi partii za dva goda s 18 oktiabria 1905 po oktyabr' 1907 g*, S.P.B. 1907.
Konstitutsionno-demokraticheskaia partiia *Pered vyborami v vtoruiu dumu*, S.P.B. 1907.
(Konstitutsionno-demokraticheskaia partiia, accounts and bulletins of party congresses in chronological order below.):
Konstitutsionno-demokraticheskaia partiia *S''ezd 12–18 oktiabria 1905 g.*, S.P.B. 1905 (also published as supplement to *Svobodnyi Narod*, 1 December 1905).
Konstitutsionno-demokraticheskaia partiia *Vtoroi vserossiiskii s''ezd* (unofficial edition), S.P.B. 1906, Bulletins 1–9. See also "Vtoroi vserossiiskii delegatskii s''ezd k.d.p.", supplement to *Pravo*, Nos 4 and 7, 1906.
Konstitutsionno-demokraticheskaia partiia *Biulleteni III obshcheimperskogo delegatskogo s''ezda partii Narodnoi Svobody*, S.P.B. 1906.
Konstitutsionno-demokraticheskaia partiia "Postanovleniia III-ego s''ezda 21–25 aprelia 1906g" (Supplement to *Vestnik Partii Narodnoi Svobody*, No. 12, 1906).
Konstitutsionno-demokraticheskaia partiia *Protokoly III s''ezda partii Narodnoi Svobody*, S.P.B., 1906. See also "III s'ezd delegatov partii Narodnoi Svobody", in *Pravo*, No. 18, 1906.
Konstitutsionno-demokraticheskaia partiia For an account of the IV Congress see the reports in *Rech'*, 26–30 September 1906, primarily under the title of "IV s'ezd partii Narodnoi Svobody".
Konstitutsionno-demokraticheskaia partiia *Protokoly Tsentral'nogo Komiteta i zagranichnykh grupp Konstitutsionno-demokraticheskoi partii 1905 – seredina 1930 gg*. Vol. I, 1905–11 gg, Moscow, Izdatel'stvo Progress – Akademiia 1994.
Konstitutsionno-demokraticheskaia partiia *S''ezdy i konferentsii Konstitutsionno-demokraticheskoi partii 1905–1920 gg*. Vol. I, 1905–7 gg, V.V. Shelokhaev (ed.), O.N. Lezhneva (compiler), Moscow ROSSPEN 1997.
Kornilov, A.A. "Agrarnyi vopros" in N.I. Astrov (ed.) *Zakonodatel'nye proekty i predpolozheniia partii Narodnoi Svobody*, S.P.B. 1907, pp. 363–86.
Krasnyi arkhiv Vol. 5: "Perepiska N.A. Romanova i P.A. Stolypina", see also Vol. 30.

Krasnyi arkhiv Vol. 10: "Pis'mo kn. E.N. Trubetskoi Nikolaiu Romanovu po povodu rospuska 1-oi Gosudarstvennoi Dumy".
Krasnyi arkhiv Vols 11–12: "Doklady S.Iu.Vitte Nikolaiu II, "Manifest 17 oktiabria", "Iz arkhiva S.Iu.Vitte".
Krasnyi arkhiv Vol. 17: "K istorii agrarnoi reformy Stolypina".
Krasnyi arkhiv Vol. 31: "Bor'ba S.Iu.Vitte s agrarnoi revoliutsiei".
Krasnyi arkhiv Vol. 32: "Mobilizatsiia reaktsii v 1906g".
Krasnyi arkhiv Vols 46 and 47–8: "Kadety v 1905–1906 gg" (Reports of Kadet Central Committee Meetings in 1905–6).
Krasnyi arkhiv Vol. 49: "P.A. Stolypin i Sveaborgskoe vosstanie".
Krasnyi arkhiv Vol. 57: "Pervaia Gosudarstvennaia Duma v Vyborge".
Kryzhanovskii, S. *Kak proshli vybory v Gosudarstvennuiu Dumu*, S.P.B. 1906.
Kryzhanovskii, S. *Vospominaniia*, Berlin 1938.
Kuskova, E.D. "Otkrytki (iz tetradki vospominanii)", *Sovremennye Zapiski*, 25, 1925.
Kuskova, E.D. "Kren nalevo: iz proshlogo", *Sovremennye zapiski*, Vol. 44, 1939.
Lenin, V.I. *Sochineniia*. Moscow-Leningrad 1931. Vols VI–IX (1904–6). See in particular "Dve taktiki sotsial-demokratii v demokraticheskoi revoliutsii", Vol. VIII, 1905.
Lokot', T.V. *Pervaia duma*, Moscow 1906.
L'vov, N.N. and Stakhovich, A.A. (eds) *Nuzhdy derevni*, 2 Vols, S.P.B. 1904 (on Witte's committees on the needs of the agricultural industry).
Maklakov, V.A. "Iz proshlogo", *Sovremennye zapiski*, Vols 38, 40–44, 46–48, 50–54, 56, 58–60.
Maklakov, V.A. *Vlast' i obshchestvennost' na zakate staroi Rossii*, 3 Vols, Paris 1936.
Maklakov, V.A. *Pervaia duma*, Paris 1939.
Maklakov, V.A. *Iz Vospominanii*, New York 1954.
Marc, P. *Au seuil du 17 Octobre 1905*, Leipzig 1914.
Martov, L. "Sotsialdemokratiia 1905–07 gg", in *Obshchestvennoe dvizhenie*, Vol. III, pp. 537–628.
Martov, L., Maslov, P. and Potresov, A. (eds) *Obshchestvennoe dvizhenie v Rossii v nachale XX-go veka*, 4 Vols, S.P.B. 1909–11.
Martynov, A. "Istoriia k.d.p.", in *Obshchestvennoe dvizhenie*, Vol. III, pp. 1–85.
Miliukov, P.N. "Bolgarskaia konstitutsiia", in Dolgorukov and Petrunkevich (eds) *Politicheskii stroi sovremennykh stran* (listed separately).
Miliukov, P.N. *Ocherki po istorii russkoi kultury*, 3 Vols, S.P.B. 1896–1901.
Miliukov, P.N. *Russia and its Crisis*, Chicago/London 1905.
Miliukov, P.N. "The Case of the Second Duma", *Contemporary Review*, Vol. 92, October 1907.
Miliukov, P.N. *God bor'by* – publisticheskaia khronika 1905–06, S.P.B. 1907.
Miliukov, P.N. "Intelligentsiia i istoricheskaia traditsiia", in *Intelligentsiia v Rossii*, K. Arsen'ev (ed.), pp. 89–191, S.P.B. 1910.
Miliukov, P.N. *Tri popytki (K istorii russkogo lzhe-konstitutsionalizma)*, Paris 1921.
Miliukov, P.N. "Sud nad kadetskim liberalizmom", *Sovremennye zapiski*, Vol. 41, 1930.
Miliukov, P.N. "Liberalizm, radikalizm, i revoliutsiia", *S.Z.*, 57, 1935.
Miliukov, P.N. "M.M. Vinaver kak politik", in *M.M. Vinaver i russkaia obshchestvennost' nachala XX veka – sbornik statei*, Paris 1937.
Miliukov, P.N. "Rokovye gody. Iz vospominanii (1904–1906)", in *Russkie zapiski*, Nos 4–21, Paris, 1938–9.
Miliukov, P.N. *Vospominaniia 1859–1917*, 2 Vols, New York 1955.

200 Bibliography

Miliukov, P.N. *Political Memoirs*, 1905–17, A.P. Mendel (ed.), Ann Arbor 1967.
Miliukov, P.N. "Sergei Andreevich Muromtsev", in D.I. Shakhovskoi (ed.) *Sergei Andreevich Muromtsev (sbornik statei)* (listed separately).
Mosolov, A.A. *At the Court of the Last Tsar*, London 1935.
Mukhanov, A.A. and Nabokov, V.D. *Pervaia Gosudarstvennaia Duma* (listed separately).
Narodnaia Svoboda, see *Svobodnyi Narod*.
Nicholas II (Emperor) *Letters of Tsar Nicholas II to the Empress Mariya Fedorovna*, J. Bing (ed.), London 1937.
Nikolai II (Imperator) *Dnevnik Imperatora Nikolaia II*, Berlin 1923.
Novoe Vremia S.P.B., daily newspaper.
Osvobozhdenie Twice-monthly periodical. Published in Stuttgart, Nos 1–56 (18 June 1902–7 September 1904).
Osvobozhdenie Paris, Nos 57–78/79 (2 October 1904–5 October 1905).
Osvobozhdenie Listok Osvobozhdeniia (special bulletins published by *Osvobozhdenie*). Stuttgart/Paris, 1904–5.
Osvobozhdenie Materialy po vyrabotke russkoi konstitutsii, 3 Vols, Paris 1905.
Osvobozhdenie "Osnovnoi gosudarstvennyi zakon Rosskiiskoi imperii, vyrabotannyi gruppoi chlenov Soiuza Osvobozhdeniia", Vol. 1 of *Osvobozhdenie*'s *Materialy po vyrabotke russkoi konstitutsii*.
Osvobozhdenie "Proekt osnovnogo zakona Rossiiskoi imperii, vyrabotannyi komissiei Biuro obshchezemskikh s''ezdov" (The so-called "Muromtsev" constitution), Vol III of *Osvobozhdenie*'s *Materialy po vyrabotke russkoi konstitutsii*.
Pares, Sir B. "The Peterhof Conference", Russian Review, Liverpool 1913.
Pares, Sir B. "The Second Duma", *S.E.E.R.*, Vol. 2, June 1923.
Pavlov, D.B. (compiler) *Protokoly tsentral'nogo komiteta Konstitutsionno-demokraticheskoi partii*, 1905–11, Vol. I, Progress-Akademia, Moscow 1994.
Pavlov, D.B. (compiler) *Liberal'noe dvizhenie v Rossii 1902–05 gg*, ROSSPEN, Moscow 2001.
Pavlovskii, G. (Pavlovsky) *Agricultural Russia on the Eve of the Revolution*, London 1930.
Pervaia Gosudarstvennaia Duma (3 Vols) A.A. Mukhanov and V.D. Nabokov (eds), S.P.B. 1907. An invaluable collection of materials and articles on the Kadets in the First Duma.
Petergofskoe soveshchanie o proekte Gosudarstvennoi Dumy, Berlin 1913.
Petrunkevich, I.I. "Iz zapisok obshchestvennogo deiatelia", Vol. XXI of *Arkhiv russkoi revoliutsii*, Berlin 1934.
Poliarnaia svezda Weekly journal of Struve, Nos 1–13, 15 December 1905–12–March 1906 (S.P.B.) (later continued as *Svoboda i Kultura* and *Duma*).
Polnoe sobranie zakonov, S.P.B., 1885–1911, Vols 24–26.
Pravo 1903–6. St. Petersburg weekly journal of the legal profession. From late 1904 it became an important organ of "Liberationist", and later of Kadet, opinion. It also contains reports of Kadet and zemstvo congresses, and other valuable material concerning the Kadets. At the same time it prints the texts of most government laws, communiqués, etc.
Prokopovich, S.N. *Soiuzy rabochikh i ikh zadachi*, S.P.B. 1905.
Protopopov, D.D. *Chto sdelala pervaia Gosudarstvennaia Duma*, Moscow 1906.
Rech' daily newspaper S.P.B. 1906– (ed. P.N. Miliukov and I.V. Gessen).
Robinson, G.T. *Rural Russia under the Old Régime*, 2nd edn, New York 1949.

Rodichev, F.I. "The Liberal Movement in Russia" (1855–91 and 1891–1905), *The Slavonic Review*, London, Vol. 2, Nos 4 and 5, June and December 1923.
Rodichev, F.I. "Iz vospominanii", *Sovremennye zapiski*, Paris 1933, No. L111.
Rodichev, F.I. "Avtobiografiia F.I. Rodicheva". Autobiographical letter to A.R. Lednitsky in *Vozrozhdenie*, Paris 1954.
Rodichev, F.I. "The Veteran of Russian Liberalism: Ivan Petrunkevich", *S.E.E.R.*, Vol. 7, 1928/9.
Russkie vedomosti (Moscow daily newspaper), *Russkie Vedomosti 1863–1913*, Moscow 1913. See especially Part II for biographical/autobiographical section on contributors to *Russkie Vedomosti*.
Russkie vedomosti: Iz istorii russkoi pechati, organizatsiia obshchestvennogo mneniia v Rossii i nezavisimaia gazeta "Russkie Vedomosti" (ed. V. Rozenburg).
Sanders, Jonathan *The Union of Unions*. PhD dissertation, Columbia University, 1985.
Savich, G.G. *Novyi gosudarstvennyi stroi Rossii*, S.P.B. 1907.
Sbornik izbiratelia na 1906 god (published by I.I. Efron), S.P.B. 1906.
Sef, S.E. *Burzhuaziia v 1905 godu*, Moscow 1926.
Shakhovskoi, Prince D.I. "Soiuz osvobozhdeniia", in *Zarnitsy*, S.P.B. 1909, No. 2, Part II.
Shakhovskoi, Prince D.I. (ed.) *Sergei Andreevich Muromtsev (sbornik statei)*, Moscow 1911.
Shelokhaev, V.V. (ed.) *Politicheskie partii Rossii: Konets XIX – pervaia tret' XX veka (Entsiklopediia). Dokumental'noe nasledie*, ROSSPEN 1996.
Shelokhaev, V.V. *S'ezdy i konferentsii Konstitutsionno-demokraticheskoi partii 1905–07 gg*, Vol. I, 1905–7, ROSSPEN, Moscow 1997.
Shelokhaev, V.V. *Liberal'noe dvizhenie v Rossii 1902–1905 gg* (D.B. Pavlov, compiler), ROSSPEN, Moscow 2001.
Shershenevich, G.F. *Programma partii Narodnoi Svobody v obshchedostupnom izlozhenii*, Moscow 1906.
Shipov, D.N. *Vospominaniia i dumy o perezhitom*, Moscow 1918.
Smirnov, S.A. (ed.) *P.N. Miliukov. Sbornik materialov po chestvovanii ego semidesiatiletiia 1859–1929*, Paris 1929.
Struve, P.B. "My Contacts and Conflicts with Lenin", *S.E.E.R.* Part I: April 1934, Vol. 12, No. 36. Part II: July 1934, Vol. 13, No. 37.
Struve, P.B. "My Contacts with Rodichev", *S.E.E.R.*, January 1934, Vol. 12, No. 35.
Svobodnyi Narod daily newspaper, S.P.B., No. 1, December 1905. Stopped by the administration on its second number, but succeeded by *Narodnaia Svoboda*, 15–20 December 1905.
The Times, London, occasional nos in 1906.
Treadgold, D.W. "The Constitutional Democrats and the Russian Liberal Tradition", *A.S.E.E.R.*, Vol. 10., 1951, pp. 85–94.
Treadgold, D.W. *Lenin and his Rivals*, London 1955.
Treadgold, D.W. *The Great Siberian Migration*, Princeton 1957.
Trotsky, L.D. *1905*, Milan 1948.
TsGAOR: Tsentral'nyi Gosudarstvennyi Arkhiv Oktiabr'skoi Revol'utsii, Moscow, fondy 523, 579 (now incorporated in GARF, see above).
Tyrkova-Williams, A. "Russian Liberalism", *Russian Review*, No. 1, 1951.
Tyrkova-Williams, A. *Na putiakh k svobode*, New York 1952.
Tyrkova-Williams, A. "The Cadet Party", *Russian Review*, Vol. 12, No. 3, 1953.
Tyrkova-Williams, A. *To, chego bol'she ne budet*, Paris 1954.

Bibliography

Vekhi, sbornik statei o russkoi intelligentsii (ed. M. Gershenzon), Moscow 1909.
Veselovskii, B.B. "Istoriia zemstva za sorok let", Vols I–IV, S.P.B. 1909–11.
Veselovskii, B.B. "Dvizhenie zemlevladel'tsev", in L. Martov (ed.) *Obshchestvennoe dvizhenie*, Vol. I, pp. 291–312.
Veselovskii, B.B. and Frenkel', Z.G. *Iubileinyi zemskii sbornik*, S.P.B. 1914.
Vestnik Partii Narodnoi Svobody S.P.B. 1906. The official journal of the Constitutional-Democratic Party.
Vinaver, M.M. *Konflikty v 1-oi Gosudarstvennoi Dume*, S.P.B. 1907.
Vinaver, M.M. *Istoriia Vyborgskogo vozzvaniia*, Petrograd 1917.
Vinaver, M.M. "M.M. Vinaver i russkaia obshchestvennost' v nachale XX veka" (Sbornik statei), Paris 1937.
Vinaver, M.M. *Nedavnee, Vospominaniia i kharakteristiki*, 3rd edn, Paris 1937.
Vitte (Witte), S.Iu. *Vospominaniia. Tsarstvovanie Nikolaia II*, 3 Vols, Berlin 1922.
Vitte (Witte), S.Iu. *Vospominaniia, memuary*, 2 Vols, Minsk Moskva 2001.
Vitte (Witte), S.Iu. *Iz arkhiva S.Iu.Vitte, Vospominaniia*, Vols I–II, S.P.B. 2003.
Vodovozov, V.V. *Sbornik programm politicheskikh partii v Rossii*, 2nd edn, S.P.B. 1905.
Vodovozov, V.V. "Osvobozhdeniia Soiuz", *Entsiklopedicheskii slovar' Brokgauz-Efron*, Supplement, Vol. II, S.P.B. 1906.
Von Laue, T.E. "Political Parties in the Russian Dumas", *Journal of Modern History*, Vol. 22, June 1950.
Von Laue, T.E. "Count Witte and the Russian Revolution of 1905", *A.S.E.E.R.*, XVII, No. 1, February 1958.
Von Laue, T.E. *Sergei Witte and the Industrialisation of Russia*, New York/London 1963.
Von Laue, T.E. *Why Lenin, why Stalin?*, New York 1964.
Von Laue, T.E. "The Chances for Liberal Constitutionalism in Russia, *Slavic Review*, 24, 1965.
Vyborg Trial *Delo o Vyborgskom vozzvanii – stenograficheskii otchët o zasedaniiakh osobogo prisutstviia Peterburgskoi sudebnoi palaty 12–18 oktiabria 1907*, S.P.B. 1908.
Vyborg Trial *Deputaty I-oi Dumy pod sudom. Delo (o Vyborgskom vozzvanii)*. Compiled by V.N. Klasson, S.P.B. 1908.

Index

academics and Kadet Party 45, 108–9, 171, 178
agrarian policies: and agrarian disorders 9; alienation of land 26–7, 41, 114, 115, 124–5, 154–5, 156–7, 159, 160–1, 164; and communes 9, 42, 163–4, 184; critique of 160–6, 184–5; after Emancipation 6, 9; and First Duma 114, 115, 116, 117–18, 124–5; government attitude to 114, 115, 124–5, 129, 131; and Kadet landlords 164–5; of Kadets 41–2, 114, 124–5, 129, 154–66; and "Memorandum of the 42" 116, 159–60, 163; and peasantry 6, 9, 129, 134, 155, 156, 159–60, 161, 162, 163, 164; and Second Duma 163–4; and socialists 117–18; and Union of Liberation 15, 26–7; and zemstvos 13, 27
Aladin 108, 117
Alexander II 1, 3, 5, 7
Alexander III 7, 49
alienation of land 26–7, 41, 114, 115, 124–5, 154–5, 156–7, 159, 160–1, 164
All-Zemstvo Congress 18, 19, 29, 31
autonomy, Kadet policies on 152–4

Bak, Yurii 80
bicameral system 17, 29, 85, 148–9
Bloody Sunday 23–4
Bogucharskii, V.Ia. 11, 16
Bolsheviks 58, 59, 117, 129, 132–3, 139, 191
Borodin, N.A. 106, 171, 173
Budgetary Rules 86
Bulgakov, Sergei 15, 16
Bulgarian constitution 52–3, 147
Bulygin, A.G. 24; Bulygin Duma 30–1, 31–2, 36–7

Bureau of the Progressive Press 133
bureaucrats in Kadet Party 172–3
businessmen in Kadet Party 171–2

Central Committee, Kadet Party: and agrarian policies 155, 156; composition of 44–5, 74, 78–9, 97, 108; and constitutional reform 74–6; and dissolution of Duma 134–5, 136, 138; and extra-parliamentary activity 133–4; and finances 176; and French loan 88–9; and grassroots 133–4; and the left 81–2, 83, 106–7; and legalization of the party 80, 97; and Miliukov 108, 110; organization of 62, 63–4, 78–9; 133–4; and party press 79, 133–4; and persecution of the party 77–8; and Second Congress 74–6, 81; and tactics 94, 97; and Third Congress 94; and Vyborg Manifesto 138
Chernenkov, N.N. 45, 155, 156, 157, 158
Chuprov, A.A. 44, 164
civil rights 9, 39, 47, 114, 149–50, 180, 181
constituent assembly 25–6, 33, 47, 52–3, 55, 56, 74–5, 76, 147
cultural self-determination 39, 152–4

December crisis 59–62, 73
decentralization 40, 150–4
deputation to the Tsar (June 1905) 29–30
dissolution of Duma 114, 119, 121, 123–4, 125–30, 133; and Vyborg Manifesto 134–9
Dolgorukov, Pavel 45, 78, 88–9, 133, 136, 137, 138, 155, 156, 165, 176
Dolgorukov, Peter 16, 110, 149
donations to party 176–7
Durnovo, P.N. 49, 54–5, 73, 78

economic policies: and economic backwardness of Russia 183–7; of Kadets 40–1, 189–91; policies of government 186–8; of Union of Liberation 26
election results (First Duma) 83–5
Emancipation of the Serfs (1861) 2–3, 6, 9
English Revolution 113
Ezerskii, N.F. 111, 127

Fedorov 175
Fifth Congress of Union of Zemstvo Constitutionalists 31
finances of Kadets 63, 134, 176–7
First Congress of Liberation 15–16
First Duma: agrarian policies 116, 117, 124–5, 129, 158–60, 161, 154–66; and coalition cabinet 122–7, 129–30; composition of 105–7; and constitutional reform 119–31, 148–50; dissolution of 114, 119, 121, 123–4, 125–30, 133, 134–9; and formation of new ministry 119–31, 148; and Fundamental Laws 90–3, 97–8, 103–4, 112; and Goremykin 104–5, 114, 125–6; government's strengthening position 114–15; and grassroots 133–5; and Kadet cabinet 123, 124, 126–31; Kadet tactics and policies 103–18, 146–66; and key offices in chamber 110; and the left wing 103, 105–8, 116, 117–18, 125, 131–3; legislative programme of Kadets 111–12, 115–18, 149–64; local government reform 150–4; mood of despair 115; and Nicholas II 104–5; Reply to the Speech from the Throne 107–8, 111–12, 113, 148–9; and revolutionaries 129, 132; and role of monarchy 112–13, 114; tactics of Kadets 113–18; and Trudoviks 105–8, 116, 117–18, 125, 132, 138; Vyborg Manifesto 135–9; and workers 154
First Duma, run up to: balance of power 72, 94–6; and constitutional reform 72, 74–5, 76–7, 84–7, 146–8; election campaign 77–8; election results 83–5; and electoral system 61, 70; and French loan 88–90; Fundamental Laws 90–3, 97–8; government in ascendancy 72–3; government limits authority of 85–8; and Kadets' electoral support 173–81; Kadets' Second Congress 73–7; Kadets' Third Congress 94–8; Laws of 20 February 85–7, 95; and the left 76–7, 80–3; and legalization of the party 80, 97; organization of Kadet party 78–83; and party press 79–80; and peasantry 84; and the right wing 82; and rural population 78, 82; and Witte's fall 93–4
First Kadet Congress *see* Foundation Congress, Kadet Party
First World War 190, 191
Fischer, G. 14
Foundation Congress, Kadet Party: election of Central Committee 44–5; lack of unity 42–3; and Miliukov 43–4; and the October Manifesto 46–50; proposals of 39–43; representation at 37, 38–9; and socialists 43–4; and strikes 38; and subscriptions 63; and support for strike 45–6; and zemstvos 43, 44–5
Fourth All-Zemstvo Congress 31
Fourth Congress of Liberation 32–3
Fourth Kadet Party Congress 137–8, 138–9
France: loan from 88–90; revolution in 113
Frank, Semeon 61
freedom of conscience 149–50
"Friends of *Liberation*" 11, 12, 14, 15
Fundamental Laws 90–3, 97–8, 103–4, 112
"Fundamental State Law of the Russian Empire, The" 17; *see also* "Union of Liberation Constitution"

Gapon, George 23
Geiden, Count 82, 114, 124, 130
Gershchenkron, Alexander 186, 187, 188
Gertsenshtein, M.Ia. 136, 156, 159, 161, 163, 164, 171, 186
Gessen, I.V. 43, 45, 65, 74, 75, 80, 92, 126
Golovin, F.A. 51–2, 93, 97, 138
Goremykin 5, 93, 96, 104–5, 114, 125, 126, 148
Grave, B. 88
Great Reforms (1860s) 3, 4, 178, 179
Gredeskul', N.A. 110, 180
Gregory, Paul R. 187
Guchkov, Alexander 37, 54, 55, 60–1, 82
Gurko, V.I. 104, 115, 119, 126, 160, 162, 186

Iakushkin, V.E. 80, 149, 155, 159–60
Ianovskii, V.V. 111, 136
industrialization 6, 8–9, 160, 184–90
intelligentsia: Central Committee, Kadet Party 45; doctrinaire intelligentsia 48;

and Kadet party membership 174, 177–80; and liberalism 10, 13, 177–80; and revisionist socialists 43; and Union of Liberation 14–15, 16–17, 18, 19, 29, 31; and Union of Unions 27–9, 31; and zemstvos 31
inviolability of the individual 39, 149, 150
Iordansky, N.I. 154
Izvolskii, A.P. 104, 119, 121, 122–4, 125–6, 128

journals *see* party press

Kadet Party, birth of: and constitutional reform 39–40, 47, 48–9, 51–3, 55–6, 61; and December crisis 59–62; and election of Central Committee 44–5; failure to recruit mass support 65–6; finances of 63; and Foundation Congress 37–47; Fourth Party Congress 137–9; and left wing 57–63; mistrust of government 48, 50, 53, 61–2; and October Manifesto 46–50; organization of 62–4; and party press 64–5; provincial groups 63–4; and right-wing 57, 60; Second Party Congress 65–6; and strikes 46, 58, 59–60; Third Party Congress 94–8; and Witte 50–9, 62; and zemstvos 36–7, 55–7, 63–4
Kadet Party deputies, composition of 170–3;
Kadet Party electoral support, social composition of 173–81
Kadet Party policy: agrarian policies 41–2, 114, 124–5, 129, 154–66; constitution and civil rights 146–50; local government and regional autonomy 150–4; social reform 154
Kaminka, A.I. 148, 176, 181
Kaufman 163, 164
Kharkov meeting 15
Kliuchevskii 127
Kokoshkin, F.F.: background of 109; and class hatred 165; and electoral privileges 165; and First Duma 75, 76, 108, 110, 112, 125; and freedom and democracy 180–1; and local government reform 150; and regional autonomy 153; and second house 148; and Vyborg Manifesto 136, 137; as a Westernist 178; and Witte 51–2, 56
Kokovtsov, V.N. 104, 119, 121–2, 188
Koliubakin, A.M. 110, 138
Komissarov, M.G. 80, 171, 176

Kornilov, A.A. 45, 64, 79, 157
Kovalevskii, M.M. 16, 92
Kovalevskii, V.I. 91–3, 119–20
Kryzhanovskii, S.E. 77–8
Kurier 131–2
Kuskova, E.D. 44
Kuzmin-Karaiev, V.D. 122, 124

land ownership *see* agrarian policies
landowners in Kadet Party 164–5, 170, 171, 173–4, 176–7
Laws of 20 February 85–6, 90, 95, 96, 116
Lazarevskii, I.I. 86
leaseholding 41, 42, 156, 159, 161, 163, 164
left wing/socialist groups: and birth of Kadet party 43–4, 57–63, 76–7; Bolsheviks 58, 59, 117, 129, 132–3, 139, 191; December crisis 59–62; and dissolution of Duma 136; and electoral campaign 80–3; in First Duma 105–8, 113–14, 117–18, 128–9, 131–3; Mensheviks 82, 117, 131–2, 132–3; Trudoviks 105–8, 116, 117–18, 125, 132, 138; and Union of Liberation 15, 16, 32–3, 43; and Union of Unions 15, 28, 31
legal profession in the Kadets 171, 172–3, 178–9
legislative process: and Duma 40, 75, 85–6, 91, 116–18; and Union of Liberation 17
legislative programme, Kadets 42, 94–5, 111–12, 115–18, 149–64
Lenin, V.I. 33
liberalism: evolution of 2–5, 10–11; and industrialization 184–90; *Liberation* (journal) 11–14; and possibility of success 183–5; post WWI 190–1; and Westernization 2, 177–80
Liberation (journal) 11–14, 15, 16, 22, 25, 26, 31
loan, from France 88–90
local government, Kadet policy on 150–4
Lokot', T.V. 107
L'vov, G.E. 51–2
L'vov, N.N. 15, 16, 45, 110, 122, 123, 130

Maklakov, V.A. 33, 46, 47–8, 52, 53, 88–9, 105, 107
Manuilov, A.A. 156, 164
"Memorandum of the 42" 116, 159–60, 163
Mensheviks 82, 117, 131–2, 132–3

206 Index

Miliukov, Pavel: and agrarian policy 155; and Bulgarian constitution 52–3, 69, 147; Bulygin Duma 31; on Central Committee 45, 108; and constitutional reform 25–6, 52–3, 55–6, 74–5, 76, 84–5, 146, 147–8, 184; and dissolution of Duma 134–5, 137; and electoral campaign 75, 77; at Foundation Congress 43–4, 45, 46, 47; and Fundamental Laws 90, 91, 92–3, 97, 98; as historian 108–9; and industrialization 185–6; and journals/newspapers 10, 11, 12, 14, 22, 65, 80; and Laws of 20 February 86, 95; and left wing 43–4, 59, 60, 106, 107, 113–14, 132; and Mirskii 22; and monarchy 52–3, 55, 112, 146–7; and Muromtsev 126–7, 177; and new ministry 103, 119, 120–1, 122, 123, 124, 125, 126–7, 128–30, 146; and October Manifesto 47, 48, 55; and revolutions 113–14; at Second Congress 73–4, 76; and Serbia 191; and Stolypin 123, 125, 128–9, 130, 146; and suffrage 74, 165–6; tactics of 94–6, 108, 109, 110, 118; and taxation 185; at Third Congress 94–6, 97; and Trepov 120–1, 130; and Union of Liberation, early days 17, 25, 27–8, 31; and Union of Unions 27–8; and Vyborg Manifesto 135, 137; and Westernization 1, 12; and Witte 52–3, 60, 93, 185; and zemstvos 31, 43, 51, 55–6, 78
minority nationalities 8, 18, 26, 39, 152–4
Mirskii (Sviatopolk-Mirskii) 18, 22–3, 24
Mosolov, A.A. 105
Mukhanov, A.A. 136, 172
"Muromtsev Constitution" 31, 35, 147–8
Muromtsev, S.A.: and constitutional reform 31, 35, 148; and Miliukov 126; and new ministry 121, 122, 124, 126; opening speech to Duma 112; as President of Duma 110; as a Westernist 177–8; and Witte 51, 56, 93

Nabokov, V.D. 45, 79, 81, 110, 112, 113, 117, 134, 172, 176
Narodnaia Svoboda 60, 65
Narodnoe Delo 80, 134
nationalities, minority 8, 18, 26, 39, 152–4
newspapers 11–14, 18, 64–5, 79–80, 133–4; *see also* individual newspaper and journal titles
Nicholas II, Tsar: attitude to Duma 104–5; character of 7–8, 49, 127; and dissolution of Duma 124; and extreme right 73; and new ministry 121–2, 122–3, 124, 127–8, 130; and October Manifesto 49; powers of 7–8, 91, 104–5; and Witte 49, 73, 104
Novoe Vremia 118

Obninskii, V.P. 185
October Manifesto 46–50, 55, 58, 72, 147
Octobrist Party 82–3, 106
Ovchinikov 96

Paris conference 18, 19
party press 11–14, 18, 64–5, 79–80, 133–4; *see also* individual newspaper and journal titles
Pavlov 117
Pavlovskii (Pavlovsky), G. 161, 162
Peasant Union 32, 36
peasantry: and agrarian policy 6, 9, 129, 134, 155, 156, 159–60, 161, 162, 163, 164; and civil equality 149; conferences of 28; and Duma election 84; and First Duma 105, 106; historically 2; and industrialization 188; as Kadet deputies 170, 172, 173; rights of 23; and taxation 185, 188; and Union of Liberation 26, 28, 32, 36; unions of 28, 32, 36; and unrest 2, 8–9, 134; and zemstvos 5, 7, 9
Peterhof Conference: on Bulygin Duma 30
Petrazhitskii, L.I. 125, 134, 136, 162, 185
Petrunkevich, I.I. 4, 10, 16, 29, 51, 56, 57, 61, 108, 110, 120, 125, 130, 165
Plehve, V.K. 8, 13, 18
Plekhanov 131–2
Pobedonostsev, Konstantin 49
Poland 40, 152–3
Poliarnaia Zvezda 60–1
Pravo 18, 23, 50, 57, 58–9, 65, 90, 93, 98
press 11–14, 18, 64–5, 79–80, 133–4; *see also* individual journal and newspaper titles
private estates 160–1, 164
professionals: and Kadets 45, 170–2, 174–5, 177–80, and liberationists 10, 19, 27; and zemstvo 5–6, 170, 174–5, 177–80
Prokopovich, S.N. 16, 28
Propper, S.M. 65

Rech' 80, 82, 84, 86, 88, 89, 91, 103, 106, 110, 113, 118, 127, 132, 137
regional autonomy 152–4
religion, and freedom of conscience 149–50

Reply to the Speech from the Throne 107–8, 111–12, 113, 148–9
revolutionaries *see* left wing/socialist groups
right-wing groups 37, 50, 56–7, 60–1, 106; Octobrist Party 82–3, 106
Robinson, G.T. 161
Rodichev, F.I. 14, 29, 108, 150, 155, 181
Russkie Vedomosti 65
Russkoe Gosudarstvo 89, 90
Russo-Japanese war (1904) 16–17, 17–18, 38
Ryutli, O.I. 163

Sabashnikov, M.A. 45, 64
Schaffhausen, Switzerland 14–15
Second Congress of Liberation 18–19
Second Congress of Union of Unions 32
Second Congress of Union of Zemstvo Constitutionalists 17
Second Duma 139, 148, 163–4, 175, 189
Second Element 170, 171, 172
Second General Strike 58
Second Kadet Congress 64, 65–6, 73–7, 81, 155–6
Second Zemstvo Congress 29, 31
Sef, S.E. 33, 61
Shakhovskoi, D.I. 14, 16, 19, 28, 29, 31, 64, 79, 110
Shershenevich, G.F. 108, 180
Shipov, D. 13, 18, 22, 29, 51, 54–5, 123–4, 127–8, 130
Sipiagin, D.S. 8, 13
Slavophiles 10
Smirnov, A. 84, 134
socialists *see* left wing/socialist groups
Special Conference on the Needs of the Countryside 13, 188
St Petersburg Assembly of Workers 23–4
St Petersburg Soviet 59
Stakhovich, M.A. 54, 130
State Council 47–8, 85–7, 91–2, 120, 148
Stishinskii 104, 115, 160, 162
Stolypin 104; and agrarian reforms 125, 130, 164; and dissolution of First Duma 123–4; 125–6, 135; and dissolution of Second Duma 139; and Miliukov 123, 125, 128–9, 130, 146; and new ministry 121, 122, 123, 128–9, 130; and premiership 125–6
strikes 38, 45–6, 58, 59–60, 62–3
Struve, Peter B.: and agrarian policy 163; and Bloody Sunday 24; and Bulygin Duma 31–2; deputation to Tsar 30; and dissolution of Duma 134; as editor of *Liberation* 11–12; and formation of Union of Liberation 14, 15, 17, 25; and Guchkov, Alexander 60–1; as liberationist 10–11, 13, 14; and Mirskii 22, 23; moves to the right 30, 60–1; and revolutionaries 60–1; at Second Kadet Congress 76; and support of workers 81; and Trubetskoi 30
subscription to Kadet Party 63, 134, 176
suffrage 25, 30, 39, 61, 74
Sviatopolk-Mirskii, Prince 18, 22–3, 24
Svobodnyi Narod 59, 65

taxation 6, 26, 41, 184, 185, 188, 189
Tennison, Ia. Ia. 111, 136
Teslenko, A. 28
Third Congress of the Union of Liberation 25–7
Third Duma 139
Third Element 5–6, 7, 10, 172
Third General Strike 59
Third Kadet Congress 82, 94–8, 103, 133, 156–8, 163, 175
Third Zemstvo Congress 29, 33
Times, The 127
town dumas 150, 152
Treadgold, D.W. 160, 161
Trepov, A.F. 119
Trepov, D.F. 24, 73, 91, 119–22, 123, 128, 130
Trubetskoi, E.N. 78
Trubetskoi, S.N. 22, 30
Trudoviks 105–8, 116, 117–18, 125, 132, 138
Tsarskoe Selo Crown Council: on the Fundamental Laws 90
Tyrkova, A.V. 74, 133

Union of Liberation: and agrarian policy 26–7; and Bloody Sunday 24–5; and Bulygin Duma 31–2; composition of 14–15, 36; and constitutional reform 17–19, 22–3, 25–6, 147, 148; council of 16–17, 18–19; deep divisions within 17; deputation to Tsar 29–31, 33; end of 32–3; final assessment of 32–4; First Congress 15–16; Fourth Congress 32–3; and "Friends of *Liberation*" 11, 12, 14, 15; and government reforms 22–3; inauguration of 14; and intelligentsia 14–15, 16–17, 18, 19, 29, 31; leftward leaning 15–16, 25; and *Liberation* (journal) 11–14; and Mirskii 22–3;

Union of Liberation *continued*
  nucleus of 10; Paris conference 18; and peasantry 26, 28, 32, 36; programme of 15–16, 19, 25–7; and Russo-Japanese war 16–17, 17–18; Second Congress 18–19; and socialists 15, 16, 43; Third Congress 25–7; and Union of Unions 27–9, 31–2; and workers 28; and zemstvos 14, 15, 16, 17, 18–19, 29, 31, 33
"Union of Liberation Constitution" 17, 31, 35, 147, 148
Union of Unions 27–9, 31–2, 36
universities 8, 38, 171, 175, 177–8, 179
Urusov, Prince 54

Vasil'ev 138
Veisman 96
Veselovskii, B.B. 3
Vestnik 79–80, 134, 148, 154, 174, 176
Vinaver, M.M. 77, 108, 109, 110, 115, 125, 134–5, 135–7, 137–8
Von Laue, T.H. 48, 50, 184, 186, 188, 190
Vyborg Manifesto 135–9

Wallace, Sir Donald Mackenzie 128–9
Westernization 177–80, 184, 186
Witte, Sergei: and agriculture 13; attempts to gain public support 50–9; and constitutional reform 47, 48–9, 51–7, 72, 85, 87; and December crisis 59, 72–3; and Durnovo 54; and election results 89–90; fall of 93–4; financial policies 185, 186; and French loan 88; and Fundamental Laws 90–1, 92–3; health of 73; and industrialization 6, 8–9, 184–5, 186, 187, 188; Kadets' attitude to 61, 87–8, 89–90; and Laws of 20 February 87; losing authority 73; and Miliukov 52–3, 60, 185; and the October Manifesto 48–50; and revolutionaries 59; and Shipov 54, 55; and zemstvos 48, 51–7

Zemstvo Bureau 51–4
Zemstvo Constitutionalists (Union of) 15, 17, 19, 25, 31, 32, 37
zemstvos: and agrarian policy 13, 27; and birth of Kadet Party 36–7, 44–5, 51–2; and Bulygin Duma 36–7; and Central Committee, Kadet Party 45; composition of 3, 4, 5–7; congresses of 13, 15, 18, 19, 23, 29, 31, 36–7, 54, 55–7, 63–4, 74; and constitutional reform 12, 19, 22–3, 25, 29–30, 51–2, 54–5; deputation to Tsar 29–30; economic work of 4–6; and evolution of liberalism 3–7, 10–11; government attitude to 7–8, 13, 14; as Kadet deputies 170, 171, 172; and *Liberation* (journal) 11, 12; and local government reform 150–2; and Miliukov 43; and Mirskii 22; mistrust of government 51–2; and opposition to government 3, 5, 7, 9–10; and peasantry 5, 7, 9; reform of 7, 12, 23; and the right-wing 37, 57; role of 4–7; and socialists 43, 78; and Union of Liberation 14, 15, 16, 17, 18–19, 29, 31, 33; and Union of Unions 28, 31; and Witte 48, 51–7

For Product Safety Concerns and Information please contact our EU representative GPSR@taylorandfrancis.com
Taylor & Francis Verlag GmbH, Kaufingerstraße 24, 80331 München, Germany

www.ingramcontent.com/pod-product-compliance
Lightning Source LLC
Chambersburg PA
CBHW062225300426
44115CB00012BA/2224